DIGITISING CULTURAL HERITAGE

This open access book investigates the role played by copyright on the digitisation of cultural heritage from three angles: the theoretical differences between cultural property law and copyright; a comparative analysis of the EU, UK, and US; and analysis of current practices and concerns, based on empirical research.

As heritage digitisation projects become increasingly common for purposes such as preservation and access, the impact of copyright is also becoming more problematic. In order to provide a full and current picture of the copyright problem, the book first introduces the reader to the debates on the scope and ownership of cultural heritage and provides an overview of the copyright implications of the digitisation process and newer uses, including 2D and 3D scanning; virtual and augmented reality; text and data mining; and artificial intelligence.

The author then divides the main critical analysis into three parts, referred to as the 'clashes with copyright'. The first, clash in theory, lies between cultural property law and copyright justification theories. The second clash is in the different legal approaches to digitising in-copyright, public domain, orphan, out-of-commerce and unpublished works in the chosen jurisdictions, focusing on the relevant rights and defences. The third clash is in the interests of stakeholders, based on public reactions to existing projects and cases, supported by interviews with heritage professionals engaging in digitisation.

By placing itself in this particular intersection of law, heritage, and technology, the book will be of interest to both intellectual property academics and cultural heritage professionals.

Volume 2 in the Art Law Library series

The Art Law Library

The Art Law Library includes books on all aspects of the law relating to art in its widest sense, including antiquities, museums, intangible cultural heritage, archives, intellectual property and human remains. Titles in the series are invaluable to those working and studying in the fields of law, museums, galleries, libraries, planning, archaeology and law enforcement. The series continues the imprint of the Institute of Art and Law.

Series Editor: Ruth Redmond-Cooper, Editor of* Art Antiquity and Law, *and founder of the Institute of Art and Law

Recent titles in the series

Volume 1: The Parthenon Marbles Dispute: Heritage, Law, Politics
Alexander Herman

Volume 2: Digitising Cultural Heritage: Clashes with Copyright Law
Pinar Oruç

Digitising Cultural Heritage

Clashes with Copyright Law

Pinar Oruç

•HART•
OXFORD • LONDON • NEW YORK • NEW DELHI • SYDNEY

HART PUBLISHING

Bloomsbury Publishing Plc

Kemp House, Chawley Park, Cumnor Hill, Oxford, OX2 9PH, UK

1385 Broadway, New York, NY 10018, USA

Bloomsbury Publishing Ireland Limited, 29 Earlsfort Terrace, Dublin 2, D02 AY28, Ireland

HART PUBLISHING, the Hart/Stag logo, BLOOMSBURY and the Diana logo are trademarks of Bloomsbury Publishing Plc

First published in Great Britain 2025

First published in hardback, 2025

Paperback edition, 2027

This publication was supported by the University of Manchester – Faculty of Humanities.

A catalogue record for this book is available from the British Library.

A catalogue record for this book is available from the Library of Congress.

Library of Congress Control Number: 2025934693

ISBN: PB: 978-1-50995-932-7
ePDF: 978-1-50995-930-3
ePub: 978-1-50995-929-7

Typeset by Compuscript Ltd, Shannon

ACKNOWLEDGEMENTS

Looking back, it is easy to connect the dots that led to this book. It started with a class discussion on orphan works, which turned into a PhD proposal, and received the Herchel Smith IP PhD funding at Queen Mary University of London. Then more inspiration came from teaching on IP and cultural heritage during my PhD, which was then followed by a posdoc at CREATe, in 'reCreating Europe: Rethinking digital copyright law for a culturally diverse, accessible, creative Europe' project, and more research on copyright, heritage and technology.

I am grateful to the people I met at QMUL and CREATe, especially Uma Suthersanen, Gaetano Dimita, Graham Dutfield, Malcolm Langley, Martin Kretschmer, Marta Iljadica and Thomas Margoni, and many other IP and heritage experts, for providing me with new ideas and perspectives. I am thankful to my interviewees from the heritage sector, who have generously shared their valuable experiences with me both in 2016–2017 and 2023–2024, proving again what an engaging field I have chosen to research. I am also grateful to the Institute of Art and Law, and the Hart Publishing team for supporting this book.

On a personal note, I want to thank my friends and family who have been so supportive, no matter the distance. Special thanks go to Greig, for cheering me up and being my thesaurus. Finally, none of this would be possible without the support and encouragement of my parents, Cahit and Zeyneti Oruç – sizi çok seviyorum.

CONTENTS

LIST OF ABBREVIATIONS

Abbreviations and Acronyms

AG	Advocate General
AHD	Authorised Heritage Discourse
AI	Artificial Intelligence
ALAI	Association Littéraire et Artistique Internationale
AR	Augmented Reality
ARROW	Accessible Registries of Rights Information and Orphan Works
BNF	Bibliothèque nationale de France – National Library of France
CC	Creative Commons
CDL	Controlled Digital Lending
CDSM	Copyright in Digital Single Market
CILIP	Chartered Institute of Library and Information Professionals
CJEU/ECJ	Court of Justice of the European Union/European Court of Justice
CMO	Collective Management Organisation
CONFU	Conference on Fair Use
DCMS	Department for Digital, Culture, Media & Sport
EC	European Commission
ECL	Extended Collective Licensing
ECS	European Copyright Society
EU	European Union
IA	Internet Archive
ICOM	International Council of Museums

IIIF	International Image Interoperability Framework
IPO	Intellectual Property Office
LACA	Libraries and Archives Copyright Alliance
LIBER	The Association of European Research Libraries
MS	Member State(s)
NPG	National Portrait Gallery
OCR	Optical Character Recognition
PLR	Public Lending Right
RAM	Random Access Memory
SCCR	Standing Committee on Copyright and Related Rights (WIPO)
SGDR	*Sui Generis* Database Right
TDM	Text and Data Mining
UK	United Kingdom
UNESCO	The United Nations Educational, Scientific and Cultural Organization
US	United States
USB	Universal Serial Bus
V&A	Victoria and Albert Museum
VOB	Vereniging van Openbare Bibliotheken
VR	Virtual Reality
WIPO	World Intellectual Property Organization

Legislation

1954 Hague Convention	Convention for the Protection of Cultural Property in the Event of Armed Conflict with Regulations for the Execution of the Convention (The Hague, 14 May 1954).
1970 Convention	Convention on the Means of Prohibiting and Preventing the Illicit Import, Export and Transfer of Ownership of Cultural Property (Paris, 14 November 1970).

2003 Convention	Convention for the Safeguarding of the Intangible Cultural Heritage (Paris, 17 October 2003).
Berne Convention	Berne Convention for the Protection of Literary and Artistic Works (Paris, 9 September 1886, as amended on 28 September 1979).
CDPA	Copyright, Designs and Patents Act 1988 (UK).
CDSM Directive	Directive (EU) 2019/790 of the European Parliament and of the Council of 17 April 2019 on copyright and related rights in the Digital Single Market and amending Directives 96/9/EC and 2001/29/EC OJ L130/92.
Database Directive	Directive 96/9/EC of the European Parliament and of the Council of 11 March 1996 on the legal protection of databases OJ L77/20.
InfoSoc Directive	Directive (EC) 2001/29 of the European Parliament and of the Council of 22 May 2001 on the harmonisation of certain aspects of copyright and related rights in the information society OJ L167/10.
MoU	Memorandum of Understanding: Key Principles on the Digitisation and Making Available of Out-of-Commerce Works (2011).
Orphan Works Directive	Directive 2012/28/EU of the European Parliament and of the Council of 25 October 2012 on certain permitted uses of orphan works Text with EEA relevance OJ L 299/5.
PSI Directive:	Directive (EU) 2019/1024 of the European Parliament and of the Council of 20 June 2019 on open data and the re-use of public sector information (recast) OJ L172/56.
Operational Guidelines	Operational Guidelines for the Implementation of the World Heritage Convention. WHC21/01, 24 September 2023.
Rental and Lending Directive	Directive (EC) 2006/115 of the European Parliament and of the Council of 12 December 2006 on Rental Right and Lending Right and on Certain Rights related to copyright in the field of intellectual property OJ L376/28.
Software Directive	Directive (EC) 2009/24 of the European Parliament and of the Council of 23 April 2009 on the Legal Protection of Computer Programs OJ L111/16.

Term Directive	Directive 2006/116/EC of the European Parliament and of the Council of 12 December 2006 on the term of protection of copyright and certain related rights (codified version) OJ L 372/12.
US Copyright Act	17 USC §§101 et seq. (2006) Pub.L.No.94-553, 90 Stat.
World Heritage Convention	Convention concerning the Protection of the World Cultural and Natural Heritage (Paris, 16 November 1972).
WCT	WIPO Copyright Treaty (Geneva, 20 December 1996).
WPPT	WIPO Performances and Phonograms Treaty (Geneva, 20 December 1996).
German Copyright Act	Act on Copyright and Related Rights, as amended up to Act of June 23, 2021 (Germany).
French Intellectual Property Code	France, Intellectual Property Code, consolidated version as of February 17, 2022 (France).

Sources

Bus.L.R.	Business Law Reports
CMLR	Common Market Law Reports
CUP	Cambridge University Press
ECDR	European Copyright and Design Report
EIPR	European Intellectual Property Review
FSR	Fleet Street Reports
Intl J Cult Prop	International Journal of Cultural Property
IIC	International Review of Intellectual Property and Competition Law
IPQ	Intellectual Property Quarterly
JIPITEC	Journal of Intellectual Property, Information Technology and E-Commerce Law
JIPLP	Journal of Intellectual Property Law & Practice
MLR	Modern Law Review
OUP	Oxford University Press
QMJIP	Queen Mary Journal of Intellectual Property

TABLE OF CASES

European Union

United Kingdom

United States

Other Jurisdictions

Australia

France

Germany

Italy

Israel

TABLE OF LEGISLATION

International

Europe

United Kingdom

United States

Other

Introduction

The starting point of this book is cultural heritage. This familiar concept covers everything and nothing, belongs to everyone and no one, and is both there for us to experience, but also just out of reach. For lawyers and non-lawyers alike, it is easy to make vague statements about the value of cultural heritage. But when actual decisions need to be made regarding its preservation, its ownership and, especially for this book, its digitisation, then the lack of precision becomes apparent. It requires asking, 'what exactly is cultural heritage, and what can we do with it, or do to it?'

However, these questions are answered differently by cultural property law and copyright law. From a copyright perspective, it is tempting to equate cultural heritage with just old objects. Doing so directs the attention to the public domain only, and so there is also no risk of infringement during its digitisation. If that option were taken, the only remaining copyright question would become: 'can we claim new copyright for digital copies?' This is also a valid question and is touched upon briefly in this book, but it is not the main issue at hand. Choosing heritage as the starting point means a wider interpretation of its scope should be embraced; the challenges about its ownership and integrity need to be taken into consideration; and its safety and availability need to be prioritised. But this wide scope also means that there will be overlap between protected subject matter, so copyright will be an obstacle to digitisation.

Before I go any further in introducing this book, I need to be clear to the reader: my position is not hidden very well if one reads the title and the subtitle without the colon: digitising cultural heritage clashes with copyright law. Perhaps holding a neutral stance at first and then deciding on a negative position would have been a surprising twist, but the simple logic is that if something is protected, this will be a problem for others wanting access to the same thing. This does not mean that this book will argue for every work being immediately digitised and freely circulated, as that would require abolishing copyright altogether. But there is room for readjusting the copyright laws for digitisation by heritage institutions.

Cultural Property Law and Copyright Law: Definitions and Problems

Before we can discuss the impact of copyright law on the digitisation of cultural heritage, the first step is to define heritage. Relevant instruments are shaped by the history, purpose and stakeholders, so their definitions are therefore of limited use.[1] Its scope is not static, and has expanded over time, together with the responsibility and the legal basis for protection. Similarly, cultural property instruments identify the responsible parties differently, thus creating further confusion on whether heritage belongs to the entirety of humankind, nations, even groups, communities and in some cases, individuals. This is further exacerbated by how different problems and solutions are prioritised in the instruments, such as protection from physical destruction, repatriation and inventory-making. Determining the scope will require asking three main questions: (i) what is the scope of cultural heritage, (ii) whose heritage is it, and (iii) what are the dangers faced by heritage? Since there is no single instrument that answers everything in a neat and tidy way, identifying patterns and goals (referred as 'principles') for cultural heritage is the next best option.

Lately there has also been a push towards digitisation, as heritage institutions are encouraged to digitise their collections.[2] The COVID-19 pandemic especially showed how fragile our access to cultural heritage institutions can be. Although making copies of objects is not a new practice, digitisation comes with its own unique complexities. It is a method that has been slowly but steadily embraced by heritage institutions in the past few decades, with some wide scale projects emerging over time.[3] Compared to older practices of copying, digitisation is mostly viewed as a method to increase access, as opposed to being viewed as solely for preservation. Newer technologies such as 3D scanning, virtual and augmented reality, and machine learning are creating more opportunities to facilitate the public's interaction with items from the past. However, when digitisation and heritage meet, several obstacles reveal themselves. Financial, technical, organisational and legal challenges can discourage heritage institutions from digitising their collections. Out of these challenges, copyright especially emerges as a strict limit to which works can be digitised, and who can subsequently view the digital copies.

The problem seems straightforward at first. If we determine the subject matter of digitisation from the perspective of cultural property law, then it includes material that is both protected and unprotected by copyright. Digitisation of the protected ones infringes the exclusive right of at least reproduction, and potentially other rights if works are placed online. Therefore, to understand the full extent of copyright's impact in the digitisation process, the following will need

[1] Observant readers might notice that so far, the subject matter is referred to as 'cultural heritage' but the law around it is referred to as 'cultural property law' in this book, due to how earlier instruments used the term 'property'. The terminology will be addressed in the next chapter.

[2] UNESCO Recommendation Concerning the Preservation of, and Access to, Documentary Heritage Including in Digital Form (Paris, 2015); Commission Recommendation (EU) 2021/1970 of 10 November 2021 on a common European data space for cultural heritage [2021] OJ L401/5.

[3] Examples include projects such as Project Gutenberg, Internet Archive, Million Book Project, Digital Public Library of America, Google Books and HathiTrust in the US, and GABRIEL, The European Library, and Europeana in Europe (also noting their overlaps in content).

to be asked: what should be taken into consideration at the beginning of projects (impact of non-legal concerns); what will be digitised (heritage overlapping with copyright); who performs digitisation (authorship and beneficiaries for defences); what is involved in digitising 2D/3D/audiovisual works (economic and moral rights); what is the purpose of digitisation (applicable defences); how to classify digital copies (new copyright);[4] and finally, what is the impact of new technologies such as artificial intelligence and virtual reality (for potential infringement and new defences). Copyright is involved in all of these questions, meaning that at best there are some uncertainties, and at worst, obstacles to digitisation. Addressing the copyright problem is needed for more digitisation from heritage institutions, thereby benefiting the public.[5]

Introducing the 'Clashes'

After answering the abovementioned questions on cultural property and the copyright implications of the digitisation process, this book embraces a three-pronged approach. These are framed as 'clashes' between copyright and digitisation of cultural heritage in this book: (i) the theory, (ii) the law, and (iii) the practice.

The first is the clash in theory, handled first since it is the underlying cause of problems. On one side we have cultural heritage, with its wide scope and multiple owners, and the aim is to keep to heritage safe and accessible through various methods including digitisation. On the other, we have copyright protection, which is needed to ensure that the author controls their work for a limited time, allowing them to monetise their labour and protect their personality. To what extent can the principles emerging from cultural property law allow overriding the justifications for copyright for the author? How this question is answered will impact on the clash of laws and will also depend on which stakeholders are listened to.

The second clash is the law, specifically on whether digitisation activity and subsequently making this available are infringing, and whether the defences/licensing allow such activities. Understanding this clash requires asking if the laws impacting digitisation are sufficiently clear and consistent. For example, if the aim is to create digital copies for preservation and never to show it to anyone, is copyright still going to be an obstacle? Or does the impact change according to the purpose of digitisation and the copyright status of the material to be digitised? This book focuses specifically on the EU, the UK, and the US as the main

[4] Some parties claim new copyright over copies, but it will be argued that the likelihood of sufficient originality is low when creating an accurate representation of heritage.

[5] 'Member States are encouraged to periodically review copyright codes and legal deposit regimes to ensure they are fully effective, with limitations and exceptions, for preserving and accessing documentary heritage in all its forms.' (UNESCO, 'Recommendation Concerning the Preservation of, and Access to, Documentary Heritage Including in Digital Form' art 4.6).

jurisdictions for their long-term digitisation efforts and different approaches to copyright – but the outcome would have been inconsistent regardless of which jurisdictions were chosen. So, an additional question emerges on whether the jurisdictional differences allow more room for digitisation. The law is shaped by the theory, and it both affects and is affected by what is happening in the practice.

The third clash is in the practice, caused by the conflicting interests of the stakeholders. There are various parties involved in digitisation (cultural heritage institutions, commercial and non-commercial users, digitisers, authors, publishers, producers and collective management organisations), but it might be possible to group them into two sides (parties that seek more protection versus parties that seek more access) whose interests need to be balanced based on the theory and the law. Understanding the impact of this clash in practice will require looking into the public reactions to developments and the use of empirical evidence, in the form of semi-structured interviews with experts in the heritage sector.

Structure and Limitations

Chapter one will set the scope by examining the history of cultural property protection and the relevant UNESCO instruments. It will then discuss the ownership and selection of cultural heritage and the role of heritage institutions, before illustrating the dangers faced by heritage to show why this requires attention. This chapter will establish the 'principles of cultural property law' to establish the patterns and goals that will support the other chapters.

Chapter two will explore the digitisation process through the perspective of copyright law, starting with the selection of material, the parties performing it, the activities required for different mediums, the purpose of digitisation, and the conditions leading to copyright infringement risk or new copyright. This chapter will also cover new uses of digital heritage, such as AI, which could lead to more copyright uncertainties.

Chapter three will focus on the theoretical clash. There are considerable differences in terms of how cultural property law and copyright law treat ownership and commodification of heritage/works, and what is left for the public. Regardless of the theory behind copyright, whether it is about rewarding the labour or protecting the personal connection with the author or about achieving a utilitarian balance, this chapter will show that copyright justifications are incompatible with the 'heritage of all humankind'.

Chapter four will address the legal clash by looking in detail at three areas. The first, digitising for preservation, will analyse the rights affected (reproduction and adaptation) and the existing preservation exceptions. The second, digitising for providing access, will focus on the rights affected when the digitised versions are shared with the public (communication to public, distribution, public display, rental and lending) and compare the methods of making them available, such as relying on copyright defences or licensing options. The third section will focus on digitising certain types of works (referred as 'special cases') including orphan works, unpublished works and out-of-commerce works. The chapter will conclude with an overview of the World Intellectual Property Office's efforts in finding an international solution.

Chapter five will turn to the practical clash. It will consider the relevant parties and their clashing interests, followed by more specific examples. The reactions to past digitisation projects and discussions in the EU and US have led to changes in copyright laws, which satisfied some stakeholders more than the others, so their analysis will help in identifying the patterns in the practice. This will then be supported by empirical research on the impact of copyright on digitisation.

Chapter six provides a conclusion with recommendations. It will summarise the patterns and will consider two different options: low impact changes (changing the scope of existing rights and defences) with specific recommendations for the chosen jurisdictions versus high impact changes (and why a new defence might face difficulties).

It is understandable that for readers with sufficient familiarity with cultural property or copyright law, it might be more appealing to directly move on the chapters dealing with the clashes or follow a mixed order while reading this book. For example, readers familiar with copyright terminology can start with the interview findings in chapter five to understand the concerns in practice, before moving to chapter one on cultural heritage.

There are also limitations to what can be covered in this book. On the cultural heritage side, the book recognises but does not fully cover the impact of authorised heritage discourse and the debates surrounding repatriation, treatment of traditional knowledge and traditional cultural expressions, or national cultural heritage codes. It focuses on the digitisation activities of cultural heritage institutions and experts, so the actions of private buyers and topics such as auctions, import and export, shipping, tax and insurance are not covered. On the legal side, the focus is on copyright law so other forms of intellectual property, contract and competition law are recognised but are only partly addressed.

Finally, it is necessary to recognise that there is no natural end to this story. The concerns are constantly changing, and the targets are moving: first, cultural heritage protection developed in a piecemeal way, then it was the start of digitisation projects, then the major lawsuits, then it was the changes in defences, combined with other legal developments on special cases. There were also technological changes to take into consideration, with the developments in 3D technology, and rapid developments in artificial intelligence, while at the same time not knowing what other technologies might emerge in the future. But unfortunately seeing the full impact of Copyright in Digital Single Market Directive, and the decisions on

AI and controlled digital lending will need more years after this book is completed. The law is accurate up until 15 September 2024.

Although this book is for supporting the digitisation of cultural heritage and working towards reducing the negative impact of copyright (and the uncertainty around it), it must be recognised early on that there is no perfect solution to this problem. However, any efforts in solving this problem will need to take theory, law and practice into consideration.

1

The Scope of Cultural Heritage

Determining the scope of cultural heritage is the first step for understanding how copyright clashes with the digitisation of cultural heritage. Historically, the boundaries of the scope of cultural heritage, and the law around it, have changed numerous times based on multiple factors, such as preceding events, the purpose of the multilateral instrument and the parties whose interests are at stake. This makes it more difficult to pinpoint exactly what counts as heritage.

In the absence of solid limitations to the scope, patterns and principles need to be identified. By discussing the scope (question of what), ownership and responsibility (question of who) and the dangers surrounding heritage (question of why), this chapter will establish three principles of cultural property law. These will then shape the subject matter to be tested against the boundaries of copyright throughout this book.

First, the chapter will examine the problem with scope of cultural heritage, which will be supported by an overview of relevant instruments from cultural property law and more recent recommendations on digital heritage, where the first 'principle' on the extent of protection will emerge. Then it will question exactly whose heritage is at risk, and what the role of the heritage institutions should be. Delving deeper into the question of who can decide 'heritage' status, and therefore exclude others, will lead to the second 'principle' on the ownership and selection of cultural heritage. Finally, the chapter will focus on the dangers surrounding cultural heritage. These dangers could cause losing access to cultural heritage permanently (such as institutions burning down), temporarily (such as the COVID-19 pandemic), or even include ethical dangers of misuse. Predicting these and taking pre-emptive measures is therefore key. The last section will establish the third principle on the responsibility for keeping heritage safe and accessible.

1.1. What is Cultural Heritage?

1.1.1. Problem with Definitions

First, 'culture' needs to be defined.[1] As suggested by Edward Burnett Tylor, culture is the 'complex whole which includes knowledge, belief, arts, moral, law, custom,

[1] 'Without a precise definition of terms, neither systematization nor precise isolation of problems is possible ... But culture has never been precisely defined according to the standards of science': A Blumenthal, 'A New Definition of Culture' (1940) 42(4) *American Anthropologist* 571, 572.

and any other capabilities and habits acquired by man as a member of society'.[2] It is 'socially inherited patterns of behaviour',[3] as the members of the group respond to each other until they form 'common modes of thinking and acting', creating shared traditions.[4]

'Heritage' is also a vague term, signifying what was left by our ancestors to be enjoyed and utilised, opening up questions on who inherits what from whom. There is also a challenging choice to be made between the terms cultural 'property' and cultural 'heritage', despite the shift towards the latter in the legal instruments.[5] There are arguments in the academic literature that see 'heritage' as broader and more valuable than 'property', because property is something that can be exploited.[6] At the same time, there is also a potential to reclaim the word 'property', but with a revised understanding of the context.[7] A deeper dive into cultural property law is needed before selecting between heritage and property at the end of this chapter. Unfortunately, using the combination of two vague terms, 'culture' with 'property/ heritage' will be therefore equally, if not more, challenging for the purpose of legal analysis.

If we turn to the academic literature in our search for a definition, we see that cultural heritage is the result of the cumulative experience of humankind; it is both what was left by previous generations and what will be preserved, developed and left for future generations. It encompasses both the past and the future, it is here the idea emerges that cultural heritage might be more than only 'old' objects.[8]

Needing a more precise definition, we have to turn to legal instruments and the historical framework of cultural property protection. An overview of cultural property law will show that each change in the definition usually reflects the

[2] EB Tylor, *Primitive Culture: Researches into the Development of Mythology, Philosophy, Religion, Language, Art, and Custom, Vol 1* (London, John Murray, 1871) 1.

[3] E Sapir, 'Cultural Anthropology and Psychiatry' (1932) 27(3) *Journal of Abnormal and Social Psychology* 229, 235–36.

[4] K Young, *An Introductory Sociology* (New York, American Book Company, 1934) 19.

[5] Lixinki frames this as a shift from a legal (property) to a non-legal (heritage) term, that signifies 'victory of non-lawyers in this area': L Lixinski, 'A Third Way of Thinking about Cultural Property' (2019) 44(2) *Brooklyn Journal of International Law* 563.

[6] M Frigo, 'Cultural Property v. Cultural Heritage: A "Battle of Concepts" in International Law?' (2004) 86 *International Review of the Red Cross* 367; LV Prott and PJ O'Keefe, '"Cultural Heritage" or "Cultural Property"?' (1992) 1(2) *Intl J Cult Prop* 307; J Blake, 'On Defining Cultural Heritage' (2000) 49 *International and Comparative Law Quarterly* 61.

[7] See especially: F Macmillan, *Intellectual and Cultural Property: Between Market and Community* (London, Routledge, 2021).

[8] 'compendium of the sufferings and genius of mankind': (SA Williams, *The International and National Protection of Movable Cultural Property: A Comparative Study* (New York, Oceana Publications Inc, 1978) 52); 'manifestations of human life which represent a particular view of life and witness the history and validity of that view': Prott and O'Keefe (n 6) 307; 'collective memory of peoples and nations around the world, shaped by humanity's unique ability to conceive meaning located in the past and recasting it to build a future': L Arizpe, 'The Cultural Politics of Intangible Cultural Heritage' in J Blake (ed), *Safeguarding Intangible Cultural Heritage: Challenges and Approaches* (Leicester, Institute of Art and Law, 2007) 25.

environment in which they were shaped, meaning that factors such as history and politics, at both national and international levels, can affect which heritage items are glorified and which are forgotten. The downside of the law developing as targeted responses to urgent problems is the sudden expansions of the scope, and uneven increases and decreases in relevant parties' responsibilities.

It will also show a pattern in the treatment of cultural heritage: first, one side's heritage is destroyed or taken away by their opponents or oppressors, while other parties condemn this. Then, rules are laid down where cultural heritage is defined according to the crisis at hand. Then another conflict arises, and cultural heritage is still destroyed or taken away, so the rules are revised with more input from different parties. Even without the threat of destruction or removal, other challenges regularly emerge (physical, moral, and technological), which means that the rules repeatedly need to be revised. This inconsistent treatment of heritage then impacts how its scope is determined.

1.1.2. Early Stages of Mistreatment: Plunder and Looting

The fate of the enemy's property during and after wars has long been a subject of debate. In line with the right of conquest, cultural heritage was routinely treated the same way as the rest of the enemy's property. This meant cultural heritage could also be taken away or destroyed by the winning side, like everything else that belongs to the losing side. This approach reflected the Roman understanding that, the moment a war was declared, the enemy's property became *res nullius* – property that belonged to no one, until the winning side captured it without distinguishing between military and civilian property.[9]

The motives for the taking of enemy property were sometimes as simple as economic gain, such as selling and even melting down valuable materials. Other times, they were also used as evidence of victory or they brought advantage in treaty negotiations.[10] At its worst, taking the enemy's heritage would be a form of cultural genocide, where the traces of their civilisation were removed, and communities' ties were severed from their land and their past.[11]

The pleas to exclude certain property from armed conflicts also have early origins. As one of the earliest supporters, in 164 BC, Polybius, a prominent

[9] C Forrest, *International Law and the Protection of Cultural Heritage* (London, Routledge, 2010) 56.

[10] See also MM Miles, *Art as Plunder: The Ancient Origins of Debate about Cultural Property* (New York, CUP, 2008) 13; T Kono, *The Impact of Uniform Laws on the Protection of Cultural Heritage and the Preservation of Cultural Heritage in the 21st Century* (Leiden, Martinus Nijhoff Publishers, 2010) 10.

[11] This could be in the form of ideological and/or religious iconoclasm, or pillage for financial gain. For a detailed account on the history of destruction of cultural heritage, see H Parzinger, 'Cultural Heritage under Attack: Learning from History' in J Cuno and TG Weiss (eds), *Cultural Heritage and Mass Atrocities* (Los Angeles, Getty Publications, 2022) 59–77.

historian, expressed his wish that the conquerors should leave forms of wealth in their original places in order to demonstrate dignity. His warning had two layers, these items did not contribute to the power of the city, but also seeing their art in a new context would cause jealousy and hatred within the defeated parties:

> There were indeed perhaps good reasons for appropriating all the gold and silver: for it was impossible for them to aim at a world empire without weakening the resources of other peoples and strengthening their own. But it was possible for them to leave everything which did not contribute to such strength, together with the envy attached to its possession, in its original place, and to add to the glory of their native city by adorning it not with paintings and reliefs but with dignity and magnanimity[12]

Another practice that emerged was affluent people privately collecting valuable objects, which was eventually followed by the emergence of public museums. The word 'museion' was originally used to define where a philosophical school assembled, one example being the Alexandria Museion which had a large hall for gathering in, famously attached to the Library of Alexandria.[13] Despite the scholarly and public interest reasoning, and the longer term preservation and access this practice allows, it also meant that objects were gathered to be displayed together in one place, therefore still taking them out of their intended context, in a less drastic fashion compared to their permanent destruction.

As time passed, the principle of proportionality emerged in relation to what can be destroyed in war, and the arguments for sparing religious sites and works were developed. In the seventeenth century, Grotius suggested not destroying sacred or artistic works when there is no military advantage, citing Polybius, Marcellus and Cicero.[14] With the growing scholarly interest, monuments and works of art were treated as a 'distinct category of property' that was the shared concern of the *respublica literaria* (republic of letters), that approach proved to be useful in increasing awareness.[15]

In 1758, Emerich de Vattel argued for sparing 'temples, tombs, public buildings and all works of remarkable beauty', because destroying them did not bring any advantage.[16] Nevertheless, Vattel commented on the inevitability of destruction

[12] Polybius, *The Histories*, Volume IV: Books 9–15, trans. by WR Paton in 1922, revised by FW Walbank and C Habicht, Loeb Classical Library 159 (Cambridge, Harvard University Press, 2011) Book IX, Ch 3, 29.

[13] One of the earliest examples is Ennigaldi-Nanna's Museum from 530 BCE: 'The World's Oldest Museums' (museums.eu) museums.eu/highlight/details/105317/the-worlds-oldest-museums. See also ED Van Buren, 'Museums and Raree Shows in Antiquity' (1922) 33(4) *Folklore* 337, 338.

[14] JH Merryman, *Thinking about the Elgin Marbles: Critical Essays on Cultural Property, Art and Law*, 2nd edn (Alphen aan den Rijn, Kluwer Law International, 2009) 114); P Gerstenblith, 'From Bamiyan to Baghdad: Warfare and the Preservation of Cultural Heritage at the Beginning of 21st Century' (2006) 37 *Georgetown Journal of International Law* 245, 249; R O'Keefe, *The Protection of Cultural Property in Armed Conflict* (Cambridge, CUP, 2006) 8–9.

[15] R O'Keefe (n 14) 8.

[16] 'It is declaring one's self an enemy to mankind, thus wantonly to deprive them of these monuments of art and models of taste': E de Vattel, *The Law of Nations or the Principles of Natural Law, applied to*

at times, especially in bombardments when they are the only means of defeating the enemy.[17] In 1772, Rousseau argued for the protection of civilian property unless it was absolutely necessary to achieve a military objective,[18] which meant that the scope of suggested protection was even wider (now covering civilian property). Combined with the destruction of remnants of the *Ancien Régime*, in 1789 the French Revolution also helped solidify the new approach to nationalising the cultural heritage, with the focus on preserving the *patrimonie*.[19]

Nevertheless, the practice of removing cultural heritage as an outcome of armed conflicts and colonialism continued well into the nineteenth century. A well-known example is the Napoleonic Wars, which systematically brought items from Italy, Austria and Egypt to the Louvre Museum between 1796 and 1812, based on the argument that France deserved them more. But instead of basing their claim on the rights of the conqueror, the basis for keeping them was that France, 'as a centre of liberty, of enlightened political thought and the pivot of Europe', should be where the whole world turned to for inspiration.[20] This argument was opposed both at national and international levels, the Duke of Wellington questioned the legality of Napoleon's acquisitions, and Lord Castlereagh and representatives of other allied powers forced France to return the items, showing an increasing consciousness for cultural heritage.[21]

Another example is the looting of the Benin Bronze by the British in 1897. The Oba had a specialist guild of bronze casters, and these were made solely for Oba, or to be gifted by him.[22] After the vice-consul of British Trading Post's expedition was killed, a punitive raid was held and countless artefacts including the Benin Bronze were collected and later sold to cover the costs of the expedition.[23] These objects are currently held in many different museums and private collections, so their return is not straightforward.[24]

the Conduct and to the Affairs of Nations and Sovereigns (1758), *Book 3: Of War* para 168. For the online version of anonymous 1797 translation, edited by B Kapossy and R Whatmore (Indianapolis, Liberty Fund, 2008) see oll.libertyfund.org/titles/2246.

[17] ibid paras 168–69.

[18] 'When a full-scale war is going on, a prince is entitled to help himself to anything in the enemy country that belongs to the public, but if he is just he will respect the lives and goods of individuals': J-J Rousseau, *The Social Contract* (1772).

[19] Parzinger (n 11) 63.

[20] Gerstenblith (n 14) 251; Williams (n 8) 7.

[21] Gerstenblith (n 14) 252; Miles (n 10) 327–329; Williams (n 8) 7.

[22] For Benin Bronze and others collected by the UK, such as Rosetta Stone and Koh-i Noor diamond, see J Greenfield, *The Return of Cultural Treasures,* 3rd edn (Cambridge, CUP, 2013) 122.

[23] ibid 124–25.

[24] There have been recent partial returns from Germany and there are ongoing developments in other countries. Now there is a new wave of discussion on whether they should be held in the Museum of West African Art or the royal collection (which is argued to be less accessible to the public). For database listing artifacts in 137 institutions across 20 countries, see Digital Benin: digitalbenin.org/catalogue. See also NA Enahoro, 'Nigeria Debates the Fate of Returning Benin Bronzes *New Lines Magazine* (2 April 2024) newlinesmag.com/reportage/nigeria-debates-the-fate-of-returning-benin-bronzes.

1.1.3. Inconsistent Legislative Developments

Around the same period, the first set of rules were created. In 1863, at the request of General-in-Chief of the Union Armies, Francis Lieber prepared a set of rules for the Union forces in the American Civil War. This instrument was aimed at controlling the actions of belligerents in the enemy's land, and it is widely seen as the first attempt at codifying the conduct of war.[25]

The Lieber Code required the protection of 'classical works of art, libraries, scientific collections, or precise instruments, such as astronomical telescopes, as well as hospitals',[26] but it also allowed the removal of 'works of art, libraries, collections, or instruments belonging to a hostile nation' by the conquering state, only to decide its ownership in a treaty of peace afterwards[27] and allowed the property to be used 'when the public service may require it'.[28] This meant that, despite attempts to regulate the conduct of war, cultural heritage could still be taken away, targeted or used in cases of necessity, further contributing to its inconsistent treatment.

The twentieth century did not immediately improve the treatment of cultural heritage either. Two peace conferences were held in 1899 and 1907. Influenced by the Lieber Code, certain buildings were spared in line with the military necessity,[29] the 1899 Hague Convention prohibited pillage,[30] but allowed destroying or seizing enemy property if it was 'imperatively demanded by the necessities of war'.[31] The 1907 Hague Convention also identified certain items as private property ('property of municipalities, that of institutions dedicated to religion, charity and education, the arts and sciences, even when State property … institutions of this character, historic monuments, works of art and science') and made their seizure, destruction and wilful damage subject to legal proceedings.[32] It was also necessary for the besieged to place distinctive and visible signs on places to be avoided by land and naval forces. This additional responsibility of indicating one's own heritage also continued in the other instruments such as the 1935 Treaty on the Protection of Artistic and Scientific Institutions and Historic Monuments (Roerich Pact), the 1954 Hague Convention for the Protection of Cultural Property and national military manuals as well.[33]

[25] J Toman, *The Protection of Cultural Property in the Event of Armed Conflict* (Brookfield, Dartmouth Publishing Company, 1996) 7.

[26] Instructions for the Government of Armies of the United States in the Field (Lieber Code), 24 April 1863, art 35.

[27] ibid art 36.

[28] ibid art 34.

[29] Forrest (n 9) 68; Gerstenblith (n 14) 256.

[30] Convention (II) with Respect to the Laws and Customs of War on Land and its annex: Regulations concerning the Laws and Customs of War on Land (The Hague, 29 July 1899) arts 28 and 47.

[31] ibid art 23(g).

[32] Convention (IV) respecting the Laws and Customs of War on Land and its annex: Regulations concerning the Laws and Customs of War on Land (The Hague, 18 October 1907) art 56.

[33] For a full overview of practice relating to this rule, see ihl-databases.icrc.org/en/customary-ihl/v2/rule38.

The protection provided by 1899 and 1907 Conventions is important for two reasons: (i) they influenced the 1954 Hague Convention;[34] and (ii) they were ratified by some States that did not later ratify the 1954 Convention.[35] These conferences were a reflection of the internationalist belief that international law can restrain wars, but their accomplishments for disarmament were insufficient.[36] A third convention was due to take place in 1914, but instead the principles were tested by World War I.

After World War I, it was recognised that the rules from 1899 and 1907 were not sufficient for protection.[37] The tendency to overlook and justify the destruction of cultural property with military objective was common: for example, the targeting of Reims Cathedral was justified by Germany since it was being used as a French military observation post, but France disagreed with this.[38] Although a list of war crimes was prepared, including the destruction of historical buildings and monuments, in the end these crimes were not tried due to the political climate at the time.[39]

The rules were poorly applied again in World War II, in which Germany caused 'unprecedented punitive destruction of heritage'.[40] Many items were carried off to Germany, and this was later charged as 'looting and plundering works of art' at the Nuremberg trials.[41] This can be interpreted as a stronger reaction to looting of cultural heritage than before. But it also requires asking whether there would be a trial for looting works of art, if the other atrocities of World War II had not taken place. Furthermore, items forcibly taken from the Jewish families were not necessarily returned to the families, but either returned to the state itself (if they were recovered by the Allied Expeditionary Force) or shipped away as a compensation for Nazi damage (if they were recovered by Soviet Trophy Brigades), not addressed until a later stage.[42]

[34] Convention for the Protection of Cultural Property in the Event of Armed Conflict with Regulations for the Execution of the Convention (The Hague, 14 May 1954). ('1954 Hague Convention').

[35] For example, the United States did not ratify it until 2008. The UK debated it for a while and ratified it in 2017. See PJ O'Keefe and LV Prott (eds), *Cultural Heritage Convention and Other Instruments – A Compendium with Commentaries* (Builth Wells, Institute of Art and Law, 2011) 16; D Gillman, *The Idea of Cultural Heritage* (Leicester, Institute of Art and Law, 2006) 28; Gerstenblith (n 14) 263; Statement by John Glen, 'Ratification of the 1954 Hague Convention and Protocols: Written Statement' (parliament.uk, 2017) www.parliament.uk/business/publications/written-questions-answers-statements/written-statement/Commons/2017-09-12/HCWS125.

[36] L Müller, *Neutrality in World History* (New York, Routledge, 2018) 119.

[37] Toman (n 25) 14.

[38] L Moffett, 'A Bridge Too Far? Attacks against Cultural Property used as Military Objectives as War Crimes: The *Prlić et al.* Case and the Mostar Bridge' (2020) 20(2) *International Criminal Law Review* 214.

[39] Forrest (n 9) 70.

[40] K Fitz-Gibbon (ed), *Who Owns the Past?* (New Brunswick, Rutgers University Press, 2005) 4; Gerstenblith (n 14) 258.

[41] Merryman, *Thinking about the Elgin Marbles* (n 14) 122.

[42] A Herman, *Restitution: The Return of Cultural Artefacts* (London, Lund Humphries, 2021) 57–58; NM O'Donnell, *A Tragic Fate: Law and Ethics in the Battle Over Nazi Looted Art* (Chicago, American Bar Association, 2017).

Following the destruction caused by two World Wars, the United Nations was formed. Under the UN Charter, which came into effect in 1945, Article 57 foresaw a specialised agency for education and culture. Constitution of the United National Educational, Scientific and Cultural Organization (UNESCO) came into force on 4 November 1946 with 20 signatories.[43] With regard to cultural heritage, UNESCO Constitution Article 1(2) stated that the organisation will:

> (c) maintain, increase and diffuse knowledge:
>
> By assuring the conservation and protection of the world's inheritance of books, works of art and monuments of history and science, and recommending to the nations concerned the necessary international conventions;

An instrument providing more permanent protection for cultural property was needed. UNESCO's General Conference instructed the Director-General to report on measures to ensure the protection of cultural property during armed conflict in 1949; the preparation of a draft conference with experts began in 1950 and a draft was finalised in 1952.[44]

They needed to find a balance between getting parties to participate and providing adequate protection, and also ensuring that these rules would be accepted by States with large and active militaries at the time of conflict and chaos; therefore the military necessity had to be taken into consideration.[45] Since the 1954 Hague Convention was drafted with war conditions in mind, and under the influence of the Lieber Code, the military was given the responsibility for preserving cultural heritage. But even with its training manuals, and the distinctive signs put up by the besieged, the military has other priorities than distinguishing what needed to be preserved during war – especially when the choice was between human lives and monuments. It is a hard decision between generations of heritage versus the safety of one generation.[46]

Military necessity is a recurring concept in the chain of events. Although this approach evolved in the twentieth century, it did not completely disappear. This is an indication of how other priorities can reduce the impact of positive developments for cultural heritage. Even when it is not about human lives, there will be other priorities that might require the immediate attention and the funds of the State. The fate of cultural heritage should not be left solely to one party, such as existing governments, which might prioritise other urgent public needs, so heritage should be a long-term and shared responsibility. But understandably, armed conflicts are a difficult time to ensure multiple parties work well together towards keeping cultural heritage safe, even with clear rules in place.[47]

[43] Constitution of the United Nations Educational, Scientific and Cultural Organization (London, 16 November 1945). See also 'History of UNESCO' www.unesco.org/en/history.

[44] R O'Keefe (n 14) 92–93.

[45] ibid 93.

[46] Also see H Slim, 'Choosing Between Human life and Cultural Heritage in War' in Cuno and Weiss (n 11) 299–307; EH Matthes, '"Saving Lives or Saving Stones?" The Ethics of Cultural Heritage Protection in War' (2018) 32(1) *Public Affairs Quarterly* 67.

[47] But parties can seek technical assistance from UNESCO, and UNESCO can also make proposals on its own initiative per art 23 of the Hague Convention.

Article 1 of the 1954 Hague Convention defines cultural property as:

(a) movable or immovable property of great importance to the cultural heritage of every people … monuments; archaeological sites; groups of building; works of art; as well as scientific collections …
(b) buildings whose main and effective purpose is to preserve or exhibit the movable cultural property … museums, large libraries and depositories of archives …
(c) centers containing a large amount of cultural property

This definition was in line with the purpose of keeping the scope narrow and clear by placing an emphasis on buildings where heritage is kept, to make it easier to distinguish under war conditions.[48] It does not differentiate according to origin or ownership,[49] and covers all heritage that fits this definition. Similar to the 1899 and 1907 Conventions, it is up to the besieged to put up easily identifiable signs on the cultural heritage.[50]

UNESCO's domain was questioned since the very beginning, especially: (i) whether it will act like a governmental or non-governmental organisation, (ii) whether it would stay limited to education and culture, or cover other domain such as science, and finally (iii) whether it would rely on a 'sense of worldwide scientific humanism' or limit itself to the interests of the majority of its members.[51] But the real difficulty lies in the enforcement of the UNESCO instruments. When something goes wrong, there is not much to do other than require the cessation of the wrongful act, or resort to countermeasures, such as trading sanctions or suspension of diplomatic relations.[52] But even when these measures are applied, and the international community disapproves, there is no guarantee that cultural heritage will be safe, as seen in the destruction caused by the Taliban or ISIS, or most recently in the example of Russia.

1.1.4. Scope Constantly Growing

After the 1954 Convention, the scope of cultural heritage continued to grow with other instruments drafted and implemented. One of the key instruments in cultural heritage protection was the Convention on the Means of Prohibiting and Preventing the Illicit Import, Export and Transfer of Ownership of Cultural

[48] Kono, *The Impact of Uniform Laws* (n 10) 109; Forrest (n 9) 85; Blake, 'On Defining Cultural Heritage' (n 6) 62.

[49] Williams (n 8) 36.

[50] To see this sign: UNESCO, 'Distinctive Emblem of the 1954 Hague Convention' www.unesco.org/en/heritage-armed-conflicts/convention-and-protocols/emblem. At the same time, there is no guarantee that these signs will be respected, as a recent example, despite both being parties to the Hague Convention, Russia has so far deliberately damaged a large amount of Ukrainian cultural heritage, even with the signs placed by UNESCO in 2022 as an emergency measure: UNESCO, 'Ukraine: over 150 cultural sites partially or totally destroyed' (Unesco.org, 24 June 2022) whc.unesco.org/en/news/2453; UNESCO, 'Damaged cultural sites in Ukraine verified by UNESCO' (UNESCO, 7 February 2024) www.unesco.org/en/articles/damaged-cultural-sites-ukraine-verified-unesco?hub=66116.

[51] K Huefner, *What can save UNESCO?* (Berlin, Frank & Timme, 2015) 16–17.

[52] Forrest (n 9) 401.

Property,[53] which was in reaction to the growing interest in archaeological excavations and the artefacts being carried to other countries. Unlike the 1954 Convention concerned with deliberate and accidental destruction to immovables, preventing illicit trade required listing different types of movables.[54]

Article 1 reads:

> For the purposes of this Convention, the term 'cultural property' means property which, on religious or secular grounds, is specifically designated by each State as being of importance for archaeology, prehistory, history, literature, art or science and which belongs to the following categories:
>
> (a) Rare collections and specimens of fauna, flora, minerals and anatomy, and objects of palaeontological interest;
> (b) Property relating to history, including the history of science and technology and military and social history, to the life of national leaders, thinkers, scientists and artist and to events of national importance;
> (c) Products of archaeological excavations (including regular and clandestine) or of archaeological discoveries;
> (d) Elements of artistic or historical monuments or archaeological sites which have been dismembered;
> (e) Antiquities more than one hundred years old, such as inscriptions, coins and engraved seals;
> (f) Objects of ethnological interest;
> (g) Property of artistic interest, such as: (i) pictures, paintings and drawings produced entirely by hand on any support and in any material (excluding industrial designs and manufactured articles decorated by hand); (ii) original works of statuary art and sculpture in any material;(iii) original engravings, prints and lithographs; (iv) original artistic assemblages and montages in any material;
> (h) Rare manuscripts and incunabula, old books, documents and publications of special interest (historical, artistic, scientific, literary, etc.) singly or in collections;
> (i) Postage, revenue and similar stamps, singly or in collections;
> (j) Archives, including sound, photographic and cinematographic archives;
> (k) Articles of furniture more than one hundred years old and old musical instruments.

Since it is based on 'compromise between exporting and importing states', the list of protected subject matter is exhaustive, excluding other forms of heritage. Article 1 also allows States to designate what is of importance. While recognising that the most accurate decisions about the nature of heritage can be achieved at a national level, this also means allowing States to determine what can be exported freely for gain.[55]

[53] Convention on the Means of Prohibiting and Preventing the Illicit Import, Export and Transfer of Ownership of Cultural Property (Paris, 14 November 1970) ('1970 Convention').

[54] 1978 Recommendation for the Protection of Movable Cultural Property art 1 also has identified 11 categories of movables, but does not fully overlap with the 1970 categories ('1978 Recommendation').

[55] Forrest (n 9) 170; IA Stamatoudi, *Cultural Property Law and Restitution* (Cheltenham, Edward Elgar, 2011) 37.

This instrument is then followed by the introduction of 'world heritage': compared to the 1954 Convention being a reaction to the losses in armed conflict and the 1970 Convention being a reaction to increased trafficking, the definition in the 1972 World Heritage Convention is shaped by the increasing tourism to and accessibility of heritage sites, and the realisation that there are other challenges to preserving heritage such as 'increasing urbanisation, industrialisation, social and economic upheaval, pollution and climate change'.[56] This Convention identifies 'world heritage' as something that concerns all humankind.[57]

The same instrument defines both cultural heritage and natural heritage separately; the definition of 'cultural heritage' in Article 1 is similar to the 1954 Convention but with more detail:

> Monuments: architectural works, works of monumental sculpture and painting, elements or structures of an archaeological nature, inscriptions, cave dwellings and combinations of features, which are of outstanding universal value from the point of view of history, art or science;
>
> groups of buildings: groups of separate or connected buildings which, because of their architecture, their homogeneity or their place in the landscape, are of outstanding universal value from the point of view of history, art or science;
>
> sites: works of man or the combined works of nature and man, and areas including archaeological sites which are of outstanding universal value from the historical, aesthetic, ethnological or anthropological point of view.[58]

The common qualifier here, 'outstanding universal value', is not defined under the 1972 Convention, but is addressed under the Operational Guidelines. Six of these criteria are for cultural heritage and the other four are more focused on natural heritage.[59]

World Heritage Status comes with a large increase in the annual number of visitors.[60] This status supports the sites and the surrounding areas, but also requires investing in preventing the over-exploitation of the sites.[61] The process involves State Parties producing a Tentative List, updated every ten years, and only some of those are nominated (one nomination per State).[62] Limiting the number of nominations means there will be some prioritisation in what State parties choose. This could lead to overlooking heritage more valuable to minorities, and/or less

[56] Forrest (n 9) 224.

[57] Convention concerning the Protection of the World Cultural and Natural Heritage (Paris, 16 November 1972) ('World Heritage Convention'). The Preamble states: 'Considering that deterioration or disappearance of any item of the cultural or natural heritage constitutes a harmful impoverishment of the heritage of all the nations of the world'.

[58] 'Natural heritage', that covers the natural features, geological and physiographical formations and natural sites, is defined under art 2 of this instrument.

[59] Operational Guidelines for the Implementation of the World Heritage Convention. WHC.24/01. These guidelines are updated regularly: whc.unesco.org/en/guidelines. ('Operational Guidelines').

[60] MT Albert and B Ringbeck, *40 Years World Heritage Convention: Popularizing the Protection of Cultural and Natural Heritage* (Berlin, De Gruyter, 2015) 139.

[61] ibid 145.

[62] Operational Guidelines (n 59).

likely to attract tourists, thus creating the risk of uneven treatment of relevant communities.[63]

This was followed by another expansion in the scope of heritage recognised by the UNESCO instruments: intangible heritage. Recognising intangible heritage in the World Heritage Convention was debated but, in the end, it was not included.[64] Throughout subsequent developments, solidified by the UNESCO Convention in 2003, intangible cultural heritage was eventually included within the protected scope.[65]

Article 2 of 2003 Convention defines its subject matter as:

> 1. The 'intangible cultural heritage' means the practices, representations, expressions, knowledge, skills – as well as the instruments, objects, artefacts and cultural spaces associated therewith – that communities, groups and, in some cases, individuals recognize as part of their cultural heritage …
>
> 2. The 'intangible cultural heritage', as defined in paragraph 1 above, is manifested inter alia in the following domains:
>
> (a) oral traditions and expressions, including language as a vehicle of the intangible cultural heritage;
> (b) performing arts;
> (c) social practices, rituals and festive events;
> (d) knowledge and practices concerning nature and the universe;
> (e) traditional craftsmanship.[66]

In terms of stakeholders, this instrument also mentions 'communities, groups, and in some cases, individuals' as the parties who should be the ones recognising these as part of their cultural heritage, and mentions that it is transmitted from generation to generation.[67] So while creating a national and international responsibility, the instrument still puts the creators of such heritage into focus.[68]

[63] C Cameron and M Rössler, *Many Voices, One Vision: the Early Years of the World Heritage Convention* (London, Routledge, 2013) 231–32.

[64] Kono, *The Impact of Uniform Laws* (n 10) 82.

[65] UNESCO World Conference on Cultural Policies 1982, Recommendation on the Safeguarding of Traditional Culture and Folklore 1989, Living Human Treasures Programme 1993, Programme of the Proclamation of Masterpieces of the Oral and Intangible Heritage of Humanity 1997, UNESCO Convention for the Safeguarding of the Intangible Cultural Heritage (Paris, 17 October 2003) ('2003 Convention').

[66] 2003 Convention, art 2.

[67] 2003 Convention, art 2. J Blake, 'UNESCO's 2003 Convention on Intangible Cultural Heritage – the Implications of Community Involvement in Safeguarding' in L Smith and N Akagawa (eds), *Intangible Heritage* (London, Routledge, 2008) 45–73.

[68] For discourses on intangible cultural heritage and intellectual property, also in the form of Traditional Knowledge and Traditional Cultural Expression, see J Blake, *Safeguarding Intangible Cultural Heritage: A Practical Interpretation of the 2003 UNESCO Convention* (Cheltenham, Edward Elgar, 2023); L Lixinski and J Blake, *The 2003 Intangible Heritage Convention: A Commentary* (Oxford, OUP, 2020); C Antons and W Logan (eds), *Intellectual Property, Cultural Property and Intangible Cultural Heritage* (London, Routledge, 2018); M Torsen and J Anderson, 'Intellectual Property and the Safeguarding of Traditional Cultures: Legal Issues and Practical Options for Museums, Libraries and Archives' (World Intellectual Property Organization, 2010); A Xanthaki, S Valkonen, L Heinämäki

In parallel, the UNESCO Charter on the Preservation of Digital Heritage also kept its focus very wide and includes both born-digital and converted to digital:

> The digital heritage consists of unique resources of human knowledge and expression. It embraces cultural, educational, scientific and administrative resources, as well as technical, legal, medical and other kinds of information created digitally, or converted into digital form from existing analogue resources. Where resources are "born digital", there is no other format but the digital object.
>
> Digital materials include texts, databases, still and moving images, audio, graphics, software and web pages, among a wide and growing range of formats. They are frequently ephemeral, and require purposeful production, maintenance and management to be retained.[69]

More recent developments include two recommendations from 2015 on heritage in digital form and protection of museums, showing that UNESCO is trying to adapt to changes in technology and heritage practices.[70] This indicates that the scope of heritage can and will change again and will be subject to inconsistent treatment, but this time due to developments other than armed conflicts and illicit trade.

Turning from international to regional approaches, it is also necessary to mention the involvement of the EU[71] and the Council of Europe in defining the scope of cultural heritage, which also consists of multiple instruments with multiple definitions:[72] The 1954 European Cultural Convention places on its Contracting Parties the responsibility to take appropriate measures to safeguard the 'common cultural heritage of Europe' and refers to 'languages, history and civilisation' and 'objects of cultural value', without providing a clearer list of subject matter.[73] The 1985 Convention for the Protection of Architectural Heritage defines its scope very similar to the 1954 Hague Convention and focuses on 'monuments, group of buildings and sites'.[74] The 1992 Convention for the Protection of the

and P Nuorgam (eds), *Indigenous Peoples' Cultural Heritage* (Leiden, Brill Nijhoff, 2017); L Lixinski, *Intangible Cultural Heritage in International Law* (Oxford, OUP, 2013); T Kono, *Intangible Cultural Heritage and Intellectual Property: Communities, Cultural Diversity and Sustainable Development* (Antwerp, Intersentia, 2009); T Janke, 'Minding Culture: Case Studies on Intellectual Property and Traditional Cultural Expressions' (World Intellectual Property Organization Publication, 2003) No. 781.

[69] Charter on the Preservation of Digital Heritage (Paris, 15 October 2003), art 1.

[70] Recommendation Concerning the Preservation Of, and Access To, Documentary Heritage Including in Digital Form (2015); and Recommendation concerning the protection and promotion of museums and collections, their diversity and their role in society (2015).

[71] See Consolidated Version of the Treaty on European Union [2008] OJ C115/13, art 3, and Consolidated version of the Treaty on the Functioning of the European Union [2012] OJ C326/47, art 167.

[72] For all standards, see 'Culture and Cultural Heritage Standards' (coe.int) www.coe.int/en/web/culture-and-heritage/standards.

[73] European Cultural Convention (Paris, 19 December 1954), arts 1–4.

[74] Convention for the Protection of the Architectural Heritage of Europe (Granada, 3 October 1985), art 1.

Archaeological Heritage of Europe protects 'structures, constructions, groups of buildings, developed sites, moveable objects, monuments of other kinds as well as their context, whether situated on land or under water'.[75]

Although focused on a limited region, the Council of Europe Framework Convention on the Value of Cultural Heritage for Society (Faro Convention) provides a wider definition than other European instruments:

> Article 2: cultural heritage is a group of resources inherited from the past which people identify, independently of ownership, as a reflection and expression of their constantly evolving values, beliefs, knowledge and traditions. It includes all aspects of the environment resulting from the interaction between people and places through time; …
>
> Article 3: … (a) all forms of cultural heritage in Europe which together constitute a shared source of remembrance, understanding, identity, cohesion and creativity, and
>
> (b) the ideals, principles and values, derived from the experience gained through progress and past conflicts, which foster the development of a peaceful and stable society, founded on respect for human rights, democracy and the rule of law.[76]

This definition is both wide and vague, in the sense that it includes intangible heritage but also other abstract concepts such as ideals, principles and values. The fact that this instrument limits itself to European heritage still does not provide a narrow scope.

Most recently, the European Commission has published a recommendation on a common European data space for cultural heritage,[77] indicating the benefits of digital technologies, especially in light of the pandemic; and encouraging Member States to digitise their heritage in line with the new technology. This recommendation defines 'cultural heritage assets' as:

> (a) tangible cultural heritage, such as monuments, archaeological sites, sound and audiovisual material, books, journals, newspapers, photographs, museum objects, archival documents;
> (b) intangible cultural heritage;
> (c) natural heritage, such as landscapes and natural sites, as defined in Article 2 of the Convention concerning the protection of the world cultural and natural heritage;
> (d) born digital heritage.[78]

The recommendation also sets ambitious goals for 3D digitising all of heritage at risk and 40 per cent of the most physically visited sites by 2030, raising further questions on how beneficial and realistic these goals are.

[75] European Convention on the Protection of Archaeological Heritage (Revised) (Valetta, 16 January 1992), art 1.

[76] Council of Europe Framework Convention on the Value of Cultural Heritage for Society (Faro, 27 October 2005), art 2.

[77] Commission Recommendation (EU) 2021/1970 of 10 November 2021 on a common European data space for cultural heritage [2021] OJ L401/5.

[78] ibid.

1.1.5. Principle One: We Need a Broad Interpretation of the Scope

The abovementioned Conventions and Recommendations show how flexible definitions can be, especially considering the later expansions in the scope for intangible heritage and separate instruments for archaeological, architectural and underwater with detailed categories. Furthermore, looking at these different definitions of cultural heritage, it becomes clear that these definitions are reactions to the event surrounding their creation and the varying levels of impact by the stakeholder. That means that it will be impossible to come up with a single definition, and a more flexible approach of 'guiding principles' will be used instead. For the scope of cultural heritage, we need a broader understanding of it.

1.1.5.1. Not Limited to the Tangible

The inclusion of intangible heritage in the protected subject matter was already very late, considering that other forms of heritage were recognised nearly 50 to 60 years ago by UNESCO. Furthermore, there were still weaknesses in the 2003 Convention that were subject to criticism. For example, the Convention requires States to identify elements of intangible culture in their territory,[79] which does not protect culture as a 'living, dynamic system'.[80] When a part of the culture that changes and grows with people is inventoried, it does not grow the same way, or it is more likely that it does not match the inventory anymore. While it is true that inventories keep a record of what is still being practiced or what is being lost, whether they fully represent the living heritage is debatable.

We should note the work of Laurajane Smith. By critical discourse analysis, Smith identified 'authorised heritage discourse' (AHD), in which there is a dominance of technical and aesthetic experts, and state cultural agencies in the determination and treatment of cultural heritage; this discourse (wrongly) prioritises 'monumentality and grand scale, innate artefact/site significance tied to time depth, scientific/aesthetic expert judgement, social consensus and nation building'.[81] Smith emphasises that all heritage is intangible instead, and argues that these places and objects that are seen as 'heritage' today, are only so because of current cultural processes and activities that give them a symbolic value.[82] But that also means that anything that falls outside this pre-determined scope is not 'heritage' and will not receive the same care and attention when AHD is prevalent. AHD therefore not only limits the scope of protected subject matter, but leads to

[79] 2003 Convention, art 11.

[80] MF Brown, 'Heritage Trouble: Recent Work on the Protection of Intangible Cultural Property' (2005) 12(1) *Intl J Cult Prop* 40, 48.

[81] L Smith, *Uses of Heritage* (London, Routledge, 2006) 11.

[82] ibid 3.

inequality and insufficient representation of certain communities whose heritage falls outside this scope of 'heritage' created by AHD.

The prevalence of AHD in the earlier stages of cultural property protection is hard to miss. The instruments discussed above, and UNESCO as an organisation, deserve criticism for prioritising tangible heritage for so long. These instruments largely focused on movable or immovable forms of tangible heritage, until the 1997 Programme of the Proclamation of Masterpieces of the Oral and Intangible Heritage and the 2003 Convention introduced inventorying systems for intangible heritage – even though the method's effectiveness for safeguarding is already uncertain. Not only were the definitions and scopes focused on the tangible, but less visible damages of the intangible heritage were not addressed. This also put the needs of communities with primarily intangible heritage at a disadvantage.

Does the inclusion of intangible heritage suddenly solve the problem with AHD? Not at all. There are still significant issues with the heritage inventories and ensuring community participation. But at least the dynamic relationship between tangible and intangible is more visible to all parties. Around the same time as the 2003 Convention, UNESCO also described heritage as 'a major vehicle of human aspirations' and argued that tangible heritage is its physical form but that it is intangible heritage that is 'the motor and the steering mechanism'.[83] So then it has to be recognised that not only does the scope of 'cultural heritage' include intangible heritage, but it becomes necessary to preserve the tangible items to indirectly safeguard the intangible.

So, the answer to the question 'does heritage have to be tangible' is no. The tangible and intangible distinction is already wrong, and viewing them as separate domains intrinsically ignores the heritage of some stakeholders. One way to achieve this would be to view 'material culture' only as one part of 'heritage' scope, and not even the important part.[84] Instead, it is the intangible aspect that gives rise to the necessity for protection of the physical.[85] While the later chapters will focus on the digitisation of heritage institutions' collections of tangible objects, it should be noted already that those are the digital copies of the entirety of heritage, both the tangible and intangible elements, whose loss should be prevented.

1.1.5.2. Not Limited to the Pleasant

Whether heritage has to be pleasant is the next question, considering how monumental and aesthetic heritage has been prioritised by experts and has dominated

[83] K Stenou, 'Universal Declaration on Cultural Diversity: a vision, a conceptual platform, a pool of ideas for implementation, a new paradigm' unesdoc.unesco.org/images/0012/001271/127162e.pdf.

[84] Blake (n 6) 68.

[85] Smith (n 81) 56; F Macmillan, 'The Protection of Cultural Heritage: Common Heritage of Humankind, National Cultural "Patrimony" or Private Property ?' (2013) 64 *Northern Ireland Legal Quarterly* 351.

the World Heritage List for a long time. This fits well with the 'Disneyfication' of heritage, where heritage has to be simplified and sanitised regarding any negative messages in order to attract tourism.[86] But in reality, cultural heritage can be manifested in various ways similar to everything that humans experience. Heritage does not have to be pleasant; it can be dark or disturbing, or it can reflect a negative event.

Looking at the wording of UNESCO instruments shows that there are multiple references to heritage being 'of great importance' (1954 Hague, 1964 Recommendation),[87] 'of importance for archaeology, prehistory, history, literature, art or science' (1970 Convention), 'of outstanding universal value' (1972 World Heritage) and 'of historical, artistic, scientific or technical value and interest' (1976 and 1978 Recommendations).[88] In contrast, later instruments' definitions rely less on the idea of value, but instead refer to being 'recognized as part of their cultural heritage' (2003 Convention) and 'a reflection of their constantly evolving values, beliefs, knowledge and tradition' (2005 Faro Convention).[89]

This is especially visible in relation to the World Heritage Convention. At the earlier stages, some parties expressed their opinion that it should be about celebrating achievements: 'the intent of the Convention on the cultural side has always been to commemorate man's great creative activities and not his negative accomplishments.'[90] Thankfully this approach was not followed by the other delegations and heritage signifying negative experiences still made the list early on.

But the problem with qualifiers such as 'outstanding universal value' remains, which is that they are vague and can be interpreted as assuming cultural heritage has to be grandiose, highly valued works of art (combined with a Western-centric view to what counts as valuable), which risks ignoring the heritage of the rest of the world. The term 'monument' is criticised for taking on particular registers such as 'power, greatness and beauty',[91] which also lead to forming a similar idea of what needs to be preserved. Relying too heavily on this way of approaching heritage and assuming cultural heritage should only consist of pleasant, aesthetic and old

[86] S Zukin, *Landscapes of power: From Detroit to Disney World* (Berkeley, University of California Press, 1991).

[87] 1954 Hague Convention; 1964 Recommendation on the Means of Prohibiting and Preventing the Illicit Export, Import and Transfer of Ownership of Cultural Property ('1964 Recommendation').

[88] Recommendation concerning the International Exchange of Cultural Property 1976 ('1976 Recommendation'); Recommendation for the Protection of Movable Cultural Property 1978.

[89] Council of Europe Framework Convention on the Value of Cultural Heritage for Society (Faro, 27 October 2005).

[90] Cameron and Rössler quote the letter from Peter H Bennett to M Raletich-Rajicic, Ottowa (24 November 1978, United States National Park Service, World Heritage archives, file 1976–1978) and give examples of a slave site at the Island of Gorée (listed in 1978), a camp at Auschwitz-Birkenau (listed in 1979), Hiroshima Peace Memorial (listed in 1996) and Robben Island which was used as a prison (listed in 1999): Cameron and Rössler (n 63) 223–24.

[91] Smith (n 81) 19.

monuments ignores the value of others that are unpleasant or even mundane,[92] and would lead to forming an incomplete understanding of heritage.

However, then there is also the question of whether all cultural practices are 'respectful of the principle of humanity' and therefore worth saving, Slim questions how we would react if 'Hitler Youth or the Interahamwe in Rwanda had insisted that we respect their club houses and the flags and uniforms … because they are key spaces of their culture'.[93] This is difficult, because on one side if the opinion of the current society is surveyed, people might disagree with the preservation of certain heritage after viewing things through current societal norms. But the outcome would have been different 50 or 100 years ago.[94] However, if current and future generations have nothing to learn from such heritage and do not want to keep it, then who exactly is the heritage valuable for, if the values of an uncertain future generation cannot be predicted?

There is also the issue of benefit for past generations versus current inhabitants. Can a heritage site lose its heritage 'value' if it turns into something more convenient for the locals living around it? In practice, it is possible to be delisted from the World Heritage List if a site loses its previous characteristics and does not take the necessary measures in time.[95] In 2009, Dresden Elbe Valley was removed from the World Heritage List due to losing its outstanding universal value after the building of Waldschlösschen Bridge to reduce traffic congestion.[96] A poll taken shortly after the delisting decision showed that the majority of the participants did not think the UNESCO title was necessary and the majority voted in favour of the bridge.[97] More recently, Liverpool (listed as 'Liverpool – Maritime Mercantile City' in 2004) was delisted by UNESCO in 2021, due to the development of Liverpool Waters damaging the outstanding universal value and its authenticity and integrity.[98] Similarly, the loss of heritage status is argued to have not affected the locals.[99] When heritage status and the goal of improving the daily lives of the communities conflict, the living might take priority – this is also an example of

[92] 'Even when it is the "bad" that is being preserved, it is very often the exceptionally "tragic" event that is commemorated, rather than unpleasantness that is more mundane or reflective of the general inequalities of human experiences' (Smith (n 81) 23).

[93] Slim (n 46) 299–307.

[94] A good example would be the different reactions to Zwarte Piet in Sinterklaas, with younger generations less inclined to keep the tradition with the same appearance: L Belder and A Figaroa, 'Living cultural heritage in the Netherlands: the debate on the Dutch tradition of Sinterklaas' in C Waelde, C Cummings, M Pavis and H Enright (eds), *Research Handbook on Contemporary Intangible Cultural Heritage: Law and Heritage* (Cheltenham, Edward Elgar, 2018) 342–62.

[95] Operational Guidelines (n 59) paras 192–98.

[96] UNESCO, 'Dresden is deleted from UNESCO's World Heritage List' whc.unesco.org/en/news/522.

[97] J Abramsohn, 'Dresden loses UNESCO world heritage status' (dw.com, 25 June 1009) www.dw.com/en/dresden-loses-unesco-world-heritage-status/a-4415238.

[98] UNESCO, 'World Heritage Committee deletes Liverpool – Maritime Mercantile City from UNESCO's World Heritage List' whc.unesco.org/en/news/2314.

[99] J Halliday, 'We don't need UNESCO listing, says new Liverpool heritage chief' *The Guardian* (23 September 2021) www.theguardian.com/uk-news/2021/sep/23/we-dont-need-unesco-listing-says-new-liverpool-heritage-chief.

different priorities in the treatment of cultural heritage, a lighter version of military necessity (and human lives) taking priority over protection of heritage in armed conflict.

1.1.5.3. Not Limited to the Old

In connection with not recognising heritage as a living thing, there might also be the perception that heritage needs to be 'old'. As noted by Smith, as part of AHD, authenticity/age of heritage became especially important in the nineteenth century, and this also means only experts are able to legitimately speak on behalf of the past.[100] This also means that the values of these past experts played a big role in what we consider as heritage now.

Except for a few, cultural property instruments rarely determine a time-range for heritage. For example, underwater heritage limits itself to traces of human existence that are partially or totally underwater for more than 100 years, because the 2001 instrument was influenced by the 1985 European Convention on Offences relating to Cultural Property.[101] Another example is Historic England, which usually requires listed buildings to be older than 30 years.[102]

Of course, the impact of past events can only be recognised and understood with full clarity after some time has passed. Likewise, on most occasions, the regular, day-to-day use of an object will end long before it is placed in a museum. But just being old is insufficient, there is also the element of intention to preserve by relevant parties, and heritage institutions will select what is displayed and cared for. For example, objects that were originally treated like garbage, such as leaflets and ticket stubs from the past, are now displayed in museums.[103] On some occasions, sites with more recent significance are also preserved.[104] So it is hard to pick an exact length of time, and also to apply this logic to the preservation of decaying heritage. In defining the scope of heritage, we must understand that it is not just the objects held in institutions but a constantly growing body of things. Insisting on limiting cultural heritage with an arbitrary definition of 'old' only puts humankind at a disadvantage.

Having a single definition and scope for cultural heritage would be convenient, but unfortunately this is not the case. The scope of protected subject matter

[100] 'The vagueness of "the past", its mystery, and "hard to pin downness", immediately works to render it subject to the judgement of experts such as archaeologists and historians': Smith (n 81) 29.

[101] Convention on the Protection of the Underwater Cultural Heritage (Paris, 2 November 2001) art 1. See also Kono, *The Impact of Uniform Laws* (n 10) 78.

[102] Historic England, 'What Are Listed Buildings?' (historicengland.org.uk, 10 July 2024) historicengland.org.uk/listing/what-is-designation/listed-buildings.

[103] For example, 'Rapid Response Collection' at the V&A Museum collects contemporary objects from major moments in recent history: www.vam.ac.uk/collections/rapid-response-collecting.

[104] Loulanski gives the examples of houses damaged in the 1995 Kobe earthquake, which are now preserved as memorials: T Loulanski, 'Revising the Concept for Cultural Heritage: The Argument for a Functional Approach' (2006) 13(2) *Intl J Cult Prop* 207, 217.

changed and grew according to historical developments and the purpose of the instrument. But limiting the scope to tangible, pleasant or old objects would only give us an a limited understanding of what is involved. Therefore, instead of having precise definitions, it is logical to draw some principles from cultural property legislation and literature and use these principles to guide the discussions in the upcoming chapters. The first guiding principle emerges here: the scope of heritage shall be construed in a wide manner, heritage is more than only the tangible, pleasant and old objects. Both tangible and their digital reproductions are vessels embodying heritage. But the inclusion of more recent heritage will then conflict with a time-limited monopoly (copyright) in the rest of the book.

1.2. Whose Heritage?

The second question is whose heritage is at stake, given that this is an area with multiple stakeholders with opposing views on ownership. This question is not just about where the tangible objects are held, but also determines what is preserved or listed, who is responsible for taking the right steps at the right time, and finally, who can access heritage. The issues around ownership especially matter for the rest of the book, when cultural property law and copyright law give different answers on who 'owns' the object and the rights.

The problem with the past is that there is no specific owner; some things are meant to belong to everyone and some need to be controlled by a certain community which understands the underlying intangible values better than others (such as nations, groups and individuals, or other overlapping groups such as researchers and the heritage sector). At the same time, no one should own the past, because it is not something to be owned in the first place.

Similar to the scope question, cultural property law is not helpful in solving this. An overview of the instruments provides us with references to 'heritage of every people' (1954), 'heritage of a country' (1964), 'peoples of the world' (1968), 'civilization and national culture' (1970), 'heritage of all nations of the world' (1972), 'in the opinion of the competent bodies in individual States' (1976), 'common heritage of mankind' (1978), 'common heritage of all Europeans' (1985), 'cultural heritage of all humanity' (2001), and 'communities, groups and, in some cases, individuals' (2003).[105]

This is where we see another inconsistency in the treatment of cultural heritage. Not only is its scope vague, but its owner is also uncertain. The tendency to associate heritage with either a specific group or the whole of humankind corresponds with the purpose of each instrument, and therefore is important in the forming of the second principle.

[105] In the same order: 1954 Hague Convention; 1964 Recommendation; 1970 Convention; 1972 World Heritage Convention, 1976 Recommendation; 1978 Recommendation; Convention for the Protection of the Architectural Heritage of Europe 1985; Convention on the Protection of the Underwater Cultural Heritage 2001; 2003 Convention.

1.2.1. Cultural Internationalism versus Nationalism

In addressing ownership disputes, it is necessary to mention John Henry Merryman, who is seen as the leading theorist on cultural property law, whose arguments have shaped the debates on cultural property over many years.[106] Merryman identified two ways of thinking about cultural property: cultural internationalism and cultural nationalism. These approaches can potentially help in addressing questions on where heritage is held, and who should be responsible for it.

Cultural internationalism is the understanding that cultural heritage is part of a common culture, regardless of its origin or current location.[107] The 1954 Hague Convention identifies heritage as something that belongs to everyone; its Preamble even states that the protected subject matter is 'the culture of all mankind, since each people makes its contribution to the culture of the world'.[108] This approach makes it a shared concern, requiring States to take responsibility for the protection of all cultural property. UNESCO itself is also mostly internationalist, with its purpose being to establish the 'intellectual and moral solidarity of mankind … to preserve peace',[109] therefore attaching a stronger meaning to its actions.

At the opposite end, cultural nationalism gives objects a national character. A significant distinction in cultural property law is dividing the world between source nations (cultural heritage-rich countries with fewer resources and less demand) and market nations (where demand for heritage exceeds supply).[110] The nationalist approach gives source nations control over the movement of cultural heritage and supports their repatriation claims. As a result of the earlier understanding that the winning State is free to take the cultural heritage of the losing State, many objects are currently kept and displayed in different countries. It is common for countries to seek to recover their cultural heritage removed due to colonialist approaches, and these efforts are supported by the 1970 Convention. The 1970 Convention is different from Hague 1954 in the sense that it does not distinguish between times of war and peace. Another major difference is that the 1970 Convention mostly shows a nationalist approach: it builds on the previous understanding of cultural property needing protection, but it gives heritage a more national character and highlights the importance of the context.[111]

[106] CL Lyons, 'Thinking about Antiquities: Museums and Internationalism' (2014) 21(3) *Intl J Cult Prop* 251; D Shapiro, 'A Universalist: Fathering Fields' (2014) 21(3) *Intl J Cult Prop* 237.

[107] JH Merryman, 'Two Ways of Thinking About Cultural Property' (1986) 80 *The American Journal of International Law* 831.

[108] 1954 Hague Convention, Preamble.

[109] Constitution of the United Nations Educational, Scientific and Cultural Organization (London, 16 November 1945).

[110] Merryman, 'Two Ways' (n 107) 832.

[111] 'cultural property constitutes one of the basic elements of civilization and national culture, and that its true value can be appreciated only in relation to the fullest possible information regarding is origin, history and traditional setting' (1970 Convention, Recital 3).

The weakness of this Convention is that it is essentially an uneasy compromise between source nations wanting their heritage back, and market nations wanting to move art and antiquities; and the latter have unevenly influenced the negotiations, thereby affecting its cut-off date, recommended measures, and subsequent participation by the States.[112]

In between these two approaches, cultural internationalism is continuously visible with the development of international rules. UNESCO instruments are one of the few opportunities to give preservation responsibility an international character, as it achieves something different from national measures. It is understandable that the references to humankind are abundant for when cultural heritage is in danger, and it makes sense to view it as a shared responsibility. However, that is more applicable for some forms of dangers. Based on the relevant instruments, armed conflicts and natural erosions are dangers that concern the whole of humankind, requiring action to be taken at the international level and ensuring that these are moved to safety and/or added to a list. But the dangers of looting and loss of the intangible require a more localised approach on who can identify and react to such behaviours, and who has more to lose.

While recognising the benefits of seeing preservation as an international responsibility, there are few problems with seeing this as an 'ownership' issue. More ardent supporters of internationalism will also argue that these humankind arguments should extend to who keeps cultural heritage where, and this conflating of ownership with responsibility is problematic; ownership and responsibility are two different things.

1.2.2. Problems with the 'Ownership' Question

1.2.2.1. Ignoring Communities within Nations

The first problem is whether the internationalist/nationalist distinction is helpful to everyone involved, given that the treatment of heritage also concerns communities within source nations. Returning objects to their source nations does not automatically solve the ownership concerns. Suggesting a 'third way of thinking', Lixinski both criticises and provides an alternative to Merryman's arguments on nationalism and internationalism, arguing that framing it as a debate between nations excludes communities from international decision-making, and therefore damages heritage in the long run, instead they should be added to this debate as a 'way of pluralizing access to law and decision making'.[113] However, it is only fair to recognise that this is not something that can be achieved by cultural property law alone, and has its roots in how minorities are treated by the majority in any given

[112] Forrest (n 9) 167.
[113] Lixinski, 'A Third Way' (n 5) 564–65.

State, which can change from year to year depending on historical and political developments at the time, and which is outside the scope of this book.[114]

Even if repatriation is achieved, determining the owner internally can be challenging. Since movable objects are transferred from place to place, it is possible for them to show the characteristics of more than one culture.[115] It is especially difficult if the object was taken in the distant past and if more than one group claim ownership of the same item. Furthermore, the community might be elsewhere, since geographical proximity does not always mean closer connection to the heritage: Smith argues that prioritising local communities due to geographical proximity may lead to ignoring displaced people such as the Indigenous groups in post-colonial countries.[116]

1.2.2.2. Conflating Ownership with Responsibility

The second problem is that cultural internationalism will always have an unfair advantage when the preservation responsibility and the right to keep the objects are treated as the same thing. In his works, Merryman gives the example of endangered works being moved to places where they can be better preserved, and describes the efforts towards the return of their heritage as 'destructive retention'.[117] According to Merryman, it is 'tragic' for these objects to be 'hoarded' by States without any resources, when they could be better preserved by other States that are able and willing to provide better care.[118] In another essay, Merryman defines cultural nationalism as 'nation-oriented', and he argues we should be more 'object-oriented', with an emphasis on three independent considerations: preservation, truth and access.[119]

In response to the 'destructive retention' argument, such recovery attempts by source nations are necessary to strengthen their cultural identity and their connection to the land. They can make better use of their cultural heritage object by displaying or using it within its original context, such as heritage sites.[120] If Merryman's aim of 'object-oriented' approach is about getting the object to reveal their 'truth',[121] would their source location not provide the best context? Even the wording of 'object-oriented' versus 'nation-oriented' already implies that only certain countries will know what is best for the object.

[114] On the role of 'community' in cultural property law, see Macmillan, *Intellectual and Cultural Property* (n 7); Blake, 'UNESCO's 2003 Convention' (n 67) 45–73.
[115] M Bruncevic, *Regulating Transnational Heritage: Memory, Identity and Diversity* (London, Routledge, 2021).
[116] Smith (n 81) 72.
[117] Merryman, 'Two Ways' (n 107) 846.
[118] ibid 849.
[119] JH Merryman, 'The Nation and the Object' (1994) 3(1) *Intl J Cult Prop* 61, 64.
[120] Forrest (n 9) 158.
[121] Merryman, 'Nation and the Object' (n 119) 64.

Another argument used by internationalists is that these museums are serving the public and therefore where they are kept should not matter as long as they are more accessible. This argument is then combined with arguments on how institutions like British Museum or the Louvre would be empty if certain objects were repatriated to their original locations, and those locations would be more difficult to visit. In an unpublished lecture, former director of British Museum Neil MacGregor argued that the British Museum could have been founded in any other European capital and is only in London because its founder wanted a place 'where it would be best used by a large number of people, international people as much as possible'.[122] To support this, it is argued that the display of a cultural heritage object in another State does not necessarily remove its national qualities. For example, in regard to the Parthenon Marbles, Merryman suggests that 'one can admire the Greekness of the Marbles … without concluding that they belong in Greece'.[123] But would these national qualities not be appreciated most in a national context? It is also often argued that if they were to be returned, they would be displayed not in their original place but in an indoor museum in Athens.[124] However, this is also a weak argument considering that the indoor museum is very close to the Parthenon, and that indoors provides better protection, so avoiding outdoor deterioration should be celebrated as 'object-oriented' as described above. The discussions on the fate of the Marbles are vast and beyond the scope of this book.[125]

1.2.2.3. Ownership is Further Complicated with the Creation of Copies

Ownership discussion is further affected by the ability to make copies. When physical boundaries are removed, this reduces the starkness of cultural internationalism/nationalism distinction.[126] If these copies are then shared online, that also reduces the context problem, by allowing users to view objects within their intended context or in connection with different items, especially if they are held in different countries that are unwilling to return the objects themselves.

A proposal for making digital copies also emerges from the plans for African cultural heritage held in France. After Emmanuel Macron promised their restitution in 2017, a report was prepared by Felwine Sarr and Bénédicte Savoy.[127]

[122] J Cuno, *Who Owns Antiquity?* (Princeton, Princeton University Press, 2008) xxxv.

[123] JH Merryman, 'Thinking about the Elgin Marbles' (1985) 83(8) *Michigan Law Review* 1880, 1916.

[124] Although the British Museum recognises that this argument is not sufficient: British Museum, 'The Parthenon Sculptures: The Trustees' statement' www.britishmuseum.org/about-us/british-museum-story/contested-objects-collection/parthenon-sculptures/parthenon.

[125] For a detailed analysis, see A Herman, *The Parthenon Marbles Dispute: Heritage, Law and Politics* (Oxford, Hart Publishing, 2023).

[126] See also NA Silberman, 'From cultural property to cultural data: the multiple dimensions of "ownership" in a global digital age' (2014) 21(3) *Intl J Cult Prop* 36.

[127] F Sarr and B Savoy, 'The Restitution of African Cultural Heritage. Toward a New Relational Ethics' (November 2018).

The authors recommended measures on objects in different categories, and came up with a three-phase plan for the return of objects. The second phase (which was foreseen between Spring 2019 and November 2022) included 'sharing of digital content', where digital copies were to be shared on an open-access platform and the 'rights of reproduction' to be subject to revision regarding requests from African countries from where the objects originated.[128] However, this report does not expand on the treatment of these copies.

Another example is the scanning of the Nefertiti Bust by two artists. Discovered in Egypt in 1912, this object has been in Germany ever since. Two artists shared the scans of the bust online in 2015, claiming that they brought their own scanner to the museum for the purpose of criticising the taking of cultural property by Western countries.[129] They subsequently shared the scans online and claimed that they were 'returning the heritage', although there were some concerns about the quality of scans.[130] The artists also decided against giving the scans to the Ministry of Culture of Egypt and decided that it is best that they remain public.[131]

The term 'digital repatriation' is increasingly used for making heritage remotely available to source communities in Europe, US and Australia.[132] This seems like a positive development at first. But in reality, nothing is repatriated, making this kind of 'repatriation' only desirable as a temporary measure or when copies need to be accessible to the multiple parties living in different locations. Not only do these copies not solve the problem of ownership, but they might even function as a distraction. Going back to the example of the Parthenon Marbles, whose cast copies were rejected in the past,[133] 3D copies online also have not stopped the repatriation efforts.[134] Similarly for Benin collections kept in European museums, it is suggested that online availability of digitised collections is being used to distract from returning them.[135] The Sarr-Savoy report's approach to digitised heritage was

[128] ibid 66–67.

[129] SK Katyal, 'Technoheritage' (2017) 105 *California Law Review* 1111, 1113.

[130] C Wilder, 'Swiping a Priceless Antiquity … With a Scanner and a 3-D Printer' *The New York Times* (1 March 2016) www.nytimes.com/2016/03/02/arts/design/other-nefertiti-3d-printer.html; FG Kahl, 'There's Something Fishy About the Other Nefertiti' (6 March 2016) thegreatfredini.com/2016/03/06/theres-something-fishy-about-the-other-nefertiti.

[131] For a presentation by the artists from 2017, see N Al-Badri and JN Nelles, 'The Other Nefertiti' aksioma.org/the.other.nefertiti.

[132] M Alivizatou, *Intangible Heritage and the Museum: New Perspectives on Cultural Preservation* (New York, Routledge, 2012).

[133] G Robertson, *Who Owns History? Elgin's Loot and the Case for Returning Plundered Treasure* (London, Biteback Publishing, 2019); British Museum, 'The Parthenon Sculptures: The Trustees' statement' www.britishmuseum.org/about-us/british-museum-story/contested-objects-collection/parthenon-sculptures/parthenon.

[134] 3D models of objects from the British Museum can be found at sketchfab.com/britishmuseum.

[135] 'Should technological advances make virtual representation as good as the physical objects, this logic would also apply to arguing that the European museums have no reason for keeping the physical objects': K Opoku, 'From Restitution to Digitalization: Looted Benin Treasures to Go Online' (Modern Ghana, 27 April 2020) modernghana.com/news/998338/from-restitution-to-digitalization-looted-benin.html.

also criticised by scholars regarding the uncertainties surrounding the ownership of intellectual property rights and the conditions of the open-access.[136]

Willingness to cooperate seems more likely when the tangible object has deteriorated or been destroyed completely. In these circumstances, having a digital copy can be positive, serving as a representation of what was lost, while still providing the same information and enjoyment to the public. But as long as originals are still in existence, the original object will always be more valuable than its copies due to its 'aura'.[137] What makes these objects valuable for stakeholders is their age and authenticity; so for heritage that still exist, repatriation requests and the debates on ownership cannot be solved by creating more copies. Digital repatriation cannot be sufficient on its own, and arguing otherwise would severely underestimate the existing tensions between nations, and between nations and communities.[138] Additionally, creation of digital copies then creates a new set of ownership disputes for the copies of heritage – especially in the realm of intellectual property that will be addressed in chapter two.[139]

1.2.3. Questions Beyond Ownership: Who Selects What is Preserved and Accessed?

It is also important to pay attention to the difference between owning heritage and controlling heritage. Even if the question of who should own cultural heritage is answered in one of the two ways identified above, it does not fully answer who would be responsible for other decisions. This is because control over cultural heritage not only means keeping it, but determining how it will be displayed (or if displayed at all), how it will be interpreted (in a context that could be inconsistent with the source country) and choosing which conditions will be applied for access. So, when this control switches to the externals, this means a great loss to the community.

[136] M Pavis and A Wallace, 'Response to the 2018 Sarr-Savoy Report: Statement on Intellectual Property Rights and Open Access relevant to the digitization and restitution of African Cultural Heritage and associated materials' (2019) 10 *JIPITEC* 115; L Lixinski, 'Digital Heritage Surrogates, Decolonization, and International Law: Restitution, Control, and the Creation of Value as Reparations and Emancipation' (2020) *Santander Art & Culture Law Review* 65; DO Oriakhogba, 'Repatriation of ancient Benin bronzes to Nigeria: reflection on copyright and related issues' (2022) 17(10) *JIPLP* 823–33.

[137] W Benjamin, 'The Work of Art in the Age of Mechanical Reproduction' (1935), trans H Zohn, ed H Arendt, *Illuminations* (New York, Schocken Books, 1968). See also Section 3.1.

[138] R Boast and J Enote, 'Virtual Repatriation: It Is Neither Virtual nor Repatriation' in PF Biehl and C Prescott (eds), *Heritage in the Context of Globalization*: Europe and the Americas (New York, Springer, 2013); K Hennessy, 'Virtual Repatriation and Digital Cultural Heritage: The Ethics of Managing Online Collections' (2009) 50 *Anthropology News* 5; P Dawson, R Levy and N Lyons, '"Breaking the Fourth Wall": 3D Virtual Worlds as Tools for Knowledge Repatriation in Archaeology' (2011) 11 *Journal of Social Archaeology* 387.

[139] For a similar analysis specifically focused on 3D digitisation see P Oruç, 'Rethinking who "keeps" heritage: 3D Technology, Repatriation and Copyright' (2022) 71(12) *GRUR International* 1138.

Also worth taking into consideration are the arguments by Warren on what is framed as an 'integrative perspective'.[140] Warren introduces 'the 3R's' which dominate the discussion on the ownership of cultural heritage (namely claims concerning restitution, restriction of imports and the rights of ownership and access) and argues that instead we should focus on the impact of conceptual frameworks, especially oppressive ones (such as Western, patriarchal, male-identified assumptions) and the language we use.[141] Especially noting the bias in how the debate is framed as an ownership dispute and a win-lose perspective, Warren suggests that an integrative perspective is embraced, where the cultural heritage debate is less focused on finding an owner, and more focused on preservation and custodianship with a diverse approach to values and a flexible approach for reaching compromises.[142]

Even the choice of which items of cultural heritage have been preserved up to this date is valuable information in itself, because it allows us to see what was considered worthy. But we already have an incomplete picture of remaining heritage that is supposed to belong to all humankind. The items preserved so far are incomplete, in the sense that, until a certain point in history, they were chosen by white, upper-class, male curators, which reflects the impact of AHD.[143]

Given that the instruments and lists originated from Europe, it is not surprising that Western and tangible heritage are receiving more attention – not unlike other imbalances in relation to resources in the treatment of heritage. Two decades after the World Heritage Convention, studies revealed that European sites and Christian monuments were overrepresented.[144] A 'Global Strategy for a Representative, Balanced and Credible World Heritage List' was developed, which encouraged going beyond the narrow definitions of heritage.[145]

The abovementioned 2003 Convention is a part of the efforts to recognise a diverse range of voices; both this Convention and its predecessor the 1997 Masterpieces programme required States to seek the widest possible level of participation from communities, groups and individuals. While the 2003 Convention was different from the previous instruments in the sense that it focused on

[140] KJ Warren, 'A Philosophical Perspective on the Ethics and Resolution of Cultural Property Issues' in PM Messenger (ed), *The Ethics of Collecting Cultural Property*, 2nd edn (Albuquerque, University of New Mexico Press, 1999) 1–25.

[141] Warren identifies nine main arguments that affect these 3Rs: on one side (i) claims based on rescuing cultural property from destruction, (ii) claims of legal ownership by foreign countries, (iii) claims based on common humanity ownership, (iv) claims based on cultural property export aiding promotion of values, (v) claims based on scholarly access, (vi) claims based on how restricting export will encourage illegal activities, and on the other side of the debate (vii) claims based on national identity and patrimony, (viii) claims based on country of origin, (ix) claims based on the risk of collection might negatively affect scholarly value and aesthetic integrity of cultural property: ibid 1–11.

[142] ibid 11–22.

[143] Smith (n 81) 23.

[144] UNESCO, 'Report of the Expert Meeting on the "Global Strategy" and thematic studies for a representative World Heritage List' (Paris, 20–22 June 1994) whc.unesco.org/archive/global94.htm.

[145] For expert meetings and reports between 1994 and 2004, see whc.unesco.org/en/globalstrategy/.

communities, as opposed to nations or humankind, there is no guarantee that the suggested cooperation would take place during heritage nominations. The Convention on the Protection and Promotion of the Diversity of Cultural Expressions is also similar in its purpose, referring to how 'cultural diversity forms a common heritage of humanity and should be cherished and preserved for the benefit of all'.[146] But even with all the good intentions in cultural property law, it is not guaranteed that the State will want the same things as the community. These instruments refer to 'experts', however who these experts are plays a much bigger role in practice; that also connects with AHD introduced above.[147] By determining what should count as cultural heritage, these experts effectively create or destroy heritage.[148] That also means that current curation decisions also have an impact on how the next generation will view the world so it is a positive development that representing diverse forms of heritage is now being taken more into consideration by scholars and heritage institutions.[149]

Looking specifically at who makes these decisions, there is not a closed list of 'memory institutions' in the UNESCO instruments. But what they have in common is that these institutions are curated by humans despite their seemingly universal and infallible positions.[150] So despite the best of intentions, curation decisions might still be influenced by external factors, such as reduction in resources, input by the funders (State or private), and an ongoing attempt to gain visitors' attention. Therefore, although these institutions do have the responsibility for these decisions, it is necessary to be collectively avoiding any potential bias in selection and access.

1.2.4. Principle Two: Heritage is 'For Everyone' – But How?

When we turn to the 'whose heritage' question, there is again the risk of contributing to the inconsistent treatment of cultural heritage. In terms of responsibility, saying that everybody is responsible also creates the risk of neglect, almost as a form of bystander effect. That is why it is vital to have clearer rules on the matter and increase public awareness of the importance of cultural heritage – something

[146] Convention on the Protection and Promotion of the Diversity of Cultural Expressions (Paris, 20 October 2005) Preamble.

[147] Smith (n 81) 50.

[148] L Lixinski, *International Heritage Law for Communities: Exclusion and Re-Imagination* (Oxford, OUP, 2019) 75.

[149] See also J Giblin, I Ramos and N Grout, 'Dismantling the Master's House: Thoughts on Representing Empire and Decolonising Museums and Public Spaces in Practice An Introduction' (2019) 33(4–5) *Third Text* 471; S Vawda, 'Museums and the Epistemology of Injustice: From Colonialism to Decoloniality' (2019) 71(1–2) *Museum International* 72; G Porter, 'Gender Bias: Representations of Work in History Museums' (1990) 3 *Continuum: The Australian Journal of Media & Culture*.

[150] WL Boyd, 'Museums as Centers of Controversy' (1999) 128(3) *Daedalus* 185.

that UNESCO strives to achieve. The rules must be clear in who is doing what, although this is not very easy when there is no one to enforce them.

While recognising guidance from organisations such as UNESCO is beneficial for international cooperation, it should not be assumed internationalism equals better preservation. Better preservation or more visibility cannot negate the need to repatriate. But cultural nationalism is also not sufficient on its own, as there could be more important urgencies at the national level. It is also important to consider risks of giving into the authorised heritage discourse,[151] ignoring the needs of other actors within nations (third way of seeing heritage)[152] or seeing this as a win-lose situation.[153]

As illustrated with the examples, international cooperation and motivation to preserve is possible, and it is even easier when the said object no longer exists, but the question of who 'owns' heritage is not going to go away as long as tangible copies exist. Copying heritage, and effectively making it accessible to everyone, is not going to make ownership less important. On top of that, 'digital repatriation' carries the risk of distracting from actual repatriation, and dematerialising heritage creates further ownership questions about who will own these copies.

Beyond the ownership of physical objects and their copies, there are also selection decisions that lead to inconsistent treatment of heritage. Unfortunately, selecting what gets to be preserved is usually far from perfect and is impacted by many factors such as the institution type, funding, motivation, existing bias and their willingness to receive attention from visitors. That is both true for the heritage that reaches us, and heritage that we are leaving for later. Decisions need to be made with diversity and inclusion taken into consideration.

Even if cultural heritage overcomes the hurdles of preservation and selection, there are also questions of access to heritage and its copies. Similar to the first part on defining cultural heritage, we are again left with multiple views and challenges. In that sense, the second guiding principle should be identified as 'heritage should be for everyone'. How that is achieved varies, and will depend on the international, national and institutional practices, and the voices of multiple stakeholders.

1.3. Heritage in Danger

The first two sections established that cultural heritage has a wide scope, and its ownership, selection and responsibility involve multiple stakeholders. However, this can also cause slow responses as the wider actions seem to be prompted by specific incidents. The attention given to cultural heritage could increase on certain occasions, but this might not be a consistent kind of attention. There

[151] Smith (n 81).
[152] Lixinski, 'A Third Way' (n 5).
[153] Warren (n 140) 1–25.

could be other priorities, especially in relation to military necessity. It is therefore important to think of keeping cultural heritage safe and accessible as a constant motivation.

1.3.1. Ethical Dangers

While the idea that heritage has to be recorded in tangible form comes from the Western understanding of permanence,[154] in line with AHD introduced earlier, it would be simplistic to assume the West only has tangible heritage: instead, cultural heritage in both East and West are subject to all forms of dangers. Ethical challenges concerning the treatment of heritage are not within the scope of this research, but they are still relevant for the treatment of tangible copies.

The underlying problem to consider is whether cultural heritage is more or less vulnerable when it is not recorded in any material form. While oral traditions are lost on a regular basis, in other instances they can last longer than tangible – for example a nomadic community leaving behind the tangible elements but carrying their traditions, or a monument being destroyed in war while the community moves away with their knowledge and memory intact.[155]

There are also circumstances where cultural heritage is recorded by externals to a community, which can have more devastating effects in the long run. The decisions made by externals, or their ancestors, might upset communities, and can lead to an altered and sterilised version of the past being displayed. In line with 'digital repatriation' introduced above, externals deciding to digitally 'repatriate' the heritage of others also carries the risk of accidentally releasing sensitive heritage to the internet.[156] At times, communities might not even be aware that any recorded versions exist. For example, Fourmile refers to the tapes of her grandfather speaking the language in 1959, coincidentally located in Australian Institute of Aboriginal Studies (currently Australian Institute of Aboriginal and Torres Strait Islander Studies): 'Some of my people have been trying to encourage and revive our language for about the last 10 years … is it deliberate government policy to limit funds to institutions … and thus maintaining our ignorance for political purposes?'[157]

It is even more concerning when these copies are created by externals who may want to commodify or limit whether their copies can be freely enjoyed by the

[154] K Knopf, *Decolonizing the Lens of Power: Indigenous Films in North America* (Amsterdam, Editions Rodopi, 2008) 83.

[155] J Cruikshank, 'Oral Tradition and Material Culture: Multiplying meanings of "words" and "things"' (1992) 8(3) *Anthropology Today* 5.

[156] See also WB Wendland, 'Managing Intellectual Property Options When Documenting, Recording and Digitizing Intangible Cultural Heritage' in T Kono (ed), *Intangible Cultural Heritage and Intellectual Property* (Antwerp, Intersentia, 2009); P Oruç, 'Documenting Indigenous Oral Traditions: Copyright for Control?' (2022) *Intl J Cult Prop* 29(3) 243.

[157] H Fourmile, 'Who Owns the Past? Aborigines as Captives of the Archives' (1989) 13 *Aboriginal History* 1.

source communities. Such are the examples of the collector who sold the tapes to Maliseet communities but refused their further copying,[158] or the copyright owner who refused to give copies of recording of the sacred 'Red Ochre Ceremony' to the Pitjantjatjara delegation who only accidentally found out that their sacred ceremony was recorded.[159] These challenges get especially complicated when IP law implications are taken into consideration, discussed in chapter three.

1.3.2. Physical Dangers

On the other hand, there is much attention on the physical dangers faced by heritage. Military necessity has been very visible throughout the development of cultural property law, and still functions as an excuse for destruction. Intentional destruction of heritage is identified as a war crime in many national and international instruments but it still occurs. Since cultural heritage is a direct reflection of human experience, damaging it functions as an effective way to erase the shared identity of the group in question.[160] An example is the destruction of the Bamiyan Buddhas in Afghanistan, which set a precedent for other violent acts of iconoclasm, such as the destruction of Iraqi heritage sites in 2015 by ISIS. These destructive activities were filmed and published by the people who performed them, which is another way to demotivate others.

Even when an attack is expected, it might not be possible to intervene or move heritage to a safer location in time, and especially in the case of immovable heritage. The Bamiyan Buddhas were built in the sixth century, survived until 2001 and were destroyed with gunfire and dynamite in only a few weeks; it becomes clear that things change very quickly for heritage that has endured many centuries.[161]

But even without armed conflict, other physical losses still occur. From the flooding of the Arno River in November 1966, which caused damage to Florence's libraries and museums,[162] to the fire that destroyed Notre-Dame

[158] AB Nicholas, 'Who Owns Indigenous Cultural and Intellectual Property?' (Policy Options, 27 June 2017) policyoptions.irpp.org/magazines/june-2017/who-owns-indigenous-cultural-and-intellectual-property.

[159] J Anderson, 'Access and Control of Indigenous Knowledge in Libraries and Archives: Ownership and Future Use' (American Library Association and The MacArthur Foundation, 2005).

[160] 'Practice Relating to Rule 38 Attacks against Cultural Property' (IHL Databases) ihl-databases.icrc.org/en/customary-ihl/v2/rule38. See also JD Kila and M Balcells, *Cultural Property Crime: An Overview and Analysis of Contemporary Perspectives and Trends* (Leiden, Brill, 2014); F Francioni and F Lenzerini, 'The Obligation to Prevent and Avoid Destruction of Cultural Heritage: From Bamiyan to Iraq' in BT Hoffman (ed), *Art and Cultural Heritage: Law, Policy, Practice* (Cambridge, CUP, 2006).

[161] It could be possible to rely on old photographs to create a copy of destroyed heritage; photogrammetry allows bringing multiple points of measurements to create a complete three-dimensional copy, which will be discussed in ch 2.

[162] P Conway, 'Preservation in the Age of Google: Digitization, Digital Preservation, and Dilemmas' (2010) 80 *The Library Quarterly* 61.

in 2019,[163] our recent history is filled with natural disasters that caused damage.[164] In most of these cases, there might not be enough time or resources, especially if disaster strikes suddenly.

If there are limited resources or more serious threats to human life, protection of heritage will very likely lose its priority. In order to avoid this decision between human lives and cultural heritage in a time of crisis, it might be safer to create copies of the cultural heritage in advance.

Even if the heritage is held in safe locations and institutions, this does not completely solve the problem of natural deterioration, which is neither deliberate nor accidental. Leaving materials as they are can cause the knowledge that is contained within them to be permanently lost. The negative impact of factors such as temperature, humidity and light also depends on the medium and how long they are left unattended. For example, paper-based objects suffer damages to the material and binding,[165] photographs start to shrink and form gas bubbles over time and decaying acetate and nitrate becomes very flammable,[166] and films can be damaged in high temperature environments.[167] Generally, it is suggested that heritage institutions should first invest in improving storage conditions and then, if they still have resources, spend them on other preservation methods.[168]

1.3.3. Role of Technology

Technology can both help and prevent the preservation of heritage: it can provide newer, faster and more efficient options for effective preservation of cultural heritage (such as improving conditions, format changes, restoration or

[163] Similarly, Moscow's Scientific Information Library and National Museum of Brazil were destroyed in fires recently, respectively in 2015 and 2018. Emma Burrows, 'Fire destroys historic documents at Moscow library' (cnn.com, 2 February 2015) www.cnn.com/2015/02/02/europe/russia-fire-library; Dom Phillips, 'Brazil museum fire: "incalculable" loss as 200-year-old Rio institution gutted' *The Guardian* (3 September 2018) www.theguardian.com/world/2018/sep/03/fire-engulfs-brazil-national-museum-rio.

[164] The causes for loss can be divided into ten categories: physical forces, vandalism, fire, water damage, pests, pollution, light, temperature, humidity and dissociation (loss of information): International Centre for the Study of Preservation and Restoration of Cultural Property (ICCROM) 'A Guide to Risk Management of Cultural Heritage (2016).

[165] A 2011 study showed: '2% brittle pages, 10% fungi, 20% loose pages, 21% uncut pages and the remaining 47% other physical damages': JA Magán et al, 'Mass Digitization at the Complutense University Library: Access to and Preservation of Its Cultural Heritage' (2011) 21 *LIBER Quarterly* 48, 55.

[166] Left untouched since 1983, Robert Waller Photography Collection was almost lost until its digitisation: L Capell, 'Digitization as a Preservation Method for Damaged Acetate Negatives: A Case Study' (2010) 73 *American Archivist* 235.

[167] After an air conditioning malfunction, an Indonesian film archive was subject to triple the amount of recommended temperature, where it took 7.5 months and $148,000 to repair one 35mm film: S Widianto, 'Inside the Fight to Save Indonesia's Decaying Film Heritage' (Vice, 2016) www.vice.com/en_id/article/pgyme9/inside-the-fight-to-save-indonesias-decaying-film-heritage.

[168] Conway (n 162) 69.

dematerialisation) and also make it easier to access it. But technology also keeps evolving at a speed where previously documented material and born-digital material can easily become obsolete, thus wasting all the effort and investment.

It is not realistic to always expect every heritage institution to own necessary equipment to display every format in their collection at any time and to keep them properly maintained.[169] Several examples can be given of analogue technologies facing problems. For instance, the projectors for 8mm films are not as common as they were 25 years ago, and if a projector cannot be found, the films are impossible to access without a format shift.[170] Similarly, Nelson Mandela's Rivonia trial speech could not be played by the National Archives of South Africa since the hardware to play dictabelts is no longer available; these recordings were restored after long attempts by audio engineers and the British Library.[171] Keeping track of which formats are becoming obsolete requires constant attention and technical knowledge.

More recently the COVID-19 pandemic had a great impact on the culture sector and access to cultural heritage.[172] Museums especially suffered from this: a May 2020 UNESCO study found that 90 per cent of museums were temporarily closed while 10 per cent may never reopen.[173] The research also highlighted the uneven availability of digital heritage in African states and Small Island Developing States.[174] The International Council of Museums (ICOM) report from 2021 also confirmed that the pandemic greatly increased the shift to digital activities and how multiple waves of lockdowns had a detrimental effect on heritage staff.[175] While its impact is greatly reduced at the time of writing, the pandemic was also a form of crisis where there were understandably other priorities, especially human lives. While it sped up the transition to digital, it also means that a similar pandemic, or other disasters such as climate change, might cause similar obstacles for cultural heritage.

[169] T Padfield, 'Preserving and accessing our cultural heritage – issues for cultural sector institutions: archives, libraries, museums and galleries' in E Derclaye (ed), *Copyright and Cultural Heritage: Preservation and Access to the Works in a Digital World* (Cheltenham, Edward Elgar, 2010) 196.

[170] P Torremans, 'Archiving exceptions: where are we and where do we need to go?' in E Derclaye (ed), *Copyright and Cultural Heritage: Preservation and Access to the Works in a Digital World* (Cheltenham, Edward Elgar, 2010) 113.

[171] R Ranft, 'Rescuing the Rivonia Trial recordings' (britishlibrary.typepad.co.uk, 6 December 2013) britishlibrary.typepad.co.uk/sound-and-vision/2013/12/rescuing-the-rivonia-trial-recordings.html. This example was also recognised in *Gower's Review of Intellectual Property* (London, HM Treasury, 2006) 65.

[172] UNESCO, 'Disruption and Resilience: UNESCO reports reveal new data on impact of COVID-19 on culture' (2021) www.unesco.org/en/articles/disruption-and-resilience-unesco-reports-reveal-new-data-impact-covid-19-culture; C Zuanni, 'Mapping museum digital initiatives during COVID-19' (2020) pro.europeana.eu/post/mapping-museum-digital-initiatives-during-covid-19.

[173] UNESCO, 'Museums around the world in the face of COVID-19' (2020) unesdoc.unesco.org/ark:/48223/pf0000373530.

[174] Ibid.

[175] ICOM, 'Museums, museum professionals and Covid-19: third survey' (2021) icom.museum/wp-content/uploads/2021/07/Museums-and-Covid-19_third-ICOM-report.pdf.

1.3.4. Principle Three: We must keep Heritage Safe and Accessible

Cultural heritage regularly faces physical and non-physical challenges. Measures are in place: for dangers such as armed conflict or looting, there are rules at the international level. For dangers such as natural disasters and natural deterioration, there are regional or national rules and internal guidelines. Obsolescence is also a problem that is taken care of as the technology moves forward.

The solutions include moving heritage from danger zones to where they can be kept safely, then invest first in the storage conditions, then preservation methods, and finally in the digitisation of the cultural heritage. But these steps need to be taken at the right time. It does not help to copy objects only after they are damaged, or try to restore obsolete formats. This does not mean everything needs to be, or can be, copied in advance, as there are limited resources. But it is something to strive for: the third principle is heritage must be kept safe and accessible. If it is not possible to keep the objects themselves, then we need to think about alternative ways to achieve preservation and access through their copies. Echoing Principle Two, if we argue that heritage concerns everyone, then keeping it safe and accessible for future generations becomes a shared responsibility.

1.4. Conclusion

Looking at the scope of heritage, neither the academic literature nor the international instruments provide a single uniform definition. Through multiple instruments, the scope of heritage has expanded. Different approaches to ownership, decision making and challenges were also introduced.

Even the terminology suffers from uncertainty. The legal instruments and academic literature have a tendency to use the terms 'cultural property' and 'cultural heritage' interchangeably. Earlier instruments tend to favour the term 'property', as instruments prior to UNESCO did not actually address the concept of cultural heritage at that point and used the term 'property' in line with property rights.[176] Although the term 'heritage' was used within the Conventions alongside 'cultural property', it was first used on its own as the main subject matter in the 1972 Convention. Some scholars argue that treating it as 'property' gives the implication that its exploitation is free, and risks the commodification of culture. In addition, the term 'cultural property' can be criticised for being a 'western concept'.[177]

[176] Kono, *The Impact of Uniform Laws* (n 10) 108.
[177] Stamatoudi (n 55) 6; Brown (n 80) 43.

In contrast, using the term 'heritage' is deemed broad and dynamic, and implies something 'valuable' is inherited that encourages its preservation.[178] For the sake of consistency, the term 'heritage' will be used in the upcoming chapters, as the term currently utilised by UNESCO.

But after examining the expansions and challenges, significant problems emerge. Having a single definition, scope and terminology would understandably make things simpler. But none of it is really that simple. In addition to the historical pattern of not prioritising heritage due to military necessity, there are further challenges regarding its ownership and selection. Even after accepting the international responsibility to keep heritage safe, there is no single answer to the internationalism/nationalism distinction, and the ownership questions might be slightly blurred but not completely solved by creating further copies.

Instead, it makes sense to proceed with principles which are: (i) broad interpretation of the scope is needed, with heritage including old and new, pleasant and unpleasant, tangible and intangible, (ii) heritage should be for everyone (which is not limited to the physical ownership, but the decisions on display and access), (iii) there is public heritage interest in keeping them safe and accessible.

The previous two sections answered the questions of 'what' and 'who', whereas the final section focused on the question 'why'. Now we have to look at the question 'how'. To keep heritage safe and accessible, it is time to assess the feasibility of making copies, specifically digital copies. The next chapter will focus the digitisation process and the copyright implications.

[178] Prott and O'Keefe (n 6) 310–11; Frigo (n 6) 369; Blake, 'On Defining Cultural Heritage' (n 6) 69.

2

Copyright Implications of the Digitisation Process

Copying cultural heritage is not a new practice. Even before digitisation was a possibility, rare and deteriorating manuscripts and paintings were copied sometimes even by their authors themselves. Similarly, three dimensional objects were copied by casting, in which melted material is poured into a mould. Cast copies were then displayed in museums in distant locations for educational purposes, even though all parties already knew they were copies.[1] Even digitisation is not a new practice, as digitisation efforts were in place as early as the 1970s.[2] Digital photographs of paintings and scanned books are already used widely for preservation and dissemination of cultural heritage.

Although it is beneficial for heritage, among the biggest obstacles to digitisation are the legal challenges and uncertainties that reveal themselves before, during and after the digitisation process. These legal challenges will cause an additional layer of inconsistency in the treatment of cultural heritage. Out of these challenges, copyright law arguably has the most complicated relationship with technology. With each development, such as the printing press, radio, television or the internet, copyright law had to adapt to new subject matter, new authorship, new ways of infringement and new potential defences. In this chapter, the digitisation process will be examined from a copyright perspective.

But, as a disclaimer, it is not the only intellectual property (IP) right involved in the treatment of heritage: patent and trade secret protection apply to traditional knowledge and skills; design law applies to the visible characteristics of heritage; and trade mark protection and geographical indications apply to signs identifying certain cultural heritage. Although the boundaries of registered rights, such as patents or trade marks, are a bit clearer compared to copyright (which does not require registration) there is no guarantee that the relevant

[1] For the historical practice of making cast copies, see R Frederiksen and E Marchand (eds), *Plaster Casts: Making, Collecting and Displaying from Classical Antiquity to the Present* (Berlin, De Gruyter, 2010); M Lending, *Plaster Monuments: Architecture and the Power of Reproduction* (Princeton, Princeton University Press, 2022); A Alexandridis and L Winkler-Horaček (eds), *Destroy the Copy – Plaster Cast Collections in the 19th – 20th Centuries: Demolition, Defacement, Disposal in Europe and Beyond* (Berlin, De Gruyter, 2022).

[2] Project Gutenberg has reproduced and shared the Declaration of Independence in 1971 (typed, not scanned): www.gutenberg.org/about/background/history_and_philosophy.html.

individuals/communities will want to proceed with registration. There are also attempts at the international level for the protection of traditional knowledge, traditional cultural expressions and genetic resources as a new form of IP.[3] In addition, depending on what is digitised, there are further legal implications for data protection and contract law; and depending on location, there are further national heritage codes limiting the use of heritage without the permission of authorities.

2.1. Digitisation: How Did We Get Here and What is Next?

Digitisation involves turning analogue materials into a binary code, which can be stored and accessed electronically. Microfilms were more common in the past as a durable method: they only work for some materials, but they can survive for hundreds of years (at least according to accelerated ageing tests) and can be viewed with any light source, even after minor damages.[4] Nevertheless, the cultural heritage sector has slowly embraced digitisation, mostly for its access benefits.

Although people may think of Google Books, the Digital Public Library of America (DPLA) or Europeana today, digitisation efforts in US and EU go back in decades. Early US projects include Project Gutenberg in 1971, Prelinger Archive in 1983, Internet Archive in 1996 and the Million Books Project, which reached 1.5 million copies in 2007.[5] Carnegie Mellon had the Universal Library project, and the Open Content Alliance included Microsoft, Yahoo and several major libraries digitising their content. Mass digitisation gained more attention from the public when Google started working on its two connected projects, one with libraries and the other with the publishers (Google Partner Program and Google Print – subsequently called Google Book Search). For publishers, the attraction was Google directing the users to purchase the full text from their websites. For libraries, especially those with limited resources, being involved in this project meant getting their collections digitised and receiving digital copies. Compared

[3] See also I Stamatoudi (ed), *Research Handbook on Intellectual Property and Cultural Heritage* (Cheltenham, Edward Elgar, 2022) chs 1–6; M Torsen and J Anderson, 'Intellectual Property and the Safeguarding of Traditional Cultures: Legal Issues and Practical Options for Museums, Libraries and Archives' (2010) WIPO. For detailed information on the work of Intergovernmental Committee on Intellectual Property and Genetic Resources, Traditional Knowledge and Folklore (IGC), see www.wipo.int/tk/en/igc.

[4] H Brown et al, 'The role of microfilm in digital preservation' in J Davidson, S Ross and M Day (eds), *DCC Digital Curation Manual* (2011) 8; A Smith, 'Why Digitize?' (1999) www.clir.org/pubs/reports/pub80-smith/pub80.html.

[5] D Marcum and RC Schonfeld, *Along Came Google: A History of Library Digitization* (Princeton, Princeton University Press, 2021); M Rimmer, *Digital Copyright and the Consumer Revolution* (Cheltenham, Edward Elgar, 2007) 229.

with early digitisation efforts, there are a few main reasons why Google's projects might have attracted more attention than previous ones: (i) the company's superior indexing; and (ii) its financial and organisational commitments to its participants.[6] But what makes this project even more significant for our purposes is: (iii) the lawsuit, settlement agreements and the application of US fair use.[7]

In Europe, prior to establishing Europeana as the main EU aggregator, there were individual national and also joint projects trying to bring digital collections from Europe together.[8] One of the first shared portals was called 'Gateway and Bridge to Europe's National Libraries' (GABRIEL) which was founded in 1997; this was followed by The European Library (TEL) between 2001 and 2016.[9] TEL acted as a contributor to Europeana from 2010 and ended its services in 2016.[10] More recently, the COVID-19 pandemic has demonstrated the need for digital heritage, when access to institutions were severely limited during lockdowns.[11] In 2021, the European Commission Recommendation on a Common European Data Space for Cultural Heritage further encouraged EU institutions to increase digitisation efforts, including 3D digitising at-risk heritage and most visited sites, especially in light of the pandemic.[12]

The challenge is not over once heritage is digitised and placed online; how digitised heritage will be experienced by users is also subject to changes in how internet developed. Web 1.0 covers the early period from 1989 to 2004 and is known as 'read-only' where few were creating content and the majority mainly accessed mostly static websites.[13] Web 2.0, on the other hand, has increased the participation and interactivity, including social media. The main difference between Web 2.0 and Web 3.0 is decentralisation, as the internet is supposedly moving away from the big companies such as Google or Meta that currently hold the vast variety of user generated content. Examples of decentralised technologies include blockchain, non-fungible tokens and the metaverse, and these go hand in hand with uses of cultural heritage for machine learning and virtual reality.[14]

[6] Rimmer (n 5) 229; J Epstein, 'Books@Google' (*The New York Review*, 19 October 2006) www.nybooks.com/articles/2006/10/19/booksgoogle.

[7] This case will be covered in Sections 4.3.4.5 and 5.2.1.

[8] The attempts in France started with the Gallica experiment in 1997, the German Digital Libraries Project started in 1998, and the Strathclyde Centre for Digital Library Research group was founded in 1999: M Dalbello, 'Cultural Dimensions of Digital Library Development, Part I: Theory and Methodological Framework for a Comparative Study of the Cultures of Innovation in Five European National Libraries' (2008) 78 *The Library Quarterly: Information, Community, Policy* 355.

[9] S Chambers and W Schallier, 'Bringing Research Libraries into Europeana: Establishing a Library-Domain Aggregator' (2010) 20 *LIBER Quarterly* 105, 107–108.

[10] ibid 107–108; The European Library www.theeuropeanlibrary.org.

[11] See also Sections 1.3.3 and 2.6 for the impact of the pandemic on heritage institutions.

[12] Commission Recommendation (EU) 2021/1970 of 10 November 2021 on a common European data space for cultural heritage [2021] OJ L401/5, Recitals 3 and 15.

[13] MR Solanki and A Dongaonkar, 'A Journey of Human Comfort: Web 1.0 to Web 4.0' (2016) 3(9) *International Journal of Research and Scientific Innovation* 75.

[14] S Gilbert, 'Crypto, web3, and the Metaverse' Policy Brief (Bennett Institute for Public Policy, March 2022).

At the same time, some of the technology giants have already secured their position in Web 3.0, such as (formerly) Facebook's investment in 'Meta'.[15]

One might wonder, what is the end goal? Is it realistic to have all the information online, to create a universal library that can be freely used by both humans and machines? Instead of thinking of them as copies of isolated objects, representing the cultures of separate States and communities, can everything be turned into a single corpus that can be used without limits?[16] This is already partially happening: digitised material placed online is regularly used to feed machine learning, which allows machines to recognise dynamic relationships between these works, and build on them with increasingly more accurate generative artificial intelligence (AI).[17]

While it is hard to predict the specific details for the future, such as the status of the metaverse or the full potential of artificial intelligence, these technologies will undoubtedly open up new ways of interacting with cultural heritage. Moving cultural heritage from analogue to digital formats is the prerequisite for embracing other new technologies ahead, and so that is what heritage institutions have been doing for some time. Therefore, it makes sense to see digitisation as just another step for cultural heritage: first, cultural heritage had to be defined, and its physical integrity had to be ensured against numerous challenges (armed conflict, illicit trade, natural changes). Now we must think about this next digital stage, and also question whether copyright law will impact the treatment of cultural heritage.

The following sections will examine the stages of digitisation and their copyright implications, namely:

- decisions prior to digitisation (non-legal challenges that will affect the process);
- selecting the material (whether it overlaps with copyright subject matter);
- parties performing digitisation (determining copyright implications for authorship, and beneficiaries for defences);
- digitisation activity (whether it overlaps with economic and moral rights);
- the purpose of digitisation (whether copyright defences can be applicable);
- the nature of digital copies (whether there is new copyright in the digital copies);
- methods and new technologies such as artificial intelligence and virtual reality (whether these new methods infringe copyright and/or create new works).

[15] S Rose, '"The metaverse will be our slow death!" Is Facebook losing its $100bn gamble on virtual reality?' *The Guardian* (7 December 2022) www.theguardian.com/technology/2022/dec/07/metaverse-slow-death-facebook-losing-100bn-gamble-virtual-reality-mark-zuckerberg; M Farokhmanesh, 'Will the Metaverse Live Up to the Hype? Game Developers Aren't Impressed' (Wired, 19 January 2023) www.wired.com/story/metaverse-video-games-fortnite-zuckerberg.

[16] M Borghi and S Karapapa, *Copyright and Mass Digitization* (Oxford, OUP, 2013); K Kelly, 'Scan This Book!' *The New York Times* (14 May 2006) www.nytimes.com/2006/05/14/magazine/14publishing.html.

[17] See Section 2.8.2.

2.2. Decisions at the Beginning of Digitisation Projects: Non-legal Issues

There are many non-legal decisions in digitisation projects for financial, organisational and technical matters. While they may seem separate from legal issues, they are connected to the availability of resources and expertise necessary for predicting copyright implications early on. If copyright is not taken into consideration when determining the feasibility of a project or when seeking funding, the sudden emergence of the unexpected costs for rights clearance can have drastic results.

Digitisation can be expensive: it requires an upfront investment for the necessary devices, which will need to be replaced regularly.[18] Once relevant devices are acquired, projects will be overseen by employees, which will also contribute to the cost. Employees have to select the material to be digitised, locate and bring the materials, match the digital data with originals, and re-shelf afterwards. If the material is coming from donors or the estates of artists, employees will have to work on building these relationships. State funding might not be sufficient or available to cover these costs, relying on private funding (or even an oppressive State who does not prioritise the minorities) creates further concerns on biased decisions on the selection of what gets to be digitised.[19] Seeking external funding might lead to additional conditions, such as Heritage Lottery Fund requiring Creative Commons licences for the digitised material placed online.[20] It is also possible to charge visitors for access to generate income for the institutions. But even with sufficient internal and external resources for funding, digitising the entirety of collections is unfeasible for most institutions.

It is also possible that, midway during preservation, the costs might exceed the expected benefit gained from the work being digitised. Mwangi describes a few challenges that were not included in their initial calculations for digitising Kenya's cultural heritage, such as the realisation that wide-format drawings and maps required special costly scanners; contractors' tendency to produce lower-quality preservation (and the need for archival staff to be present at all times to ensure quality); extra funds for ensuring consistency in the filing system; and problems with access (insufficient service providers capacity).[21]

[18] For project planning, see JM Perrin, *Digitizing Flat Media: Principles and Practices* (Lanham, Rowman & Littlefield, 2015); C Hintz et al, *Finding Balance: Collaborative Workflows for Risk Management in Sharing Cultural Heritage Collections Online* (The University of Kansas Libraries, 2023).

[19] See also Q McCrary, 'The Political Nature of Digital Cultural Heritage' (2011) 20 *LIBER Quarterly* 357, 360.

[20] Heritage Lottery Fund, 'Digital Good Practice Guide' www.heritagefund.org.uk/funding/good-practice-guidance/digital. See also Section 4.3.3 for more on Creative Commons.

[21] FG Mwangi, 'The Road to Providing Access to Kenya's Information Heritage' in L Duranti and E Shaffer (eds) *UNESCO The Memory of the World in the Digital Age: Digitization and Preservation Conference Proceedings* (Vancouver, 26–28 September 2012).

Another concern is whether the digitisation process can damage original material, as it is not acceptable to sacrifice originals for a process that does not create very stable results. Digitisation, even with gloves, means subjecting copies to added pressure, light and heat. Furthermore, using flat scanners, and handling pressing brittle and bound material could cause additional damage. For example, when Google was scanning the collections in the University of Michigan Library, damages to the originals were reported.[22]

Digitised heritage will also need to be maintained. There is no such thing as selecting a perfect format that will never go obsolete; formats preferred by institutions are often replaced by newer ones. For example, in 2000 the Canadian Museum of Civilization was placed in a challenging position when approximately half a million of its digitised images needed migration due to the Kodak Photo CD format going obsolete.[23] Another example is from the British Library, which started a project to preserve digital content held on CDs through the use of emulators and legacy software.[24] Born-digital material is subject to similar challenges: for example once a website is taken down, user generated material uploaded on there also becomes inaccessible, similarly, changes in link shorteners can lead to millions of hyperlinks no longer working.[25] Even if every attempt is made to keep up with new formats, digitised material can still become inaccessible due to malfunctions. Keeping more than one digital copy might help, but that would then increase the need for storage.

There are also differences between the formats used by heritage institutions, making it harder for both repositories and users working with digitised collections of multiple institutions. These differences have been addressed more recently by the International Image Interoperability Framework (IIIF), which is being embraced in order to increase users' ability to access multiple images, but also compare and manipulate digitised heritage.[26] However, it is not fully certain how compatible rights statements are for works that are not in the public domain (or when heritage institutions claim copyright over their digitised materials).[27]

[22] A Green, 'Big digitisation: where next?' (Digital Resources for the Humanities and Arts Conference, Belfast, 8 September 2009).

[23] L Renaud and JME Vincent, 'Photo CD PCD To Tiff Migration Case Study' (2006) library.imaging.org/admin/apis/public/api/ist/website/downloadArticle/archiving/3/1/art00028.

[24] M Day et al, 'The preservation of disk-based content at the British Library: Lessons from the Flashback Project' (2016) 26(3) *Alexandria: The Journal of National and International Library and Information Issues* 216.

[25] B Farrand, 'Born Digital: Law, policy and the preservation of videogames as digital cultural heritage' in Stamatoudi (n 3) 502–16.

[26] See generally: International Image Interoperability Framework: iiif.io/community/consortium. See also Stanford Library: library.stanford.edu/iiif, Cambridge University Library: www.lib.cam.ac.uk/research/digital-humanities/case-studies/dynamic-digital-library-iiif-scoping-project.

[27] M de Vos, 'IIIF – The digitized manuscripts revolution we've all been waiting for!' blog.digitizedmedievalmanuscripts.org/iiif-international-image-interoperability-framework.

2.3. Selecting the Material to be Digitised: Overlaps with Copyright Subject Matter

Chapter one established that the scope of cultural heritage needs to be interpreted widely and go beyond the unnecessary distinctions of tangible/intangible, old/new or pleasant/unpleasant. But when we turn to cultural heritage institutions digitising their collections, their resources and capabilities are not limitless.

Multiple decisions affect the visibility of cultural heritage; important decisions are already made when objects are acquired and placed in heritage institutions. Considering that heritage institutions do not have unlimited space, there is then the question of which physical objects should be prioritised in terms of display, maintenance, and further curation decisions such as how much is displayed, in what context, where it should be displayed and whether loans from other institutions are needed for a specific collection or exhibition.

Digitisation requires an additional set of decisions for heritage. Multiple factors can affect the priority of digitisation, such as the medium of the object (audiovisual is harder than paper-based materials) or their fragility (fragile items can be harmed during digitisation, but the subsequent access to their copies might be more valuable). Some institutions might choose to prioritise standard-sized and sturdy material to speed digitisation up. There are also decisions between particularly valuable inaccessible material that researchers are interested in that will be expensive and slow, versus 'dull' manuscripts that researchers are not aware of that would otherwise not get digitised.[28] Usually there is no clear cut or consistent way to prioritise materials, so it will depend on the goals of projects. Amongst these decisions, copyright status of the material also has a big role and will require looking into the scope of copyright.

Similar to the uncertainties around the scope of cultural heritage, copyright's subject matter is also uncertain. For the scope of copyright law, we must turn to international and national instruments. In the Berne Convention, there is an illustrative list for protected subject matter in Article 2, which is protected in all contracting countries:[29]

> the expression 'literary and artistic works' shall include every production in the literary, scientific and artistic domain, whatever may be the mode or form of its expression, such as books, pamphlets and other writings; lectures, addresses, sermons and other works of the same nature; dramatic or dramatico-musical works; choreographic works and entertainments in dumb show; musical compositions with or without words; cinematographic works to which are assimilated works expressed by a process analogous

[28] C Fabian and C Schreiber, 'Piloting a National Programme for the Digitization of Medieval Manuscripts in Germany' (2014) 24(1) *LIBER Quarterly* 2.

[29] Berne Convention for the Protection of Literary and Artistic Works (Paris, 9 September 1886, as amended on 28 September 1979) ('Berne Convention'), art 2(1).

> to cinematography; works of drawing, painting, architecture, sculpture, engraving and lithography; photographic works to which are assimilated works expressed by a process analogous to photography; works of applied art; illustrations, maps, plans, sketches and three-dimensional works relative to geography, topography, architecture or science

While not making any explicit references to cultural heritage, Berne Convention Article 15(4) refers to the 'unpublished works of unknown authors'.[30] Countries like France and Germany have an open list approach to what is protected by copyright, other countries, such as the UK, keep a closed (exhaustive) list.[31] The US also provides a non-exhaustive list for 'original works of authorship fixed in any tangible medium of expression'.[32]

When viewing UNESCO definitions through the lens of copyright law, there are references to works protected by copyright. For example, in the 1970 Convention Article 1, there are mentions of collections, monuments, properties of artistic interest, sculptures, engravings, prints, montages, manuscripts, old books, documents, photographic and cinematic works and articles of furniture. They easily fit into the subject matter of copyright law.

Being in the right category is not sufficient, there are other requirements for copyright protection. To receive copyright protection, works need to be 'original'.[33] There are references to originality in the UNESCO 1970 Convention subject matter, but it is not certain that it means the same level of 'originality' requirement in copyright.[34] The Berne Convention allows contracting countries to embrace different levels of originality for protection. So, when open-list countries apply the originality threshold to determine the subject matter, it requires assessing previously unconsidered categories such as the smell of perfumes or the taste of cheese for copyright protection.[35] The originality standard in CJEU decisions is that the work has to be the 'author's own intellectual creation', and this can only be present when the author can make 'free and creative choices' not dictated by their

[30] The idea of including the term 'folklore' in the Berne Convention was first suggested by the Indian delegation in 1967, however delegates had differing opinions on which aspects of 'folklore' should be in the public domain: S Ricketson and JC Ginsburg, *International Copyright and Neighbouring Rights: The Berne Convention and Beyond Vol.1.*, 3rd edn (Oxford, OUP, 2022). See also *Guide to the Berne Convention for the Protection of Literary and Artistic Works* (Paris Act, 1971).

[31] Although, there might be different interpretations in the future: *SAS Institute v World Programming* [2013] EWCA Civ 1482, [2014] RPC 8. L Bently, B Sherman, D Gangjee and P Johnson, *Intellectual Property Law*, 6th edn (Oxford, OUP, 2022) 64–66.

[32] See for a detailed account, JAL Sterling, *Sterling on World Copyright Law*, 6th edn (London, Sweet & Maxwell, 2022) ch 6; JC Ginsburg and E Treppoz, *International Copyright Law: U.S. and E.U. Perspectives: Text and Cases* (Cheltenham, Edward Elgar, 2015) 5.2.; Ricketson and Ginsburg (n 30) ch 8.

[33] The originality requirement will be revisited in Section 2.7.

[34] '(ii) original works of statuary art and sculpture in any material; (iii) original engravings, prints and lithographs; (iv) original artistic assemblages and montages in any material' Convention on the Means of Prohibiting and Preventing the Illicit Import, Export and Transfer of Ownership of Cultural Property (Paris, 14 November 1970), art 1.

[35] E Bonadio and N Lucchi, 'How far can copyright be stretched? Framing the debate on whether new and different forms of creativity can be protected' (2019) 2 *IPQ* 115; J McCutcheon, 'Levola Hengelo BV v. Smilde Foods BV: The Hard Work of Defining a Copyright Work' (2019) 82 *MLR* 936.

technical function.[36] The traditional UK standard of 'labour, skill and judgment' is also being moved away from.[37] The United States also requires originality for copyright protection, which is described as 'independently created by the author and possesses a minimal degree of creativity'.[38]

Another requirement for copyright protection is fixation. The Berne Convention leaves it to Member States to determine if this is a requirement.[39] Embedding the work in a stable physical matter is required for copyright protection in the UK[40] and the US,[41] but not in most civil law countries. But those civil law countries also have it in their laws that the work needs to be perceivable by a human or machine, even if it is temporary.[42] This is reminiscent of the tangible and intangible distinction in heritage, where tangible forms should not be prioritised. In any case, material that can be digitised will be sufficiently 'fixed' by their nature.

In summary, heritage institutions hold a wide range of material ranging from paintings to rocks and utensils – some might enjoy copyright protection, some do not. In practice, for most objects held in heritage institution, their lack of copyright does not reduce their value for the visitors. The visitors will likely care about other things, such as their age, aesthetic value and which civilisations have held the item. But for institutions wanting to avoid copyright infringement, it makes sense to prioritise the digitisation of works in the public domain. Therefore, in addition to the previously discussed distinctions between tangible/intangible, pleasant/unpleasant or old/new; there is another: heritage protected by copyright versus cultural heritage in the public domain.

2.4. Who Performs Digitisation?

There is no closed list of such institutions in UNESCO instruments, but the definition usually encompasses at least the libraries, museums, galleries and archives, and sometimes educational institutions (and their libraries). These institutions differ in the items they hold: library collections include published and printed

[36] Case C-5/08 *Infopaq International A/S v Danske Dagblades Forening* ECLI:EU:C:2009:465, [2009] ECR I-6569; Case C-145/10 *Eva-Maria Painer v Standard Verlags GmbH and Ors* ECLI:EU:C:2011:798, [2011] ECR I-12533, para 89.

[37] Bently and Sherman (n 31) 100–128, see also Section 2.7.2 below.

[38] *Feist Publications, Inc v Rural Telephone Service Co*, 499 US 340 (1991).

[39] Berne Convention, art 2(2).

[40] Copyright, Designs and Patents Act 1988 (CDPA), s 3.

[41] US Copyright Act of 1976, s 101.

[42] 'Accordingly, for there to be a "work" as referred to in Directive 2001/29, the subject matter protected by copyright must be expressed in a manner which makes it identifiable with sufficient precision and objectivity, even though that expression is not necessarily in permanent form': Case C-310/17 *Levola Hengelo v Smilde Foods BV* ECLI:EU:C:2018:899, [2018] Bus.L.R. 2442, para 40. See also Sterling (n 32) ch 6.

materials that also exist in other places.[43] Archives also hold usually two dimensional material, similar to libraries, but their collections are more unique.[44] This also means the collections held in the archives, unlike commercially published materials, serve more as a unique documentation of the history of their communities.[45] Archives are usually grouped together with libraries under copyright, but scholars have pointed out that archives experience different challenges due to their greater proportion of orphan and unpublished material.[46] There could also be concerns other than copyright for archives: official archives may hold items that require strict confidentiality (such as personal or governmental secrets) and sometimes be subject to public access laws to require disclosure.[47] Unlike libraries and archives, museums usually hold unique objects that are both two and three-dimensional, ranging from works of art (concerns copyright), to minerals and plants (does not concern copyright).[48] It can be suggested that the provenance and aura of museum collections receive more scrutiny than other heritage institutions.[49]

An unusual category is legal deposit libraries. The legal deposit system requires a copy of each work to be submitted after publication, the types of works and the selected institutions depending on national laws. It is usually not limited to printed works, and also covers sound recordings, films, and even material published online (such as websites) in some jurisdictions.[50] This practice does not function as a pre-requisite for copyright protection (per Article 5(2) of the Berne Convention). Legal deposit status does not allow these institutions to copy everything in their collection, and they will still have to rely on authorisation or defences like other institutions.

Another way to categorise these institutions is their approach to digitisation, namely one-off (request) versus systematic digitisation of the collections. Heritage

[43] For a useful comparison, see CH Rasmussen and B Hjørland, 'Libraries, archives and museums (LAM) Conceptual issues with focus on their convergence' in B Hjørland and C Gnoli (eds), *ISKO Encyclopedia of Knowledge Organization*, www.isko.org/cyclo/lam.

[44] ibid.

[45] ibid; KE Foote, 'To Remember and Forget: Archives, Memory and Culture' (1990) 53(3) *The American Archivist* 378, 380.

[46] R Deazley and V Stobo, 'Archives and Copyright: Risk and Reform' (2013) CREATe Working Paper No. 3, 46–47.

[47] KD Crews, 'Archives Copyright Exceptions: Typology Analysis' WIPO SCCR/39/5 (2019).

[48] Rasmussen and Hjørland (n 43).

[49] See also International Council of Museums definition: 'not-for-profit, permanent institution in the service of society that researches, collects, conserves, interprets and exhibits tangible and intangible heritage': icom.museum/en/resources/standards-guidelines/museum-definition. See also JF Canat and L Guibault, 'Study on copyright limitations and exceptions for museums' WIPO SCCR/30/2 (2015); P Oruc and U Suthersanen, 'Intellectual property and cultural heritage issues for museums of archaeological materials' in Stamatoudi (n 3) 392–412.

[50] For origins and justifications, see also Sterling (n 32) 15.09–15.10; KD Crews, 'Legal Deposit in Four Countries: Laws and Library Services' (1998) 80(4) *Law Library Journal* 551; J Gilchrist, 'Copyright Deposit, Legal Deposit or Library Deposit: The Government's Role as Preserver of Copyright Material' (2005) 5(2) *Queensland University Technical Law & Justice Journal* 177. Some examples include the Legal Deposit Libraries Act 2003 and Legal Deposit Libraries Regulations SI 2013/777 (UK), Code du patrimonie art L131-1 to L133-1 (France), 17 USC s 407 (United States).

institutions, especially libraries, have been making copies of their collections for much longer than digitisation technology. In some circumstances, what starts out as a request-based digitisation could turn into a wider digitisation project once the initial hurdles and costs of devices and employees are covered.

The majority of these decisions depend on the resources available for institutions. For example, in the UK the support received by national museums is different from local authority museums.[51] Government support is dwindling in the US, with institutions instead relying on donors and revenues.[52] There could also be other priorities for funding, such as caring for the remaining collections or even keeping the institution open, which may take precedence over digitisation.[53] Combined with the concerns on the impact of AHD on the curation by white, upper-class males, previously introduced under Section 1.2.3, receiving private funding might create the risk of bias in the selection of objects. But more importantly for copyright, funding also has an impact on the caution levels in decision making. Particularly when funding is limited, copyright uncertainty and the costs of rights clearance deter institutions with limited resources. There are multiple studies on how comfortable these institutions are with making copyright law decisions.[54] There is also a distinction between State versus private heritage institutions, for example in the US, State entities enjoy sovereign immunity from suit, while privately affiliated institutions (including some university libraries) will have to be more careful about copyright infringement.[55]

Who performs digitisation will have two main copyright implications: first, it will determine whether they can rely on copyright defences. Defences allow otherwise infringing activities for certain beneficiaries, and some can be narrow

[51] DC Research and Wavehill, 'Research to understand the levels of public investment in museums' (Arts Council England, January 2024) www.artscouncil.org.uk/research-and-data/research-understand-levels-public-investment-museums. See also House of Commons Library Briefing on Local Museums (March 2018): researchbriefings.files.parliament.uk/documents/CDP-2018-0059/CDP-2018-0059.pdf and N Mendoza 'The Mendoza Review: an independent review of museums in England' (DCMS, November 2017) www.gov.uk/government/publications/the-mendoza-review-an-independent-review-of-museums-in-england.

[52] FW Bell, 'How are museums supported financially in the U.S.?': static.america.gov/uploads/sites/8/2016/03/You-Asked-Series_How-Are-Museums-Supported-Financially-in-the-US_English_Lo-Res_508.pdf.

[53] An ICOM study established that multiple waves of lockdowns during the COVID-19 pandemic had a detrimental effect on institutions: 9.6% of staff and 15% freelancers laid off: ICOM, 'Museums, museum professionals and Covid-19: third survey' (2021).

[54] C Morrison and J Secker, 'Copyright Literacy in the UK: a survey of librarians and other cultural heritage sector professionals' (2015) 39(121) *Library and Information Research* 74; P Hatch, C Morrison and J Secker, 'A study of copyright specialists in UK educational and cultural institutions: Who are they and what do they do?' (December 2017): reshare.ukdataservice.ac.uk/853176; KD Crews, *Copyright Law for Librarians and Educators: Creative Strategies and Practical Solutions*, 4th edn (Chicago, ALA Editions, 2020); P Vizvary et al, 'Copyright Literacy of Cultural Heritage Workers in the Czech Republic with a Focus on Librarians' (7th European Conference on Information Literacy, Virtual, 20–23 September 2021).

[55] US Copyright Office, 'State Sovereign Immunity Study' (2021); GA Rub, 'Reimagining Digital Libraries' (2024) Forthcoming 113 *Georgetown Law Journal*, Ohio State Legal Studies Research Paper No. 848, 58–59.

or unclear about the categories of beneficiaries. For example, museums were at a more disadvantaged position compared to libraries and archives in some jurisdictions in the EU, but the preservation defence has been recently harmonised through the CDSM Directive.[56]

The second copyright implication is the authorship of the digitised copies. Section 2.7 will evaluate the rare circumstances where digitisation creates new works protected by copyright, so who actually carries out the digitisation internally becomes important for potential authorship of this digitised copy. Some heritage institutions have specific teams that perform digitisation in-house, while others receive outside help. The nature of employment will matter, as most civil law countries have rules assuming the employee is the author unless there is a contractual provision. Common law countries, conversely, usually assume that the works created during employment belong to the employer.[57] Another option would be to rely on an outside team for digitisation and commission them to undertake the project. There are no international or regional instruments clarifying the ownership of commissioned works, but there are national provisions with different approaches on who holds the copyright (commissioner or commissioned).[58] Especially in those cases, cultural heritage institutions should be clear in their contracts with the digitising parties to avoid any authorship conflicts that may become a problem later.[59]

There is also copyright protection for computer-generated works in the UK that protects the 'person by whom the arrangements necessary for the creation of the work are undertaken',[60] which could potentially apply in rare circumstances, such as a conveyor belt digitisation. This is unlikely, but not impossible.

2.5. Digitisation Begins: Risk of Infringing Economic and Moral Rights

Any legal uncertainty about the nature of the digitisation process is likely to discourage digitisation and reduce its suitability for cultural heritage. The digitisation process has some differences based on the medium, but all works are turned to the same binary language afterwards. A brief overview of the digitisation process will be followed by the relevant exclusive rights of the author.

[56] Directive (EU) 2019/790 of the European Parliament and of the Council of 17 April 2019 on copyright and related rights in the Digital Single Market and amending Directives 96/9/EC and 2001/29/EC OJ L130/92 ('CDSM') Copyright defences are covered in ch 4.

[57] Sterling (n 32) 5.92–5.110; P Goldstein and PB Hugenholtz, *International Copyright: Principles, Law and Practice*, 4th edn (New York, OUP, 2019) 236–38; Crews, *Copyright Law* (n 54) 61–68.

[58] Sterling (n 32) 5.111.

[59] T Margoni, 'The Digitisation of Cultural Heritage: Originality, Derivative Works and (Non) Original Photographs' (2014) Institute for Information Law 54; B Savenije and A Beunen, 'Cultural Heritage and the Public Domain' (2012) 22 *LIBER Quarterly* 84.

[60] CDPA, s 9(3).

2.5.1. Copying Audio and Video

In order to play sounds or videos, analogue devices rely on the physical differences in the material, such as the bumps on a recording or the magnetisation on tapes. These works are at a higher risk of obsolescence, and it is also possible that institutions holding them might not have access to the devices that are able to play them.

Digitising them involves transfer of data into binary form. While this process involves no additional contribution from the digitisers, further edits and restorations might. Digital formats allow the content to be read and edited by computers, while analogue formats can only play what was originally recorded on them, therefore increasing the possibility of additions. Digital copies also do not degrade with repeated use like analogue copies.[61] A challenge with audiovisual works is that sometimes their content might not be accessed until after being switched to a different format, meaning that their copyright status cannot be determined until after digitisation occurs.

2.5.2. Two-Dimensional Copying

For most literary and artistic works, two-dimensional copying methods can be sufficient. Earlier methods for reproducing two-dimensional works include: (i) relief printing, where solid material was carved until the desired print was left as a raised area, and (ii) intaglio printing where the desired print was cut into the material, as a reverse of the first method, (iii) planographic printing where there is no carving or etching, and instead material with a flat surface is used.[62]

Digital reproduction, on the other hand, relies on photography, which relies on light. For two-dimensional materials, a scanner will be needed. When a document is placed in the scanner, generally using a flatbed or specifically designed angled surface,[63] the image is captured at the desired resolution, although it might make sense to differentiate between different resolutions as higher resolution copies are more attractive for commercial uses.[64] During and after scanning, it is possible to process the image further, such as colour optimisation or image sharpening, but this might reduce the quality of the initial scan and/or lead to an inaccurate representation of cultural heritage.

[61] See also B Lyons, 'Audiovisual archives & digital preservation' (22 November 2018, Digital Preservation Coalition) www.dpconline.org/blog/wdpd/audiovisual-archives-digital-preservation; State Records NSW, 'Digitisation of analogue audio and video' staterecords.nsw.gov.au/recordkeeping/guidance-and-resources/digitisation-analogue-audio-and-video.

[62] V&A, 'What is print?' www.vam.ac.uk/articles/what-is-print.

[63] For linear book scanner used by Google Books, see code.google.com/archive/p/linear-book-scanner.

[64] Some institutions might only release low-resolution copies freely while keeping high-resolution ones for commercial licensing. For example, in the dispute between the National Portrait Gallery and Derrick Coetzee, multiple low-resolution images on the website were brought together by Coetzee to create a full, high-resolution copy of the works, which was uploaded to Wikimedia. It will be assessed in Section 2.7.

2.5.3. Three-Dimensional Copying

Three-dimensional objects were already copied by sculpting or casting, but technology now allows the creation of nearly perfect 3D scans, which can also be edited and printed. But this new technology creates further copyright questions about the nature of these copies.[65]

Two of the most common methods are laser scanning and photogrammetry.[66] For laser scanning, laser light is sent to the surface without any contact. It allows higher accuracy and is especially useful for large structures, but requires potentially expensive equipment.[67] Types of laser 3D scanning can be grouped as triangulation, pulse and phase, differing in the distance and amount of detail captured.[68] Once the data is gathered, the raw data needs to be processed, where there is room for human input such as the removal of supporting material (that the object was leaning on), correcting errors, removing reflections and noise reduction.[69] To facilitate sharing, the model can be simplified or edited further.[70]

Photogrammetry, on the other hand, calculates the measurements between specific points in images. The accuracy of these 3D models depends less on the device capturing the images, and more on the software that collates the information.[71] For large objects, there are decisions to be made regarding the use of manned or unmanned aircrafts, methods to capture elevations and problem areas in the photogrammetry of buildings and structures, using tripods and deciding on the right surface and light conditions for excavation areas.[72] For smaller objects, there are decisions to be made about camera lenses, lighting and turntables.[73] This method is especially useful for lost heritage, for example, the Bamiyan Buddhas destroyed by the Taliban in 2001 were digitally recreated this way. One of the

[65] 3D printing concerns other areas of intellectual property (eg replicating patented inventions, or infringing shape marks or design) that are outside the boundaries of this book: S Bradshaw, A Bowyer and P Haufe, 'The Intellectual Property Implications of Low-Cost 3D Printing' (2010) 7 *SCRIPTed* 1, 26; LS Osborn, *3D Printing and Intellectual Property* (Cambridge, CUP, 2019); D Mendis, M Lemley and M Rimmer (eds), *3D Printing and Beyond: Intellectual Property and Regulation* (Cheltenham, Edward Elgar, 2019).

[66] P Oruç, '3D Digitisation of Cultural Heritage: Copyright Implications of the Methods, Purposes and Collaboration' (2020) 11(2) *JIPITEC* 149.

[67] A Davis et al 'Pilbara Rock Art: Laser Scanning, Photogrammetry and 3D Photographic Reconstruction as Heritage Management Tools' (2017) 5 *Heritage Science* 25; Historic England, '3D Laser Scanning for Heritage: Advice and Guidance on the Use of Laser Scanning in Archaeology and Architecture' (2018) 2.

[68] Historic England, '3D Laser' ibid 7–8.

[69] G Tucci, D Cini and A Nobile, 'Effective 3D Digitization of Archaeological Artifacts for Interactive Virtual Museum' (2011) *International Archives of the Photogrammetry, Remote Sensing and Spatial Information Sciences* 414, 417; Historic England, '3D Laser' (n 67) 23–29.

[70] Tucci, Cini and Nobile (n 69) 417.

[71] Lanmar Services, 'Laser Scanning vs. Photogrammetry' lanmarservices.com/2014/11/07/laser-scanning-vs-photogrammetry.

[72] Historic England, 'Photogrammetric Applications for Cultural Heritage: Guidance for Good Practice' (2017) 53–73.

[73] ibid 73–76.

projects relied on three sources: while the internet and tourist images were only useful to an extent, a 3D model was mainly based on metric images acquired in 1970, which provided more precise information about the measurements.[74]

2.5.4. Introduction to Economic Rights

Next, we need to consider whether the activity of copying audiovisual, 2D and 3D works overlaps with any of the exclusive economic rights of the author. Out of these rights, reproduction right is the most relevant.

Reproduction right in the Berne Convention includes all types of copying ('in any manner or form').[75] The World Intellectual Property Organization (WIPO) Copyright Treaty (WCT) also states that it 'fully applies in the digital environment' and that storage of a protected work in digital form in an electronic medium counts as reproduction.[76] The reproduction right under the InfoSoc Directive also includes reproduction 'in any form'.[77] The Copyright, Designs and Patents Act 1988 (CDPA) gives the owner of the copyright the exclusive right to copy the work.[78] In the UK, section 17(2) of the CDPA initially mentions 'reproducing work in any material form', but 'storing the work in any medium by electronic means' is also included, thus clarifying the inclusion of digital material. US copyright law also gives the copyright owner the exclusive right 'to reproduce the copyrighted work in copies or phonorecord', and the definition of a 'copy' includes 'work fixed by any method now known or later developed'.[79] Given that reproduction encompasses any method, using future digital methods will still concern copyright law in these jurisdictions.

Economic rights other than reproduction will also be affected when access to cultural heritage is provided: if any of these activities involve sharing the digitised heritage with visitors on and off premises, communication to public right will be infringed. If this access allows visitors to take copies from the heritage institution, this will likely infringe distribution right in the form of digital distribution. Depending on the activities of the heritage institution, these digitised works might be displayed, performed, or lent.[80]

[74] A Grün, F Remondino and L Zhang, 'Photogrammetric Reconstruction of the Great Buddha Of Bamiyan, Afghanistan' (2004) 19(107) *The Photogrammetric Record* 177, 182; E Delman, 'Afghanistan's Buddhas Rise Again' *The Atlantic* (10 June 2015) www.theatlantic.com/international/archive/2015/06/3d-buddhas-afghanistan/395576.

[75] Berne Convention, art 9(1).

[76] WIPO Copyright Treaty (Geneva, 20 December 1996) Agreed Statement concerning art 1(4).

[77] Directive (EC) 2001/29 of the European Parliament and of the Council of 22 May 2001 on the harmonisation of certain aspects of copyright and related rights in the information society OJ L167/10 ('InfoSoc Directive').

[78] Copyright, Designs and Patents Act 1988 ('CDPA'), s 16 (acts restricted by copyright in a work) and s 17 (infringement of copyright by copying).

[79] US Copyright Act of 1976, s 106.

[80] Rights and defences arising in digitisation, both for preservation and access, will be discussed in ch 4.

Infringement criteria in most jurisdictions include: causal connection and access; similarity between works; the copied part to be the expression and not the idea; the copied part to be substantial (qualitative); there has to be a direct or indirect reproduction (in some jurisdictions making an adaptation is included in reproduction).[81] Despite the different definitions of 'infringement' in the chosen jurisdictions, copying is at the heart of it. Therefore, we must assess the nature of copies made during digitisation for infringement purposes.

For most projects, digitising the entire work is preferable. While is possible to digitise only a certain part of the work, especially with literary works, it can be even more time-consuming and costly for the digitising team to review and determine which parts will be most useful. Additionally, complete works are more useful for text and data mining purposes.[82] It is important to re-emphasise that the reproduction in the abovementioned instruments do include partial taking but there are some references to 'substantiality': under UK law, reproduction 'as a whole or any substantial part of it' can be infringement.[83] Under US law, proof of copying must include substantial copying.[84] As for sound recordings, the copy should directly or indirectly reproduce the sounds fixed in the recording.[85]

2.5.5. Introduction to Moral Rights

While economic rights are focused on controlling the commercial exploitation of protected works, moral rights protect the personality of the author and their connection to their work.[86] Moral rights are rooted in international instruments such as the Berne Convention, TRIPS Agreement,[87] WIPO Copyright Treaty and Beijing Treaty. Berne Convention Article 6bis reads:

> (1) Independently of the author's economic rights, and even after the transfer of the said rights, the author shall have the right to claim authorship of the work and to object to any distortion, mutilation or other modification of, or other derogatory action in relation to, the said work, which would be prejudicial to his honor or reputation
>
> (2) The rights granted to the author in accordance with the preceding paragraph shall, after his death, be maintained, at least until the expiry of the economic rights …

The idea of protecting the author's reputation and integrity had already developed in civil law countries; however, introduction of such rights in the Berne

[81] Sterling (n 32) 13.05–13.23; Goldstein and Hugenholtz (n 57) 284–85.

[82] Text and data mining is revisited again in Section 2.8 and Section 4.3.4.3.

[83] CDPA, s 16(3).

[84] JC Ginsburg and R Gorman, *Copyright Law* (New York, Thomson Reuters, 2012) 134.

[85] US Copyright Act of 1976, s 114.

[86] Sterling (n 32) ch 8, Goldstein and Hugenholtz (n 57) ch 10.

[87] However, it is worth noting that art 9(1) clarifies that Members will have no rights or obligations in respect of rights in Berne 6bis: Agreement on Trade-Related Aspects of Intellectual Property Rights (Marrakesh, 15 April 1994) ('TRIPS').

Convention originally met with a 'reserved' reaction from common law countries.[88] There are differences in the national application of moral rights. In terms of duration, they last at least until the expiry of economic rights but are perpetual in others, and in most jurisdictions they can still be exercised by their heirs.[89] They remain with the author even when economic rights are assigned, although it might be possible to waive them in some countries, including the UK.[90] The US resisted incorporating Article 6bis into national law and only introduced these two rights in 1990, that apply only to 'works of visual art' that are not more than 200 copies.[91] There are also rights that are not included in international instruments that are even less harmonised, such as the right to disclose (divulgation), which is relevant for digitising unpublished works.[92]

Paternity (also referred to as attribution) right means the author needs to be recognised unless they wanted to publish pseudonymously or anonymously. This right supports the management of the work (including royalties), improves the interpretation of the work (in connection to the authors' identity) and rewards the author.[93] In terms of subject matter, this right will only be granted for some works (usually works requiring originality), and not others (such as computer programs or computer-generated works). In some jurisdictions, this right needs to be asserted.[94] The circumstances where attribution is required are also not harmonised, although it seems to be a common requirement for commercial exploitation.[95]

Integrity right allows the author to oppose derogatory treatment of their work, although what counts as derogatory is determined on a case-by-case basis, trying to seek a balance between the author's subjective opinions and objective risk of harm. On whether it requires actual modification of the work and whether the scope of integrity right allows the prevention of the destruction of work (which can be especially complicated if the work is held by someone other than the author), these are also inconsistent across jurisdictions.[96]

[88] Sterling (n 32) 8.03, quoting G Dworkin, 'Moral Rights and the common law countries' (1994) *Australian Intellectual Property Journal* 5.

[89] For example, moral rights have the same duration as economic rights in the UK and Germany, but they are perpetual in France: Sterling (n 32) 18.77.

[90] ibid.

[91] US Copyright Act, ss 106A and 101. See also Goldstein and Hugenholtz (n 57) 338.

[92] This right is not in Berne art 6bis. However, it can be supported by Berne arts 10 and 10bis. See also Sterling (n 32) 8.12; G Davies and K Garnett, *Moral Rights*, 2nd edn (London, Sweet & Maxwell, 2016); C Sappa and B Widla, 'Framing texts and images: critical and posthumous editions in the digital Single Market' (2023) 54 *IIC* 1359; J McCutcheon, 'Death rights: legal personal representatives of deceased authors and the posthumous exercise of moral rights' (2015) 3 *IPQ* 242. See also Section 4.1.1 on unpublished works.

[93] Bently and Sherman (n 31) 306.

[94] For the UK, see CDPA, s 78.

[95] Bently and Sherman (n 31) 309.

[96] Sterling (n 32) 8.19–8.22, G Dutfield and U Suthersanen, *Dutfield and Suthersanen on Global Intellectual Property Law*, 2nd edn (Cheltenham, Edward Elgar, 2020) 132.

The unharmonised nature of moral rights becomes even more challenging in the digital environment.[97] When cultural heritage is shared online it also concerns jurisdictions where moral rights do not expire, requiring the recognition of paternity rights without any local and temporal limits.[98] An online environment makes it easier for works to be separated from their authors if they are shared with incomplete or incorrect attribution. Without accurate information, it is also harder to determine the age of the original works that were digitised, leading to potential mistakes with their copyright status.

Partial taking can also affect the moral rights of the author. These copies carry a greater risk of losing the attribution. Once taken out of context, it could have negative effect on the integrity of the author. A similar problem occurs when a partial copy survives, and the original work deteriorates. Furthermore, decisions to alter the work during or after digitisation can also affect moral rights. This could be in the form of omissions: in a French case, *Saint Claire v Malerbi*, cutting parts of photographs during reframing was found to be an infringement of moral rights.[99] Similarly in *Pasterfield v Denham*, the Court had to address whether omitting some of the features on the edges and changes in colouring amounts to distortion of the work that was used in a leaflet, where the differences were found to be trivial but not affecting the honour or reputation of the artist (therefore not derogatory).[100] The changes in restoration could also be more than trivial; while it was held that faithful restorations do not require consent in Germany,[101] colourising an older film without authorisation was held to be an infringement of integrity right in *Turner Entertainment v Huston*.[102] Even with the best intentions, digital copies could lead to poor quality copies with smaller size or insufficient sharpness, which has led to different outcomes in the UK and French cases, the latter more likely to recognise it as an infringement of integrity.[103]

However, reproducing faulty works without alteration might also be a problem, as this might create an inauthentic version of the work.[104] For example, in *Nova Stradivarius v Berio*, the composer was able to oppose the further circulation of defective sound recordings in CD-format, as they provided an inaccurate

[97] See Section 3.3.2 for personhood, moral rights and digitisation.

[98] P Torremans, 'The protections of cultural heritage by copyright and related rights' in Stamatoudi (n 3) 52.

[99] *Saint-Claire v Malerbi*, CA Paris, 11 June 1990, RIDA 146, 293 (1990), as cited in Sterling (n 32) 8.110.

[100] *Pasterfield v Denham* [1999] FSR 168.

[101] Upper Regional Court of Düsseldorf, judgment made 20 February 2019–20 U 134/17.

[102] *Turner Entertainment Co v Huston*, Cass. 28 May 1991, 149 RIDA 197 CA Versailles 10 December 1994 164 RIDA 256 – as cited in Sterling (n 32) 8.110.

[103] Borghi and Karapapa (n 16) 127–28, see also *Tidy v Natural History Museum Trustees* [1995] 37 IPR 501 (reducing cartoons in size); cf *H & K, André R v Google*, CA Paris, 5 February 2011 TGI Paris, 3e ch, (cropped photographs on Google Images); *Moulinsart, Fanny R v Neret-Minet*, Court d'appel de Paris, 4 è me chambre, 14 March 2007 (low quality digitisation of Tintin cartoons).

[104] Borghi and Karapapa (n 16) 130.

version of the work and infringed the integrity right.[105] But then it is difficult to decide (i) if the author wanted natural deterioration, and (ii) at which stage of natural deterioration can something be digitised. The relationship between digitisation and moral rights is complicated. Altering the work too much, or not being able to achieve an accurate copy (due to technological constraints) can all affect integrity.

Borghi and Karapapa recognise two dimensions in ensuring the integrity of the work: its structural integrity is negatively affected when interventions affect the appearance of the work, however contextual integrity is negatively affected when the work is displayed outside its context, for example in association with other works.[106] The latter is especially challenging, considering that placing digital reproductions in a different context does not even require human involvement. Especially lately, artificial intelligence can easily read and merge previously unrelated works together, creating further uncertainty on how to oppose (for example, derogatory) context when there are less obvious decisions made beyond human understanding which are also not visible in any AI-generated output.

2.6. Purpose of Digitisation

Considering that the activity of digitisation carries a significant risk of infringing both economic and moral rights, that leaves the digitisers few options: (i) only focus on the public domain, (ii) risk copyright infringement, (iii) seek authorisation, and (iv) rely on defences.[107] In determining the best option and whether any defences will be applicable, the purpose of digitisation is important.

In terms of preservation, developments in technology allow accurate representations that can be reproduced indefinitely with the same quality. Digital copies can decrease the handling of the originals, which indirectly supports their preservation. Especially when placed online, millions can view the same source but without the negative effects of handling, light, humidity and temperature they would otherwise endure. This would help the originals to remain in good condition for a longer period. However, whether digitisation itself is a preservation method is doubtful, and its access benefits far outweigh the preservation purpose. In a 2020 survey, more than 80 per cent of the participating museums cited 'increased visibility' as their main reason for digitising their collections (although 'preservation' does not seem to be an option).[108] Another survey cited in this report, ENUMERATE Core

[105] *Nova Stradivarius v Berio*, Corte di Appello di Milano, 3 June 2003, Italy, *Il diritto di autore*, April–June 2002, as cited in Borghi and Karapapa (n 16) 121–22.

[106] Borghi and Karapapa (n 16) 126.

[107] These options will be revisited in Section 4.1.

[108] Network of European Museum Organisations, 'Final report: Digitisation and IPR in European Museums' (March 2020).

Survey, showed an average of 92 per cent of heritage institutions reported having collections that needed to be preserved for future generations.[109]

Digitisation can also be used for restoration. It allows for noticing new details, completing missing pieces, recovering sound recordings and films, and even increasing their quality with digital technology. But despite the amount of work needed, the level of restoration described here is for bringing an old work back to its original state and, on most occasions, it would not create a new work, as discussed in the next section. When the deterioration is so severe, and photographing the originals or copying from microfilms is insufficient, digitisation can help. One example of digitisation helping recovery of information is the Great Parchment Book, a manuscript that was destroyed by fire in 1786 with brittle and creased pages. This was later photographed from multiple angles and then flattened digitally to enable its contents to be read.[110] Additionally, once a work is digitised, parties in different locations can work on the same project, cross-border support from teams with more experience and resources can help.

Once a digital copy is created, the next step is providing access to it, in line with the public missions of heritage institutions. While researchers with specific targets can request one-off digitisation, mass digitisation can be more helpful for users undecided on a specific source, and users who increasingly expect works to be in searchable formats.[111] At the same time, mass digitisation requires an additional layer of diligence with the accuracy of digitised material. For example, the Google Books project was criticised for having metadata errors, in which the year 1899 was used as a placeholder for some books with unknown details, thereby creating confusion among researchers.[112]

Another access benefit is being able to use digitised versions for new purposes that were not possible to accomplish with originals. Digitised material can be arranged in different ways so that they tell more than one story and allow the user to interpret them freely.[113] Presenting old works in a new context might give a new range of possibilities, such as interactive exhibitions sharing digitised works. For example, the X Degrees of Separation project allows the user to choose two digitised art works. The programme then analyses the visual characteristics of these works and shows other artworks resembling them, thus creating a chain between these two works.[114] Similar projects allow artificial intelligence to interact

[109] 'Europeana DSI 2-Access to Digital Resources of European Heritage D4.4 Report on ENUMERATE Core Survey' (2017).

[110] 'Project History' (Great Parchment Book) www.greatparchmentbook.org/the-project/.

[111] E Hudson and AT Kenyon, 'Digital Access: The Impact of Copyright on Digitisation Practices in Australian Museums, Galleries, Libraries and Archives' (2007) 30 *University of New South Wales Law Journal* 12, 13.

[112] G Nunberg, 'Google Books: A Metadata Train Wreck' (upenn.edu, 1 September 2009) languagelog.ldc.upenn.edu/nll/?p=1701.

[113] J Langdalen, 'Editing Historical Music in the Age of Digitization' in L Duranti and E Shaffer (eds), *UNESCO The Memory of the World in the Digital Age: Digitization and Preservation Conference Proceedings* (Vancouver, 26–28 September 2012).

[114] M Klingemann and S Doury, 'X Degrees of Separation': artsexperiments.withgoogle.com/xdegrees.

with digitised heritage, to see patterns that are not visible to the human eye.[115] Furthermore, digitised heritage being used to support generative AI allows newer machine-generated works, that will also be part of our heritage.[116]

In practice, digitisation could be performed for a range of different purposes that are not always clear-cut as to where one purpose ends and other begins. Digitisation does not provide long-term preservation, and will require further maintenance, but it is useful for increased access. At the same time, although preservation and access are both equally important, they will have different copyright implications, further discussed in chapter four.

2.7. Nature of the Copies: Can Digitisation Create a New Copyright Work?

2.7.1. Public Domain and Copyfraud

Given how costly and uncertain digitisation can be, the chance of relying on new copyright for digitised copies is a great incentive. Digitising only the works in the public domain is an easy way to both avoid the risk of copyright infringement but also to recover the costs of digitisation. There are ways other than relying on copyright in monetising the digital copies, such as charging visitors for viewing digital copies on premises, charging for making copies online or on the premises, only releasing watermarked or low-quality versions and charging for full access. These institutions can limit the access to public domain works on-site or rely on contractual provisions when giving access to digital copies.[117] However, none of these methods provide the certainty that copyright provides, so copyright has turned into a convenient catch-all solution for enhancing the control over the copies in the public domain.

The practice of falsely claiming copyright over public domain (also referred as 'copyfraud') is increasingly common.[118] This approach does not have to be malicious, and could be due to lack of knowledge, but the outcome is all the same: it pulls cultural heritage that was in the public domain back into the domain of copyright that belongs to a new author – the digitiser. This practice works in the favour of parties making these claims, and reduces what is left for the public to

[115] M Borghi and S Karapapa, 'Non-Display Uses of Copyright Works' (2011) 1 *QMJIP* 21, 23.

[116] See also Section 2.8.2 below.

[117] J Dryden, 'Copyfraud or Legitimate Concerns? Controlling Further Uses of Online Archival Holdings' (2011) 74(2) *The American Archivist* 522.

[118] J Mazzone, 'Copyfraud' (2006) 81(3) *New York University Law Review* 1026; G Petri, 'The Public Domain vs. the Museum: The Limits of Copyright and Reproductions of Two-dimensional Works of Art' 12(1) *Journal of Conservation and Museum Studies* arts 8, 7–10; KC Butler, 'Keeping the World Safe from Naked-Chicks-in-Art Refrigerator Magnets: The Plot to Control Art Images in the Public Domain through Copyrights in Photographic and Digital Reproductions' (1998) 21 *Hastings Communications and Entertainment Law Journal* 55, 128.

build upon.[119] Especially when it comes to the treatment of cultural heritage that is not meant to be seen or shared, such as Indigenous material, for an outsider to claim control over both the physical ownership of the material and their subsequent copies is something to be cautious about.[120]

The incentive of copyright can be beneficial for bringing forgotten works back into circulation, which would otherwise be ignored.[121] This could benefit the public, there is the question of whether the intention of the authors can be predicted, were they planning to let the work disappear, or were they planning a different strategy for further circulation and monetisation? This is especially impossible in the case of works covered in Section 4.4 below. This will also be also an important issue for the UK unpublished works that are entering into the public domain in 2039, which might be promptly digitised with claims of new copyright.

2.7.2. How is Law Adapting to Copyright Claims Over Public Domain?

A significant obstacle to treating copies of public domain works as new copyright works is the originality requirement.[122] Although a considerable amount of skill and labour is needed for digitisation, the contribution in digitisation is not always sufficient for originality.[123] The copyright status of photographic copies of public domain works have been keeping courts busy since at least the 1869 *Graves' Case* in the UK. In this case, the photographs of an engraving were found to be original under the 1862 Fine Arts Copyright Act, emphasising that all photographs are copies of some object.[124]

More recently, in *Bridgeman v Corel*, public domain works of art in Bridgeman art library were reproduced on CD-ROMs sold in the US, UK and Canada.[125] It was held that photographic copies of public domain works could not receive

[119] Mazzone (n 118) 1030.

[120] See also previous work that touches on Indigenous material and another on digital surrogates: P Oruç, 'Documenting Indigenous Oral Traditions: Copyright for Control?' (2022) *International Journal of Cultural Property* 29(3) 243 and P Oruc, 'Rethinking who "keeps" heritage: 3D Technology, Repatriation and Copyright' (2022) 71 (12) *GRUR International* 1138. See also Section 1.2.2.3.

[121] For theoretical arguments for protecting digitised copies of rare documents with copyright, see S Mendis, A *Copyright Gambit: On the Need for Exclusive Rights in Digitised Versions of Public Domain Textual Materials in Europe* (Berlin, Springer, 2019).

[122] There are other non-copyright obstacles to copying public domain, which will be assessed in Section 4.3.2.

[123] Originality requirement was first introduced under Section 2.3. See also AM Sullivan, 'Cultural Heritage & New Media: A Future for the Past' (2016) 15 *J Marshall Rev Intell Prop L* 604, 614; Margoni (n 59) 19.

[124] *Graves' Case* (1869) LR 4 QB 715. For subsequent developments, see R Deazley, 'Photography, copyright, and the South Kensington experiment' (2010) 3 *IPQ* 293; E Cooper, *Art and Modern Copyright: The Contested Image* (Cambridge, CUP, 2018).

[125] *Bridgeman Art Library v Corel Corp*, 36 F Supp 2d 191 (SDNY 1999).

protection under the UK law, and the result would have been the same if US law was applied instead.[126] In the subsequent re-consideration, the court applied US law with the same outcome. It was held that the copies could not be protected because the result was not original enough, in line with case law in the US.[127] The discouraging impact of the *Bridgeman* decision has been widely discussed; although it was a US decision, applying US law and commenting on UK law, and scholars have also questioned whether Bridgeman means the *Graves' Case* is no longer good law.[128] Such a scenario was already mentioned in passing in *Interlego v Tyco*, that producing a good copy by painting or photographing takes great skill, labour and judgement but it would not be sufficient for originality.[129] While some scholars argued that photographing was different from photocopying and accurate copying should receive copyright protection, and, in the vein of *Walter v Lane* (court reporters noting down a speech verbatim), others agreed with the *Bridgeman* outcome.[130] In *Antiquesportfolio*, photographs showing different aspects of antique furniture received protection, when a traditional UK test of originality was applied (skill and labour).[131]

In 2009, Derrick Coetzee accessed the National Portrait Gallery's (NPG) website, acquired and uploaded high resolution copies of public domain paintings to Wikipedia. This activity brought not only copyright issues, but database right and breach of contract (as terms on NPG website do not allow reproduction without permission) and involved jurisdictional issues (US citizen downloading from UK servers, then sharing online and worldwide), but NPG never sued.[132] If they did, the case would have provided useful guidance on the copyright implications of merging low-resolution versions.

[126] ibid.

[127] 'distinguishable variation' in *Gerlach-Barklow v Morris&Bendien* 23 F 2d 159 (SDNY 1927); 'something more than merely trivial, something recognizably his own' in *Alfred Bell v Catalda Fine Arts* 191 F 2d 99 (2d Cir 1951); 'substantial as opposed to trivial variation … an element of creativity' in *L Batlin & Son v Snyder* 536 F 2d 486 (2d Cir 1976); as quoted in RC Matz, 'Bridgeman Art Library, Ltd. v. Corel Corp.' (2000) 15 *Berkeley Technology Law Journal* 3. For the US approach, see also *Meshworks, Inc. v Toyota Motor Sales USA, Inc.*, 528 F.3d 1258 (10th Cir. 2008); *Osment Models, Inc. v Mike's Train House, Inc.*, No. 2:09-CV-04189-NKL, 2010 WL 5423740; cf. *Alva Studios, Inc. v Winninger*, 177 F. Supp. 265 (SDNY 1959) and *Lucky Break Wishbone Corp. v Sears Roebuck & Co.*, 373 F. App'x 752, 755 (9th Cir. 2010).

[128] TS Kogan, 'Photographic Reproductions, Copyright and the Slavish Copy' (2012) 35 *The Columbia Journal of Law & the Arts* 445; MC Wojcik, 'The Antithesis of Originality: Bridgeman, Image Licensors, and the Public Domain' (2008) *Hastings Communications and Entertainment Law Journal* 257; RJ Allan, 'After Bridgeman: Copyright, Museums, and Public Domain Works of Art' (2007) 155 *University of Pennsylvania Law Review* 961; KL Kelley, 'The Complications of "Bridgeman" and Copyright (Mis)use' (2011) 30(2) *Art Documentation: Journal of the Art Libraries Society of North America* 38.

[129] 'Skill, labour or judgment merely in the process of copying cannot confer originality': *Interlego v Tyco* [1989] AC 217.

[130] *Walter v Lane* [1900] AC 539; K Garnett, 'Copyright in Photographs' (2000) *EIPR* 229; R Deazley, 'Photographing Paintings in the Public Domain: A Response to Garnett' (2001) 22(5) *EIPR* 179; S Stokes, *Art and Copyright*, 3rd edn (Oxford, Hart Publishing, 2021) 130–38.

[131] *Antiquesportfolio v Rodney Fitch & Co Ltd* [2001] FSR 23.

[132] Stokes (n 130) 153–56; Petri (n 118). For correspondence between parties, see material uploaded by Mr Coetzee, who argued these NPG photographs of public domain paintings were not protected by copyright: commons.wikimedia.org/wiki/User:Dcoetzee/NPG_legal_threat.

Although the originality criteria and status of portrait photography was previously clarified by the CJEU,[133] a dispute involving a German museum took place in 2016, where Reiss-Engelhorn-Museum filed a lawsuit against a visitor who scanned exhibition catalogues, took photographs on-site and uploaded them to Wikimedia. The court recognised that the museum's photographs can potentially receive lower protection given to non-original photographs in Article 72 of German Copyright Act because they were producing a faithful copy. The court also held that by entering an exhibition a visitor agreed to its terms and conditions, which includes no photography on the premises, otherwise this would be an infringement of the museum's property rights.[134]

The status of the public domain was further clarified in the EU by Article 14 of the CDSM Directive.[135] Originally intended as a paragraph under the Article 6 on preservation, this provision then became a self-standing provision.[136] This Article clarifies that the reproductions of public domain will not receive copyright protection unless they are the author's own intellectual creation.[137] It is useful for emphasising the EU originality criteria and ensuring that the works in the public domain are not pulled back under copyright control. This Article also limits the protection afforded to non-original photographs, such as the one in the Reiss Engelhorn case mentioned above, although it is not yet tested. Recital 53 provides some clarification for the rationale for this provision: 'circulation of faithful reproductions of works in the public domain contributes to the access to and promotion of culture, and the access to cultural heritage'.

But Article 14 has some shortcomings too, both due to the digital environment and differing national rules affecting cross-border dissemination. The Directive does not sufficiently clarify what counts as a 'work of visual art' and whether it includes all kinds of visual works, including two and three-dimensional and even audiovisual works.[138] At the implementation stage, countries whose laws were

[133] Case C-5/08 *Infopaq International A/S v Danske Dagblades Forening* [2009] ECDR 16; Case C-145/10 *Eva-Maria Painer v Standard VerlagsGmbH and Ors* [2012] ECLI:EU:C:2011:798.

[134] German Federal Court of Justice (Bundesgerichtshof), *Museumsfotos*, decision of 20 December 2018 – I ZR 104/17. See also S Michel, 'Digitisation of art in the public domain–museum urges Wikimedia to take down reproductions of out-of-protection artworks' (2019) 14(6) *JIPLP* 427.

[135] European Copyright Society, 'Comment of the European Copyright Society on the Implementation of Art. 14 of the DSM Directive 2019/790' (2020) 11 *JIPITEC* 22; A Wallace and E Euler, 'Revisiting Access to Cultural Heritage in the Public Domain: EU and International Developments' (2020) 51 *IIC* 823; G Dore and P Turan, 'When Copyright Meets Digital Cultural Heritage: Picturing an EU Right to Culture in Freedom of Panorama and Reproduction of Public Domain Art' (2024) 55 *IIC* 37; C Sappa, 'Hosting the public domain into a minefield: the resistance to art.14 of the DSM Directive and to the related rules that transpose it into national law' (2022) 17(11) *JIPLP* 924.

[136] E Rosati, *Copyright in Digital Single Market* (Oxford, OUP, 2021) 240–41.

[137] CDSM, art 14.

[138] Europeana, 'Recommendations on Copyright and its role in the Digital Transformation of the Cultural Heritage Sector' (March 2021) 8: pro.europeana.eu/files/Europeana_Professional/Publications/Recommendations%20on%20copyright%20and%20its%20role%20in%20the%20digital%20transformation%20of%20the%20cultural%20heritage%20sector.pdf.

already in line with protecting only original works, decided not to implement Article 14.[139] But more importantly, even though Article 14 looks like a significant change for preventing copyright claims over the public domain, it is still very much subject to originality requirements. Most methods would only give way to new copyright in very rare circumstances due to the lack of originality in the scanning process, which needs to be assessed case by case, causing legal uncertainty.

In the US, 'copyright misuse doctrine' has been defined through case law, as a rule that prevents 'the use of the copyright to secure an exclusive right or limited monopoly not granted by the Copyright Office'.[140] An interesting example is *Highsmith v Getty*: in this case the artist had already donated her photographs to the Library of Congress and gave the public the right to reproduce and distribute them, but was later contacted by Getty Images unlawfully claiming copyright over her images (charging licensing fees and threatening individuals and companies).[141] However, Highsmith's claim was dismissed by the court on the grounds that these works were in the public domain, and other claims were settled outside court. It is worth noting how Getty argued that image libraries are permitted to charge fees, quoting their services for image search and delivery; but this normally should not amount to being able to charge for image licensing.[142]

In the UK, the status of public domain works was recently confirmed in *THJ v Sheridan*.[143] This case was about graphic displays, specifically regarding originality in charts as artistic works. On appeal, the EU originality standard was applied, as opposed to the UK originality standard of skill and labour. The decision confirmed that the necessary originality threshold will not be met when the 'free and creative' choices are dictated by technical considerations.[144] Given that the UK has not implemented the CDSM Directive and there is no equivalent of Article 14, this case is useful in clarifying the UK courts' approach to the originality and the treatment of copies of public domain works. While it reduced the chance of heritage

[139] For more detailed information on its implementation, see T Nobre, 'The Post-DSM Copyright Report: Public Domain and cultural heritage rights' (9 February 2024): communia-association.org/2024/02/09/the-post-dsm-copyright-report-public-domain-and-cultural-heritage-rights. The clashes with national codes also remain, which are most recently seen in Italy's transposition of Article 14 without any prejudice to the Italian Code of Cultural Heritage and Landscape, therefore still controlling the works of Italian heritage in the public domain. This will be addressed in Section 4.3.2.

[140] *Lasercomb Am. Inc v Reynolds*, 911 F.2d970, 977 (4th Cir. 1990), as cited in Sullivan (n 123) 633.

[141] *Highsmith v Getty Images (US), Inc.*, No. 16-CIV-5924 (SDNY 2016).

[142] VP Kohli and S Teilmann-Lock, 'Copyright and Public Domain Works: Highsmith v Getty' in E Bonadio and A O'Connell (eds), *Intellectual Property Excesses: Exploring the Boundaries of IP Protection* (Oxford, Hart Publishing, 2022) 71–86. For the now removed statement by Getty Images, see web.archive.org/web/20170312030940/; press.gettyimages.com/statement-regarding-highsmith-claim/.

[143] *THJ Systems Limited & Anor v Daniel Sheridan & Anor* [2023] EWCA Civ 1354, [2024] ECDR 4.

[144] 'What is required is that the author was able to express their creative abilities in the production of the work by making free and creative choices so as to stamp the work created with their personal touch. This criterion is not satisfied where the content of the work is dictated by technical considerations, rules or other constraints which leave no room for creative freedom': *THJ v Sheridan* (n 143) para 16. See also D Clark, 'Skill and labour not enough for copyright – but software-generated art still original' (2024) 35(3) *Entertainment Law Review* 128.

institutions relying on copyright, some commentators argued that this case will lead to stricter terms of use on museum websites.[145]

2.7.3. Seeking Originality in Contributors, Methods and Purpose

Turning to the specifics of the digitisation process is useful to reach a conclusion on the chances of originality in the digitisation of cultural heritage. There are three questions to ask in order to determine the level of originality involved, on a case-by-case basis: (i) were there human decisions involved? (ii) which methods were used? (iii) was the purpose more than faithful representation?[146]

For the first question, Section 2.4 above has covered the types of institutions, but it is necessary to look at the decisions of the humans involved. If the process is completely automated (such as a conveyor belt digitisation and no input from the digitiser is possible, then it is not likely to be original. There could still be input through the choice of material to be digitised, but the act of reproduction is not performed by them if digitisation is fully automated.[147] If the process is semi-automated, where a human determines certain things, then originality might be possible. An example would be aerial photos of Paris taken from a plane; the photographer (human element) only determined the time of the shoots but not the angle or light.[148] Finally, if it is done completely by humans, with free and creative choices, applying their own labour, skill, judgement and personality, then there might be sufficient originality.

Answering the second question requires looking at the methods of digitisation and the complexity of the technological process. For example, the digitisation of 2D works or converting audiovisual works from analogue format to digital formats is less likely to be sufficiently original.[149] Even considering the technological developments for art reproduction photography bringing more illumination and higher detail, such differences would hardly be more than trivial input.[150] However, more

[145] D McCarthy, 'After THJ Sheridan' (13 January 2024): douglasmccarthy.com/2024/01/after-thj-v-sheridan; N Korn and S Waterman, 'How does a recent landmark ruling change museums' understanding of copyright?' (Museums Association, 8 February 2024): www.museumsassociation.org/museums-journal/opinion/2024/02/how-does-a-recent-landmark-ruling-change-museums-understanding-of-copyright.

[146] This structure is based on a previous work specifically focusing on the methods, purposes and collaboration in 3D digitisation: Oruç, '3D Digitisation' (n 66).

[147] Margoni (n 59) 5–6.

[148] This was found to be not original enough; they would be the same if another technician was placed in the same situation: Margoni (n 59) 34; citing TGI Paris, 6 October 2009, RIDA, 2010, no. 226, 506 (on aerial photographs).

[149] Mendis also assesses the process of 2D scanning of rare textual materials against the EU originality criteria and reaches the conclusion that a digitised version will not be protected as it would not be original: S Mendis (n 121) 192.

[150] Matz (n 127) 16.

complicated decisions are made in relation to 3D scanning and other processes, as opposed to 2D.

Originality might be possible in the 3D scanning methods, such as laser scanning and photogrammetry.[151] Positioning of the objects plays a big role in the desired outcome, and it was reported that deciding on the right position can take up as much as half of the data acquisition time.[152] The *Painer* decision also shows that the lighting and positioning of the object can impact the originality of the outcome.[153] *Painer* also mentions situations after the image is captured for adding a 'personal touch'.[154]

In arguing for originality for laser scanning, levels of human involvement are relevant. For example, the level of free and creative choices could be different between the scanning of an object placed on a turntable versus the scanning performed by hand-held or backpack-mounted scanners. Depending on the size of the scanned location, the use of drones adds another layer to the scanning stage, where original decisions can be made on how they are guided. Even if there is only one possible angle (such as an excavation with limited access), there could be input in the additional editing to complete the missing parts. While some argue that lighting, colour and shadows disappear during the processing stage, especially if they are aiming for accuracy, there could be further choices during this stage, such as removing errors or editing textures.[155]

As for photogrammetry, even though it relies on facts and measurements not protected by copyright, the underlying material (photographs) might already be protected, and their reproduction would require permission. There could be decisions on how these photographs and other materials holding measurement data are interpreted and brought together, which might provide sufficient originality. If this is done entirely by a computer program, without any human involvement, the outcome is less likely to be original. Alternatively, one could argue that the collection of these measurement points can be treated as an original database in which the outcomes are individually accessible.[156] The closest example would be

[151] First introduced in Section 2.5.3.

[152] Tucci (n 69) 416.

[153] See also *Painer* (n 36), *Antiquesportfolio* (n 131); Margoni (n 59) 19; D Mendis, 'Clone Wars Episode II – The Next Generation: The Copyright Implications Related to 3D Printing and Computer-Aided Design (CAD) Files' (2014) 6 *Law, Innovation and Technology* 265, 277–78.

[154] 'In the preparation phase, the photographer can choose the background, the subject's pose and the lighting. When taking a portrait photograph, he can choose the framing, the angle of view and the atmosphere created. Finally, when selecting the snapshot, the photographer may choose from a variety of developing techniques the one he wishes to adopt or, where appropriate, use computer software': *Painer* (n 36) para 91.

[155] LS Osborn, 'Of PhDs, Pirates,and the Public: Three-Dimensional Printing Technology and the Arts' (2014) *Texas A&M Law Review* 811, 831; F Remondino, 'Heritage Recording and 3D Modeling with Photogrammetry and 3D Scanning' (2011) 3 *Remote Sensing* 1104.

[156] A database is defined as 'a collection of independent works, data or other materials arranged in a systematic or methodical way and individually accessible by electronic or other means': Database Directive, art 1(2).

the recreation of a map, in which the CJEU confirmed that it could be protected.[157] Alternatively, it could fit under the creation of a *sui generis database* that needs to be protected based on the substantial investment in obtaining, verifying or presenting the contents of the database.[158]

Furthermore, we must remember that not all choices for the 3D scanning process will have an impact on the originality of the outcome. For example, the decisions made for the models' printing, such the colour or material might not matter in the final object.[159] Similarly, when the CAD file is converted into STL file, they lose features such as lighting and shadows (as they are not needed for the printing),[160] which means that the original decisions regarding those aspects also disappear.

As for sounds recordings and films, which are subject to different originality requirements, their digitisation involves transfer of data from analogue forms (cellulose films, and bumps on the recording) into binary form, and this does not require any creative or personal input from the digitiser. Therefore, unless there is additional input such as changes to improve quality, this conversion between formats also does not provide sufficient originality.

After considering the human element and the method, the final question in the determination of originality is on the purpose of digitisation: if the purpose is 'faithful representation', to be used in preservation, research, or even 'virtual repatriation', that rarely leaves enough room for originality.[161] For example, the aforementioned Recommendation on a common European Data Space for cultural heritage requires Member States to digitise 50 per cent of their most physically visited cultural and heritage monuments and 100 per cent of the heritage at risk by 2030 – but these would be faithful reproductions of cultural heritage.[162]

However, if a new two- or three-dimensional work is being created with creative purposes, or if the restoration work involves making free and creative choices, there could be originality. When the purpose is restoration, such as removing weather damage or smoothing of the edges, changing scale, or purposefully separating a single model into separate models, it is possible that the result will be

[157] '… Article 1(2) of Directive 96/9 must be interpreted as meaning that geographical information extracted from a topographic map by a third party so that that information may be used to produce and market another map retains, following its extraction, sufficient informative value to be classified as "independent materials" of a "database" within the meaning of that provision.' Case C-490/14 *Freistaat Bayern v Verlag Esterbauer* EU:C: 2015:735 [2015] Bus L.R. 1428, para 29; see also Bently and Sherman (n 31) 73.

[158] Database Directive, art 7; Case C-444/02 *Fixtures Marketing Ltd v Organismos prognostikon agonon podosfairou AE (OPAP)* ECLI:EU:C:2004:697, [2004] ECR I-10549.

[159] S Yamada, 'Who Moved My Masterpiece? Digital Reproduction, Replacement, and the Vanishing Cultural Heritage of Kyoto' (2017) 24(3) *Intl J Cult Prop* 295, 302; MJ Wachowiak and BV Karas, '3D Scanning and Replication for Museum and Cultural Heritage Applications' (2009) 48 *Journal of the American Institute for Conservation* 141, 147.

[160] M Antikainen and D Jongsma, 'The Art of CAD: Copyrightability of Digital Design Files' in RM Ballardini, M Norrgård and J Partanen (eds), *3D Printing, Intellectual Property and Innovation: Insights from Law and Technology* (Alphen aan den Rijn, Kluwer, 2017) 260.

[161] ibid 269; Osborn, *3D Printing* (n 65) 168; J Hornick, '3D Printing and IP Rights: The Elephant in the Room' (2015) 55 *Santa Clara Law Review* 801, 812.

[162] Commission Recommendation on Data Space (n 12) 5.

original – although not necessarily historically accurate. Based on past court decisions, restorations can be capable of being protected as original works in the EU.[163] It is possible that extra input in the public domain, such as performing editions of a public domain musical work, can lead to sufficient originality, when solving missing pieces is akin to 'assembling the pieces of a jigsaw puzzle' where reaching the full picture is going to require a lot of work.[164]

A famous example is the reconstruction of Dead Sea Scrolls, where access to the important fragments was exclusively provided to a group small of international researchers.[165] Professor Qimron worked on compiling the fragments into a single document, and also completed (or 'deciphered') the missing parts based on their own research. Before it could be published, the copies of the texts (including the deciphered work) were released to the public and were subsequently published by Eisenman without authorisation. It was held that while there was no copyright infringement for copying an ancient text, Qimron's reconstruction was protected as a compilation (literary work).[166]

It becomes even easier to claim a new work is created when the 3D scanning is for creative purposes, going even beyond restoration: scholars refer to them as 'expressive scans' where the outcome significantly differs from the original objects and therefore displays sufficient originality.[167] For example, there are various 3D models of the previously mentioned Nefertiti bust online, where additional contributions have created printable models for different objects such as plant pots and accessories based on an identical copy of the bust.[168] Being able to further modify and print these objects might provide the users with a better understanding of cultural heritage.

To sum up, copyright is often claimed by the relevant stakeholders, but might not be suitable for this purpose, due to originality threshold. Courts have also clarified, on multiple occasions, that public domain should not be pulled back to copyright. A closer examination in this section reveals that there are only a rare set of circumstances where copies of public domain can be protected by copyright – mainly in 3D digitisation that requires new human input for restoration and creative purposes.

[163] A Rahmatian, 'Copyright protection for the restoration, reconstruction and digitization of public domain works' in E Derclaye (ed), *Copyright and Cultural Heritage: Preservation and Access to the Works in a Digital World* (Cheltenham, Edward Elgar, 2010) 51–77; P Torremans, 'Legal issues pertaining to the restoration and reconstitution of manuscripts, sheet music, paintings and films for marketing purposes' in P Torremans (ed), *Copyright Law: A Handbook of Contemporary Research* (Cheltenham, Edward Elgar, 2007) 28–48.

[164] C Cronin, 'Intellectual property implications of 3D printing of cultural heritage' in Stamatoudi (n 3) 572; *Eisenman v Qimron*, CA. 2790/93, 2811/93, 54(3) PD 817. See also MD Birnhack, 'The Dead Sea Scrolls Case – Who is an Author?' (2001) 23(3) *EIPR* 128.

[165] *Eisenman v Qimron* (n 164).

[166] ibid.

[167] M Weinberg, '3D Scanning: A World without Copyright' (2016) *Shapeways* 10; SK Katyal, 'Technoheritage' (2017) 105 *California Law Review* 1111, 1147.

[168] The scanning of the bust was first mentioned in Section 1.2.2.3. For the scans of bust and subsequent works, see 'Nefertiti Hack' nefertitihack.alloversky.com; Thingiverse, www.thingiverse.com/tag:Nefertiti.

Additionally, some scholars suggest alternative types of protection: shorter protection for lower originality photographs, which exist in some European jurisdictions, including Germany, Austria, Spain and Italy, can be a less impactful alternative for digitised public domain.[169] Others suggest that collections of non-original photographs can be potentially protected as a *sui generis database right* (SGDR) that needs to be protected based on the substantial investment in obtaining, verifying or presenting the contents of the database; therefore making their lack of originality less of a problem.[170]

2.8. New Uses of Digital Copies

The new uses covered under this part, VR and AI, provide new opportunities for the use and circulation of cultural heritage, but at the same time they highlight existing copyright uncertainties, and create further concerns on subsistence and ownership.

2.8.1. Use of 3D Heritage in Virtual Reality

Virtual reality (VR) technology allows the creation of a real or edited environment and exploring it with equipment (such as headsets and gloves). It allows full immersion; some headsets also emit sounds.[171] VR sets are getting less expensive over time; companies such as Meta and Sony are also developing their own sets, creating new VR platforms and adapting existing games to VR, while there are also sceptics as to whether these investments will be profitable in the long run.[172] Nevertheless, users who are discouraged by the costs of headsets can still enjoy heritage institution exhibitions that provide a VR device temporarily, allowing for a deeper understanding of art and history.[173]

[169] Margoni (n 59); Sunimal Mendis recommends such protection for digitised public domain rare documents, which both provides an incentive but also not at the same level as copyright protection. S Mendis (n 121).

[170] F Truyen and C Waelde, 'Copyright, Cultural Heritage and Photography: A Gordian Knot?' in KJ Borowiecki, N Forbes and A Fresa (eds), *Cultural Heritage in a Changing World* (Cham, Springer, 2016) 85. For SGDR, see Directive 96/9/EC of the European Parliament and of the Council of 11 March 1996 on the legal protection of databases OJ L77/20 ('Database Directive'), art 7.

[171] It allows experiencing specific moments in history, such as the Battle of Dunkirk or a Viking battle: S Leslie, 'The Key Role of VR in Preserving Cultural Heritage' (Arts Management & Technology Laboratory, 6 May 2022) amt-lab.org/blog/2022/4/motivating-usages-of-virtual-reality-in-cultural-heritage.

[172] G Hopkin, 'Top 10 companies leading in virtual and augmented reality' (AIMagazine. 17 February 2023) aimagazine.com/top10/top-10-companies-leading-in-virtual-and-augmented-reality; J Vanian, 'VR market keeps shrinking even as Meta pours billions of dollars a quarter into metaverse' (CNBC, 19 December 2023) www.cnbc.com/2023/12/19/vr-market-shrinking-as-meta-pours-billions-of-dollars-into-metaverse.html.

[173] J Richardson, 'Virtual Reality Is a Big Trend in Museums, But What Are the Best Examples of Museums Using VR?' (MuseumNext, 24 January 2024): www.museumnext.com/article/

Augmented reality (AR), on the other hand, overlays 3D objects and supporting information onto the real world and does not require full immersion. Even a smartphone can overlay digital information over the surroundings captured by the phone camera, for purposes such as tourism, gaming or online shopping. The location matters more, especially when AR takes the surroundings into consideration. For example, Smartify overlays information about the collection, and it allows for saving the scanned material.[174]

The use of VR and AR in cultural heritage is increasing.[175] Once 3D models of cultural heritage are created, they can be inserted into such projects. There are already options to view 3D models of cultural heritage online, including a newer project where each of the 27 EU Member States will submit one 3D digitised heritage asset.[176] From a copyright perspective, the use and editing of material used in VR/AR projects, such as the information text (literary work) or photographs (artistic work) and films, could infringe both economic and moral rights of the copyright holder, so permission will be needed. Even if the underlying work is in the public domain, these works could be edited with sufficient originality using the 3D methods explained above.

These experiences and their ability to benefit the audiences of heritage institutions are also recognised by the European Commission:

> In addition to serving preservation and restoration purposes, 3D technologies may also provide increased opportunities for cultural heritage institutions to reach wider audiences with more immersive experiences that include virtual access to places which are normally inaccessible (e.g. underwater) or temporarily closed, or to reach persons with visual impairments by offering, for example, accessible tactile experiences.[177]

There are also diverging views on how to categorise the 3D models as subject matter. They could be seen as 'mini-programs' or 'preparatory design',[178] which makes

how-museums-are-using-virtual-reality; A Theodoropoulos and A Antoniou, 'VR Games in Cultural Heritage: A Systematic Review of the Emerging Fields of Virtual Reality and Culture Games' (2022) 12(17) *Applied Sciences* 8476.

[174] The National Gallery, 'Apps' www.nationalgallery.org.uk/visiting/apps, as introduced in Stokes (n 130) 108.

[175] For a detailed analysis of AR usage in heritage and copyright, see C Sappa, 'Participating in Cultural Life via Augmented Reality on Cultural Goods: What Role for Copyright?' (2022) 71(7) *GRUR International* 618. For AR and VR in creating art, see O Jean-Baptiste, 'Augmented and virtual reality art: a new frontier of legal protection' (2021) 4(2) *Interactive Entertainment Law Review* 102.

[176] Google: artsandculture.google.com/project/openheritage; Sketchfab: sketchfab.com/categories/cultural-heritage-history; Smithsonian: 3d.si.edu/; 'Virtual tours of the National Gallery' www.nationalgallery.org.uk/visiting/virtual-tours; Twin It: pro.europeana.eu/page/twin-it-3d-for-europe-s-culture.

[177] Commission Recommendation on Data Space (n 12) recital 11.

[178] D Mendis, 'In Pursuit of Clarity: The Conundrum of CAD Software and Copyright – Seeking Direction Through Case Law' (2018) 40(11) *EIPR* 694; D Mendis, 'Clone Wars' (n 153); Bradshaw (n 65) 26; K Dolinsky, 'CAD's Cradle: Untangling Copyrightability, Derivative Works, and Fair Use in 3D Printing' (2014) 71 *Washington and Lee Law Review* 591; Osborn, *3D Printing* (n 65); I Silverman, 'Optimising Protection: IP Rights in 3D Printing' (2016) 38(1) *EIPR* 5.

sense considering the definition of computer programs.[179] Another approach would be seeing them as literary works, similar to instructions given to create something new, such as a knitting pattern or circuit diagram, based on the cases from the UK.[180] As yet another alternative, some scholars argue for viewing CAD files as artistic works (in addition to literary works), based on the fact that they are scans of existing artistic works[181] or the fact that they carry instructions to create a new artistic work.[182] Some also argue that these works are protectable as databases, provided that they are the 'authors own intellectual creation',[183] which is not always the case.[184] There is also the additional question on whether the VR or AR can be protected as a separate work, and which category would be more applicable (film, artistic work, software).[185]

Relying on defences can be partially helpful if the VR/AR application has public benefit, such as research and education.[186] But it is also common for this technology to be used for commercial purposes, such as to offset the costs of such exhibitions, making it less likely to rely on a copyright defence for the use of underlying materials. This would then require relying on licensing.

Furthermore, if AR applications encourage the users to photograph their surroundings there will be originality and authorship questions, based on how much of the contribution comes from the application itself and the built-in models, and how much of it comes from the photographer. Considering that VR/AR experiences could require the scanning of the entire surroundings, as opposed to individual objects, freedom of panorama is worth mentioning. This right is described as 'the legal right in some countries to publish pictures of artworks, sculptures, paintings, buildings or monuments that are in public spaces, even when they are still in copyright'.[187] It is included in Article 5(3)(h) of the InfoSoc

[179] Computer programs are defined as 'programs in any form, including those which are incorporated into hardware … also includes preparatory design work leading to the development of a computer program provided that the nature of the preparatory work is such that a computer program can result from it at a later stage': Software Directive, Recital 7.

[180] See also *Abraham Moon & Sons v Thornber* [2012] EWPCC 37, [2013] FSR 17; *Anacon Corporation v Environmental Research Technology* [1994] FSR 659; *Brigid Folley v Ellot* [1982] RPC 433; D Mendis, 'In Pursuit' (n 178).

[181] Antikainen and Jongsma (n 160) 258; D Mendis, 'Back to the Future'? From Engravings to 3D Printing – Implications for UK Copyright Law' in Mendis, Lemley and Rimmer (n 65); A Daly, *Socio-Legal Aspects of the 3D Printing Revolution* (London, Palgrave Macmillan, 2016); H Dasari, 'Assessing Copyright Protection and Infringement Issues Involved with 3D Printing and Scanning' (2013) 41 *AIPLA Quarterly Journal* 279.

[182] D Mendis, 'In Pursuit' (n 178).

[183] Database Directive, art 3(1).

[184] Antikainen and Jongsma (n 160) 272; Osborn, *3D Printing* (n 65) 168.

[185] Stokes (n 130) 108; A Dunne, 'Copyrighting Experiences: How Copyright Law Applies to Virtual Reality Programs' (2019)12 *The Journal of Business, Entrepreneurship & the Law* 329.

[186] Eurocities, 'Three dimensions of a city': eurocities.eu/stories/three-dimensions-of-a-city; C Green, 'VR project shows how Romans built their houses to be eye-catching' (Heritage Tribune, 24 March 2022) heritagetribune.eu/italy/vr-project-shows-how-romans-built-their-houses-to-be-eye-catching.

[187] M Dulong de Rosnay and PC Langlais, 'Public artworks and the freedom of panorama controversy: a case of Wikimedia influence' (2017) 6(1) *Internet Policy Review*. See also P Combe, 'Copyright

Directive, but it is not harmonised across Europe. The unharmonised nature of this right makes it complicated, not just for VR/AR, but for the use of heritage in public spaces in general.[188]

2.8.2. Using Heritage for Text and Data Mining and Artificial Intelligence

Artificial intelligence can achieve many things for heritage, such as restoration, classification, translation and transcription, analysis and interpretation, metadata enhancement, AI-created VR and AR environments and personalised experiences, and creating further artistic expressions based on the extracted material.[189] This could involve helping humans, such as AI being used to restore damaged ancient texts and improving the accuracy in comprehending ancient texts.[190]

For example, data mining technology can view material and answer specific questions or create new categorisations. It does not have to be limited to textual analysis. One project found that the colour most used by painters has changed from orange to blue by analysing 13,000 digitised paintings from the 1800s onwards.[191] Another project analysed the content from digitised newspapers from the nineteenth century and found that all of the faces in photographs were well-dressed, white men.[192] But this technology goes beyond computers quickly devouring material and answer specific questions, digitised cultural heritage can also be used to train machine learning to create new works entirely.

From a technical perspective, machine learning has different types. For example, supervised learning relies on labelled data, whereas unsupervised learning can use unlabelled data for training, the resulting algorithm able to detect patterns but unable to interpret them. Reinforcement learning relies on trial and error to reach the maximum reward for an activity.[193] As an advanced form of machine

Protection of Works Displayed in Public Places: Challenges over the Freedom of Panorama Exception' (2018) 23 *Art Antiquity & Law* 313; K Galilee, 'To what extent should uses of public architectural works be permitted under European copyright law ?' (2018) *Stockholm Intellectual Property Law Review* 1(2) 18; M Iljadica, 'Copyright and the Right to the City' (2017) 68(1) *Northern Ireland Legal Quarterly* 59.

[188] Dore and Turan (n 135) 37.

[189] See generally: S Münster et al, 'Artificial Intelligence for Digital Heritage Innovation: Setting up a R&D Agenda for Europe' (2024) 7 *Heritage* 794.

[190] In this project the accuracy was improved from 25% to 72% with the use of deep neural networks: Y Assael et al, 'Restoring and attributing ancient texts using deep neural networks' (2022) 603 *Nature* 280. See also M Mishra and PB Lourenço, 'Artificial intelligence-assisted visual inspection for cultural heritage: State-of-the-art review' (2024) 66 *Journal of Cultural Heritage* 536.

[191] M Bellander, 'The Colors of Paintings: Blue Is the New Orange' (2015) blog.martinbellander.com/post/115411125748/the-colors-of-paintings-blue-is-the-new-orange.

[192] 'Nineteenth-Century Newspaper Analytics' (NC State University) ncna.dh.chass.ncsu.edu/imageanalytics/analyses.php#portraits.

[193] Cambridge Consultants, 'Use of AI in Online Content Moderation' (Ofcom, 2019).

learning, deep learning relies on artificial neural networks carrying data through complicated neural networks,[194] each layer making it harder to interpret the sources and reasoning. Depending on the purpose (natural language processing or computer vision), the type of data required also changes (text or visual materials).[195] However, the stages remain similar: data is collected either by obtaining free or paid datasets,[196] and/or scraping off the internet; then the data has to go through pre-processing where it is cropped, resized, broken into smaller units, or normalised so that it becomes sufficiently standardised for training.[197] Once the algorithm is trained, it can be further improved with newer and/or augmented data.

From a copyright perspective, heritage and artificial intelligence raises two issues when the data set includes works still protected by copyright: (i) whether heritage can be used to train AI,[198] and (ii) whether new copyright emerges from the changes (such as restoration or additional augmented data) made by AI. If there are changes being made to the work, that could also infringe the moral rights of the rightsholder.

For the first issue, if we turn to the machine learning process again, it is possible that the data scraped from online resources will include copyright protected material. More subject-specific datasets will likely include material that falls under the scope of both cultural heritage and copyright subject matter and will require authorisation. However, works that are not protected by copyright or SGDR might be subject to even stricter contractual terms. In *Ryanair v PR Aviation*, PR Aviation's price comparison site was screen scraping from Ryanair, while Ryanair terms and conditions explicitly limited the use to non-commercial purposes such as making and changing bookings. Although they allowed the third parties who had sought a licence with them, PR Aviation did not have such a licence. Ryanair claimed that their copyright and/or database right was infringed by PR Aviation. After the Dutch courts dismissed Ryanair's claim, Supreme Court has referred the case to the CJEU. The Court was asked if the freedom to use databases, which are not protected by SGDR or copyright, can be limited contractually. The court clarified that the rights established for lawful users are not applicable in non-protectable

[194] WIPO Technology Trends 2019: Artificial Intelligence (2019) 146.

[195] For case studies on natural language processing, computer vision and data scraping, and the relevant copyright implications, see M Kretschmer, T Margoni and P Oruç, 'Copyright Law and the Lifecycle of Machine Learning Models' (2024) 55 *IIC* 110.

[196] Some companies, such as Microsoft, Google, or Meta, already hold large datasets that help them develop their own AI algorithms. Similarly, these companies may choose to make their labelled datasets, or the algorithms developed on these datasets available to the public. Examples include: Open Images Dataset V7 and Extensions: storage.googleapis.com/openimages/web/index.html; Azure Open Datasets: azure.microsoft.com/en-gb/products/open-datasets; FACET Dataset: ai.meta.com/datasets/facet.

[197] J Nelson, 'What is Image Preprocessing and Augmentation?' (2020): blog.roboflow.com/why-preprocess-augment; Appen, How to Create Training Data for Computer Vision Use Cases (2019): www.appen.com/blog/how-to-create-training-data-for-computer-vision-use-cases.

[198] The relevant copyright defence is covered in Section 4.3.4.3.

databases and that such contractual provisions are allowed. It is especially problematic for sole-source databases, where the database owner is the one producing the data.[199]

The use of protected works for machine learning will likely not be transient enough to be covered by the temporary copying defence, especially when the training material must be retained for AI accountability. Depending on where this training material is kept, such as cloud services, there could also be additional platform liability for holding copyright protected material.

For the second issue on whether AI interactions with digital heritage could lead to new copyright, there are two stages in the training that could be relevant. One is the data augmentation, where AI can artificially augment the datasets by introducing AI-generated material into the existing training dataset. The second relates to the changes made to the digitised material by AI, such as restoration, including predicting and completing missing parts. In line with the discussion in the previous section, it is possible that new works protected by copyright will emerge, but this will be subject to originality requirements. Who should be the new copyright holder in the material generated or edited by AI creates a new set of ownership problems, although there are different recommendations on who should be the copyright holder in AI works.[200]

2.9. Conclusion

If we look at digitisation from the perspective of the Cultural Property Principles established in chapter one, limitlessness and speed of digitisation make it a suitable alternative for the wide scope of cultural heritage (Principle One), it partly addresses ownership issues and gives more access to a wide range of people (Principle Two) and can save the heritage from physical challenges so it satisfies heritage public interest (Principle Three).

Digitising cultural heritage is the next logical step, but it also means copyright law now contributes to the inconsistent treatment of heritage. As illustrated in this chapter, even before copyright problems become truly visible, availability of resources will have an impact on what gets to be digitised and maintained post-digitisation. The scope of cultural heritage and copyright subject matter overlaps,

[199] Case C-30/14 *Ryanair Ltd v PR Aviation* ECLI:EU:C:2015:10, [2015] ECDR 13. See also E Derclaye, 'An Economic Analysis of the Contractual Protection of Databases' (2005) 1(2) *University of Illinois Journal of Law, Technology and Policy* 247.

[200] The copyright status of AI generated works is outside the scope of this book. See generally: DJ Gervais, 'The Machine as Author' (2019) 105 *Iowa Law Review* 2053; A Guadamuz, 'A Scanner Darkly: Copyright Liability and Exceptions in Artificial Intelligence Inputs and Outputs' (2024) 73(2) *GRUR International* 111; E Bonadio and L McDonagh, 'Artificial Intelligence as Producer and Consumer of Copyright Works: Evaluating the Consequences of Algorithmic Creativity' (2020) 2 *IPQ* 112; T Kongolo, 'The extent of the public domain in the age of new technologies including artificial intelligence (AI)' (2023) 45(1) *EIPR* 589.

unless digitisation is limited to public domain. The type and funding of the digitiser determines their decisions, including their caution levels for copyright. The digitisation activity itself, whether audiovisual, two-dimensional or three-dimensional, carries the risk of infringing economic and moral rights, and the purpose of digitisation determines the applicability of solutions such as licensing and copyright defences, to be assessed in depth in chapter four. However, there is a possibility of digitisation also creating new works which are going to be protected by new copyright, depending on the specifics of digitisation activity. Furthermore, the new technological uses for digitised heritage, such as virtual reality and artificial intelligence, create new questions and amplify existing uncertainties for copyright.

Perhaps, in the future, a new dematerialisation method will become widespread, and some works will be re-scanned, processed and transferred to this format. Until then, this is the method that we need to understand and facilitate as part of the long-term responsibility of keeping heritage safe and accessible. These copyright implications identified here will demonstrate that a clash between copyright and digitised cultural heritage is inevitable. This does not mean that digitisation should be ruled out, or that cultural heritage should be left as it is. On the contrary: the advancements of today have been achieved by standing on the shoulders of giants and it is only fair to use these developments for the future of technological and scientific advancements. That is why this chapter establishes that digitisation is the next logical step for cultural heritage institutions, while recognising the clash between copyright and digitising heritage.

The next three chapters will divide this into three 'clashes': theory, law and the practice. The clash in theory will be first: the tension between protecting the author and the public interest of cultural heritage causes this underlying, less visible clash. But the theoretical incompatibility is more impactful than it first seems, as it causes and strengthens the other clashes. Now that we know copyright protection will be infringed by digitisation, it is time to question whether justifications for copyright protection can be overridden for the purpose of keeping heritage safe and accessible.

3

Clash in Theory: The Principles of Cultural Property Law versus Copyright Justifications

In the exploration of copyright's role in digitisation, it is time to turn to the very first clash, which is at the theory level. As discussed earlier, the scope and owners of heritage are defined differently according to the purpose of each cultural property law instrument. Heritage both belongs to everyone and no-one, but its loss concerns all humankind. But due to its unclear and wide scope, cultural heritage also includes material that is temporarily protected by a different area of law: copyright. So, a conflicting force emerges, which is the protection provided to the author, justified by multiple theories. Their rights are at risk of being infringed and their interests need to be taken into consideration.

Copyright law already struggles with establishing a balance between different stakeholders, namely the author versus the public; so the tensions specific to cultural heritage (such as the uncertainties about its scope, owner and challenges) further complicate this balancing act. This chapter will show that there is a limit to how much weight the special public interest in cultural heritage can carry in this debate, when the authors interests are placed at the opposite ends of the scale.

The main question in this chapter is how will the justification theories for copyright measure against the principles of cultural property, in the specific scenario of digitisation? Will the goals for cultural property, and especially the public interest in digitisation, justify a significant recalibration in the existing protection for authors?

These theories impact multiple instruments, such as the wording of the constitution, or in intellectual property laws of a country.[1] Their influence can also be seen in court decisions and opinions. For copyright law, the influence of theories can be seen in provisions on copyright term, subject matter, protection criteria (especially originality), the economic and moral rights of the author, and copyright defences.

[1] For example, US Constitution, art I, s 8, cl 8: 'To promote the Progress of Science and Useful Arts, by securing for limited Times to Authors and Inventors the exclusive Right to their respective Writings and Discoveries.'

3.1. Different Viewpoints: Scarcity and Commodification

Citing Rawls and Hume, Waldron suggests that scarcity is 'presupposition of all sensible talk about property,' and if there was no scarcity, the questions about nature and justification of property would come to an end.[2]

Cultural heritage, broadly defined, is both scarce and not. Following Walter Benjamin's ideas about the 'aura of the original', most artefacts are valued due to their presence in time and space.[3] Cronin argues that we perceive the objects in the same way we perceive ancestors: for example, the Parthenon is not only revered for its aesthetic value, but because it is very old and has been created and touched by individuals of an ancient civilisation over 2,000 years ago.[4] But there is also heritage that is not 'old' in the same sense.

There are occasions where alteration over a long period of time creates a new object: for example, Ise Grand Shrine in Japan was first built 2,000 years ago, and it is a part of tradition to rebuild it with new wood every 20 years (*Shikinen Sengu*).[5] Does it mean this object is valued because of its scarcity, or because of what it represents? In a sense, the same logic applies to digital copies without aura. They do not replace damaged heritage or solve repatriation issues, they merely provide representations, without aura.[6]

Ownership of heritage is also different from other objects. Tangible forms of heritage are sometimes held in distant locations, whereas intangible forms of heritage, including digital, are easier to share. Some forms of heritage have unknown and/or multiple contributors over multiple generations and need to be accessible to all members of that community. Cultural 'property' cannot be owned the same way as other property and cannot be sold or disposed of freely, which is usually prevented by national and international rules.

On the other side, IP rights are separate from the tangible objects. Underlying ideas or inventions can be easy to reproduce, therefore IP creates an artificial scarcity in the form of time limited monopoly.[7] During the monopoly, only the

[2] J Waldron, *The Right to Private Property* (Oxford, Clarendon Press, 1988) 31–32.

[3] W Benjamin, 'The Work of Art in the Age of Mechanical Reproduction' (1935), trans H Zohn, ed H Arendt, *Illuminations* (New York, Schocken Books, 1968) Note 5.

[4] C Cronin, '3D Printing: Cultural Property as Intellectual Property' (2015) 39 *The Columbia Journal of Law & the Arts* 1.

[5] Japan Woodcraft Association, 'Traditions: Shikinen Sengu': japanwoodcraftassociation.com/2020/02/13/traditions-shikinen-sengu. The shrine is included under the 'Fujisan, sacred place and source of artistic inspiration', inscribed in 2013: whc.unesco.org/en/list/1418.

[6] F Cameron and S Kenderdine, *Theorizing Digital Cultural Heritage: A Critical Discourse* (Cambridge, Massachusetts, MIT Press, 2010); NA Silberman, 'From cultural property to cultural data: the multiple dimensions of "ownership" in a global digital age' (2014) 21 *International Journal of Cultural Property* 365; Cronin (n 4); SK Katyal, 'Technoheritage' (2017) 105 *California Law Review* 1111. See also Section 1.2.2.3.

[7] Lemley argues that IP rights 'artificially replicate scarcity where it would not otherwise exist': MA Lemley, 'IP in a World Without Scarcity' (2015) 90 *New York University Law Review* 460. See also MA Carrier, 'Limiting copyright through property' in H Howe and J Griffiths (eds), *Concepts of Property in Intellectual Property Law* (Cambridge, CUP, 2013).

rightholders can take advantage of it, instead of the rest of humankind. Their term of protection is not yet over. Their commodification is not frowned upon but welcomed and sought after by the author.

The main underlying difference in these two areas, then, is the commodification of works. The aim of IP, protecting the individual and their opportunity for commodification, is the exact opposite of what cultural heritage needs. That is not to say opposing arguments regarding the commodification of cultural heritage do not exist; going back to Merryman's work in the area, he argues that 'the work of art itself is somehow reduced or sullied by being bought and sold … surely does not bear scrutiny'.[8] It is even argued that creating a licit market would both reduce the illicit activities, and make way for an internationalist approach to heritage, where resources will move from market nations towards source nations,[9] though this view is not very common and does not fit with the previously introduced UNESCO instruments and the academic literature, since there are safeguards against the commodification of cultural heritage.

If the subject matter of cultural property and copyright overlaps, and the former belongs to everyone (but should not be commodified) and the latter belongs to a specific member of the public (and can be commodified) for a limited time, where does one end and the other begin? Is it as simple as assuming things that belong to an 'author' for a limited duration then gain some inherent value just by being older and entering into the public domain, and therefore start receiving different treatment? Does that make the public domain more valuable (as it is now 'heritage') or less valuable (as in everyone can edit or distort)? Or can we rethink the theories behind the existence of copyright, and bend them to the point that they fit the purpose of keeping heritage safe and accessible through digitisation?

The boundary between what concerns the author and what concerns the public is already unclear. Authors are also a part of the public, and their works build on existing heritage around them. Seeking more digitisation and more access is generally beneficial to the creation of new works. However, whichever theory lies behind why an author needs protection is tested, it will be challenging to argue for reducing the copyright protection. The first two theories (labour and personhood) are important for scrutinising why the author deserves this protection in the form of a private property right. The remaining two theories (utilitarian and culture) are more relevant for seeking a balance between the author and the public, while achieving an efficient or culturally beneficial distribution of rights and duties.

[8] JH Merryman, 'A Licit International Trade in Cultural Objects' (1995) 4(1) *Intl J Cult Prop* 13, 38. Merryman cites Spanish Minister of Culture's comments on how they cannot allow their 'historical artistic heritage' becoming an 'object of common trade': J Thomas, 'Goya Portrait to go back to Spain' *The New York Times* (11 April 1986) www.nytimes.com/1986/04/11/arts/goya-portrait-to-go-back-to-spain.html.

[9] ibid.

3.2. Labour Theory

According to the Lockean theory, humans are entitled to the result of their work on common raw goods.[10] This argument is based on the argument that a person owns their body and labour, and therefore should own whatever they mix their labour with:

> God gave the world to men in common; but since he gave it them for their benefit, and the greatest conveniences of life they were capable to draw from it, it cannot be supposed he meant it should always remain common and uncultivated. He gave it to the use of the industrious and rational, (and labour was to be his title to it;) not to the fancy or covetousness of the quarrelsome and contentious.[11]

This was then supported with the assumption that 'every person has a property in their own person', and therefore mixing own labour with the commons should make it their property ('he hath mixed his Labour with, and joined to it something that is his own, and thereby makes it his Property').[12]

Labour theory has two additional conditions, 'no spoilage' and 'enough and as good'. The first requires not taking more than one can use:

> As much as any one can make use of to any advantage of life before it spoils, so much he may by his labour fix a property in. Whatever is beyond this is more than his share, and belongs to others.[13]

Works in the public domain do not spoil but might become less appealing over time. On the other hand, there are also rare examples of public domain works regaining value at a later stage.[14] In that sense, digitisation can save them from being 'spoiled', by providing more access to them and facilitating their revival. Spoilage goes beyond merely destroying one's own property through using it, it means neglecting or deliberately destroying things that could be otherwise used by others.[15] So letting a work disappear (through physical deterioration or obsolescence of format), also leads to 'spoilage' of resources.[16]

[10] J Locke, *Two Treatises of Government* (1690) Essay Two, Chapter V. Locke's main purpose was not only discussing private property, but to reconcile the idea of commons with individual appropriation, that fits within his theory of government. For more on the labour theory, see L Zemer, 'The Making of a New Copyright Lockean' (2006) 29(3) *The Harvard Journal of Law & Public Policy* 891; R Merges, *Justifying Intellectual Property* (Cambridge MA, Harvard University Press, 2011); EC Hettinger, 'Justifying Intellectual Property' (1989) 18 *Philosophy & Public Affairs* 31; CJ Craig, 'Locke, Labour, and Limiting the Author's Right: A Warning Against a Lockean Approach to Copyright Law' (2002) 28 *Queen's Law Journal* 1.

[11] Locke (n 10) para 34.

[12] ibid para 26.

[13] ibid para 31.

[14] Zemer (n 10) 924.

[15] Waldron explains how Locke means 'negligent or deliberate loss of use-value without use so that an object becomes useless for any human purpose': Waldron (n 2) 208.

[16] For a detailed summary of 'waste' under Lockean proviso in relation to unpublished works, see P Masiyakurima, *Copyright Protection of Unpublished Works in the Common Law World*, paperback edn (Oxford, Hart Publishing, 2021) 130–34.

As for the 'enough and as good' proviso, the right of property is conditional upon a person leaving in the commons 'enough and as good' for the other commoners. Ideas are non-rivalrous goods, but the human potential to use existing information to create a new idea is limited by the current state of cultural and scientific data available at that moment.[17] Likewise, the use of tangible cultural heritage objects is subject to physical conditions, meaning that only the person who is holding the item can use it – unless it is dematerialised. In that sense, digitising and providing access can instead leave 'enough and as good' for others. However, as long as the initial property right is justified and copyright protection exists, this unexpected fit between the proviso and the benefits of digitisation does not justify overriding or reducing this protection.

While adding own labour to commons provides a fair basis for deserving a reward, it also requires asking what the right type of reward is. A common criticism directed towards the labour theory is whether exclusive property rights are the right reward for the labour, especially when it can be argued for other rewards, which could have a less intrusive effect on the rest of the society.[18] More importantly, proponents of this theory also overlook that its application to intellectual property law is controversial, as Locke did not necessarily have intellectual property in mind when he focused on the connection between labour and ownership;[19] in his other writings, Locke criticises the excessive monopoly of Company of Stationers and the length of (especially sole) printing privileges, arguing that this limits the dissemination of knowledge.[20]

3.2.1. Heritage as 'Commons'

In this justification, there are two main components: labour and commons. The first component is labour. As Waldron asks, what distinguishes the appropriator from the rest of mankind? What are the crucial actions that justify the taking?[21] For copyright to emerge, this labour has to come from the author, and it has to be the right kind of labour. A question that emerges from the labour theory is whether labour should be defined as unpleasant labour or 'activity one would rather not

[17] P Drahos, *A Philosophy of Intellectual Property* (ANU eText, 2016) 51.

[18] L Bently, B Sherman, D Gangjee and P Johnson, *Intellectual Property Law*, 6th edn (Oxford, OUP, 2022) 41.

[19] Zemer suggests that most academics try to apply Locke's general theory to intellectual property law and ignore his explicit arguments in his other works 'The Essay concerning Human Understanding' and 'Liberty of the Press'. While the concepts of 'intellectual commons' and IP are not addressed in *Two Treatises*, Locke's other works display a 'collectivist and social approach' to copyright, instead of the exclusivity foreseen labour theory: Zemer (n 10) 892; SV Shiffrin, 'Lockean Arguments for Private Intellectual Property' in S Munzer (ed), *New Essays in the Legal and Political Theory of Property* (Cambridge, CUP, 2001) 139–40; Drahos (n 17) 47.

[20] Zemer (n 10) 901–905, also quoting 'Liberty of Press' by John Locke.

[21] Waldron (n 2) 172.

engage in',[22] because many authors enjoy the process of intellectual creation. But usually, most works would involve some kind of contribution that would justify the protection for the works. This labour needs to be added to the commons.[23]

This second component, commons, is vaguer. The material owned by the community as a whole includes 'the universe of facts, languages, cultural heritage, the set of ideas currently apprehended by at least one person but not owned by anyone, the set of ideas currently apprehended by at least one person, the set of all reachable ideas, the set of all possible ideas'.[24] Turning to the concept of community in Locke's writing, two ways to view the commons emerge: in 'negative community', commons belong to no one and parts of it can be appropriated, whereas in 'positive community', the commons belong to all.[25] In embracing positive community, Locke then has to justify how one can use the commons, without the permission of the community, and that can only be achieved through labour.[26]

When previously introduced approaches to the ownership of heritage (cultural internationalism and cultural nationalism) are considered together with the Lockean understanding of 'God hath given the world to men in common', there is a parallel with the assumptions on the 'common heritage of all humankind'. But this parallel is imperfect, as there are limits to the commons. In explaining the 'intellectual commons', Drahos limits it to 'part of the objective world of knowledge which is not subject to the following: property rights or some other conventional bar (contract, for instance); technological bars (for example, encryption) or a physical bar (hidden manuscripts), however he recognises that intellectual property rights do not automatically means things become inaccessible, just subject to some restrictions (such as licence fee), at least while the property right is protected.[27] The previous chapter established that cultural heritage overlaps with the protected subject matter of copyright. But the works whose term has ended, together with ideas, facts and forms of intangible heritage, might be treated as 'commons'.

Even though the tangible and intangible distinction is not helpful for limiting the scope of cultural heritage, it provides a way to categorise the 'commons': tangible objects allow some certainty about who holds them, but intangible heritage is much more open to being assumed as common resources by the public. While access to tangible heritage is rivalrous, intangible heritage is something that can be potentially used without being depleted. This is reminiscent of a familiar concept

[22] Hughes argues that the main question is not whether the activity is unpleasant but whether it is less desirable than other activities: J Hughes, 'Philosophy of Intellectual Property' (1988) 77 *Georgetown Law Journal* 287, 304.

[23] The understanding of 'commons' is connected to the understanding of economists and has not developed the same way in civil and common law jurisdictions. See S Dusollier, 'The commons as a reverse intellectual property – from exclusivity to inclusivity' in H Howe and J Griffiths (eds), *Concepts of Property in Intellectual Property Law* (Cambridge, CUP, 2013).

[24] W Fisher, 'Theories of Intellectual Property' in Munzer (n 19) 186.

[25] Drahos (n 17) 83.

[26] ibid 53–54, quoting J Tully, *A Discourse on Property* (Cambridge, CUP, 1980) 4.

[27] Drahos (n 17) 65.

under intellectual property: idea/expression dichotomy. Every work usually reflects the author's experiences in society.[28] But ideas cannot be protected by copyright unless turned into expressions, and therefore ideas and knowledge shared across communities and generations could potentially be treated as 'commons' and open to exploitation. This does fit the labour theory view of adding one's own labour to common ideas.

If some cultural heritage is part of the commons, and adding labour to commons creates new works that eventually become part of cultural heritage, this creates a predictable loop of heritage building on itself, sandwiched between a continuously expanding time length (that is copyright duration) to be spent out of commons. However, with intangible heritage, there are both ethical concerns (such as secret/sacred knowledge and guidelines developed at national and international level, specifically for Indigenous heritage), and there are also attempts at protecting them as traditional knowledge and traditional cultural expressions at the WIPO level. This requires questioning when a work stops belonging to an individual and becomes something shared to be built on, and more importantly, whether copyright term is the right instrument for this determination.

For heritage entering into commons, it does not seem fair that the ending of a copyright term is a prerequisite for switching to a different from of protection under a different area of law. It seems rather arbitrary that extending the length of a property right indirectly 'postpones' heritage status. This is especially hard to comprehend, given that copyright term has been extended multiple times, so each time it takes longer for works to come back to being 'heritage'.

3.2.2. External Labour

Another angle is whether labour on (perceived) commons automatically justifies ownership by everyone. Returning to the distinction between negative and positive community, whether the commons belong to no one or everyone, it is also possible to limit the ownership to either every member of the community, or only to some members of the community. There are also different levels of willingness to share heritage between nations, for example, heritage-rich countries might hesitate to share their heritage, but similarly other nations with more developed technology and medicine might hesitate to share their intellectual property.[29] That means the 'common heritage' idea will face different levels of resistance from different stakeholders. It makes sense for each State to determine how much can be used, and who can use them, based on own interests and needs of communities.

Ownership of heritage, as argued, is already filled with tensions, but there are also circumstances where labour might indeed qualify someone external as the

[28] Hettinger suggests 'Invention, writing, and thought in general do not operate in a vacuum; intellectual activity is not creation ex nihilo': Hettinger (n 10) 37–38.

[29] Drahos (n 17) 67.

'author', but this might not be in the best interest of the source community. This occurs especially when intangible heritage is only documented by an outsider to the group.[30]

The first example is the Strehlow collection, in which an Australian researcher documented secret Aboriginal rituals and artefacts by promising secrecy. These documents were later shared with the researcher's university, and others, which led to legal proceedings between the Aboriginal community and the university.[31] In this example, Strehlow has gathered and documented the secret and sacred heritage by putting labour into the process. But this action was incompatible with the ownership of that heritage belonging to the community.

The second example is the treatment of sketches of Navajo dry paintings found in Peabody Museum: being aware that the originals are normally destroyed after the ritual, the museum was concerned that keeping them is a form of disrespect and sought the advice of Navajo consultants to decide if these should be preserved or allowed to decompose.[32] In this example, the first work (dry painting) is created in sand with the intention of being destroyed. So, the labour that went into their creation was not for individual ownership (as the object belonged to the entire community) and it did not guarantee protection. At the same time, when an external made copies of such works and later donated their field notes or recordings to a museum, they did not do that with the assumption that it will be destroyed. It is understandable that these institutions also have a responsibility towards these donors as well.

The third example are the recordings depicting Warumungu culture, in which researchers (who created the recordings) willingly chose to set up different levels of access when sharing them. This meant that if a ritual could be attended only by people with a certain standing in that community, its recording would also be only shown to people with the same standing.[33] In this example, the researchers have put in the labour and created the work but chose to limit the exploitation of their own works, to protect the Indigenous community.

These examples show us that the connection between labour and ownership is not always clear in the realm of cultural heritage practices. There are also circumstances where the externals can rely on their copyright and refuse to share their works with the source community, such as the examples of Maliseet elders and recordings of the Red Ochre ceremony.[34]

[30] For a discussion of copyright protection for externals documenting Indigenous oral traditions, see P Oruç, 'Documenting Indigenous Oral Traditions: Copyright for Control?' (2022) 29(3) *Intl J Cult Prop* 243–64.

[31] LV Prott and PJ O'Keefe, '"Cultural Heritage" or "Cultural Property"?' (1992) 1 *Intl J Cult Prop* 307, 314; J Morton, 'The Strehlow collection of sacred objects' www.clc.org.au/wp-content/uploads/2021/03/The-Strehlow-collection-of-sacred-objects.pdf.

[32] MF Brown, 'Can culture be copyrighted?' (1998) 39(2) *Current Anthropology* 193.

[33] K Christen, 'Gone Digital: Aboriginal Remix and the Cultural Commons' (2005) 12(3) *Intl J Cult Prop* 315, 316.

[34] These examples were provided in Section 1.3.1. See also AB Nicholas, 'Who Owns Indigenous Cultural and Intellectual Property?' (2017) policyoptions.irpp.org/magazines/june-2017/who-owns-

To sum up, labour theory holds strong. It does not leave much room for readjusting copyright protection in line with the previously established principles for keeping heritage safe and accessible. Cultural heritage overlaps but does not match the scope of 'commons' in Lockean theory, and whether externals can rely on 'labour' to claim ownership over heritage is also not always straightforward. Interpreting Locke's idea of commons this widely would require expanding the borders of 'common heritage' to the point where it would require arguing for removing copyright protection altogether, or at least introducing some way of reducing the author's rights over their own work.

3.3. Personhood Theory

The next theory requires questioning to what extent can the personal connection between the author and their work be challenged, and if there is any merit in arguing for severing this tie for public interest in digitisation. Personhood theory is rooted in the work being a manifestation of the author's personality, and that interest is best protected by a property right. The focus is very much on the author.

Kant explains how the work 'speaks' for the author in his essay 'On the wrongfulness of unauthorized publication of books':

> This right of the author is, however, not a right to the thing, namely to the copy (for the owner can burn it before the author's eyes), but an innate right in his own person, namely, to prevent another from having him speak to the public without his consent, which consent certainly cannot be presumed because he has already given it exclusively to someone else.[35]

Hegel explains how the author's will becomes a 'thing' that is protected towards the others:

> A person has as his substantive end the right of putting his will into any and every thing and thereby making it his, because it has no such end in itself and derives its destiny and soul from his will. This is the absolute right of appropriation which man has over all 'things … property is the first embodiment of freedom.'[36]

But there is also the question of whether private property is the right way to address this connection. Waldron suggests that Hegel did not believe in a distinction between the interests of the community, and its members, but the individual

indigenous-cultural-and-intellectual-property; J Anderson, 'Access and Control of Indigenous Knowledge in Libraries and Archives: Ownership and Future Use' (2005) American Library Association and The MacArthur Foundation.

[35] I Kant, 'On the wrongfulness of unauthorized publication of books' (1785) trans and ed by MJ Gregor in *Practical Philosophy* (Cambridge, CUP, 1996).

[36] GWF Hegel, *Philosophy of Right* (1820) trans by TM Knox (Oxford, Clarendon Press, 1952) §44-45.

had to grow into this by establishing a clear sense of themselves as an 'individual right-bearer'; so private property was necessary as 'a stage in one's individual and social development'.[37] Fisher has categorised how owning private property can contribute to human flourishing: peace of mind, privacy, autonomy, self-realisation as a social being, self-realisation as an individual, security and leisure, responsibility, identity, citizenship and self-expression.[38] The work is deemed to reflect the will of the individual, who is aiming to actualise themselves on the external sphere.[39]

The assumption is that property rights are necessary to protect the author's will in an output, and to ensure that the author is the only one speaking to the public, a fact which is not meddled with.[40] So how to ensure that the embodiment of will is safe when the author authorises others to exercise economic rights? The answer is moral rights, which are protected unevenly in different jurisdictions, generally more prominent in continental Europe.[41] Both the attribution and integrity of works need to be secured based on the author's connection with their works, and such rights exist across multiple jurisdictions.[42]

3.3.1. Interpretation of Personhood

In its application to IP rights, this theory relies on an abstract idea of 'personhood'.[43] Within the jurisdictions embracing the personality theory, copyright is used to protect the romantic notion of the artist, who is a 'uniquely sensitive soul', and to 'reinforce the status of the genius'.[44] But in practice, how does personhood show itself?

The first issue is whether the work, once released into the public, is still part of the author's personhood. With regard to whether the author can alienate the right to prevent reproduction of their work, Fisher suggests that Kant would reject that and argue that 'authors' interest in deciding how and when to speak is an inalienable part of his personality', but that Hegel would argue that 'expressions of mental aptitudes are external to the author and can be alienable'.[45] Although its role in the development of moral rights is important, the personality theory does not fully

[37] Waldron (n 2) 347.
[38] Fisher connects various philosophers and academics with each specific need, see Fisher (n 24).
[39] Hughes (n 22) 330–31.
[40] This personal connection argument does not equally apply to all forms of intellectual property, some forms, such as trade marks or patents, do not necessarily display the personality of their creator and/or receive any protection similar to moral rights.
[41] Moral rights were previously introduced in Section 2.5.5.
[42] See also Waldron (n 2); Hughes (n 22); Merges (n 10).
[43] Fisher claims that it requires either a better description of human nature or being tied to a more specific culture: Fisher (n 24) 192.
[44] A Barron, 'Copyright Law and the Claims of Art' (2002) 4 *IPQ* 368, 369.
[45] Fisher (n 24) 191.

justify the economic monopoly of the author once works are revealed to the public; it fails to explain why authors have rights that are wider than just preventing harmful changes.[46]

Kant argues for owning the object onto which one has projected their will, but this can perhaps be seen as a way to 'implicitly elevate the interests of creators to a very high level'.[47] This does not necessarily mean creating something from scratch or continuously using it, a person could still project their will on something without changing it or labouring on it.[48] Projecting one's will onto something is vague, which requires thinking of authorship as an 'activity or process' deserving of protection, that is separate from the object.[49] In that sense, personhood in the work is very abstract. Drahos questions whether this justifies authors' personalities being protected more than other property owners who might also claim they have 'poured' their personality into their property.[50]

Secondly, this theory disregards how authors are affected by their surroundings. Craig argues that, currently, copyright focuses too much on the author–work link, whereas it should be structured 'with deference to the public–work link'.[51] Hegel takes into consideration the author's interaction with the outside and how their mental processes are shaped by the outside; the first step for the author's self-realisation can be seen as appropriating the outside world and acting on it.[52] Would it also not require protecting the autonomy of communities that these works originate from? Copyright law is rarely able to recognise joint authorship, in cases where heritage is used by one of the members of the community, in a way that conflicts with the community's wishes.[53] Especially for intangible heritage, when multiple generations are involved, whose will and personhood is actually reflected in the work? But under IP, protection for communities is never as strong as the protection for the individual author.[54] Copyright does not allow the

[46] N Netanel, 'Copyright Alienability Restrictions and the Enhancement of Author Autonomy: A Normative Evaluation' (1993) *Rutgers Law Review* 24; C Shevlin, 'The Difficulties in Finding a Single Theory to Justify Copyright' (2015) 3 *North East Law Review* 49, 52.

[47] 'This way of thinking about property removes creators from jostling of interest and utilitarian trade-offs; it makes of them a class of special concern.' (Merges (n 10) 81).

[48] Hughes gives the example of a rock (a natural object) from a holiday location that carries significance for its owner, without the owner wanting to change it or labouring upon it: Hughes (n 22) 334.

[49] Barron (n 44) 399.

[50] Drahos (n 17) 96.

[51] Although focused more on Lockean theory, Craig argues that focusing too much on the role of the relationship between the author and the work results in neglecting the common good: Craig (n 10) 1, 6.

[52] Hughes (n 22) 333.

[53] For an example of community not agreeing with a member's circulation of heritage: *Yumbulul v Reserve Bank of Australia* [1991] FCA 331, 21 IPR 481. See also T Janke, 'Minding Culture: Case Studies on Intellectual Property and Traditional Cultural Expressions' (2003) WIPO Publication No. 781; MM Carpenter, 'Intellectual Property Law and Indigenous Peoples: Adapting Copyright Law to the Needs of a Global Community' (2004) 7 *Yale Human Rights and Development Law Journal* 51.

[54] J Christman, 'Autonomy, social selves and intellectual property claims' in A Lever (ed), *New Frontiers in the Philosophy of Intellectual Property* (Cambridge, CUP, 2012) 33–57.

same kind of recognition for the surrounding community (whose personhood might be there as well), collective ownership for traditional knowledge and traditional cultural expressions are seen as more suitable to address with *sui generis* protection.[55]

Third, what happens to personhood in works, in the case of (unaltered) preservation, are they not better protected? Even if we ignore the second point (the impact of surroundings on the creation of the work), is there any room for arguing personal interest can be overridden for leaving a fuller picture of history to the society? Can we argue that copying people's works gives them an immortality, which serves their interests in the longer term, as opposed to the limited term copyright protection? Fisher uses Radin's argument on property rights, allowing 'the ability to project a continuing life plan into the future', and argues that modifying or damaging the works disturbs this continuing life plan, also in line with moral rights.[56] But this can also be interpreted differently, by assuming the author might want to prevent physical damage to their work by default. Would it then make sense to argue that all authors inherently wish for accurate immortality, and therefore preserving their work actually contributes more to their self-realisation?

Doing so would justify digitising for the purpose of preserving the work (and therefore preserving the author's connection to their work). But this is a very big leap in the argument, stretching the understanding of what an author may or may not want. Even if this argument was successful for the purpose of preservation, the purpose of providing further access to digitised works conflicts too much with this theory.

3.3.2. Digitisation and Moral Rights

Especially in the online environment, the line between the author and the public is blurred. Anyone can disseminate the works they created with sufficient ease, but it is also much easier to lose control of the work once it is placed on the internet. In that sense, digital environment increases the risk towards the personhood.

As discussed in Section 2.5.5, there is a greater risk of damage after digitisation. For example, when unpublished works are digitised and placed online, this would affect the disclosure/divulgation right, which does not exist in every jurisdiction. Furthermore, attribution is much easier to alter in the online environment, so identifying the author could be challenging. This could also lead to false attribution,

[55] See also Section 1.1.4, fn 68 for discourses on intangible cultural heritage and intellectual property.

[56] Fisher (n 24); M Radin, *Reinterpreting Property* (Chicago, University of Chicago Press, 1993). For example, Masiyakurima disagrees with the assumption that works are created for the benefit of 'dozens of successive generations of heirs': Masiyakurima (n 16) 4.

where a digitised work seems as though it belongs to another author who would not want to be associated with it. It also makes it much harder for authors to detect their works, withdraw, or opt-out where necessary.

There is also an increased risk of suffering from any changes made to the work's integrity during digitisation. There could be problems when the work is altered for the digital format (such as low-quality images not depicting the work correctly, or a book being digitised with some pages missing). This then requires placing additional safeguards on the use of works, even when defences are present. For example, most copyright defences require attribution when possible. However, the lack of resources or copyright awareness, or the peculiarities of the online environment might still cause digitisers to inadvertently neglect moral rights.

Overall, personhood theory is also not very compatible with the principles of cultural property, especially on how heritage should be for everyone, and it should be kept safe and accessible. This theory provides a very strong basis for protecting the author and cannot be overridden by assuming that the individual should want the same things as their community. Having to consider the needs of the individual will also pose an obstacle to the digitisation of special cases (orphans, unpublished and out of commerce are discussed in the next chapter), because even when there is no one to come forward, the personal connection is still there, there is still someone 'speaking' through their works. Furthermore, the moral rights of the author are more likely to be negatively affected by online uses, making this theory also not very compatible with digitisation. So far, the theories that have the author's self and their contribution (labour and personhood) at their centre cannot be reinterpreted differently for the sake of heritage and it is time to turn to theories that equally consider the interests of the rest of the public.

3.4. Utilitarian Theory

The purpose of the utilitarian theory is to achieve the greatest good for the greatest number and to achieve the greatest social welfare.[57] When applied to intellectual property, there is a focus on how such time-limited rights can serve as an incentive, so that the society will benefit in the long run.[58] This theory has historically

[57] For more on the utilitarian theory, see J Bentham, *Introduction to the Principles of Morals and Legislation* (1789); JS Mill, *Principles of Political Economy* (1848); PS Menell, 'Intellectual Property: General Theories' in B Bouckaert and G de Geest (eds), *Encyclopedia of Law & Economics: Volume II* (Cheltenham, Edward Elgar, 2000); WM Landes and RA Posner, 'An Economic Analysis of Copyright Law' (1989) 18 *The Journal of Legal Studies* 325; EE Johnson, 'Intellectual Property and the Incentive Fallacy' (2012) 39 *Florida State University Law Review* 623.

[58] 'Utilitarian theory of exclusive rights allows a taking from or enclosure of the cultural commons in the near term to create richer commons in the long term' (L Hyde, *Common as Air: Revolution, Art and Ownership* (New York, Farrar, Straus and Giroux, 2010) 49).

developed in parallel to the evolution of the modern State. By granting monopolies and incentivising creation, States became more powerful.[59]

> The principle stating that the greatest happiness of all those whose interests are involved is the right and proper – and the only right and proper and universally desirable – end of human action; of human action in every situation, and in particular in the situation of functionaries exercising the powers of Government[60]

In relation to protection of inventions, Bentham argues:

> With respect to a great number of inventions in the arts, an exclusive privilege is absolutely necessary, in order that what is sown may be reaped. In new inventions, protection against imitators is not less necessary than in established manufactures protection against thieves. He who has no hope that he shall reap, will not take the trouble to sow.[61]

In order to achieve an effective system, more attention will be needed as regards finding a balance on the needs of different parties, as opposed to mainly focusing on one side. There are a few issues to address here: first, is a property right the right kind of incentive; and second, how much weight can the public interest carry?

3.4.1. IP as Incentive

Fisher identifies three general ways in which a strong intellectual property system can be beneficial for social welfare:[62] First, stronger rights increase the incentive to create.[63] It is logical for authors to want protection against free riders and to have a guarantee that they will have rights over their own works. This means that limiting the public's usage of works today leads to the creation of the works in the future. Second, it optimises patterns of productivity. Since creators can observe what consumers want, they can adjust what they produce accordingly. There is the risk that creators, who are expecting big rewards, might 'overinvest' in certain intellectual products.[64] Third, it is argued to eliminate or reduce duplicative activity. While it can increase the pace of development, it can also have the wasteful result of many people spending resources on being the first.[65] This again relies on

[59] On the historical development of intellectual property and its relation to state monopoly, see also C May and SK Sell, *Intellectual Property Rights – A Critical History* (Boulder, Lynne Rienner Publishers, 2006).

[60] Bentham (n 57) (First published in 1789, this definition added in 1823 in the 'A New Edition, corrected by the Author').

[61] ibid 71.

[62] Fisher (n 24) 178.

[63] W Patry, *How to Fix Copyright* (Oxford, OUP, 2011).

[64] GS Lunney, 'Reexamining Copyright's Incentives – Access Paradigm' (1996) 49 *Vanderbilt Law Review* 485; Fisher (n 24).

[65] Fisher (n 24) 182.

the assumption that people only create where there is an incentive to do so. But some of these arguments are perhaps more suited to registered rights like patents, where independent creation is not rewarded and only the one that registers first is able to monetise their time and investment.

Negative spaces, when applied in an IP context, cover fields and communities that are traditionally not addressed by IP law; their existence is evidence of how innovation can occur without the promise of IP protection.[66] In relation to incentive theory, Sprigman highlights the issue of how copyright is shaped more by producer interests (such as lobbying), as opposed to the public interest, especially in the absence of evidence of copyright acting as an incentive.[67]

Going back to the incentive argument, should this incentive be in the form of exclusive and lengthy protection? First of all, policies to incentivise are not necessarily uniform, for example incentives that increase one type of work, or in one jurisdiction may not work for the other.[68] Some parties do not create with the expectation of monetary gain.[69] There are various other reasons that urge authors to create, such as prestige, fame, conveying a particular message or furthering a certain ideology.[70] Copyright is only one of many ways to increase the stability of authors' lives.[71]

This is not to say that copyright protection should depend on the expectation of any gain, which can be hard to predict. But it at least requires asking whether the existing protection should be so lengthy?[72] Protecting one side for a long term means that there will be some deadweight losses along the way, especially in the case of orphans and out-of-commerce works. While copyright could have been an

[66] See also K Raustiala and CJ Sprigman, 'The Piracy Paradox: Innovation and Intellectual Property in Fashion Design' (2006) 92(8) *Virginia Law Review* 1687; K Raustiala and CJ Sprigman, 'When Are IP Rights Necessary? Evidence from Innovation in IP's Negative Space' in B Depoorter and P Menell (eds), *Research Handbook on the Economics of Intellectual Property Rights* Vol. 1 (Cheltenham, Edward Elgar, 2019); K Darling and A Perzanowski (eds), *Creativity without Law: Challenging the Assumptions of Intellectual Property* (New York, New York University Press, 2017).

[67] CJ Sprigman, 'Copyright and Creative Incentives: What Do(n't) We Know?' in RC Dreyfuss and ESK Ng (eds), *Framing Intellectual Property in the 21st Century: Integrating Incentives, Trade, Development, Culture, and Human Rights* (Cambridge, CUP, 2018) 33–34.

[68] Patry (n 63) 77.

[69] DL Zimmerman, 'Copyrights as Incentives: Did We Just Imagine That?' (2011) 12 *Theoretical Inquiries in Law*; Shevlin (n 46) 51.

[70] Johnson refers to these reasons as 'inherent motivation': Johnson (n 57) 624.

[71] For example, Zimmerman suggests patronage, including stipends and grants, as a way to increase creation: Zimmerman (n 69) 21.

[72] Lunney quotes 'It is good that authors should be remunerated; and the least exceptionable way of remunerating them is by a monopoly. Yet monopoly is evil. For the sake of the good we must submit to the evil; but the evil ought not last a day longer than is necessary for the purpose of securing the good' from *The Speeches of Macaulay* 235, 240–41 (1900), as cited in Lunney (n 64). See also R Pollock, 'Forever Minus a Day? Calculating Optimal Copyright Term' (2009) 6(1) *Review of Economic Research on Copyright Issues* 35; PJ Heald, 'How Copyright Keeps Works Disappeared' (2014) 11(4) *Journal of Empirical Legal Studies* 829; J Flynn, R Giblin and F Petitjean, 'What Happens When Books Enter the Public Domain? Testing Copyright's Underuse Hypothesis Across Australia, New Zealand, the United States and Canada' (2019) 42(4) *University of New South Wales Law Journal* 1215.

incentive in their creation, most works have a short span where they are profitable; afterwards copyright uncertainty just disadvantages the public.

In fact, for the safety of cultural heritage, the incentive argument matters more when such works are being revived. Since digitisation is costly, digitising and reviving public domain works requires an incentive. Providing a shorter term of protection to digitised works can be an option, as suggested by Mendis, for incentivising the digitisation of rare documents.[73] So, the incentive argument applies twice: it both justifies the copyright protection of the first work, and therefore make its digitisation harder until the copyright term ends, but then the promise of a new copyright protection in digital copies acts as an incentive for their revival. However, this incentive also causes some institutions to overclaim their contribution, sometimes even in the form of 'copyfraud'.[74] But if the options are between completely losing these works, or giving the incentive to the 'wrong' party, the latter at least allows the revival of works that can benefit the public in the long run.

3.4.2. Who is the 'Public'?

When we say the needs of the public are placed against the authors, who exactly is the 'public', whose interests are all merged together?

> The interest of the community is one of the most general expressions that can occur in the phraseology of morals: no wonder that the meaning of it is often lost. When it has a meaning, it is this. The community is a fictitious body, composed of the individual persons who are considered as constituting as it were its members. The interest of the community then is, what? – the sum of the interests of the several members who compose it[75]

In practice, the public does not have a single goal when dealing with protected subject matter. Some members of the public have more commercial goals in mind, understandably wanting to improve their livelihood. Some need access for research, others need them for education. These various goals require careful adjustment of copyright defences, limiting the access and use. The author is also part of the public, both needing protection and needing access to older works to build on them.[76]

[73] S Mendis, *A Copyright Gambit: On the Need for Exclusive Rights in Digitised Versions of Public Domain Textual Materials in Europe* (Berlin, Springer, 2019).

[74] As discussed in Section 2.7.

[75] Bentham (n 57).

[76] It is impossible to calculate the true effect of old works in the creation of new ones. In an article discussing factors for calculating the optimal copyright duration, Pollock also suggests that the level of reliance on former works cannot be a factor: Pollock (n 62) 36.

There is also public interest in keeping heritage safe and accessible. As established in chapter one, heritage is at constant risk of disappearing, through deliberate destruction, accidental loss, natural deterioration or technological obsolescence. When these negative outcomes cannot be prevented by moving heritage elsewhere, the best possible solution is to digitise the work. But few would argue that preservation alone is enough if access is not also provided. The interest in accessing heritage also concerns the future public, such as future authors and researchers who need works created today, and even previously unconsidered new users of heritage, such as artificial intelligence.

This again brings us back to the difference in approaches between copyright law and cultural property law. Protection under cultural property law means different measures depending on the instrument, such as physical protection or inventory making, these measures do not override or replace each other. But protection under copyright law involves conflicting interests on how the subject matter will be treated, protecting one side means preventing the others, requiring a balance. This balance is skewed often, due to some stakeholders being louder than the others. So, the public interest under copyright law is even less stable than the public interest under cultural property law and will require a significant look into the stakeholders in chapter five.

Compared to the other theories discussed above, utilitarian theory can be more lenient towards giving more weight to the public interest. It does not mean that this public interest can automatically override copyright, but it will require recalibrating the balance for the scope of protection versus defences. But perhaps there needs to be an additional prioritisation for the policymakers to push said balance towards a different direction, so it is time to turn to the final justification theory.

3.5. Culture (Social Planning) Theory

This theory supports the idea that property rights should help with reaching 'a just and attractive culture'.[77] Similar to labour theory, it aims to ensure a fair and just allocation of rights, but also seeks to give everyone a fair chance for self-expression. This viewpoint takes fundamental human needs into account, similar to personality theory, but these needs are considered differently, giving less weight to the author–work connection. It argues for a balance for a more attractive society, as does the utilitarian theory, but argues that the law should guide people's behaviour instead of leaving decisions to them.[78]

[77] Fisher (n 24) 172.

[78] This comparison relies on Fisher's Lecture 10.1, available on ipxcourses.org/lectures. Fisher, who focused on identifying this theory among debates on philosophy, political theory, psychology, economics and law, argues this is the most 'congenial and powerful' of other justifications.

Culture theory easily fits the purposes of cultural heritage. The first layer is the wider public interest in preserving works, although Fisher points out that for rare works, their integrity is very important (such as destroying the single copy of a painting), whereas changes in non-rare works that can aid further dissemination might be welcomed (such as colourising old films). The second layer is the access to these works; Fisher suggests that libraries should be unburdened by copyright, to ensure their functioning and contribution to the culture.[79] Netanel also acknowledges that reviving old works (such as re-printing, maintaining and especially digitising) requires a big investment that should be encouraged.[80]

3.5.1. Distributive Justice

Distributive justice is important for this theory: Rawls suggests that when assigning rights and duties and determining the distribution of benefits, principles of social justice should be taken into consideration.[81] Recognising that not everyone has the same starting position in life, the aim should be to even these inequalities. So, it is not about distributing everything evenly to stakeholders in different starting positions, but to ensure that everyone is brought to a fair situation, which can only be achieved if parties decide this just distribution under the 'veil of ignorance' (without knowing how the alternatives will affect their own cases).[82] The principles of justice are summarised in two formulations by Rawls:

> First: each person is to have an equal right to the most extensive scheme of equal basic liberties compatible with a similar scheme of liberties for others.
>
> Second: social and economic inequalities are to be arranged so that they are both (a) reasonably expected to be to everyone's advantage, and (b) attached to positions and offices open to all.[83]

If the aim is increasing access to knowledge, this would then threaten the previously mentioned artificial scarcity created by intellectual property. Once created, knowledge is not scarce and can be provided to all members of society equally. At the same time, copyright is not only about the society 'knowing', it prevents further copying of the protected works. However, this can only be achieved with State interference, giving them power to restrict individual freedoms.[84]

This causes a new set of concerns about whether the State knows what is best; conflicts between majority and minorities about their own culture; and whether

[79] Lecture 10.2 on ipxcourses.org/lectures.
[80] NW Netanel, *Copyright's Paradox* (Oxford, OUP, 2008).
[81] J Rawls, *A Theory of Justice* (1971) rev. edn (Cambridge MA, Belknap Press, 1999).
[82] ibid 118.
[83] ibid 53.
[84] For an alternative (entitlement theory), see R Nozick, *Anarchy, State and Utopia* (Oxford, Blackwell, 1974) 151. See also S Ang, *The Moral Dimensions of Intellectual Property Rights* (Cheltenham, Edward Elgar, 2013) 64–76.

cultural heritage should strictly be a State concern. Since this theory is aimed at 'what is good for the public', it can be criticised for relying on the 'controversial theories of good', meaning that the authority figure decides what is good for the people and decreases rights accordingly.[85] It is reminiscent of the decisions made for the selection of cultural heritage; it has the risk of being biased and is affected by existing priorities and opinions of the parties that govern heritage institutions.

As Drahos points out, distributive justice does not mean eliminating private property, but continuous adjustments in the rights of property.[86] For copyright, this would be by readjusting the length and scope of protection.[87] Copyright defences, such as education and visual impairment, are both examples of how law can prioritise the needs of certain stakeholders for a just and attractive culture. This would also involve readjusting IP based on the imbalances between certain groups, and between nations, and placing an obligation to share knowledge.[88]

An interesting example of seeking justice is Access to Knowledge (A2K).[89] Coined in 2004, this movement is focused on increasing access to knowledge and reducing the impact of limits such as intellectual property. It followed the example of the access to medicine movement, which was mainly successful, and built on existing discussions around Open-Source Software, Creative Commons and Free Culture movements.[90] The goals of this movement also involve access to cultural heritage, the A2K Coalition has even drafted a preservation treaty permitting all activities for access and reproduction for heritage institutions.[91]

3.5.2. Participation or Appropriation

The relationship between access to culture and being able to participate more as citizens is at the core of this theory. It seeks to achieve what is good for the

[85] Fisher (n 24) 192.

[86] 'gradually and continually to correct the distribution of wealth and to prevent concentrations of power': Rawls (n 81) 245; Drahos (n 17) 209.

[87] See also S Yanisky-Ravid, 'The Hidden Though Flourishing Justification of Intellectual Property Laws: Distributive Justice, National Versus International Approaches' (2017) 21 *Lewis & Clark Law Review* 1.

[88] M Chon, 'Intellectual Property "from Below": Copyright and Capability for Education' (2007) 40 *UC Davis Law Review* 803, 807; Drahos (n 17) 213.

[89] G Krikorian and A Kapczynski (eds), *Access to Knowledge in the Age of Intellectual Property* (New York, Zone Press, 2010); A Kapczynski, 'The Access to Knowledge Mobilization and the New Politics of Intellectual Property' (2008) 117 *Yale Law Journal* 804; S Bannerman, *International Copyright and Access to Knowledge* (Cambridge, CUP, 2016); T Vathitphund, 'Access to knowledge difficulties in developing countries: A balanced access to copyrighted works in the digital environment' (2010) 24(1) *International Review of Law, Computers & Technology* 7. See also Access to Knowledge Coalition www.a2k-coalition.org/about/.

[90] A Abdel-Latif, 'The Emergence of the A2K Movement: Reminiscences and Reflections of a Developing-Country Delegate' in Krikorian and Kapczynski (n 89).

[91] 'Proposed Instrument on Preservation of Cultural Heritage': www.a2k-coalition.org/issue/3-cultural-heritage/.

community, but this also raises the question of participation. There are some examples of participation being taken into consideration when deciding on copyright policy, such sentiments are repeated in copyright instruments.[92] If the aim is to allow members of a community to feel included and to participate freely in the discussion, the internet can be the right place to do this. This helps with the argument about providing access to cultural heritage in the online environment. But at the same time, considering the previous examples of secret and sacred heritage, this 'participation' cannot amount to digitising the perceived public domain and claiming new copyright.[93]

By giving priority to encouraging diversity and participation of different stakeholders, this theory is more compatible with the principles of cultural property discussed above, although not perfectly. To achieve a more diverse and culturally rich society, the selection of 'what is good for the public' should be considered in a sensitive manner.[94] Even if copyright was no longer an obstacle and if it were possible to preserve and provide access to more heritage, this should be done carefully for equal representation. This means copyright needs to be constantly readjusted to find a delicate balance, but this must be done with the specific purpose of achieving an attractive culture. Overall, this theory could be the most lenient for readjusting the reach of copyright but would still need very careful consideration of what is right for society and how to best achieve this.

3.6. Conclusion

The first two principles from chapter one, when brought together, would mean that every work belongs to everyone, and that assumption would simply not work in a world in which copyright exists, given the overlaps in the protected subject matter. After evaluating the copyright theories, these principles are not compatible with the justifications of copyright law. It is especially incompatible with the labour and personality theories. The last principle – 'heritage should be kept safe and

[92] 'Recalling the principles of non-discrimination, equal opportunity, accessibility and full and effective participation and inclusion in society' (Marrakesh Treaty to Facilitate Access to Published Works for Persons Who Are Blind, Visually Impaired or Otherwise Print Disabled (Marrakesh, 27 June 2013) Preamble); 'The policy options are also assessed in relation to their general social impacts (cultural diversity, the possibility for end users to have access to digitised cultural heritage, and influence on the general societal impacts of digitisation) and as to the impacts on fundamental rights (property right, freedom of the arts and sciences, and right to education)' Impact Assessment on the modernisation of EU copyright rules accompanying the document Proposal for a Directive of the European Parliament and of the Council on copyright in the Digital Single Market SWD (2016) 301 final).

[93] 'Local or territorially based cultural objects may be appropriated for use in global markets. Those with a comparative advantage in the generation, appropriation and delivery of abstract objects become colonisers of a different kind. Sacred objects become commercial objects': Drahos (n 17) 227.

[94] Netanel argues that the scope of copyright should both 'assure the vitality of civil society's communicative sphere … and not be too broad to smother expressive diversity': N Netanel, 'Copyright and a Democratic Civil Society' (1996) 106 *Yale Law Journal* 283, 386.

accessible' – requires focusing more on public interest and can be partly compatible with the utilitarian and culture theories.

These justification theories have impacted the development of intellectual property, but they are not completely clear-cut and immediately recognisable. There are also other factors, such as the needs of stakeholders, the current political climate and lobbying efforts, that also shape copyright policy. It is argued that Anglo–American jurisprudence does not have a unitary theory, and that multiple theories must be taken into account when trying to justify copyright.[95] The personhood theory is more prominent in civil law countries. Moral rights, developed more in continental Europe, were argued to be 'quite foreign' to Anglo–Saxon jurisprudence.[96] The labour theory is more prominent in the UK.[97] For the US, both labour and utilitarian theories are argued to be influential.[98]

Labour theory's application to IP is very solid in explaining why the author needs protection, and how copyright is the right instrument to reward this labour. There are overlaps between cultural heritage and what is in the 'commons' to add labour to. But once copyright protection emerges, this theory does not leave much room for arguing for less copyright.

Personhood theory is also hard to reinterpret in the light of principles from cultural property law and digitisation. It is impossible to ignore the author's personhood in the work, even when the works are revealed outside the author. Trying to justify digitisation and access by claiming that all authors would want immortality to preservation is also not realistic. Especially in the jurisdictions where moral rights are strong, placing digitised works online causes concerns on the integrity and attribution in the work.

Utilitarian theory is logical for giving more weight to what the public needs, but whether the incentive argument is justified is a problem. Also, for cultural heritage and digitisation, there are many stakeholders seeking different things, so the greatest benefit for the greatest number of people might not necessarily be compatible with principle of cultural property (keeping heritage safe and accessible): this might require further intervention.

Finally, culture (social planning) theory can be useful because it tries to give everyone the equal chance to flourish, including access to knowledge. When this theory is used to justify copyright, it can support the argument of copyright being adjusted to allow for a better culture. But it causes concern about what aspects of cultural heritage should be treated as freely available for a just and attractive culture, and whether this requires more sensitivity.

When testing these theories against the principles of cultural property for the purpose of digitisation, it looks as though the most lenient theory, that allows

[95] Shevlin (n 46) 54.

[96] Hughes (n 22) 289. For moral rights, see also G Davies and K Garnett, *Moral Rights*, 3rd edn (London, Sweet & Maxwell, 2010).

[97] Shevlin (n 46) 49; Zemer (n 10) 894.

[98] Fisher (n 24) 175.

room for readjustment of copyright, is the culture theory, which is based on idealistic models of how to achieve distributive justice and reach a greater culture. This does not mean other theories or jurisdictions that embrace these theories give less importance to cultural heritage. On the contrary, it could be argued that the laws and the hesitance of European jurisdictions on allowing the private sector to deal with heritage show great concern and respect for culture.[99] Despite the attempts from WIPO to find a harmonised solution, a complete international harmonisation seems unlikely in this area, and their theoretical differences is just one of the reasons for this.

The author has safeguards regarding the duration, formalities, and the scope and interpretation of defences. In some countries, the author also has the opportunity to receive remuneration and/or opt-out their work from certain systems. This leaves the heritage institutions with very few options on how to digitise works protected by copyright and works with uncertain copyright status. It is too early to comment on the overall clash, and evaluating the clash in laws and clash in practice is still necessary. However, so far, this chapter has showed that neither cultural property protection nor digitisation motivation can override the justification for copyright and can entirely take away the author's chance for commodification of their works. And this is causing the first and underlying clash between copyright and digitising heritage. But two themes emerge here, (i) there are at least two sides to these debates (author versus public) and (ii) it is unlikely to abolish private property, so it will be more likely to remain a matter that needs constant readjustment.

[99] See Section 5.2.2 for European reactions to digitisation projects and cases.

4

Clash of Laws: A Comparative Analysis of the Rights and Defences Related to Digitisation in the Chosen Jurisdictions

The first clash between copyright and the digitisation of cultural heritage was in the theory, where the principles of cultural heritage were insufficient in overriding the justification for copyright protection. The theoretical basis for copyright's existence is firmly in place, but there is some room for readjustment to find a balance between the author and the public. It is time to turn to a more visible clash, which is in the laws of the chosen jurisdictions, namely the rights, defences and other solutions. These are further complicated by regional and national legal differences, causing an uncertain environment for heritage institutions digitising their collections.

Understandably these laws did not change in a vacuum. Instead, the law is intertwined with what happens in practice, and the next chapter will investigate large-scale digitisation projects and stakeholder reactions. For now, it is worth mentioning some relevant developments: Previously introduced in chapter two, the Google Books project and subsequent case has changed the awareness on copyright law and the interpretation of fair use. The approach in the US could have also gone a different way; if the proposed settlement had succeeded, Google's Books Rights Registry would give a private company an unprecedented amount of control over digitised heritage. Similarly, the same issue would have been handled very differently in jurisdictions without fair use.

This project also served as a catalyst for digitisation at the European level, corresponding with existing digitisation efforts.[1] The i2010 Initiative was significant for the creation of digital libraries to make European heritage accessible to everyone and the forming of Europeana.[2] This was also followed by other legal

[1] For a summary of public-private partnerships in Europe at the time, see P Ayris, 'The Status of Digitisation in Europe: Extensive Summary of the Second LIBER-EBLIDA Workshop on the Digitisation of Library Materials in Europe' (2010) 19 (3/4) *LIBER Quarterly* 193, 198. See also S Chambers and W Schallier, 'Bringing Research Libraries into Europeana: Establishing a Library-Domain Aggregator' (2010) 20 *LIBER Quarterly* 105.

[2] 'i2010: Digital libraries' eur-lex.europa.eu/EN/legal-content/summary/i2010-digital-libraries.html.

developments for orphan works and the expansion of library exceptions.[3] The Directive on Copyright in Digital Single Market of 2019 has also led to significant changes for preservation defence, out-of-commerce works, text and data mining, and collective licensing.[4] The UK has not implemented this Directive due to Brexit and now has to rely on its own copyright defences (most recently amended in 2014 and still mostly harmonised with the EU) and its own orphan works regime. This does not mean that the UK is unable to develop a more flexible approach to the digitisation in the future, but currently it is lagging behind. At the international level, the World Intellectual Property Organization (WIPO) is also working on addressing limitations and exceptions for libraries, archives and museums. Unable to reach an agreement on a more significant compromise between States (such as a new instrument), WIPO has opted for the creation of toolkits – a preservation toolkit was released in 2023, and a toolkit on access is expected by the end of 2025.[5]

These developments have not benefitted all sides equally, and a full understanding of the copyright problem requires an investigation into the clash in practice in the next chapter. Without being aware of practice, some of these legal changes might seem more positive or negative than they actually are. But without being familiar with the laws, the projects and stakeholder reactions might look unnecessary or insufficient.

4.1. (Re)Introducing Options and Concerns

When digitising, institutions will have a few options: (i) only digitising public domain, (ii) risking copyright infringement, (iii) relying on defences, and (iv) seeking authorisation. One or more of these options can be used, depending on the type of works and the purpose of digitisation.[6]

Only focusing on public domain is helpful for avoiding any legal risks, but determining the status of works (especially orphans) might be challenging when

[3] Commission Recommendation of 24 August 2006 on the digitisation and online accessibility of cultural material and digital preservation [2006] OJ L236/28.

[4] Directive (EU) 2019/790 of the European Parliament and of the Council of 17 April 2019 on copyright and related rights in the Digital Single Market and amending Directives 96/9/EC and 2001/29/EC OJ L130/92 ('CDSM Directive' or 'CDSM').

[5] RE Pantalony, KD Crews and D Sutton, 'WIPO Toolkit on Preservation for Cultural Heritage Institutions' SCCR/43/4 (2024) ('Preservation Toolkit'); 'Draft implementation plan for the work program on limitations and exceptions and preliminary comments received by March 29, 2024' WIPO SCCR/45/6 (2024).

[6] These options were first introduced in Section 2.6. For digitising public domain, see Sections 2.7 and 4.3.2. For licensing, see Section 4.3.3. For defences, see Sections 4.2.2 and 4.3.4. The risk management option will not be addressed separately, see generally: R Deazley and V Stobo, 'Archives and Copyright: Risk and Reform' (2013) CREATe Working Paper No.3. Hudson identifies risk management factors, especially when the use is non-commercial, and the perceived risk is low: E Hudson, *Drafting Copyright Exceptions: From the Law in the Books to the Law in Action* (Cambridge, CUP, 2020) 89.

the resources are limited. Since copyright term is long, deteriorating works with uncertain status could be ignored or delayed. It would also leave an incomplete picture to later generations who will use digitised copies. However, the upside is that digitised public domain material can then be used freely, sometimes even to cover the costs of digitisation. However, there are non-IP obstacles to using public domain works, discussed below.

The second and opposite option is taking the risk of copyright infringement but proceeding with caution. Taking a calculated risk is not at all uncommon in the heritage sector. Especially in circumstances where no author is likely to come forward, it might make sense to proceed with digitisation and take down the copy later if needed. At the same time, a litigious rightholder and a lengthy lawsuit can quicky deplete the resources of the institution and damage their reputation. The risk can be partially addressed by limiting the liability of such institutions, with carefully set conditions. Furthermore, it is not straightforward to detect or remove the works once they are released into the public, such as the protected material used in machine learning algorithms.

The third option that heritage institutions can embrace is seeking the rightholder's authorisation where possible, usually through individual licences or going through the collective management organisations. This approach provides certainty and can be the best option when only a few works will be used for commercial purposes. Seeking licences can be expensive and time consuming for mass digitisation. The burden of procedural complexity can be partly reduced with collective management. Where there is no copyright holder to be found, licences can still be sought in jurisdictions with extended collective licensing (systems where collective management organisations reaching a certain representation threshold can also represent non-members).

The fourth option for these institutions is to rely on copyright defences (in the form of a copyright exception and limitation,[7] or fair use depending on the jurisdiction). The chances of success heavily depend on the purpose of digitisation: whether the works are reproduced to set aside for preservation, or reproduced and shared with the public for access, will then determine which rules apply and how much of it can be digitised. However, by their nature, copyright defences are not guaranteed until tested in court and do not provide certainty. Their scope is also inconsistent across jurisdictions, for example, most exceptions listed under the Information Society Directive are optional,[8] causing different implementations in Member States (MS) that will be addressed below. Similarly, US fair use is also vague enough to be interpreted differently in courts.

[7] For the difference between exceptions and limitations, see J Pila and P Torremans, *European Intellectual Property Law*, 2nd edn (Oxford, OUP, 2019) 322–23.

[8] Directive (EC) 2001/29 of the European Parliament and of the Council of 22 May 2001 on the harmonisation of certain aspects of copyright and related rights in the information society OJ L 167/10 ('InfoSoc Directive') art 5.

One might ask why States are not embracing much wider defences, and why these defences are not interpreted in the widest way possible by the courts. In line with the need to balance the interests of different stakeholders, there are safeguards on the circumstances where the exclusive right of reproduction can be limited by national rules. The rule that determines the scope of exceptions to reproduction right is called the 'three-step test'. The elements of this test can be found in the Berne Convention, Article 9(2); under the WIPO Copyright Treaty (WCT) Article 10; and under the Information Society Directive, Article 5(5).[9] It requires exceptions to: (i) apply only to special cases, (ii) not interfere with the normal exploitation of the work, (iii) not interfere with the legitimate interests of the rightholders.[10]

This provision makes it unlikely for Member States to introduce exceptions that can overhaul the exclusive right of the author, and affects how the exceptions will be interpreted by the courts. But there are also concerns about this test; the lack of legal certainty in its application arguably makes this test an unsuitable legal tool, even with the suggestion of embracing a flexible manner in its interpretation.[11] Scholars point out that many purposes would fall outside 'normal' exploitation in the second step,[12] and CJEU's application of the test has become increasingly more rigid over time.[13] The three-step test will be revisited in Section 6.3, where it will be applied to recommendations for addressing the copyright clash.

The purpose of digitisation is therefore very important to determine the applicability of defences to specific purposes in the light of the three-step test. A way to analyse the feasibility of digitisation is to divide the discussion between only preserving works (preservation purpose), and subsequently sharing them with the public (access purpose), as introduced in Section 2.6 earlier. At the same time, there are other works that do not neatly fit into these headings, the same way as

[9] Berne Convention for the Protection of Literary and Artistic Works (Paris, 9 September 1886, as amended on 28 September 1979) ('Berne Convention'); WIPO Copyright Treaty (Geneva, 20 December 1996) ('WCT'); Directive (EC) 2001/29 of the European Parliament and of the Council of 22 May 2001 on the harmonisation of certain aspects of copyright and related rights in the information society OJ L 167/10 ('InfoSoc Directive').

[10] See also InfoSoc Directive, recital 22: 'The objective of proper support for the dissemination of culture must not be achieved by sacrificing strict protection of rights or by tolerating illegal forms of distribution of counterfeited or pirated works.'

[11] J Griffiths, 'The "Three-Step Test" in European Copyright Law: Problems and Solutions' (2009) 4 *IPQ* 428; D Jongsma, 'The Nature and Content of the Three-Step Test in EU Copyright Law: A Reappraisal' in E Rosati (ed), *The Routledge Handbook of EU Copyright Law* (London, Routledge, 2021) 338–53; M Senftleben, *Copyright, Limitations and the Three-Step Test: An Analysis of the Three-Step Test in International and EC Copyright Law* (The Hague, Kluwer Law International, 2004); M Senftleben, 'The International Three-Step Test: A Model Provision for EC Fair Use Legislation' (2010) 1 *JIPITEC* 67; RM Hilty and V Moscon, 'An International Instrument on Permitted Uses in Copyright Law' in S Balganesh, N Wee Loon and H Sun (eds), *The Cambridge Handbook of Copyright Limitations and Exceptions*, paperback edn (Cambridge, CUP, 2023) 59–73.

[12] Griffiths (n 11) 441.

[13] Jongsma (n 11); Hilty and Moscon (n 11).

in-copyright works. Therefore, the rest of this chapter will be divided into three main headings: preservation, access, and the specific rules for orphans, out-of-commerce, and unpublished works, collectively referred as 'special cases'. An ideal solution should not separate preservation from access – both are necessary for cultural heritage. Similarly, the scope of heritage includes works that are in-copyright, but also public domain and special cases. These headings are only relied on for the sake of clearer analysis.

4.2. Preservation

The first purpose to be discussed is preservation, which is less likely to conflict with the authors' interests and receive negative reactions from the relevant stakeholders. It is also a logical place to start addressing digitisation, both as an easier purpose and the very first step in creating digitised copies in the first place. But it is also questionable whether it is logical or economically feasible to embark on a costly digitisation project, without ever intending to make it available to the public. This Section will focus on the rights and defences relevant for the preservation purpose.

4.2.1. Affected Rights

4.2.1.1. Reproduction

Reproduction is an essential part of digitisation. Depending on the type of the work, reproduction would cover scanning (2D and 3D) or transforming old analogue formats (wax cylinders, cassette, gramophone record – anything that relies on the bumps on the material) into digital formats.[14]

Most of the original signatories to the Berne Convention already had provisions against straightforward copying in their national laws but there was no similarity among them, especially for less common forms of copying made available by technology.[15] This fragmented approach was addressed with the introduction of the general reproduction right in the 1967 revision.[16] At the EU level, the scope of reproduction right in InfoSoc Directive Article 2 is in line with the Berne Convention. For example, the German Copyright Act defines it as a 'right to make copies by whatever method and in whatever quantity' (Article 16(1)), while the French Intellectual Property Code refers to another right: 'reproduction

[14] Reproduction right was first introduced in Section 2.5.4.

[15] S Depreeuw, *The Variable Scope of the Exclusive Economic Rights in Copyright* (Alphen aan den Rijn, Wolters Kluwer, 2014) 5–9.

[16] Berne Convention, art 9.

shall consist in the physical fixation of a work by any process permitting it to be communicated to the public in an indirect way' (L.122-3).[17] In the United States, copies are defined as 'material objects, other than phonorecords, in which a work is fixed by any method now known or later developed, and from which the work can be perceived, reproduced or otherwise communicated, either directly or with the aid of a machine or device'.[18]

When assessing the risk of infringement, it is also important to see how long this copy exists for. An important question about digitisation of cultural heritage is whether a digital work is sufficiently 'fixed', as it transitions from one medium to another.[19] It can exist for a short time (a tiny fraction of a second) but it would still count if it was stored in the computer for a short time.[20] The duration of the copy will also affect whether the temporary copying defence in the InfoSoc Directive can apply:

> Temporary acts of reproduction referred to in Article 2, which are transient or incidental and an integral and essential part of a technological process and whose sole purpose is to enable: (a) a transmission in a network between third parties by an intermediary, or (b) a lawful use, of a work or other subject-matter to be made, and which have no independent economic significance, shall be exempted from the reproduction right provided for in Article.[21]

It was clarified by the CJEU that the temporary copying exception covers copies in the cache created while browsing.[22] In the *Infopaq* case, newspapers were scanned for commercial purposes. These scans went through optical character recognition (OCR), allowing a keyword search, to understand which page contained which phrase. The system then deleted the image file of the scan as well as the text file. It was decided that the InfoSoc conditions that would allow the reproduction to be exempt did not exist in this case. The newspaper articles were deleted after the search, but the printed-out copy could continue to exist. The Court found that this process should not be dependent on human decisions and should not take longer than needed. The copies were found to be 'not transient'.[23]

[17] P Goldstein and PB Hugenholtz, *International Copyright: Principles, Law and Practice*, 4th edn (New York, OUP, 2019) 287. German Act on Copyright and Related Rights (Copyright Act, as amended up to Act of June 23, 2021) ('German Copyright Act'); France, Intellectual Property Code, consolidated version as of February 17, 2024 ('French Intellectual Property Code').

[18] 17 USC §§101 et seq. (2006) Pub.L.No.94-553, 90 Stat ('US Copyright Act') s 101.

[19] AM Sullivan, 'Cultural Heritage & New Media: A Future for the Past' (2016) 15 *John Marshall Review of Intellectual Property Law* 604, 614.

[20] J Blomqvist, *Primer on International Copyright and Related Rights* (Cheltenham, Edward Elgar, 2014) 107.

[21] InfoSoc Directive, art 5(1).

[22] 'Article 5 of Directive 2001/29 must be interpreted as meaning that the on-screen copies and the cached copies made by an end-user in the course of viewing a website satisfy the conditions': Case C-360/13 *Public Relations Consultants Association Ltd v Newspaper Licensing Agency Ltd and Others* ECLI:EU:C:2014:1195 [2015] RPC 13, para 63.

[23] Case C-5/08 *Infopaq International A/S v Danske Dagblades Forening* ECLI:EU:C:2009:465, [2009] ECR I-6569, paras 66–74.

US law also states: 'any amount of time'.[24] The law on digital temporary copies is not completely clear in the US, but there are court decisions involving works existing for a few seconds.[25] Under UK law, making temporary copies of works (other than computer programs) is allowed if 'the copy is transient and incidental, it is an integral or essential part of the technological process'[26] and for the specific purposes mentioned, and the temporary copy should have no economic significance.[27] There are cases in which a face painting,[28] a layer of coloured sands[29] or a living garden[30] were not deemed 'fixed enough'.

For cultural heritage, the scans are stored permanently, and multiple copies are created each time someone accesses the work via a website or on-site dedicated terminals. So, the first copy is not transient or incidental, but the subsequent copies, which are created when someone views the digitised work, might be sufficiently transient. Either way, reproduction right will be infringed when protected works are digitised without authorisation.

It is worth mentioning a different type of reproduction that arguably does not lead to any access – at least by humans. When works are reproduced for the purpose of data mining and computational analysis, this could be permissible under the relevant defences. However, it is also possible that these copies will at least be accessed for purposes such as standardisation and augmentation, and for supervised machine learning (such as inserting labels).[31]

4.2.1.2. Adaptation

Depending on the jurisdiction, the adaptation right could also be infringed by preservation and conservation efforts, such as colour and size changes. At the international level, the adaptation right is under Article 12 of the Berne Convention,

[24] Creating a copy in random access memory (RAM) is within the scope of the exclusive rights of the rights holder, but the statute does not define the transitory duration: US Copyright Office, 'DMCA Section 104 Report' (2001) 109–10.

[25] In *Cartoon Network v CSC*, the Appeals Court held that the District Court had focused too much on the embodiment requirement and ignored the duration, and it held that 1.2 seconds was not long enough to be counted as 'fixed', and data was 'rapidly and automatically overwritten'. This decision also refers to the *MAI Systems* decision, in which a copy was created to view the system error log; but that data remained in computer's RAM until device was turned off: *Cartoon Network, LP v CSC Holdings, Inc*, 536 F 3d 121 (2d Cir 2008); *MAI Systems Corp. v Peak Computer Inc.*, 991 F.2d 511 (9th Cir. 1993). See also J Ginsburg and R Gorman, *Copyright Law* (New York, Thomson Reuters, 2012) 130; DMCA Section 104 Report (n 24)113.

[26] One example is *ITV Broadcasting v TVCatchup Ltd* [2011] EWHC 2977, [2012] ECDR 10, concerning the buffering of films as part of a technological process.

[27] Copyright, Designs and Patents Act 1988 ('CDPA'), s 28A.

[28] *Merchandising Corp of America Inc v Harpbond* [1983] FSR 32 CA (Civ Div).

[29] *Komesaroff v Mickle* [1988] RPC 204 (Sup Ct (Victoria)).

[30] *Kelley v Chicago Park District* 635 F 3d 290 (7th Cir 2011).

[31] See also Section 2.8.2 for use of heritage for text and data mining, and Section 4.3.4.3 for the EU text and data mining defence. This monograph's position is text and data mining defences serve more to 'access' purpose, as opposed to 'preservation' purpose.

giving the authors of literary and artistic works the exclusive rights to make or authorise 'adaptations, arrangements and other alterations of their works'. There is also 'right of translation' in Article 8 for literary and artistic works. In some countries, such as France and the Netherlands, adaptation is handled together with the reproduction right.[32]

This right exists as a separate right in the UK and US. The UK adaptation right is only infringed if certain acts are done to the work: for literary and dramatic works, adaptation covers translation, converting dramatic work into non-dramatic and vice versa, conveying the work by means of pictures; for computer programs and databases, this right covers arrangement, alteration or translation (including computer languages).[33] But in the US, all derivative works are covered by this right:

> A 'derivative work' is a work based upon one or more preexisting works, such as a translation, musical arrangement, dramatization, fictionalization, motion picture version, sound recording, art reproduction, abridgment, condensation, or any other form in which a work may be recast, transformed, or adapted. A work consisting of editorial revisions, annotations, elaborations, or other modifications which, as a whole, represent an original work of authorship, is a 'derivative work'.[34]

In comparison to the narrower UK approach, US law has an imprecise but much broader scope.[35] The argument about digitised literary work being a derivative work was also brought up in *Authors Guild v Google*.[36] It was argued by the Authors Guild that Google's activities were depriving the authors of the derivative rights in its 'search functions'. It was held that the scope of a derivative work is 'ordinarily those which re-present the protected aspects of the original work i.e. its expressive content' and it would be infringing if Google was providing digitised copies to the users. But Google's use was transformative, they were not making the copies publicly available.[37]

There is also the question of whether optical character recognition (OCR), which converts images of text into machine-readable text, would count as translation in these jurisdictions.[38] Under the Software Directive, reproduction,

[32] Goldstein and Hugenholtz (n 17) 299.

[33] CDPA, s 21.

[34] US Copyright Act, s 101 Definitions.

[35] Goold compares the UK and US and suggests that their differences are caused by historical differences within the development of the intellectual property: PR Goold, 'Why the U.K. Adaptation Right Is Superior to the U.S. Derivative Work Right' (2014) 92 *Nebraska Law Review* 843, 846–47 and 869.

[36] *Authors Guild v Google, Inc* 770 F Supp 2d 666 (SDNY 2011); *Authors Guild, Inc. v Google Inc.*, 954 F. Supp. 2d 282 (SDNY 2013); *Authors Guild, Inc. v Google, Inc.*, 804 F.3d 202 (2d Cir 2015).

[37] ibid; see also M Borghi and S Karapapa, 'Non-Display Uses of Copyright Works' (2011) 1 *QMJIP* 21, 25.

[38] Goldstein and Hugenholtz suggest Berne art 8 is broad enough to include 'not only translations from one spoken language to another, but also translations from one computer language to another': Goldstein and Hugenholtz (n 17) 299.

adaptation or transformation of the form of the code is considered to be infringement, unless it is required by technical circumstances.[39] Digitisation of works that are not computer programs is not likely to fit this description, since the transformation does not occur at the formation of the code.

Another concern for adaptations with more significant changes is the infringement of moral rights.[40] Given that accuracy is needed for accurate preservation of heritage, it is unlikely that it will lead to changes which amount to derogatory treatment or cause the removal of any attribution. At the same time, if moral rights are weak in a jurisdiction, relying on adaptation can be useful for authors wanting to stop undesirable changes to their works. For example, in the US derivative works that involve cutting up and rearranging of the original work were found to be an infringement of a plaintiff's adaptation right – therefore covering the lack of moral rights in that jurisdiction.[41]

Given the uncertain scope of adaptations and derivative works, it is possible that digital copies and their subsequent arrangements (such as restorations or creative copies) could infringe the adaptation right. However, this uncertainty is not a big problem: for works still protected by copyright, the author can already object to the reproduction of their work. The boundaries of such activities will become more difficult to distinguish with the increase of automated copies.[42]

4.2.2. Preservation – By Relying on Defences

Seeking authorisation for preservation, both when works first enter collections or when digitisation projects are being planned, is likely to succeed. But the rightholders might be less enthusiastic when works are only temporarily loaned to heritage institutions.[43]

Given that at least reproduction right will be infringed during digitisation, in the absence of authorisation, copyright defences will be needed for preservation. Copyright should adapt to new technologies, so preservation exceptions should ideally provide heritage institutions the same opportunities for digitisation as they would have with preserving analogue copies. In other words, as the custodians of heritage, heritage institutions deserve some protection against copyright

[39] Directive (EC) 2009/24 of the European Parliament and of the Council of 23 April 2009 on the Legal Protection of Computer Programs OJ L111/16, recital 15 ('Software Directive').

[40] Moral rights were addressed in Sections 2.5.5 and 3.3.2.

[41] *National Geographic Society v Classified Geographic, Inc.*, 27 F.Supp.655 (D.Mass.1939); Goldstein and Hugenholtz (n 17) 300.

[42] Ginsburg and Gorman question whether derivative work is infringed when there is original authorship and what happens to automated adaptations (such as 'computer generated translations, colorization of motion pictures'), and suggest that the author would still have the option of relying on reproduction right: Ginsburg and Gorman (n 25) 150).

[43] Noting also the examples provided in Sections 1.3.1 and 3.2.2, where externals to communities made decisions on copying. See also S Corbett, 'Immaterial Cultural Property and the Private Owner: How Copyright and Trade Law Might Address Access and Preservation' (2019) 9 *QMJIP* 262.

infringement during digitisation, but they were only provided these defences with some delays and shortcomings.

The re-adjustment of copyright against the purpose of preservation is achieved through EU and UK preservation exceptions, and sections 107 and 108 of the US Copyright Act.

4.2.2.1. EU Preservation Exceptions before the CDSM

There is an optional InfoSoc exception relating to the activities of libraries and archives in Article 5(2)(c), but it is quite wide in the sense that it only provides a list of institutions and requires the reproduction to not be for economic gain:

> Member States may provide for exceptions or limitations to the reproduction right provided for in Article 2 in the following cases: …
>
> (c) in respect of specific acts of reproduction made by publicly accessible libraries, educational establishments or museums, or by archives, which are not for direct or indirect economic or commercial advantage ….

If we look at the EU Member States' earlier preservation exceptions,[44] they were not fully harmonised prior to the CDSM Directive.[45] In some jurisdictions, general library exceptions included multiple purposes that could be interpreted to include preservation. For example, library exceptions of Austria, Croatia, Italy, Malta and Romania previously made no reference to preservation, but there was also nothing implying otherwise. The Cyprus exception emphasised 'for use in public interests', which could be interpreted to include preservation.[46]

The purpose of 'replacement' was not stated in the InfoSoc Directive, but in some Member States, preservation and replacement exceptions were handled together (Estonia, Finland, Latvia, Netherlands, Slovakia, and Ireland). Some Member States (Denmark, Sweden and Finland) also included 'completion' as a purpose, which applies to incomplete works that were published in parts and where the missing part cannot be acquired in the market. For most replacement exceptions, it must be 'impossible to acquire the works from the market or general trade', or even vaguer phrases such as Ireland's 'reasonably practicable to purchase a copy'.[47] The Czech replacement exception requires authorities 'to verify by reasonable effort that the work is not being offered for sale' and the Greece library use exception requires that the additional copy 'cannot be obtained in the market

[44] For a comprehensive list, see KD Crews 'Study on copyright limitations and exceptions for libraries and archives: updated and revised 2017 edition' WIPO SCCR/35/6 (2017) ('Crews Study') The exceptions listed in this 2017 Study were then compared against the most recent versions of national laws prior to the implementation of CDSM.

[45] Directive (EU) 2019/790 of the European Parliament and of the Council of 17 April 2019 on copyright and related rights in the Digital Single Market and amending Directives 96/9/EC and 2001/29/EC OJ L130/92 ('CDSM Directive' or 'CDSM').

[46] Crews Study (n 44).

[47] Crews Study (n 44).

promptly and on reasonable terms'.[48] The question of 'what is reasonable' needed clarification, for example, what should happen if the works are available on the market, but drastically above their original price? Or what if only partly damaged, second-hand copies are available? How about different editions of books?

Before CDSM, there was also a lack of harmonisation regarding the beneficiaries of preservation exception, which caused difficulties for cooperation across different institutions across the EU. Throughout the EU, the list of beneficiaries almost always included libraries and archives. However, museums were not allowed in a few of the jurisdictions, which could be due to the 'one-of-a-kind' nature of most of the objects they hold. Educational institutions were also not allowed to perform preservation activities in some jurisdictions (Belgium, Denmark, Estonia, Finland, France, Ireland, Latvia, Lithuania, Romania, Spain, Sweden and UK),[49] but the status of university libraries was not fully clear. Although educational institutions had more flexibility when it comes to research defences, they are not necessarily thought of as places where items are preserved.

In line with the three-step test, most of these exceptions were limited to 'non-profit institutions' or for 'non-commercial purposes' (both preservation-specific, and general library exceptions). However, the nature of 'non-commercial' is not always clear-cut, given that there are corporations providing free, non-commercial services for the public, and similarly heritage institutions might want to commercially use their preserved material at a later stage. Large scale digitisation projects achieved by public–private partnerships might also face some uncertainty about their commercial nature, depending on the agreements between parties about controlling the material.[50]

Allowed methods of copying were also not consistent in these exceptions. While some Member States allowed any kind of reproduction 'by any means', others did not specify the method of copying at all.[51] Even when the allowed method of copying was described as 'any kind of reproduction', it could be assumed that digitisation is included. Another issue was that the number of allowed preservation copies were not specified, except in Latvia and Greece.[52] Not limiting the number of copies makes sense, these copies remain within the institution, so it is safer to keep as many copies as needed while also not conflicting with the normal exploitation of works.

In terms of subject matter, some jurisdictions simply mentioned 'works', but it is not clear if these countries wanted to preserve everything, or left it vague without intending to do so. Other national exceptions excluded software

[48] ibid.
[49] ibid.
[50] B Savenije and A Beunen, 'Cultural Heritage and the Public Domain' (2012) 22 *LIBER Quarterly* 84, 90; N Poole, 'The Cost of Digitising Europe's Cultural Heritage' (2010) Report for Comité des Sages of European Commission 30.
[51] Crews Study (n 44).
[52] ibid.

from the scope of preservation.[53] Excluding software was common for library exceptions and private use exceptions, the Software Directive does not allow contracts preventing the making of a back-up copy for 'observation, study or testing of the functioning of a program'.[54] Some national exceptions excluded unpublished works, such as letters and diaries.[55] Most exceptions specifically mentioned 'works in collections/in permanent collections'.[56] 'Permanent collection' normally excludes items on loan or borrowed for temporary exhibitions, but it was not fully clear when the exceptions only mentioned, for example, 'works in collection'.

4.2.2.2. EU Preservation Exception in CDSM Article 6

The CDSM Directive provided a mandatory exception in Article 6 titled 'Preservation of Cultural Heritage':

> Member States shall provide for an exception to the rights provided for in Article 5(a) and Article 7(1) of Directive 96/9/EC, Article 2 of Directive 2001/29/EC, Article 4(1)(a) of Directive 2009/24/EC and Article 15(1) of this Directive, in order to allow cultural heritage institutions to make copies of any works or other subject matter that are permanently in their collections, in any format or medium, for purposes of preservation of such works or other subject matter and to the extent necessary for such preservation.

Its beneficiaries recognised in Recital 13 are wider and more clearly defined compared to the unharmonised approaches in the past:

> publicly accessible libraries and museums regardless of the type of works or other subject matter that they hold in their permanent collections, as well as archives, film or audio heritage institutions. They should also be understood to include, inter alia, national libraries and national archives, and, as far as their archives and publicly accessible libraries are concerned, educational establishments, research organisations and public sector broadcasting organisations.

Recitals 26–28 of CDSM also recognise further difficulties such as cross border cooperation, technological obsolescence and the need for third party support for technical expertise. Similar to before, preservation is still limited to permanent collections (Recital 27), but this is defined as 'copies of such works or other subject matter are owned or permanently held by that institution, for example as a result of a transfer of ownership or a licence agreement, legal deposit obligations or permanent custody arrangement'.[57] While restoration can be included under this provision, the limits of what can be digitally restored are uncertain.[58]

[53] ibid.
[54] Software Directive, art 5.
[55] Crews Study (n 44).
[56] ibid.
[57] CDSM, Recitals 27 and 29.
[58] E Rosati, *Copyright in Digital Single Market: Article-by-article Commentary to the Provisions of Directive 2019/790* (Oxford, OUP, 2021) 137. Digital restoration of previously digitised heritage

In terms of implementation, Member States with similar exceptions could implement the provision as it is and embrace the use of digital methods with a list of activities that fit 'preservation'.[59] But they also had the option to go above Article 6, such as preserving temporary works and allowing other internal uses.[60] In practice, some Member States embraced a list of beneficiaries that is broader than Article 6, such as educational institutions and public sector broadcasting organisations (Germany, Hungary, Italy, Austria).[61] Similarly with the scope, some Member States did not limit the exception to 'permanent' collection (France and Hungary), and in addition to allowing reproduction, some countries included lending (Austria) and distribution (France and Hungary) of the digitised copies.[62]

This Article is a positive development for digital preservation in the EU, and is an improvement compared to the previous state of national preservation laws of the Member States. Its mandatory nature helps the expansion and harmonisation of the scope of subject matter, beneficiaries and methods. Preservation provision did not meet the same resistance and organisational challenges for provisions for increasing access in CDSM; WIPO's approach to addressing preservation separately is reminiscent of this, preservation emerges as the solvable part of the problem.[63]

4.2.2.3. UK Exception for 'Copying by Librarians Etc: Replacement Copies'

In the UK, both the 2006 Gowers and 2011 Hargreaves Reviews urged the making of improvements to the UK law, which led to significant changes being made to the CDPA in 2014.[64] These changes included the exceptions for private copying, caricature, parody and pastiche, quotation, research and private study, text and data mining, education and teaching, archiving and preservation, public administration and accessible formats for the disabled.

can also lead to further questions on the originality, which is tied to art 14 of CDSM, introduced in Section 2.7.

[59] Communia, 'Article 6 Preservation Exception' (2020): www.communia-association.org/wp-content/uploads/2020/07/Webinar-Presentation-Preservation-Art.6.pdf; V Proudman et al, 'Transposing the Directive on Copyright in the Digital Single Market: A Guide for Libraries and Library Associations' (2019).

[60] ibid.

[61] C Sganga et al, 'D2.3 Copyright flexibilities: mapping and comparative assessment of EU and national sources' (2023) 541.

[62] ibid 542.

[63] See Section 4.3.4.3 for text and data mining, Section 4.4.3 for out-of-commerce and Section 4.5 for WIPO.

[64] A Gowers, *Gowers Review of Intellectual Property* (London, HM Treasury, 2006); I Hargreaves, *Digital Opportunity: A Review of Intellectual Property and Growth* (2011). See also R Burrell, 'The Changing Judicial Politics of Copyright Exceptions in the UK' in Balganesh (n 11).

In the CDPA there were various defences to certain actions of libraries and archives from section 37 onwards, and definitions for libraries, museums, and 'conducted for profit' in section 43A.[65] The amendments in 2014 repealed CDPA sections 37–40, but also clarified and improved the existing provisions. It became easier to preserve works in permanent collections, and museums were included under the beneficiaries allowed to preserve and replace.[66] Under CDPA section 42, institutions can copy items to preserve or replace reference-only items that are not accessible to the public or available on loan only to other institutions. It also applies only when it is not reasonably practicable to purchase a replacement.[67]

Following Brexit, the UK has lost out on many positive changes by not implementing the CDSM, but preservation is less of a problem due to the helpful changes in 2014. The differences between the UK and the EU will become more significant when it comes to providing access to the digitised heritage.

4.2.2.4. US Exception for Reproduction by Libraries and Archives

Compared with the approach in the EU and the UK, the US system of library exceptions is deceptively straightforward. Reproduction by libraries and archives is addressed under section 108 of the US Copyright Act, but it should be assessed together with the benefits of the section 107 fair use provision to fully appreciate the flexibility of US libraries and archives. Historically, section 108 was created as a reaction to widespread photocopying of books in libraries and as a compromise among libraries, authors and publishers.[68] To sum up very broadly, subsections (a), (f), (g) and (i) set out general conditions, (b–c) address preservation and replacement, (d–e) address user requests for private study, and (h) only apply to works in their final 20 years.[69]

Section 108(a) sets forth that library reproduction will not be an infringement if it is not for commercial advantage, the institution is open to the public and there is a copyright notice on the reproduction or distribution of the work. The subject matter set out in section 108(i) excludes certain works but these limits do not apply to rights granted in subsections (b) and (c) for preservation and replacement.[70]

Preservation and replacement are addressed specifically: Section 108(b) allows the reproduction of unpublished works for preservation or depositing to

[65] See also Hudson (n 6) 123–42.

[66] Intellectual Property Office, 'Exceptions to Copyright : Libraries, Archives and Museums' (2014).

[67] CDPA, s 42, as amended by The Copyright and Rights in Performances (Research, Education, Libraries and Archives) Regulations 2014 (SI 2014/1372).

[68] US Copyright Office, 'Section 108 of Title 17 – Discussion Document' (2017) ('108 Discussion Document 2017') 5–6.

[69] US Copyright Act, s 108. Only part of s 108 (b–c) will be considered under 'preservation' purpose, and s 107 and s 108 (d–e) will be discussed for 'access' purposes, under Section 4.3.4.5.

[70] 'musical work, a pictorial, graphic or sculptural work, or a motion picture or other audiovisual work other than an audiovisual work dealing with news'.

another library. However, if it is in digital format, it cannot be distributed or made available to the public outside the premises. Section 108(c) allows the reproduction of published works for replacement, provided that the work 'is damaged, deteriorating, lost, or stolen, or if the existing format in which the work is stored has become obsolete'.[71] It means that it can be applied to analogue formats and requires that the machine or device necessary to make the work 'perceptible' is no longer manufactured or 'reasonably available' in the commercial marketplace. While it is useful that the Article defines obsoletion, it is unclear what counts as 'reasonable', what is manageable for one institution might not be so for the other.

One other section that might be relevant to digitisation for preservation is section 108(h), which allows a library or an archive or an educational institution that functions as such to reproduce (including digital reproduction), distribute, display or perform the works in the last 20 years of its copyright term for the purposes of preservation, scholarship and research, unless: (i) it is for commercial gain; (ii) the work can be obtained at a reasonable price; and (iii) the copyright owner provides a notice claiming one of the first two conditions.[72] However, it does not apply to any other subsequent users. The same concerns on what is 'reasonable' also apply to section 108(h).[73]

Various points in section 108 need improvement; the section 108 Study Group worked for three years to identify the problems between 2005 and 2008,[74] followed by another meeting in 2012 and publication of a Discussion Document in 2017.[75]

First, the Study Group had difficulty in determining the line between allowing 'non-commercial' preservation, versus 'commercial' uses of works that might also include 'long-tail' markets in the digital environment.[76] A 2017 Discussion Document suggested giving more access to the 'dark archive', where digital preservation copies of unpublished works remain unseen, the solutions proposed were: (i) access only on premises, (ii) lending the physical media that stores the material off-site, and (iii) limited time one-off access, also noting that this kind of access

[71] For an overview of recent developments on the ability to break digital locks of DVD and Blu-ray, see K Klosek, 'Library Copyright Alliance Supports US Copyright Office Exemption for Libraries, Archives, and Museums Breaking Digital Locks to Create Preservation Copies' (Association of Research Libraries, 27 October 2023) www.arl.org/news/library-copyright-alliance-supports-us-copyright-office-exemption-for-libraries-archives-and-museums-breaking-digital-locks-to-create-preservation-copies, citing this Notice of proposed rulemaking: www.govinfo.gov/content/pkg/FR-2023-10-19/pdf/2023-22949.pdf.

[72] US Copyright Act, s 108. See also E Townsend Gard, 'Last Twenty (L20) Collections: Applying Copyright's Section 108(h) in Libraries, Archives and Museums including the New Music Modernization Act for Pre-1972 Sound Recordings' (2018) 22(3) *UCLA Journal of Law and Technology* i.

[73] DR Hansen, 'Copyright Reform Principles for Libraries, Archives, and Other Memory Institutions' (2014) 29 *Berkeley Technology Law Journal* 1559, 1584.

[74] 'The Section 108 Study Group Report' (2008) ('108 Report 2008').

[75] 108 Discussion Document 2017.

[76] 108 Report 2008, 29.

could also prevent technical problems by periodically checking and refreshing these files.[77]

Another issue is the number of copies foreseen in section 108(c). This provision allowed only one copy until 1998; the Digital Millennium Copyright Act (DMCA) has increased it to three copies, which is still criticised as it is not compatible with what can be done with digital technology.[78] It was suggested in the 2017 Discussion Document that it had to be replaced with a 'reasonably necessary' standard.[79]

The discussions of section 108 also addressed the 'unnecessary' distinction between published and unpublished works.[80] The 2017 Discussion Document suggests that this should be replaced with 'disseminated' and 'not disseminated', which would make it easier to distinguish these works (as opposed to determining what is published) and would also include born-digital works.[81] The Study Group's recommendation for preserving publicly available online content (web archiving) was not followed, but is still achieved in practice based on fair use.[82] Making digital copies of both published and unpublished works is currently possible, but only physical copies can be circulated, therefore causing institutions to keep two copies (one digital, and one analogue that can be circulated).[83] This approach leaves the physical copies (CDs, DVDs) open to use and deterioration, while the digital copies stay confined to use on premises.[84]

The beneficiaries should also be increased; section 108 only allows libraries and archives, but in practice it includes university libraries. It was suggested that museums should be included under the scope of section 108, but only after carefully determining what counts as a 'museum'.[85] There are also questions on whether physical premises are necessary to be eligible for protection as libraries and archives.[86]

If the aforementioned changes were made to section 108 it would improve preservation and replacement, but so far, the provision remains the same. At the

[77] 108 Discussion Document 2017, 26–27 and 51.

[78] RR Kwall, 'Library Reproduction Rights for Preservation and Replacement in the Digital Era: An Author's Perspective on §108' (2005) 29 *The Columbia Journal of Law & the Arts* 343; M Rasenberger, 'Copyright Issues and Section 108 Reform' (2010) *The Columbia Journal of Law & the Arts* 15, 20–21; Hansen (n 73) 1585.

[79] 108 Discussion Document 2017, 25.

[80] 108 Report 2008, 47; Kwall (n 78).

[81] 108 Discussion Document 2017, 24; See also K Fisher, 'Copyright and Preservation of Born-digital Materials: Persistent Challenges and Selected Strategies' (2020) 83(2) *The American Archivist* 238.

[82] 108 Discussion Document 2017, 42.

[83] KD Crews, *Copyright Law for Librarians and Educators: Creative Strategies and Practical Solutions*, 4th edn (Chicago, ALA Editions, 2020) 173.

[84] Crews suggests that the reason for limiting the accessibility of digital copies is to prevent the libraries from 'intruding on the conventional activities of publishers' that could affect the market: ibid 173.

[85] The study group explained it by how museums share 'fundamental missions' with other institutions, namely the collection, preservation and access to material of cultural and scientific importance: 108 Report 2008, 31; 108 Discussion Document 2017.

[86] 108 Report 2008, 17; Hansen (n 73); Townsend Gard, 'Last Twenty' (n 72).

same time, the section 108 exceptions also do not prevent relying on fair use.[87] Without the safety provided by fair use, perhaps this section would have been amended to include more lenient provisions a long time ago, which would have also given more certainty to US heritage institutions.

So far, copyright law is not really an obstacle to the preservation purpose. Preserving (without providing subsequent access) involves the reproduction and potentially adaptation right, and can be achieved through copyright defences: CDSM Article 6 allows increased harmonisation in the beneficiaries, works and methods for preservation in the EU Member States; the UK has also benefitted from a clearer and wider preservation exception since 2014, and the US Copyright has an adequate defence in section 108 and the safety net of section 107. The leniency towards preservation purpose fits with goals of cultural property law for keeping heritage safe, and rarely disrupts the balance between authors and public. Even when the exceptions are insufficient or unclear, contacting the rightholders for permission to preserve is also less controversial. However, looking at the purpose of digitisation, is one purpose (preservation) more important than the other (access)? Is digitisation without any access even worth the cost and effort? But if everything qualifies as 'heritage', does wanting more access to heritage mean we have to be against copyright?

4.3. Access

Providing access to digitised heritage is significantly more challenging, where multiple rights are potentially infringed, and each solution has its shortcomings. There are several decisions to be made by heritage institutions: their methods could involve providing access at a time and place chosen by the user, or at a specific time to an audience determined by the institution. Access might be provided in a way that allows or prevents further reproduction and/or storing copies. It might come with or without a copyright notice or attribution. As a wider concern, laws are territorial so who can view the heritage institutions' websites might be important.[88] When making these decisions for access, copyright will matter.

This part will introduce the exclusive rights of the copyright holder that are likely to be infringed by access purpose (communication, public performance and display, distribution and lending), followed by three options for providing access: (i) only digitising public domain, (ii) licensing, or (iii) defences (library, research and text and data mining), then move on to the digitisation of special cases.

[87] 'Nothing in this section – (4) in any way affects the right of fair use as provided by section 107, or any contractual obligations assumed at any time by the library or archives when it obtained a copy or phonorecord of a work in its collections.': US Copyright Act, s 108(f)(4). Fair use is covered in Section 4.3.4.5 in this chapter.

[88] For territoriality of copyright, see generally: JAL Sterling, *Sterling on World Copyright Law*, 6th edn (London, Sweet & Maxwell, 2022) 12.113–12.117; R Tryggvadóttir, *European Libraries and the Internet: Copyright and Extended Collective Licences* (Cambridge, Intersentia, 2018) 273–311.

4.3.1. Affected Rights

As already established, digitising heritage will infringe the reproduction right. But whether it affects other economic rights depends on what is exactly being done with the work afterwards.[89] Providing access to digitised might infringe other exclusive economic rights of the author, through activities such as:

- Sharing digitised material online,
- Sharing both born-digital and digitised material online, one copy at a time, for a limited time,
- Sharing digitised material on dedicated terminals on premises,
- Playing or displaying digitised materials on premises.

The assessment of relevant rights here (communication, public performance and display, distribution and lending) will reveal unclear aspects and jurisdictional differences; for example an act that is considered communication to the public in the EU is more likely to be treated as distribution in the US. Since the scope of heritage is very wide, the lending of books will also be discussed here, although a large portion of these activities are left to the control of publishers who view (especially electronic) lending as a commercial matter.

4.3.1.1. Communication to the Public

'Communication to the public' broadly covers three groups of activities: communication to the public (the general act, including the following two); broadcasting (simultaneous reception); and making available (individual communication at a time and place chosen by the audience).[90] Variations of communication right exist under the Berne Convention, the Agreement on Trade-Related Aspects of Intellectual Property Rights (TRIPS) and the WCT and the WIPO Performances and Phonograms Treaty (WPPT).[91] Both the WCT and the WPPT include the same wording: 'making available in such a way that the public may access at any place and at a time individually chosen by them', this technology-neutral wording including future methods of releasing works to the public.

Prior to WCT introducing a new right of making available (as a category of communication right), the scope of the Berne Convention was no longer sufficient

[89] As an important caveat, the activities discussed here are not temporary enough to benefit from the temporary copying defence, previously discussed under Section 4.2.1.1.

[90] L Bently, B Sherman, D Gangjee and P Johnson, *Intellectual Property Law*, 6th edn (Oxford, OUP, 2022) 159.

[91] Berne Convention, arts 11, 11*bis*, 11*ter*, 14 and 14*bis*; WCT, art 8; WPPT, arts 2, 10, 14 and 15. The fragmented nature of Berne right can be explained with the technological changes taking place at different times: Depreeuw (n 15) 246.

as it did not embrace digital transmissions.[92] Other solutions for digital dissemination proposed before WCT included treating on-demand transmissions as distribution, public display or renting, or establishing a new right.[93] However, policy makers reached the decision that it should be kept neutral, in order to allow members to decide how they want to approach the matter.[94] Being a party to the WCT or the WPPT does not prevent Contracting States from implementing a different right in their national laws:[95] The US Copyright Act places broadcasting and recitation under 'public performance', has a separate 'public display' right in section 106, and other similar acts are handled under the exclusive right of distribution.[96]

At the EU level, the InfoSoc Directive definition is also technology-neutral:

> communication to the public of their works, by wire or wireless means, including the making available to the public of their works in such a way that members of the public may access them from a place and at a time individually chosen by them.[97]

The Court of Justice of the European Union (CJEU) defines this act in two steps: whether an act of communication has occurred, and whether it was to the 'public', with some complementary, interdependent criteria:[98] (i) there has to be an act of transmission or making available, such as installing TV sets and playing ambient music in a hotel,[99] offering an internet TV broadcasting service to show programmes,[100] providing links to newspaper articles found online,[101] hyperlinking to illegally published photographs[102] or indexing metadata to allow users to search and share protected works via peer-to-peer networks.[103] These acts should be done by the intervention of the user and should not have been otherwise possible. Location of the act of communication is not clarified in the EU, except in the Satellite and Cable Retransmission Directive,[104] (ii) communication is made either

[92] Blomqvist (n 20) 146; J Koo, *The Right to Communication to Public in the EU Copyright Law* (Oxford, Hart Publishing, 2019) 81.

[93] T Aplin and J Davis, *Intellectual Property Law: Text, Cases and Materials*, 4th edn (Oxford, OUP, 2022) 184.

[94] ibid.

[95] J Reinbothe and S von Lewinski, *The WIPO Treaties on Copyright*, 2nd edn (Oxford, OUP, 2015) 135.

[96] 'to distribute copies or phonorecords of the copyrighted work to the public by sale or other transfer of ownership, or by rental, lease, or lending' (US Copyright Act, s 106(3)).

[97] InfoSoc Directive, art 3.

[98] Case C-135/10 *Societa Consortile Fonografica v Marco Del Corso* ECLI:EU:C:2012:140 [2012] ECDR 276, para 79.

[99] Case C-306/05 *Sociedad General de Autores y Editores de España (SGAE) v Rafael Hoteles SA* ECLI:EU:C:2006:764 [2006] ECR I-11519.

[100] Case C-607/11 *ITV Broadcasting Ltd v TVCatchup Ltd* ECLI:EU:C:2013:14 [2013] 3 CMLR 1.

[101] Case C-466/12 *Svensson v Retriever Sverige AB* ECLI:EU:C:2014:76 [2014] 3 CMLR 4.

[102] Case C-160/15 *GS Media BV v Sanoma Media Netherlands BV and Others* ECLI:EU:C:2016:644 [2017] 1 CMLR 30.

[103] Case C-610/15 *Stichting Brein v Ziggo BV* ECLI:EU:C:2017:456 [2017] ECDR 19.

[104] For the location of communication, see N Caddick; G Harbottle; U Suthersanen (eds), *Copinger & Skone James on Copyright*, 18th edn (London, Sweet & Maxwell, 2021) paras 7-249–258; Sterling (n 88) 9.174–9.202; Tryggvadóttir (n 88) 61, Koo (n 92) 143–63.

with the same technical means to a new public (one that was not taken into consideration during the initial communication of the work) or with different technical means to a public. The 'new public' criterion is criticised for being too complex and conflicting with international treaties and EU Directives,[105] (iii) the motivation of profit is not required but if the use is made for profit, knowledge of illegality will be presumed,[106] (iv) the communication should be made with the knowledge of infringement. For example, the CJEU held that providing hyperlinks to a work already freely available on the internet was not communication to the public, but if the work is posted illegally and if the person knows or ought to know about its illegality, it is an act of communication to the public.[107]

Under UK law, the right of communication by electronic transmission includes '(a) broadcasting …, and (b) making available to the public of the work by electronic transmission in such a way that members of the public may access it from a place and at a time individually chosen by them'.[108] Electronic transmission is further defined, which covers the digital transmission within digitisation projects.[109] So far it is still in line with the EU communication to public right.

Turning to the activities of heritage institutions, it is not straightforward to determine their intended audience, other than referring to the general public and/or visitors. But in any case, sharing the digitised content on the website of the cultural heritage would count as 'new technical means'.[110] As for dedicated terminals, it depends on the visitors. It would not be possible to say that visitors to heritage institutions are 'consistent and determinate and not persons in general'.[111] For example, the CJEU held that patients at a rehabilitation centre who were enjoying television were a 'new public' because they were 'persons in general'.[112] However, the outcome was different for a dental clinic's patients enjoying radio programmes,[113] because the CJEU was focused on the profit-making side of the

[105] ALAI, 'Opinion on the criterion "New Public", developed by the Court of Justice of the European Union (CJEU), put in the context of making available and communication to the public' (2014) www.alai.org/en/assets/files/resolutions/2014-opinion-new-public.pdf. See also PB Hugenholtz and SC Van Velze, 'Communication to a new public? Three reasons why EU copyright law can do without "a new public"' (2016) 47 *IIC* 797–816.

[106] Case C-306/05 *Sociedad General de Autores y Editores de España (SGAE) v Rafael Hoteles SA ECLI*:EU:C:2006:764 [2006] ECR I-11519, para 44.

[107] The CJEU decided that when the hyperlink is provided for profit, it will be assumed that the user must have checked the content is published legally in Case C-160/15 *GS Media BV v Sanoma Media Netherlands BV and Others* ECLI:EU:C:2016:644 [2017] 1 CMLR 30, paras 49–51.

[108] CDPA, s 20(2).

[109] 'electronic means actuated by electric, magnetic, electro-mechanical energy, and in electronic form means in a form usable only by electronic means' (CDPA, s 178: 'Minor Definitions').

[110] CDPA, s 20.

[111] *Societa Consortile Fonografica* (n 98).

[112] Case C-117/15 *Reha Training Gesellschaft für Sport- und Unfallrehabilitation mbH v Gesellschaft für musikalische Auffuhrungs- und mechanische Vervielfältigungsrechte* EU:C:2016:379 [2016] 3 CMLR 40.

[113] It was found that the patients were a determinate group, background music was not aimed at bringing in more patients: *Societa Consortile Fonografica* (n 98).

rehabilitation clinic's communication to the public.[114] Hyperlinking to an already freely available work does not count as 'communication to the public' according to the CJEU, because it was not a new public.[115] So aggregators of cultural heritage which merely provide a link to the existing websites would not be communicating this work to a new public. As for the profit motivation, even if it is assumed that having more content to show on dedicated terminals would attract more visitors and indirectly bring in money, it does not mean that this is being done for profit. However, for any profit-seeking activities, such as selling merchandise, institutions should either obtain licences or ensure that the work's status does not require seeking permission. Therefore, in the absence of licences or defences, very common activities of EU and UK heritage institutions will risk infringing communication, such as placing digitised heritage on their websites, or sharing it with visitors on premises – but this could also concern the rights of public performance or display, depending on the type of the work and jurisdiction.

4.3.1.2. Public Display and Performance

The scope of rights for public performance and display overlap with communication. For public performance, it is logical to exclude 'the cases whereby means of wire or wireless technology or transmission of sounds and/or moving images take place to a public situated at another locality'.[116] However, national laws sometimes use the term 'performance' in a wider way that encompasses 'communication to the public'.[117]

At the international level, the Berne Convention covers rights in various actions that are related to public performance, covering public performance of dramatic, dramatico-musical and musical works and their translations, public communication of literary and artistic works by loudspeaker or other analogous instruments, public recitation of literary works, public performance of cinematographic adaptations.[118]

The rights are not harmonised at EU level. In the past, CJEU has distinguished live performance from the communication right, suggesting that the communication right did not include when the performance before the public is in direct physical contact with the performers, and left the matter to the national laws.[119] For example, public performance is listed under the 'communication' right, and the display right is covered as 'right of exhibition' and 'right of presentation' in

[114] B Clark and S Tozzi, '"Communication to the Public" under EU Copyright Law: An Increasingly Delphic Concept or Intentional Fragmentation?' (2016) 38 *EIPR* 715, 716.

[115] Case C-466/12 *Svensson v Retriever Sverige AB* ECLI:EU:C:2014:76 [2014] 3 CMLR 4.

[116] *Copinger* (n 104) 7-174.

[117] Blomqvist (n 20) 130–31.

[118] Berne Convention, arts 11, 11*bis*, 11*ter*, 14 and 14*bis*.

[119] Case C-283/10 *Circul Globus București (Circ & Variete Globus București) v Uniunea Compozitorilor și Muzicologilor din România* ECLI:EU:C:2011:772 [2011] ECR I-12031; Pila and Torremans (n 7) 295.

Germany;[120] whereas in France, 'représentation' (performance) covers exhibition and communication to the public.[121]

In the UK, this right is in section 19 of the CDPA 'Infringement by performance, showing or playing of work in public' and applies to literary, dramatic and musical works. Public performance right is different from communication to the public, but they could overlap. For literary, dramatic and musical works, public performance would include 'any mode of visual and acoustic presentation' (such as loudspeaker, television or otherwise) and that act would fall under public performance and communication to public.[122] For sound recordings, films and broadcasts, their communication would also fall under public performance.[123]

Under US law, the exclusive rights of the author under section 106 include performing the work and displaying the work and (for sound recordings) the means of digital audio transmission. It does not have to be done in person. Any rendering by any device fits under the definition of 'performance'.[124] Under the definitions in the US Copyright Act, performing or displaying a work publicly includes both doing these in an open place and transmitting by means of any device and process to people receiving it in separate places.[125] Under section 109(c) the owner of a lawfully made copy is entitled 'to display that copy publicly, either directly or by projection of no more than one image at a time, to viewers present at the place where copy is located' without the authorisation of the copyright owner.

For heritage institutions, public display and performance rights could be affected if the digitised work is shared with the visitors on premises. This occurs when, for example, films or sound recordings are converted from analogue format to digital, and afterwards played inside the premises of a cultural heritage institution. These could be recent works that would require authorisation, for example, if the exhibition aims to provide context on a recent event. When looking at visitors to heritage institutions, an important question is whether 'the persons coming together to form the audience are bound together by a domestic or private tie, or by an aspect of their public life'.[126] In the case of cultural heritage institutions, the

[120] '"Right of exhibition" means the right to display in public the original or the copies of an unpublished artistic work or an unpublished photographic work. (Art 18 of German Copyright Act) "Right of presentation" means the right to make an artistic work, a photographic work, a cinematographic work or illustrations of a scientific or technical nature perceivable to the public by the use of technical devices. The right of presentation does not include the right to make the radio broadcast or the making available to the public of such works perceivable to the public (section 22)': German Copyright Act, art 19(4)), translation from www.wipo.int/wipolex/en/text/586964.

[121] German Copyright Act, art 15(2); French Intellectual Property Code, L122-1(1). See Goldstein and Hugenholtz (n 17) 305.

[122] *Copinger* (n 104) 7-175.

[123] ibid 7-176.

[124] Ginsburg and Gorman (n 25) 165.

[125] US Copyright Act, s 101.

[126] Australian Performing Right Association Ltd v Commonwealth Bank of Australia (1992) 25 IPR 157 para 171, as cited in *Copinger* (n 104) 7-185.

connection is public, not private. Therefore, works that are performed and shown in cultural heritage institutions might be infringing these rights, while also overlapping with other rights addressed in this chapter.

4.3.1.3. Distribution

Another economic right that would be infringed is the distribution right. At the international level, distribution right was not consistently defined under the Berne and Rome Conventions.[127] A more detailed distribution right can be found in the WCT Article 6, where the method of distribution is 'through sale or other transfer of ownership', but it was left to the Contracting Parties to determine the conditions of exhaustion of this right (whether works can be freely circulated after the first sale).[128]

At the EU level, this right exists in various Directives and a regional exhaustion regime is embraced: distribution is described as 'by sale or otherwise' under the InfoSoc Directive,[129] 'any form of distribution to public' under the Database Directive,[130] and 'make available to public, including the rental' under the Software Directive.[131] Its boundaries with 'communication to public' are harder to determine in the digital environment, compared to the distribution of tangible goods.[132] A specifically problematic aspect of this right is 'digital exhaustion'.

Since the Software Directive did not include a 'communication to public' right, the distribution right was extended to cover the online re-selling of a computer program (transfer of licence) in the case of *UsedSoft v Oracle*.[133] The court reasoned that the ownership was transferred to the new owner, therefore communication to the public would no longer be applicable.[134] The court suggested that at the point of resale, the user must make their copy unusable in order to avoid infringing the right of reproduction.[135] It was held that the downloading of the software (in return for a fee) was 'sale' and has exhausted the right of distribution.[136]

This decision caused uncertainty about how the exhaustion rule designed for tangible copies should be applied to online copies of works other than software.[137]

[127] *Copinger* (n 104) 7-139.
[128] WCT, art 6.
[129] InfoSoc Directive, art 4, see also Recitals 28 and 29 (disseminating online copies will not exhaust right of distribution).
[130] Directive (EC) 96/9 of the European Parliament and of the Council of 11 March 1996 on the Legal Protection of Databases, art 5(c).
[131] Software Directive, art 4(c).
[132] For an overview of the overlaps between exclusive rights in the EU, see Koo (n 92) 121–35. See also C Sganga, 'A Plea for Digital Exhaustion in EU Copyright Law' (2019) 9 *JIPITEC* 211, 218–20; S Karapapa, 'Reconstructing copyright exhaustion in the online world' (2014) 4 *IPQ* 304.
[133] Case C-128/11 *UsedSoft GmbH v Oracle International Inc* ECLI:EU:C:2012:407 [2012] 3 CMLR 44.
[134] *Usedsoft* (n 133) para 52. However, as Koo argues, this approach fails to recognise only copies of the software are being transferred here and the original work still belongs to Oracle: Koo (n 92) 133–34.
[135] *Usedsoft* (n 133) para 78.
[136] ibid para 88.
[137] Aplin and Davis (n 93) 177.

In *Tom Kabinet*, the supplying of second-hand e-books for permanent use was handled under communication right instead of distribution right, and therefore the right was not exhausted.[138] This case has clarified that the digital exhaustion foreseen in *UsedSoft* did not apply to works other than software. In their reasoning, CJEU relied on the 'historic, teleological and systematic analysis of the relevant legal sources', including the *travaux* and recitals, instead of AG Szpunar's detailed opinion,[139] and highlighted that e-books are perfect substitutes, and could therefore affect the market.[140] One way to summarise is that 'the legislator intended to treat digital and analogue copies in the same way as regards to the Software Directive, but not as regards to the InfoSoc Directive'.[141] As this right currently stands, the question of whether a different approach to digital exhaustion would be more favourable for the EU copyright system remains.[142] This approach to distribution also affects e-lending, addressed in the next section.

In the UK, the right to issue copies to the public under section 18 of the CDPA ('Infringement by issue of copies to the public'), is limited to the act of putting circulation of copies not previously put in circulation in the UK and the European Economic Area, without the consent of the rightholder.[143] Following Brexit, there is a possibility for change for digital exhaustion.[144]

In the US, distribution is dealt with under section 106(3) of the Copyright Act, defined as 'to distribute copies or phonorecords of the copyrighted work to the public by sale or other transfer of ownership, or by rental, lease, or lending'. The first sale doctrine is in section 109(a), which allows the owner of a lawfully made copy to sell or otherwise dispose of that copy.[145] A key case for digital exhaustion

[138] Case C-263/18 *Nederlands Uitgeversverbond and Groep Algemene Uitgevers v Tom Kabinet Internet BV and Others* ECLI:EU:C:2019:1111 [2020] 2 CMLR 20.

[139] ibid Opinion of AG Szpunar; S Ghosh and P Mezei, 'The Elusive Quest for Digital Exhaustion in the US and the EU: The CJEU's Tom Kabinet Ruling a Milestone or Millstone for Legal Evolution?' (2020) *Hungarian Yearbook of International Law and European Law* 249, 255.

[140] 'from an economic point of view, the sale of a computer program on a material medium and the sale of a computer program by downloading from the internet are similar …. The supply of a book on a material medium and the supply of an e-book cannot, however, be considered equivalent from an economic and functional point of view …. dematerialised digital copies, unlike books on a material medium, do not deteriorate with use, and used copies are therefore perfect substitutes for new copies …' *Tom Kabinet* (n 138) paras 57–58.

[141] A Kaiser, 'Exhaustion, Distribution and Communication to the Public – The CJEU's Decision C-263/18 – Tom Kabinet on E-Books and Beyond' (2020) 69(5) *GRUR International* 489, 495.

[142] Sganga, 'A Plea' (n 132); C Sganga, 'Is the digital exhaustion debate really exhausted? Some afterthoughts on the Grand Chamber decision in Tom Kabinet (C-263/18)' (Kluwer Copyright Blog, 19 May 2020) copyrightblog.kluweriplaw.com/2020/05/19/is-the-digital-exhaustion-debate-really-exhausted-some-afterthoughts-on-the-grand-chamber-decision-in-tom-kabinet-c-263-18/; S Karapapa, 'Exhaustion of rights on digital content under EU copyright: positive and normative perspectives' in T Aplin (ed), *Research Handbook on Intellectual Property and Digital Technologies* (Cheltenham, Edward Elgar, 2020); Ghosh and Mezei (n 139).

[143] CDPA 1988, s 18.

[144] Bently and Sherman (n 90) 162–65.

[145] It does not apply to the phonorecord and computer programs rental rights: US Copyright Act, s 109(b).

is *Capitol Records, LLC v ReDigi*,[146] on the re-selling of digital music, where the software ensured that the old copy was deleted when the work was re-sold. The court held that exhaustion does not permit re-copying the work to share with the new owner, but it was possible to sell the medium (such as the PC).[147]

So how does distribution apply to the actions of heritage institutions? At the EU level, any material acquired in a tangible format can be transferred in a tangible format, and the author's right is already exhausted. However, that exhaustion in the tangible copy does not mean that heritage institutions are allowed to reproduce and distribute more copies without permission, as that would infringe the reproduction right. Materials that are acquired in a digital format, on the other hand, cannot be circulated further without authorisation, as they do not trigger a distribution right, but instead a communication right (as clarified by *Tom Kabinet*) – it will therefore require permission. In the US, the same activity will trigger both a reproduction and distribution right. The differences of communication and distribution rights, and the different approaches in the EU and US, will continue to cause complexity.[148] Furthermore, the interpretation of digital exhaustion will also have an impact on activities performed by heritage institutions for electronic lending, addressed in the next section.

4.3.1.4. Rental and Lending

The author has the exclusive right to rent and lend their works to the public. Out of all heritage institutions, the scope of lending is mostly important for libraries whose visitors regularly borrow in-copyright works. This right is significant in the light of increasing demand for the lending of digital copies, especially since the COVID-19 pandemic.[149] While relying on licences to acquire digital copies and send them to the users does not concern 'digitisation' of heritage, the line gets blurry when institutions start making and lending the copies of works they already hold in their physical collections.

The rental right exists in TRIPS, Articles 11 and 14, WCT, Article 7 (for authors of computer programs, cinematographic works and works embodied in sound recordings), and WPPT, Articles 9 and 13 (protection for also the performers and producers of sound recordings). However, the lending right is not addressed at an international level.

[146] *Capitol Records, LLC v ReDigi Inc.*, 934 F. Supp. 2d 640 (SDNY 2013).

[147] Ghosh and Mezei (n 139) 265.

[148] L Determann, 'Digital Exhaustion: New Law from the Old World' (2018) 33(1) *Berkeley Technology Law Journal* 185; Ghosh and Mezei (n 139).

[149] When the libraries were shut down due to the pandemic, big increases in ebook borrowing were reported: R Giblin and K Weatherall, 'Taking Control of the Future: Towards Workable Elending' in J Coates, V Owen and S Reilly (eds), *Navigating Copyright for Libraries* (Berlin, De Gruyter Saur, 2022).

In the EU, this right was harmonised in Directive (EC) 92/100 on rental right and lending right (revised version is Directive 2006/115).[150] Both rental and lending involve 'making available for use, for a limited period', but 'rental' is for direct or indirect economic or commercial advantage, whereas 'lending' is not for any advantage and is made through 'establishments which are accessible to the public'.[151]

The part of the Directive that concerns heritage institutions is Article 6, which allows Member States to 'derogate the exclusive rental and lending right in respect of public lending and determine the remuneration in accordance with cultural promotion objectives'.[152] Therefore, depending on the implementation, public libraries are exempt from infringing the exclusive rights of the author, in return for remuneration. However, public lending right (PLR) schemes in the EU countries are inconsistent, such as: (i) schemes being handled by government or collecting societies; (ii) remuneration calculation factors including number of loans/total books/library users; and (iii) where authors are being compensated.[153]

It is more common for libraries in the EU to 'lend' electronic books based on the licences obtained from publishers for such use.[154] There are usually limits to such uses that imitate the principles of the lending of physical copies, requiring multiple licences for popular items.[155] A new licence is needed after a determined number of loans, to imitate the ageing process of physical copies.[156] The copies usually become unavailable once the lending period ends, so it should not be seen as transfer of ownership, despite the concerns of publishers about e-lending leading to piracy.[157]

In relation to e-lending, the case of *Vereniging Openbare Bibliotheken v Stichting Leenrecht (VOB)* has clarified that the public lending exception applied to books as well.[158] It was held by the CJEU that e-lending practices similar to the lending of printed works (one copy at a time, for a limited time) should be covered under the derogation under Article 6(1) of the Rental and Lending Rights Directive.[159]

[150] Directive (EC) 2006/115 of the European Parliament and of the Council of 12 December 2006 on Rental Right and Lending Right and on Certain Rights related to copyright in the field of intellectual property OJ L376/28 ('Rental and Lending Directive'). See Sterling (n 88) 28B.01-28B.60; J Reinbothe and S von Lewinski, *The EC Directive on Rental and Lending Rights and on Piracy* (London, Sweet & Maxwell, 1993).

[151] Rental and Lending Directive, art 2 'Definitions'.

[152] ibid art 6(1).

[153] S Richly, 'Scoping Study on Public Lending Right' WIPO SCCR/45/7 (2024); GA Rub, 'Reimagining Digital Libraries' (2024) Forthcoming 113 *Georgetown Law Journal*, Ohio State Legal Studies Research Paper No. 848. EBLIDA, 'First European Overview on E-Lending in Public Libraries' (June 2022) www.eblida.org/News/2022/first-european-overview-elending-public-libraries.pdf.

[154] S Dusollier, 'A Manifesto for an E-Lending Limitation in Copyright' (2014) 5 *JIPITEC* 213, 214.

[155] ibid 217.

[156] R Matulionyte, 'E-Lending and a Public Lending Right: Is It Really a Time for an Update?' (2016) 38 *EIPR* 132, 133.

[157] Dusollier (n 154) 213, 224; Matulionyte (n 156) 133.

[158] Case C-174/15 *Vereniging Openbare Bibliotheken v Stichting Leenrecht* ECLI:EU:C:2016:856 [2017] ECDR 3 ('*VOB*').

[159] ibid paras 52–54.

AG Szpunar was in favour of a dynamic interpretation of the Directive, suggesting that it would fit with technological advancements.[160]

This case did not address the matter of digital exhaustion, and managed to avoid the strictness of InfoSoc and WCT on exhaustion, by treating the Rental Directive as *lex specialis* – the same way the *UsedSoft* case did with Software Directive.[161] Subsequent case law on distribution (*Tom Kabinet*) does not fit the *VOB* case and causes confusion on how to treat e-lending.[162] If there is no exhaustion for non-software, then it creates confusion on why e-lending is not treated under the communication right (which cannot be derogated).[163] More importantly, if there is no digital exhaustion (as clarified by *Tom Kabinet*) for e-books, then these books need to be acquired subject to licence terms.[164] Even if it is recognised that libraries have the opportunity to digitise their collections, this is only for dedicated terminals and not going to help with e-lending.[165] The interaction between distribution and lending rights at EU level can therefore be summarised as follows:

- Distribution (tangible copies): Once the object is sold, the right is exhausted.
- Distribution (software): Authorised download is treated same as 'sale', therefore the distribution right is exhausted (*UsedSoft*).
- Distribution/Communication (non-software/e-books): This act falls under communication, not distribution, therefore the right is not exhausted. (*Tom Kabinet*).
- Lending (tangible): Heritage institutions can lend their collections, but authors receive remuneration (PLR system in Rental and Lending Directive, Article 6).
- Lending (e-books): Libraries can digitise their collections but it should be treated the same as tangible lending (same number of copies), and only with remuneration (*VOB*).
  - But electronic works that libraries can lend can only be acquired through licences, as they are not exhausted when they first enter the collections. (*Tom Kabinet*)
  - Alternatively, libraries can digitise their own tangible books, but can only display them on dedicated terminals (*Darmstadt*), and this act is reproduction and communication.

[160] ibid Opinion of AG Szpunar, para 28.
[161] Sganga, 'A Plea' (n 132) 227.
[162] Sganga, 'Is the digital exhaustion debate really exhausted?' (n 142).
[163] One way to interpret this is that e-lending might be treated as communication, but if e-lending is done lawfully, then it is not a communication to a 'public': Bently and Sherman (n 90) 168.
[164] In other words, *VOB* means libraries are free to lend digital books, but Tom *Kabinet* means these digital books can only be acquired from publishers: Rub (n 153) 24; Giblin and Weatherall (n 149) 362; M Frigeri, M Kretschmer and P Mezei, 'Copyright and eLending in public libraries: an incomplete revolution?' (2024) 15 *JIPITEC* 156.
[165] C de Castell, 'Unintended Consequences of the Digital Shift' in Coates (n 149) 158–60; Rub (n 153) 27. EU copyright exception for research on dedicated terminals and *TU Darmstadt v Eugen Ulmer* case are discussed in Section 4.3.4.2 below.

Therefore, these developments leave the e-lending at public EU institutions in an uncertain position, pushing the matter under the control of licensing. This will need to be addressed at the EU level at a later stage.[166]

In the UK, the public lending right has existed since 1979.[167] It is under sections 18A, 36A, 40A and 93A of the CDPA, which have been amended in line with the EU developments. Following a review of e-lending, PLR was extended to cover audiobooks and e-books in 2014.[168]

Such a PLR system does not exist in the US. This means that once purchased, US libraries can lend tangible copies freely, without any remuneration to authors. Under the US law, it is handled mostly under the distribution right, which is subject to first sale doctrine/digital exhaustion. Through the influence of other countries (especially the UK), there have been attempts to introduce such a right since the 1980s, and it was supported by authors, academia, the press and politicians, but this led to only two bills in the US Senate, both of which subsequently failed.[169]

However, finding a solution for digital that is comparable to the tangible lending is difficult, so two main practices emerged in the US: The first is the institutions lending e-books to their users by relying on licences (allowing publishers to charge libraries with a higher price than licences for individual users).[170] The second, and disputed, option is the practice of Controlled Digital Lending (CDL) where libraries scan and share digital copies of the printed copies they hold. Once scanned, the physical copy is removed from circulation, therefore the library is still circulating the same number of copies (maintaining 'owned to loaned' ratio), which is supported by technical measures preventing further copies.[171] While controlled forms of digital lending is not a new practice, it become apparent during the COVID-19 pandemic that libraries were unable to fulfil their functions for physical lending. The Internet Archive established the National Emergency Library

[166] Frigeri, Kretschmer and Mezei suggest multiple solutions involving judicial and legislative interventions to increase the effectiveness of *VOB* decision for e-lending: (n 164).

[167] Public Lending Right Scheme Order 1982.

[168] See generally W Sieghart, 'An Independent Review of E-Lending in Public Libraries in England' (2013) and DCMS, 'Government Response to the Independent Review of E-Lending in Public Libraries in England' (2013), available at www.gov.uk/government/publications/an-independent-review-of-e-lending-in-public-libraries-in-england; DCMS, Independent Library Report for England (2014) assets.publishing.service.gov.uk/media/5a7d910aed915d3fb9594860/Independent_Library_Report-_18_December.pdf. See also Dusollier (n 154) 218; Bently and Sherman (n 90) 402.

[169] For historical perspective and predictions see JH Foley, 'Enter the Library: Creating a Digital Lending Right' (2001) 16 *Connecticut Journal of International Law* 369; R LeComte, 'Writers Blocked: The Debate over Public Lending Right in the United States during the 1980s' (2009) 44(4) *Libraries & the Cultural Record* 395.

[170] Rub notes that digital dissemination is not subject to the same obstacles as tangible lending (time, effort, wear and tear), but suggests that leaving it to the market to balance itself also causes publishers to freely apply competitive prices: Rub (n 153) 28–40.

[171] L Bailey et al, 'Position Statement on Controlled Digital Lending by Libraries', available at controlleddigitallending.org/statement/. See also DR Hansen and KK Courtney, 'A White Paper on Controlled Digital Lending of Library Books' (2018); IFLA Position on Controlled Digital Lending (2021).

and suspended 'owned to loaned' ratio, therefore giving free access to works. This example of CDL was held to be not covered by fair use (*Hachette v Internet Archive*), as recently confirmed by the Appeals Court.[172]

In the US, there is also an argument for making changes at the state level, as opposed to the federal level. For example, Maryland passed a law requiring publishers to offer e-book licences to libraries on reasonable terms.[173] But this led to a lawsuit from the Association of American Publishers and this Act was held to be unconstitutional,[174] therefore reducing the likelihood of state-level solutions.[175]

To sum up, e-lending is also a part of heritage institutions' way of providing access to cultural heritage. In the EU, *VOB* provided a temporary understanding that the issue was solved, which was complicated again by *Tom Kabinet*. In the US, in the absence of a PLR remuneration, the restrictions on heritage institutions are causing an unbalanced situation that favours the publishers. While CDL can be a useful method for increasing access to digital materials, *Hachette v Internet Archive* has demonstrated that it requires caution. When discussing the ideal scope for lending, we must acknowledge that different considerations should apply to digital books. For tangible works, the inconvenience of borrowing (travel, wear and tear) might not deter users with no resources, whereas other users prioritising comfort and permanence will continue to purchase books, therefore not necessarily damaging to the publishers.[176] With digital copies, these physical restraints do not exist.[177] Unlike museums and archives with one of a kind materials, libraries hold works that can be replacements for the market. This brings the question of whether leaving this matter completely to publisher licences is beneficial for the public, especially if overly restrictive contracts become the norm.[178] This would

[172] *Hachette Book Group Inc. v Internet Archive*, 664 F. Supp. 3d 370 (SDNY 2023), *Hachette Book Group Inc v.Internet Archive* 115 F.4th 163 (2 Cir 2024). The fair use aspect of this case will be discussed in Section 4.3.4.5. however, it is important to acknowledge in advance that libraries can implement differing CDL schemes, and this case is about the implementation chosen by the Internet Archive. It should not be treated as courts' blanket rejection of all forms of CDL.

[173] An Act Concerning Public Libraries – Electronic Literary Product Licenses – Access, House HB518; Senate SB432 (Maryland General Assembly 2021).

[174] *Association of American Publishers, Inc. v Frosh*, 586 F. Supp. 3d 379, 383 (D. Md. 2022). See also E Townsend Gard, 'Nine Copyright Things Every Library and Archive Should Know in 2023' (2023) 41 *Cardozo Arts & Entertainment Law Journal* 485.

[175] It is worth keeping in mind that state-owned libraries enjoy sovereign immunity, whereas privately owned libraries (including private university libraries) do not have the same assurance against being sued: Rub (n 153) 58–59.

[176] ibid 56–57.

[177] Rub explains how digital lending can potentially be structured in a way that benefits multiple users, even if a single digital copy is in circulation by: (i) setting the borrowing time to a few hours, (ii) automatic returns when not used, (iii) rotating borrowers during the daytime in different time zones, and (iv) not having to replace digital books, as their condition remains the same: ibid 33–34.

[178] It was found that half of the randomly selected contracts of the British Library were incompatible with the exceptions: P Davies, 'Access v Contract: Competing Freedoms in the Context of Copyright Limitations and Exceptions for Libraries' (2013) 35 *EIPR* 402, 406. See also Dusollier (n 154) 221; G Spedicato, 'Digital lending and public access to knowledge' in JC Lai and AM Dominicé (eds), *Intellectual Property and Access to Im/material Goods* (Cheltenham, Edward Elgar, 2016) 156.

jeopardise the public interest mission of these institutions and would not fit policy rationale for lending regimes that were foreseen for tangible copies, causing a disadvantage for digital activities.

4.3.1.5. Classifying the Activities for Access

When we revisit activities for providing access, we see a fragmented picture of which other economic rights of the author might be infringed:

- Sharing digitised material online: communication to public (EU, UK), distribution (US).
- Sharing both born-digital and digitised material online, one copy at a time, for a limited time: lending if done by certain institutions, subject to remuneration (EU, UK), distribution (US).
- Sharing digitised material on dedicated terminals on premises: communication to public (EU, UK) or distribution (US).
- Playing or displaying digitised materials on premises: communication (EU, UK) and/or public display and performance (EU, UK, US).

Therefore, providing access to digitised works will require the heritage institutions to select at least one of the options discussed below: digitising only the public domain, relying on licensing, and copyright defences.

4.3.2. Providing Access – Public Domain Only

The simplest way to avoid infringement altogether is to only provide access to the digitised works that are in the public domain. The rest of the works that are not in the public domain can still be digitised for preservation but would not be shared with the public. Such a risk-averse option only keeps part of cultural heritage safe and accessible and is therefore not compatible with the principles determined in chapter one.

Although digitising the public domain seems to be the easiest option for heritage institutions, there are two additional aspects in using public domain works. The first is whether new copyright can and should emerge from digitising the public domain, which was discussed in Section 2.7.

The second is the impact of the non-IP issues for digitising the public domain. One of these issues is the impact of national cultural heritage codes, which prevent the use of digitised cultural heritage without permission from local authorities determined by law, such as the ones in Italy.[179] Recent disputes

[179] Italian Code of Cultural and Landscape Heritage (Legislative Decree 42/2004) provides a definition of cultural property in art 10, which excludes works by living authors up to 50 years from their creation, which provides a different length from the current copyright term.

include Michelangelo's David with a machine gun in an advertisement,[180] David on unofficial tickets and tourism brochures,[181] a model posing as David on the cover of *GQ* Magazine,[182] Botticelli's Birth of Venus on clothing,[183] and the use of Leonardo da Vinci's drawing of Vitruvian Man used in a jigsaw puzzle[184] – which all led to either removals (without going to court), or injunctions and damages. Scholars have commented on whether this approach is going too far in functioning as a separate non-IP obstacle on access to public domain, and also how it fares with existing copyright law on freedom of panorama (does not exist in Italy) and the CDSM, Article 14 (Italy transposed it without prejudice to their heritage code).[185]

Another non-IP issue for access to the public domain is the impact of Directive on Public Sector Information (PSI Directive), which originally came into force in 2003, subsequently amended in 2013 and 2019.[186] The aim of this Directive is to address the barriers to the wide re-use of public sector and publicly funded information, and to be able to exploit PSI for the benefit of European economy and society.[187] The scope of PSI is clarified in Article 1, and it excludes 'documents for which third parties hold intellectual property rights'. However, the problem stems from the inclusion of publicly funded libraries, museums and archives in its scope in the 2013 amendment. Subject to Article 3(2) of the Directive, the

[180] Armalite advertisement was removed by the company after reactions from the Italian parties: A Bellan, 'Exclusive rights in classical art works: the "armed David" case' (IPKat, 11 March 2014) ipkitten.blogspot.com/2014/03/exclusive-rights-in-classical-art-works.html.

[181] E Rosati, 'Florence court prohibits unauthorized commercial use of David's image' (IPKat, 25 November 2017) ipkitten.blogspot.com/2017/11/florence-court-prohibits-unauthorized.html.

[182] *Ministry of Culture and Tourism v Edizioni Condè Nast* Court of First Instance of Florence, Civil Division, Section II (Tribunale di Firenze, Sez. II Civ.), judgment of 20 April 2023 – 1207/2023. See also E Rosati, 'Is it a breach of the Italian Cultural Heritage Code to feature on GQ a model posing like Michelangelo's David? Yes, says Florence Court' (IPKat, 6 June 2023) ipkitten.blogspot.com/2023/06/is-it-breach-of-italian-cultural.html.

[183] E Rosati, 'Uffizi museum sues Jean Paul Gaultier over unauthorized reproduction of Botticelli's Venus on fashion garments' (IPKat, 11 October 2022) ipkitten.blogspot.com/2022/10/uffizi-museum-sues-jean-paul-gaultier.html.

[184] AM Stein, 'The Italian Code of Cultural Heritage and the "Vitruvian Man" Case Comment' (2023) 45(8) *EIPR* 497–99; D De Angelis and B Vézina, 'The Vitruvian Man: A Puzzling Case for the Public Domain' (2023) communia-association.org/2023/03/01/the-vitruvian-man-a-puzzling-case-for-the-public-domain.

[185] R Romano, 'Copyright law and cultural heritage in Italy: work in progress' (2018) 13(9) *JIPLP* 694; G Dore and G Priora, 'The EU imperative to a free public domain: The case of Italian cultural heritage' (2024) Communia Independent Expert Opinion, available at communia-association.org/publication/the-eu-imperative-to-a-free-public-domain-the-case-of-italian-cultural-heritage; R Caso, 'Michelangelo's David and cultural heritage images. The Italian pseudo-intellectual property and the end of public domain' (Kluwer Copyright Blog, 15 June 2023) copyrightblog.kluweriplaw.com/2023/06/15/michelangelos-david-and-cultural-heritage-images-the-italian-pseudo-intellectual-property-and-the-end-of-public-domain; D De Angelis and G Giardini, 'Tales of public domain protection in Italy' (Communia, 10 July 2023) communia-association.org/2023/07/10/tales-of-public-domain-protection-in-italy.

[186] Directive (EU) 2019/1024 of the European Parliament and of the Council of 20 June 2019 on open data and the re-use of public sector information (recast) OJ L172/56 ('PSI Directive').

[187] ibid.

documents held in these institutions should be re-usable for commercial or non-commercial purposes in accordance with the Directive, and Article 6 foresees that these institutions can charge above marginal costs, that should not exceed 'the cost of collection, production, reproduction, dissemination, preservation and rights clearance, together with a reasonable return on investment'.[188] The Directive also allows cooperation with private partners for digitisation and giving them exclusivity over the digitised resources to recoup their investments, but that should be limited to 'as short a time as possible in order to comply with the principle that public domain material should stay in the public domain once it is digitised', which cannot exceed 10 years.[189] Giving the digitising institutions and external parties the opportunity to charge for digitised public domain, even if temporarily, could result in reduced access to the public domain.[190]

4.3.3. Providing Access – By Collective Licensing

If the planned access involves more than the works in the public domain, and/or if there are commercial motives, then the institutions should consider seeking authorisation. Obtaining an exclusive or non-exclusive licence from the right-holder would provide legal clarity to use the in-copyright work without fearing infringement.[191]

It can be challenging to rely on licensing for all works in the collection, but the procedural difficulty can be at least be reduced by collective management organisations (CMOs) acting on behalf of their members (and sometimes non-members as explained below).[192] Once a copyright holder is registered with a collective

[188] ibid arts 3 and 6, recital (38).

[189] Ibid art 12 and recital (49).

[190] See also P Keller et al, 'Re-Use of Public Sector Information in Cultural Heritage Institutions' (2014) 6 *International Free and Open Source Software Law Review* 1; R Polcak, 'Digitisation, Cultural Institutions and Intellectual Property' (2015) 9(2) *Masaryk University Journal of Law and Technology* 121; SPARC Europe, 'The Directive on Open Data and the Re-Use of Public Sector: Information Briefing for national legislative implementation in the interest of supporting Open Access to research data and its re-use' (2019); The National Archives, 'Guidance on the implementation of the Re-use of Public Sector Information Regulations 2015 for the cultural sector' (January 2019).

[191] This section only provides an introduction to collective management and extended collective licensing, that will be revisited in Section 4.4.3. It does not provide a list of organisations and/or provide licensing advice.

[192] Directive 2014/26 on collective management of copyright and related rights and multi-territorial licensing of rights in musical works for online use in the internal market [2014] OJ L84/72. It is implemented in the UK with Collective Management of Copyright (EU) Directive Regulations 2016 (SI 2016/221). For comprehensive analysis of CMOs, see WIPO, 'Collective Management of Copyright and Related Rights, Third Edition' (2022) www.wipo.int/edocs/pubdocs/en/wipo-pub-855-22-en-collective-management-of-copyright-and-related-rights.pdf; D Gervais (ed), *Collective Management of Copyright and Related Rights*, 3rd edn (Alphen aan den Rijn, Wolters Kluwer, 2015); D Gervais, 'The cultural role(s) of collective management organizations' (2018) 40(6) *EIPR* 349; European Commission, 'Study on emerging issues on collective licensing practices in the digital environment' (2021) Available at ec.europa.eu/newsroom/dae/redirection/document/81239.

agency, that agency will be the one collecting royalties on their behalf, usually also charging a fee for their efforts. There are many decisions to be made by institutions when seeking permission (specifying the work and planned use, determining if the activities require a licence, identifying and contacting the rightholders, drafting the request including the length and conditions of access).[193]

In some jurisdictions, an extended collective licensing (ECL) system is in place. The ECL system expands the CMO's repertoire to include non-members' works, if they fulfil the necessary criteria (such as representing a certain portion of the rightholders in the same area). Under normal circumstances, it is up to the rightholder to be represented by collective management, but on rare occasions this decision can be assumed. The unrepresented rightholders are still able to exercise their rights by opting out (which makes it different from copyright exceptions).[194]

ECL systems have existed in countries such as Sweden, Norway, Denmark, Finland and Iceland since the 1960s.[195] It started with the broadcasting of musical and literary works, then expanded to reprography and re-transmission of broadcasts later.[196] While not uniform in all of these countries, three elements are deemed the same: (i) all are based on negotiations with CMOs representing a substantial number of authors, (ii) the application of agreement is extended to non-represented members by a provision in national copyright laws, (iii) there are measures to secure the rights of outsiders (remuneration, opt-out and transparency).[197] Their national differences provide 'much more leeway for Member States to tailor the tool to their own needs and goals'.[198] It is also common for these systems to limit themselves to works with certain status. The ECL system foreseen in CDSM is in Article 8 (mandatory for MS, only for heritage institutions and only for out-of-commerce) and Article 12 (optional for MS, only for narrow, well-defined areas).

A significant question in establishing a working ECL system is how to determine what is 'a substantial number of authors' that would justify the representation of outsiders (based on percentage and geographic boundary). Another question is what to do when there is no CMO for a specific type of work, which can be overcome with the creation of a back-up exception for such circumstances. The

[193] Crews, *Copyright Law* (n 83) 251–60.

[194] M Ficsor, 'Collective Rights Management from the Viewpoint of International Treaties, with Special Attention to EU "Acquis"' in Gervais, *Collective Management* (n 192) 74.

[195] It is used as a 'support mechanism for freely negotiated licensing agreements to cover certain activities in libraries, museums and archives': G Colangelo and I Lincesso, 'Law versus technology: looking for a solution to the orphan works' problem' (2012) 20(3) *International Journal of Law and Information Technology* 178, 198.

[196] T Koskinen-Olsson and V Sigurdardottir, 'Collective Management in the Nordic Countries' in Gervais, *Collective Management* (n 192) 243.

[197] For comparison and evaluation of individual Nordic provisions on these elements and their specific provisions for libraries and archives, see Tryggvadóttir (n 88) 139–209.

[198] C Sganga, 'From Soulier to the EU Copyright Law Reform: What Future for Non-Voluntary Collective Management Schemes?' (2018) 19 *ERA Forum* 137.

system is also criticised for not being compatible with Article 5(2) of the Berne Convention on the prohibition of formalities, meaning that it puts extra formality on the shoulders of the rightholder by requiring them to opt out from the ECL system.[199]

Some jurisdictions are more hesitant about embracing an ECL system. For example, the settlement agreement in the *Authors Guild v Google* case attempted to assume that authors accepted having their works digitised by Google, unless they opted out.[200] A similar regime was also considered in the 2015 US Copyright Office Orphan Works and Mass Digitization Report, which did not amount to a concrete change.[201]

Licensing is more common for some works than others; for example, they are commonly used for e-books in libraries, but they are less likely to be used in relation to rare documents with uncertain copyright status. Even with the increased ease of CMOs, (especially if the ECL option becomes widely embraced) this authorisation can be expensive and territorial, only for a short duration – any of these inconsistencies need to be tracked and renewed accordingly. So, it does not seem likely that a heritage institution would spend resources on obtaining individual licences to fulfil daily requests from users. It can be worth the effort of seeking a licence, if the work in question is the missing piece for an exhibition or if it is indispensable for teaching or research at that educational institution. Given these considerations about licensing, it is understandable why defences are a more attractive solution for increased access, although not always applicable and do not provide the same level of certainty.

As an additional matter, institutions also have to decide on what kind of licences they will use when placing digitised works online. Use of Creative Commons (CC) licences is common, there are various models of CC, depending on factors such as what others can do with the work (commercial, non-commercial, or making changes) or whether attribution is required, both simplifying and providing control on how works will be used. However, it might also be a funding requirement to release digitised material on CC or similarly lenient licence terms, which might not be very desirable if the copyright status of the underlying work is unclear.[202]

[199] D Gervais, 'Collective Management of Copyright: Theory and Practice in the Digital Age' in Gervais, *Collective Management* (n 192) 24–26.

[200] M Borghi and S Karapapa, *Copyright and Mass Digitization* (Oxford, OUP, 2013) 16.

[201] US Copyright Office, 'Orphan Works and Mass Digitization' (2015).

[202] See generally: L Lessig, 'The Creative Commons' (2004) 65 *Montana Law Review*; L Lessig, *Free Culture* (New York, Penguin Press, 2004); N Elkin-Koren, 'Exploring Creative Commons: A Skeptical View of a Worthy Pursuit' in PB Hugenholtz and L Guibault (eds), *The Future of Public Domain* (Alphen aan den Rijn, Kluwer, 2006); U Suthersanen, 'Creative Commons – the Other Way?' (2007) 20 *Learned Publishing* 59. For example, in the UK, the Heritage Lottery Fund requires a specific CC licence, requiring works to be free to share and adapt, with attribution: Heritage Lottery Fund, 'Digital Good Practice Guide' www.heritagefund.org.uk/funding/good-practice-guidance/digital. Europeana also has 14 different types of rights statements existing to show users what they can do with the work online: 'Understanding the rights statements used by Europeana' (Europeana, 2024): pro.europeana.eu/page/available-rights-statements.

4.3.4. Providing Access – By Relying on Copyright Defences

Copyright defences are necessary for finding a balance between the needs of different sides, in line with the previously discussed justification theories and three-step test. Providing access based on defences is more difficult compared to preservation; these defences are also more likely to be limited to non-commercial use or be at the risk of contractual override.[203] It is also important to remember that the previous two options are still very much available for activities and jurisdictions not covered by these activities. So, risk-averse institutions can just focus on the public domain or turn to licensing solutions if funds allow.

Three relevant EU exceptions will be discussed here: (i) library use, (ii) research on dedicated terminals, and (iii) text and data mining (TDM). The first two are less harmonised due to the optional nature of the InfoSoc Directive, while the third one is still in the relatively early stages. The UK provisions for libraries and research are still similar to the corresponding EU exceptions, but TDM is already going in a different direction. The potential for access seems more promising for the US, due to the wide scope of the library exception in section 108 and the safety net provided by fair use section 107, whose limits were recently tested in courts for CDL and AI.

There are also other exceptions that are more suited for museums, such as the exhibition of physical works, and using works in exhibition catalogues (InfoSoc, Article 5(3)(j): 'use for the purpose of advertising the public exhibition or sale of artistic works, to the extent necessary to promote the event, excluding any other commercial use'), these exceptions are less problematic and their very limited scope is less relevant for access purpose.[204] Exceptions such as private copying, criticism or education are also outside the scope of this chapter, as they are more important for what users of heritage can do.

An additional challenge to defences is moral rights. When digitising for preservation or access, both attribution and integrity will be at risk. These rights are subject to different and narrow exceptions. For example, the UK moral rights in CDPA, sections 77 (attribution) and 80 (integrity), also have their (limited) exceptions respectively in sections 79 and 81, excluding certain acts such as reporting current events. It is usually not sufficient for the author to negatively react to the

[203] For example, Benhamou and Ferland argue for such exceptions for cultural heritage institutions to be given a mandatory character: Y Benhamou and J Ferland, 'Digitization of GLAM Collections and Copyright: Policy Paper' (2022) 71(5) *GRUR International* 403, 408.

[204] WIPO's 2015 study on limitations and exceptions applicable to museums would give an useful overview: JF Canat and L Guibault, 'Study on copyright limitations and exceptions for museums' WIPO SCCR/30/2 (2015); KD Crews, 'Museum Policies and Art Images: Conflicting Objectives and Copyright Overreaching' (2012) 22 *Fordham Intellectual Property, Media & Entertainment Law Journal* 796; M Dahlström, J Hansson and U Kjellman, '"As We May Digitize"– Institutions and Documents Reconfigured' (2012) 21 *LIBER Quarterly* 455, 460.

use of their work, there are references to 'legitimate' interests in most systems.[205] Furthermore, in some jurisdictions, moral rights do not expire as the economic rights in some jurisdictions, and authors could claim their moral rights are infringed during digitisation.[206]

4.3.4.1. EU Exception for Specific Acts of Reproduction by Publicly Accessible Cultural Heritage Institutions

Article 5(2)(c) of InfoSoc, previously introduced under Preservation purpose, also provides the basis for certain institutions to make copies of their collections and provide them for non-commercial purposes.

> Member States may provide for exceptions or limitations to the reproduction right provided for in Article 2 in the following cases:) … in respect of specific acts of reproduction made by publicly accessible libraries, educational establishments or museums, or by archives, which are not for direct or indirect economic or commercial advantage.[207]

This exception is mainly useful for one-off requests, as opposed to digitising collections in full. EC reports have also clarified that Article 5(2)(c) is not a 'blanket exception to digitise their entire collections'.[208]

Similar to the preservation exceptions before CDSM, these exceptions are also not harmonised in the EU, due to the optional nature of the InfoSoc Directive. The institutions and methods of copying are identified differently in the MS: some of them merge purposes for preservation, restoration, internal uses and/or providing copies under one Article, while others are more specific.[209] Non-commercial nature is indicated explicitly in most MS exceptions. But even when it is not explicitly mentioned, there are further conditions to ensure it stays limited to non-commercial copies, for example the Polish exception foresees giving free access 'within the scope of their tasks as stated under statute'.[210]

The types of works allowed under such exceptions are also inconsistent. Some of these exceptions are for works that are 'published' or 'disclosed', some cover only 'works in collection' and some exclude certain works (such as computer programs, databases or sheet music).[211] Some national exceptions have conditions about how

[205] See also Borghi and Karapapa, *Copyright and Mass Digitization* (n 200) ch 6; A Dietz, 'The Moral Right of the Author: Moral Rights and the Civil Law Countries' (1994) 19 *Columbia VLA Journal of Law & the Arts* 199; US Copyright Office, 'Authors, Attribution, and Integrity: Examining Moral Rights in the United States' (April 2019) 30–33.

[206] Moral rights were previously discussed in Sections 2.5.5. and 3.3.2.

[207] This provision was previously mentioned under Section 4.2.2.1.

[208] EC Green Paper: Copyright in the Knowledge Economy, COM(2008) 466 Final, 4; Tryggvadóttir (n 88) 102.

[209] For a full list of exceptions, see Crews Study (n 44), translations of more up-to-date national laws were used for confirmation.

[210] Copyright and Related Rights Act of Poland, No. 83 (4 February 1994), as amended through No. 1923 (25 September 2015, effective 20 May 2016), art 28(1).

[211] Crews Study (n 44).

such copies are provided to users. Some of them allow only one copy and some provisions limit themselves to 10 per cent of books, therefore preventing sharing works in full.[212]

Furthermore, MS exceptions are inconsistent about which uses are subject to remuneration to authors, which uses are excluded from remuneration and how remuneration is collected.[213] Given the current state of library use exceptions, they are unlikely to be harmonised unless a mandatory exception is created similar to the preservation exception in Article 6 CDSM.

4.3.4.2. EU Exception for Research on Dedicated Terminals

Another relevant InfoSoc exception is Article 5(3)(n) for allowing access via dedicated terminals:

> use by communication or making available, for the purpose of research or private study, to individual members of the public by dedicated terminals on the premises of establishments referred to in paragraph 2(c) of works and other subject-matter not subject to purchase or licensing terms which are contained in their collections.

If we look at individual exceptions of MS, there are inconsistencies: Beneficiaries in some MS do not include museums and education institutions.[214] Non-commercial purpose is not emphasised in the dedicated terminal exceptions of some Member States.[215] But these exceptions already have the purpose of research/private study, and the beneficiaries are usually public institutions, so it can be assumed that it will be used for non-commercial purposes. The types of works allowed under these defences are not harmonised, some exceptions are for 'works', most specify 'works in collection'. Some of these MS specifically require such works to be published.[216]

The access method is 'terminals'. Determining the specifics of terminals is left to the institution, but they are usually on the premises. Whether they allow printing or copying the works and whether they have internet connection depends on the institution as well. For example, in the Netherlands and Spain, dedicated terminal exceptions specify a closed network, whereas the other exceptions mention only on-site terminals.[217] It can lead to risky decisions when the task of setting up such terminals is left to the institutions, who might have limited

[212] ibid.

[213] ibid, see also Section 4.3.1.4 for PLR.

[214] For example, in Sweden: Act 1960:729 on Copyright in Literary and Artistic Works, as amended up to Act 2020:540, art 16.

[215] Crews Study (n 44).

[216] For example, the Consolidated Act on Copyright of Denmark, No. 1144 (23 October 2014) §16a mentions published works. Lithuanian Law No. VIII-1185 of May 18, 1999, on Copyright and Related Rights (consolidated 2022) Art 22(3) also only applies to published works.

[217] Crews Study (n 44).

awareness of copyright.[218] Although this access does not specifically have to be 'on-demand', this exception also does not amount to mass digitisation.

These exceptions rely on Article 5(3)(n) of the InfoSoc Directive, in which it is stated that this exception is for subject matters 'not subject to purchase or licensing terms which are contained in their collections'. This means that the work cannot be made available on dedicated terminals if there are contract terms against it. However, this was clarified by the CJEU in *Technische Universität Darmstadt v Eugen Ulmer*.[219]

In this case, a university library digitised a textbook that they physically owned, and made it available to students on electronic terminals, which also allowed printing or taking copies on USB sticks. The publisher offered a licence for the e-book version of the textbook but this was rejected by the TU Darmstadt.[220] The regional court held that the TU Darmstadt could rely on the existing German exception and the only way that it could be overruled would be if the publisher and the university already had an agreement on digital use of the work.[221] The court allowed the initial digitisation, but prohibited allowing work on terminals to be removed from the premises by printing or by using USB sticks.[222] When it was appealed, the Federal Court of Justice referred the case to the CJEU.

The CJEU held that the rightholder offering a licence does not mean that the work was subject to 'purchasing or licence terms'.[223] The concept of 'terms' was used to imply contractual terms between parties, thus reaching the conclusion that it requires the parties to have an agreement to overrule the German exception. With regard to the act of digitisation, the court held that digitisation is an act of reproduction and making copies available on terminals is an act of communication, meaning that digitisation of the works in collection should be allowed when it is for the purpose of making them available. However, in order not to prejudice the normal exploitation (referring to the three-step test in InfoSoc Directive), the number of copies available on dedicated terminals should be limited to the number of copies available in the library, and institutions would have to pay remuneration to the rightholder.[224] Finally, the CJEU held that activities such as printing out or copying onto USB sticks were acts of reproduction, performed by the users

[218] LACA and CILIP, 'Dedicated Terminals Exception to Copyright: FAQs on What It Means for Libraries' (June 2016) uklaca.org/wp-content/uploads/2020/09/6e61f-dedicated-terminals-exception-to-copyright-faqs.pdf.

[219] Case C-117/13 *Technische Universität Darmstadt v Eugen Ulmer* KG ECLI:EU:C:2014:2196 [2014] ECDR 23.

[220] ibid.

[221] ibid.

[222] ibid.

[223] 'The interpretation favoured by Ulmer implies that the rightholder could, by means of a unilateral and essentially discretionary action, deny the establishment concerned the right to benefit from that limitation and thereby prevent it from realising its core mission and promoting the public interest' (ibid at para 28).

[224] ibid paras 36–49.

(not the institution) and would not be covered by exceptions from Article 5(3)(n) of the InfoSoc Directive.[225]

What did the *Darmstadt* case mean for the digitisation activities of heritage institutions? First, it clarified that the act of digitisation involves the exclusive rights of reproduction and communication to the public. It also clarified that EU institutions can digitise their physical copies for the purpose of making them available on dedicated terminals (an ancillary right of digitisation). But in order to satisfy the three-step test, the number of copies available via terminals should be kept in line with the actual number of physical copies, and a remuneration must be paid to the author. Although it is an important case, its impact on digitisation practices is limited due to the *VOB* and *Tom Kabinet* cases.[226]

4.3.4.3. EU Exceptions for Text and Data Mining in CDSM Articles 3 and 4

The final EU exception introduced here is not an obvious candidate for access purposes, but its boundaries still concern institutions whose digitised collections are accessed for a new type of research.[227]

Although it is not possible for humans to read all of the digitised data, artificial intelligence could read digitised material and detect patterns, making it a lucrative reason for private parties to digitise.[228] Heritage institutions, on the other hand, can support such uses by digitising vast collections, and potentially license or release freely this content for parties interested in data mining.[229] The line is even more blurred if the heritage institutions are involved in TDM projects with external parties, or support colleagues in other departments (especially in the case of university libraries). Furthermore, if an algorithm is created based on works with uncertain copyright status and uncertain defences, and if it is later revealed that some works should not have been used, it is difficult to partially remove the training data from the final algorithm.[230]

[225] ibid paras 50–57.

[226] Therefore e-lending and research on dedicated terminals are not the same activity. Dedicated terminals exception makes the work available only on the premises, whereas e-lending can make works available off-premises as well. See also Section 4.3.1.4.

[227] Earlier sections explain the process for using heritage for machine learning (Section 2.8.2), and it is briefly mentioned under Reproduction (Section 4.2.1.1).

[228] Michel et al used Google Books as an example: 'If you tried to read only English-language entries from the year 2000 alone, at the reasonable pace of 200 words/min, without interruptions for food or sleep, it would take 80 years' (JB Michel et al, 'Quantitative Analysis of Culture Using Millions of Digitized Books' (2011) 331 *Science* 176).

[229] HA Izquierdo, 'Artificial Intelligence and Text and Data Mining: Future Rules for Libraries' in Coates (n 149) 497–540.

[230] For projects in this area, see 'Machine "Unlearning" Helps Generative AI "Forget" Copyright-Protected and Violent Content' (UY News, 21 March 2024) news.utexas.edu/2024/03/21/machine-unlearning-helps-generative-ai-forget-copyright-protected-and-violent-content; A McConnon, 'Teaching large language models to "forget" unwanted content' (IBM, 9 September 2024) www.ibm.com/blog/machine-unlearning.

Under the EU law, CDSM Directive Articles 3 and 4 are relevant. Both are mandatory exceptions for the reproduction of works protected by copyright and *sui generis* database rights. Article 3 is only for research organisations and cultural heritage institutions, for the purposes of scientific research, and allows the text and data mining of works to which they have lawful access. There are a few issues in this article: (i) the listed beneficiaries, further clarified in Article 2, leave research organisations with commercial partners in an uncertain position,[231] (ii) the lawful access is difficult to determine especially in automated data collection, (iii) while interpreted widely in Recital 14 to include freely available content, there is the risk of restrictive licensing terms from publishers limiting what can be lawfully accessed (such as a TDM reservation in e-books and databases),[232] (iv) Article 3(2) specifically allows storing the copies to verify scientific results, but it is up to Member States to decide who can store, and whether externals can access.[233]

Article 4, on the other hand, is for a larger set of beneficiaries for the reproduction and extraction of works, as long as the works are lawfully accessible and the rightholder has not expressly reserved their right in an appropriate manner. Article 4 is a last-minute addition[234] as the proposal version received much criticism about the limited scope.[235] For Article 4, it is also worth keeping an eye on the impact of the EU AI Act, especially because any potential requirement to disclose training data will in turn make it easier for rightholders to detect use of their material, and it creates a burden of complying on EU copyright law, even for generative algorithms developed outside which are put on the EU market.[236]

[231] This is partly addressed in Recital 11, where research organisations are allowed to carry out research activities involving TDM in public-private partnerships. See also J Griffiths, T Synodinou and R Xalabarder, 'Comment of the European Copyright Society Addressing Selected Aspects of the Implementation of Articles 3 to 7 of Directive (EU) 2019/790 on Copyright in the Digital Single Market' 72(1) *GRUR International* 22.

[232] See also T Margoni and M Kretschmer, 'A Deeper Look into the EU Text and Data Mining Exceptions: Harmonisation, Data Ownership, and the Future of Technology' (2022) 71(8) *GRUR International* 685; M Kretschmer, T Margoni and P Oruc, 'Copyright Law and the Lifecycle of Machine Learning Models' (2024) 55 *IIC* 110; Izquierdo (n 229) 497–540.

[233] Recital 15 clarifies that Member States can appoint trusted bodies to store the copies, and unauthorised access should be prevented.

[234] P Samuelson, 'Regulating technology through copyright law: a comparative perspective' (2020) 42(4) *EIPR* 214, 218.

[235] C Geiger, G Frosio and O Bulayenko, 'Text and Data Mining in the Proposed Copyright Reform: Making the EU Ready for an Age of Big Data?' (2018) 49 *IIC* 814; European Copyright Society, 'General Opinion on the EU Copyright Reform Package' (24 January 2017); R Hilty and H Richter, 'Position Statement of the Max Planck Institute for Innovation and Competition on the Proposed Modernisation of European Copyright Rules Part B Exceptions and Limitations (Art. 3 – Text and Data Mining)' (2017) Max Planck Institute for Innovation & Competition Research Paper No. 17-02.

[236] Regulation (EU) 2024/1689 of the European Parliament and of the Council of 13 June 2024 laying down harmonised rules on artificial intelligence and amending Regulations (EC) No 300/2008, (EU) No 167/2013, (EU) No 168/2013, (EU) 2018/858, (EU) 2018/1139 and (EU) 2019/2144 and Directives 2014/90/EU, (EU) 2016/797 and (EU) 2020/1828 (Artificial Intelligence Act) OJ L, 2024/1689.; See also M Kretschmer, T Kretschmer, A Peukert and C Peukert 'The risks of risk-based AI regulation: taking liability seriously'(2023) CEPR Discussion Paper No. 18517.

The implementation of CDSM is also uneven, with most recently Poland arguing that CDSM was drafted prior to current capabilities of AI and therefore Article 3 should exclude being used for the 'creation of generative models of artificial intelligence'.[237] The differing opt-out mechanisms are slowly being developed by the Member States, and will be significantly affected by the AI Act.[238] While the CDSM Directive is mostly a positive development, the EU might be at a disadvantage compared to more lenient jurisdictions, due to these exceptions being mostly for non-commercial use, and either subject to certain beneficiaries and/or subject to an opting-out regime.[239]

4.3.4.4. UK Exceptions for Access

In the UK, the previously mentioned 2014 changes improved library exceptions (including museums under beneficiaries) and introduced an exception for research on dedicated terminals (CDPA, s 40B), in line with the InfoSoc Directive.[240] This means that in terms of library and research exceptions, the UK provisions are still very similar to the EU ones discussed above and same concerns are applicable regarding the non-commercial scope. It is possible that this might change in the future as UK copyright develops separately from the EU.

Text and data mining exception is already going in a different direction. The 2014 text and data mining exception was the earliest one in the EU; section 29A in the CDPA 1988 allows copies made by a person who has lawful access to the work, for the purpose of non-commercial computational analysis, accompanied with sufficient acknowledgement. Under the UK exception, contracts to the contrary are unenforceable. The CDSM Directive was not implemented due to Brexit, and therefore the UK did not receive an open-ended exception like Article 4. Seeking next steps, the UK Intellectual Property Office has run a consultation on three specific AI and IP questions between October 2021 to January 2022, namely on copyright protection for AI generated works, patent protection for AI inventions, and copyright exceptions for text and data mining. Although the possibility of introducing a new exception that was even more lenient than Article 4 (not limited to non-commercial, cannot be opted-out by the

[237] P Keller, 'TDM: Poland challenges the rule of EU copyright law' (Kluwer Copyright Blog, 20 February 2024) copyrightblog.kluweriplaw.com/2024/02/20/tdm-poland-challenges-the-rule-of-eu-copyright-law.

[238] P Keller and Z Warso, 'Defining best practices for opting out of ML Training' (2023) Open Future Policy Brief #5: openfuture.eu/wp-content/uploads/2023/09/Best-_practices_for_optout_ML_training.pdf; L Löbling et al, 'Navigating the Legal Landscape: Technical Implementation of Copyright Reservations for Text and Data Mining in the Era of AI Language Models' (2023) 14 *JIPITEC* 499.

[239] See also Section 4.3.4.5 for the applicability of US fair use on data mining.

[240] The Copyright and Rights in Performances (Research, Education, Libraries and Archives) Regulations 2014 (SI 2014/1372); Intellectual Property Office, 'Exceptions to Copyright : Libraries, Archives and Museums' (2014). For the development of the UK library exceptions from 1952, see Hudson (n 6) 109–13.

rightholders) was considered, suggesting it will 'make most of the greater flexibilities following Brexit' and 'help make the UK more competitive as a location for firms doing data mining',[241] this plan was cancelled within a year, citing a negative response from stakeholders.[242] In the meantime, the UK does not have the same flexibilities as the EU, or the other more lenient approach of the US fair use discussed in the section below.

4.3.4.5. US Library Exception and Fair Use

To understand the full extent of US defences for access, sections 107 and 108 of the US Copyright Act should be considered together.[243] Section 108(a–c)(h) was partially introduced for preservation purpose in Section 4.2.2.5 above. Section 108(d) and (e) serves a different purpose of user requests made to libraries for the purposes of private study and research.

These provisions apply to libraries and archives and are all subject to conditions under section 108(a)[244] and (i).[245] While 108(d) is for partial copying, such as an article or a small part of a work, provided on request, 108(e) is for the complete works. For the entire work to be copied and provided under subsection 108(e), the library or archive has to determine, 'on a basis of reasonable investigation', that a new copy cannot be obtained at a 'fair price' – which could lead to some uncertainty. Both (d) and (e) require the use to be for 'private study, scholarship and research' and require the inclusion of a copyright warning where users place orders for such copies. Subsection 108(h) is for copying during the last 20 years and covers the purpose of 'scholarship and research', along with the purpose of preservation based on specific conditions.[246]

There are multiple points of criticism that are illustrated by the Section 108 Study Group Report,[247] and the Section 108 Discussion Document,[248] and

[241] Intellectual Property Office, 'Artificial Intelligence and Intellectual Property: copyright and patents: Government response to consultation' (28 June 2022) www.gov.uk/government/consultations/artificial-intelligence-and-ip-copyright-and-patents/outcome/artificial-intelligence-and-intellectual-property-copyright-and-patents-government-response-to-consultation.

[242] See also Section 5.2.3.

[243] For an overview of US developments for libraries since 1955, see P Samuelson, 'Justifications for Copyright Limitations & Exceptions' in R Okediji (ed), *Copyright Law in an Age of Limitations and Exceptions* (New York. CUP, 2017); Hudson (n 6) 114–17 and 334–36. For a detailed overview of s 108, see Crews, *Copyright Law* (n 83) 169–81; P Hirtle, E Hudson and AT Kenyon, *Copyright & Cultural Institutions: Guidelines for Digitization for U.S. Libraries, Archives & Museums* (New York, Cornell University Library, 2009), especially the flowchart in 110 and checklist in 127 in this source.

[244] Not for commercial advantage, in institutions open to the public and with a copyright notice.

[245] This is about the subject matter; s 108(i) excludes 'musical work, a pictorial, graphic or sculptural work, or a motion picture or other audiovisual work other than an audiovisual work dealing with news' from the reproduction and distribution right – except for preservation, replacement and copies in the last 20 years.

[246] Townsend Gard, 'Nine Copyright Things' (n 174).

[247] 'The Section 108 Study Group Report' (2008).

[248] 108 Discussion Document 2017.

there have been no other significant developments on amending this section. In connection to Access purpose, the Study Group Report had suggested the following: including museums under the allowed institutions; section 108(d) and (e) to include more than single copies and to be more flexible; taking measures to ensure that electronic copies were to be provided only to requesting users, and unauthorised reproduction and distribution is not allowed; and also the subject matter to include non-text-based works, after investigating how it will affect the market.[249]

For allowing on-site access to preserved material, the Report concluded that it should be only on site, because allowing off-site access would equal 'distribution privileges in new media formats',[250] but this does not prevent forming contracts for e-lending with publishers.[251] The Study Group did not reach an agreement on the matter of display and performance of unlicensed digital works. Some Study Group members proposed a recommendation to clarify section 109(c) instead, which provides an exception to public display rights for publicly displaying on site. But some members of the Study Group had concerns that expanding the scope to the performance and display of digital copies and allowing temporary copies for such performances might lead to harmful consequences.[252]

In 2017, the US Copyright Office revisited suggestions in relation to section 108, and suggested: (i) adding exceptions to public display and public performance rights; (ii) clarifying that digital distribution can be possible upon request; (iii) including non-text-based works, with additional conditions not to affect the market; (iv) expanding section 108(h) 'copying in last 20 years', to both published and unpublished works.[253] The 2017 Discussion Document highlighted that the law still does not allow providing 'different types of digital access to a wide selection of their collections without first seeking permission',[254] so the lack of clarity in section 109(c) is unresolved.

Section 108 would benefit from a wider scope but change has been very slow.[255] The US Copyright Office also noted that it was inevitable that heritage institutions still rely on fair use for some of their activities.[256] As noted earlier,

[249] 'The Section 108 Study Group Report' (2008).

[250] ibid 67.

[251] This can be interpreted as the publishers in the US being concerned about losing control over the works in the online environment: L Gasaway, 'Archiving and preservation in the U.S. copyright law' in E Derclaye (ed), *Copyright and Cultural Heritage: Preservation and Access to the Works in a Digital World* (Cheltenham, Edward Elgar, 2010) 132.

[252] 'The Section 108 Study Group Report' (2008) 117–19.

[253] 108 Discussion Document 2017.

[254] ibid 23.

[255] Crews predicts any change in s 108 will be 'slow and contentious', and any prediction about amendments would be a 'hazardous endeavor indeed': Crews, *Copyright Law* (n 83) 179. See also M Rasenberger, 'Copyright Issues and Section 108 Reform' (2010) 34 *The Columbia Journal of Law & the Arts* 15, 20–21; Hansen (n 73) 1585.

[256] 'Even a revised section 108 cannot address every situation in which public policy would deem it reasonable' (108 Discussion Document 2017, 43). See also Hudson (n 6) 334–36.

section 108 does not prevent relying on fair use and vice versa.[257] The existence of fair use both fills the gaps of section 108 but also reduces any urgency for its improvement.

Section 107 on fair use, on the other hand, does not provide certainty. Fair use factors have started out as judge-made rules and have been refined over time.[258] There are also some initiatives in developing guidelines, including the initiative of the Conference on Fair Use (CONFU) that did not get past the proposal stage, and the more recent Codes of Best Practices developed by the Center for Media & Social Impact at American University, based on interviews and focus groups.[259]

Section 107 has four factors for determining fair use:

> In determining whether the use made of a work in any particular case is a fair use the factors to be considered shall include—
>
> (1) the purpose and character of the use, including whether such use is of a commercial nature or is for nonprofit educational purposes;
> (2) the nature of the copyrighted work;
> (3) the amount and substantiality of the portion used in relation to the copyrighted work as a whole; and
> (4) the effect of the use upon the potential market for or value of the copyrighted work.

The first factor is focused on the 'purpose and character' and indicates that commercial uses are less likely to be covered under fair use. When a work is altered into a new work,[260] or used in a new manner, the use is more likely to be considered as transformative.[261] The second factor is the 'nature' of work, where the characteristic

[257] Copyright Act, s 108(f)(4): 'Nothing in this section … in any way affects the right of fair use as provided by section 107'. There are also circumstances when fair use is insufficient but s.108 can be used., the Study Group Report gives the example of copying deteriorating prints of motion pictures being evaluated as fair use in the House Report accompanying the Copyright Act, and the Congress stating that photocopies that may not satisfy the fair use exception can still be covered by s 108: 108 Report 2008, 22.

[258] *Folsom v Marsh* 9 F Cas 342 (CCD Mass 1841) (No 4901). See also P Leval, 'Toward a Fair Use Standard' (1989) 103 *Harvard Law Review* 1105; Samuelson, 'Justifications' (n 243); Kwall (n 78) 355.

[259] The Conference on Fair Use, Final Report to the Commissioner on the Conclusion of the Conference on Fair Use (November 1998) www.uspto.gov/sites/default/files/documents/confurep_0.pdf; Center for Media & Social Impact Codes of Best Practices, cmsimpact.org/report-list/codes/. For a full a detailed list of Guidelines since 1976, see Crews, *Copyright Law* (n 83) 127–35.

[260] *Cariou v Prince*, 714 F.3d 694 (2d Cir. 2013).

[261] In *Warhol v Goldsmiths* case, courts have also unevenly focused more on the first factor when applying fair use: *Andy Warhol Foundation for the Visual Arts, Inc. v Goldsmith*, 143 S.Ct. 1258, 1279 (2023). See also W Patry, 'Andy Warhol Foundation for the Visual Arts, Inc. v Goldsmith: did the U.S. Supreme Court tighten up fair use?' (2023) 18(9) *JIPLP* 628. Transformative use can be hard to identify and also impacts the fourth factor: D Tan, 'Taking the Mickey out of Disney: A Cultural Approach to the Transformative Use Doctrine in Copyright Law' in RC Dreyfuss and ESK Ng (eds), *Framing Intellectual Property in the 21st Century: Integrating Incentives, Trade, Development, Culture, and Human Rights* (Cambridge, CUP, 2018); M Marciszewski, 'What Do Andy Warhol and Google Have in Common? Transformative Uses and the Effect upon the Potential Market: The next Question for Fair Use and the Right to Prepare Derivative Works' (2023) 92 *UMKC Law Review* 291.

of the work is assessed.[262] Fair use is more likely to cover published (as opposed to unpublished), and non-fiction (as opposed to fiction).[263] The nature of out-of-commerce is inconsistent, as the courts note that even such works could be offered for licence.[264] The third factor is regarding the amount and substantiality, which is determined both quantitively and qualitatively. There might be circumstances where fair use can still apply when the entire work is used, as demonstrated in the example of the *Google Books* case below.[265] The final factor is the effect of use on the market, which aims to reduce the impact on the author; for example, if a use reduces or removes the chance for sale or licence, it is less likely to be fair.[266] Only three cases will be assessed here (*Google Books*, *HathiTrust*, *Hachette*), however the case law on fair use is extensive.[267]

The application of fair use criteria in *Authors Guild v Google* is very important for digitised materials.[268] Fair use criteria were applied to the dispute at the District Court in 2013, where the court had focused on the public benefits of the project, and even echoed the utilitarian perspective in the US Constitution: 'it advances the progress of the arts and sciences, while maintaining respectful consideration for the rights of authors and other creative individuals, and without adversely impacting the rights of copyright holders.'[269] When the case was appealed, the plaintiffs argued that: (i) the copying was not transformative under existing case law; (ii) even without advertisements, Google still gained revenue by dominating the search market; (iii) it infringed the derivative rights in search functions; (iv) the storing of digitised content was open to the risk of hacking; (v) Google's distribution of copies to its member libraries was not transformative and caused the risk of loss of sales.[270] The Court of Appeals held that the 'search' and 'snippet' functions were highly transformative and also decided that it was fair use.

But what was deemed fair use for Google might not be applicable for uses by heritage institutions. For example, the highly transformative use by Google for

[262] Earlier case law (*Harper & Row v Nation Enterprises*, 471 U.S. 539 (1985)) shows that unpublished works are excluded from fair use, however this has changed over time: Crews, *Copyright Law* (n 83) 106.

[263] Crews, *Copyright Law* (n 83) 105–107.

[264] *Basic Books, Inc v Kinko's Graphics Corp*, 758 F Supp 1522 (SDNY 1991).

[265] Crews, *Copyright Law* (n 83) 107.

[266] In some circumstances it is argued that although initially damaging, the activity brings long-term public attention and greater sales – but this argument is usually rejected. For more on the final factor, see C Sandalow, 'I Did You a Favor by Taking Your Work: Reconsidering the Harm-Based Approach to the Fourth Fair Use Factor' (2022) 46 *The Columbia Journal of Law & the Arts* 457.

[267] For cases on use of thumbnail images online, see *Kelly v Arriba Soft Corporation* 336 F.3d 811 (9th Cir. 2003); Grant of partial injunctive relief: *Perfect 10 v Google*, Inc., 416 F. Supp. 2d 828 (C.D. Cal. 2006); S Stokes, *Art and Copyright*, 3rd edn (Oxford, Hart Publishing, 2021) 142–48; Hudson (n 6) 163–74. For more fair use cases, see Sterling (n 88) 10.147–10.171.

[268] *Authors Guild v Google, Inc* 770 F Supp 2d 666 (SDNY 2011); *Authors Guild, Inc. v Google Inc.*, 954 F. Supp. 2d 282 (SDNY 2013); *Authors Guild, Inc. v Google, Inc.*, 804 F.3d 202 (2d Cir 2015). For the early days of the project and reactions to it, see Section 5.2.1.

[269] *Authors Guild, Inc. v Google Inc.*, 954 F. Supp. 2d 282 (SDNY 2013).

[270] *Authors Guild, Inc. v Google, Inc.*, 804 F.3d 202 (2d Cir 2015).

finding works and allowing snippets[271] is not the same as a heritage institution allowing full access to its users. The nature of the copied works was mostly non-fiction in *Google Books*, and was found to be fair in that case,[272] but most collections cover more than just non-fiction. The full text would be digitised, meaning that amount and substantiality criteria would not be fulfilled (it was also questionable in the *Google* case).[273] Finally, unlike providing snippets like Google, the heritage institutions would normally provide full works which would have a different effect on the market.

Another case was mentioned in *Google Books*: HathiTrust project and the subsequent case provides an even clearer fair use argument.[274] This project had started in 2008 and included both public domain and in-copyright works digitised by Google, Internet Archive and other initiatives.[275] When HathiTrust was first sued by the Authors Guild, it was suggested that if a settlement were to be reached in the *Google Books* case, this would provide an example for HathiTrust.[276] Instead, the *HathiTrust* case set an example for Google. The decision in the *HathiTrust* case was appealed, and it was argued by claimants that Congress had never intended that fair use should be used for the justification of mass digitisation projects.[277] This project allowed full search function (only showing page numbers, not full works), preservation, and provided full digitised copies for print disabled users, these benefits were recognised by the Court and their use was found to be transformative in 2014.[278]

Even more recently *Hachette v Internet Archive* tested the limits of fair use on the controlled digital lending practices in the United States.[279] The Internet Archive has been scanning books without authorisation and providing digital copies while removing the originals from circulation (lending only limited numbers).

[271] *Authors Guild, Inc. v Google Inc.*, 954 F. Supp. 2d 282 (SDNY 2013).

[272] ibid.

[273] ibid.

[274] *Authors Guild, Inc. v HathiTrust*, 902 F. Supp. 2d 445, 448 (SDNY 2012). The two main differences between Google Books and HathiTrust were identified as displaying works in copyright (HathiTrust does not, while Google shows snippets) and that Google was not a non-profit educational entity like HathiTrust.

[275] HathiTrust, ''Member List' (hathitrust.org) www.hathitrust.org/member-libraries/member-list. M Helft, 'An Elephant backs up Google's Library' *The New York Times* (13 October 2008) bits.blogs.nytimes.com/2008/10/13/an-elephant-backs-up-googles-library.

[276] J Bosman, 'Lawsuit Seeks the Removal of a Digital Book Collection' *The New York Times* (12 September 2011) www.nytimes.com/2011/09/13/business/media/authors-sue-to-remove-books-from-digital-archive.html.

[277] *Authors Guild, Inc. v HathiTrust*, 755 F.3d 87 (2d Cir. 2014); Authors Guild, 'Remember the Orphans? Battle Lines Being Drawn in HathiTrust Appeal' (authorsguild.org, 7 June 2013) www.authorsguild.org/advocacy/remember-the-orphans-battle-lines-being-drawn-in-hathitrust-appeal; A Panezi, 'A Public Service Role for Digital Libraries: A Case of Emergency Electronic Access to Library Material and the Unequal Battle against Misinformation through Copyright Law Reform' (2021) 31 *Cornell Journal of Law and Public Policy* 65.

[278] Hudson (n 6) 192–93.

[279] *Hachette Book Group Inc. v Internet Archive*, 664 F. Supp. 3d 370 (SDNY 2023). This case was previously introduced under Section 4.3.1.4.

This lending capacity was significantly increased in 2018, with the 'Open Libraries' project, if a book existed in one of the partner libraries, Internet Archive has increased the number of digital copies that can be borrowed. Therefore, when the pandemic closed the libraries, the Internet Archive launched the 'National Emergency Library' in March 2020 and removed the limit of books that can be borrowed. This ended in June 2020, shortly after the publishers filed a lawsuit. In assessing the first factor, the Court rejected the argument that the Internet Archive's copying is transformative – there was no criticism or commentary, there was nothing new added, the books were scanned as they were.[280] The Court compared this to HathiTrust and Google Books, where a full-text searchable database did not provide the readers with the opportunity to view any portion of the works, but 'just enough context surrounding the search term'.[281] In relation to non-commercial nature, the Court emphasised that monetary gain does not have to be the sole motivation, however the Internet Archive, without paying the customary price, was still getting new members and donations, and receiving portions from sales of used books from their links to Better World Books.[282] The courts have also rejected the first-sale doctrine argument of the Internet Archive.[283] The courts also commented that even after the Internet Archive returned to owned-to-loaned rations, their reproduction of books was not excused, citing the *ReDigi* case.[284] For the second factor, the Court rejected the argument that most books were past five years since publication, suggesting that copyright does not expire after five years.[285] For the third factor, the Court noted that the books were copied in full. For the fourth factor, the Court found that it has impacted the potential licensing revenues that the publishers are entitled to as the copyright holders.[286] It was held that this was not covered by fair use.[287]

This decision of *Hachette v Internet Archive* has been criticised, especially since it ignored the fact that the Internet Archive has already owned the copies and provided limited access, and also equated making unlimited copies available with CDL, which might impact other libraries in the long run.[288] HathiTrust also provided a similar service called the Emergency Temporary Access Service and were not sued; in their *amicus curiae* brief for the *Hachette* case, HathiTrust

[280] ibid.
[281] ibid.
[282] ibid.
[283] ibid.
[284] ibid, see also *ReDigi* (n 146) addressed in Section 4.3.1.3.
[285] *Hachette* (n 279).
[286] ibid.
[287] The Internet Archive has not relied on s 108, however the Publishers argued that recognising their activities as fair use would 'undermine the Congressional intent' behind s 108: ibid.
[288] MM Wu, 'Hachette, Controlled Digital Lending, and the Consequences of Divorcing Law from Context' (2023) 42(2) *Legal Reference Services Quarterly* 129; D Marcum and RC Schonfeld, *Along Came Google: A History of Library Digitization* (Princeton, Princeton University Press, 2021) 205–10; B Kahle, 'The US library system, once the best in the world, faces death by a thousand cuts' *The Guardian* (9 October 2023) www.theguardian.com/commentisfree/2023/oct/09/us-library-system-attack-digital-licensing.

also noted that the court was wrong in equating the Internet Archive's conduct to all CDL.[289]

The case was then appealed, and the Appeals Court also applied fair use factors: for the first factor, they also found that the Internet Archive's use was not transformative, and the books served the exact same purpose as the originals, 'making lending more efficient' and 'enabling other uses not possible with print books' (physical borrowing) was not sufficient for enabling transformation. But they disagreed with the district court's finding on commercial use (regarding donations and providing links to Better World Books). For the second factor, they found that even though the digitised material included nonfiction, both fiction and nonfiction books are still protected. For the third factor, they noted that this copying was nothing like Google or HathiTrust, it was to reveal the full work. For the fourth factor, the court held that the Internet Archive had not disproven market harm.[290] They affirmed the finding of the district court:

> The parties in this case represent potentially serious interests. On the one hand, eBook licensing fees may impose a burden on libraries and reduce access to creative work. On the other hand, authors have a right to be compensated .... IA asks this Court to bless the large scale copying and distribution of copyrighted books without permission from or payment to the Publishers or authors. Such a holding would allow for widescale copying that deprives creators of compensation and diminishes the incentive to produce new works. This may be what IA and its amici prefer, but it is not an approach that the Copyright Act permits.[291]

While it is understandable that this will have a chilling effect on CDL, if this case goes to the Supreme Court or if there is another case with a more limited interpretation of CDL in the future, which is then found to be fair use, that would give heritage institutions more clarity on this matter.

So far, with sections 107 and 108 combined, the United States might be in a better position for providing access to digitised cultural heritage. The scope of what was allowed in the *Google Books* case would not be possible with the current exceptions in the EU. As has been argued in the previous chapters, such differences are due to historical and cultural differences and justifications for intellectual property. At the same time, US case law after *Google Books*, especially *Hachette*, has shown that fair use indeed is far from perfect. There is also a new wave of ongoing cases on whether training data used for generative artificial intelligence will be covered by fair use; some of these cases already being partially dismissed is a good indication that such uses can be covered by fair use.[292]

[289] Brief of Amicus Curiae Hathitrust in Support of Neither Party, available at www.courtlistener.com/docket/67801014/109/hachette-book-group-inc-v-internet-archive/.

[290] *Hachette Book Group Inc v Internet Archive* 115 F.4th 163 (2 Cir 2024).

[291] ibid.

[292] These cases include *Andersen et al v Stability AI, DeviantArt and Midjourney*, U.S. District Court for the Northern District of California, No. 3:23-cv-00201 (class action of visual artists); *Getty Images (US) v Stability AI*, U.S. District Court for the District of Delaware, No. 1:23-cv-00135

4.4. Special Cases

The above assessment of the licensing and defence options in the chosen jurisdictions has shown that the rules are more fragmented, and it is more difficult to provide access to digitised heritage, compared to the preservation purpose. However this chapter has so far mostly addressed works protected by copyright,[293] and unfortunately it is even more complicated for other works (collectively referred to here as 'special cases') which constitute a considerable part of heritage collections: orphan works are when the author cannot be identified or located, out-of-commerce works are no longer available for purchase, and unpublished works have not been placed on the market at all.

Orphan and out-of-commerce works are mostly a result of the connection between the author and the work being severed in some form. The reasons are similar for both types of works: (i) abolition of formalities makes it harder to keep track of authors,[294] (ii) copyright term is too long so authors or their estates might stop paying attention as only a small portion of works stay profitable for the full length of copyright term, (iii) receiving authorisation from all rightholders is particularly difficult for works with multiple authors, combined with exponential increase in rightholders due to inheritance, (iv) internet sharing also increases the risk of (intentional or accidental) removal of attribution from digital works.[295]

Although they are grouped together here, there is not a single solution to all three types of special cases. It is difficult to predict what the author may have wanted for their works, but keeping such works inaccessible is not beneficial for the greater public. Orphan and out-of-commerce works are similar in the sense that they were made available to the public by the author in the past and the authors have already enjoyed the benefits of their labour/personhood, which might also mean less inclination to come forward. On the other hand, one of a

(Getty's 12 million photographs used in training); *Silverman v OpenAI and Meta*, U.S. District Court for the Northern District of California, No. 3:23-cv-03416 (class action of writers); *Authors Guild v OpenAI*, U.S. Southern District of New York, No. 1:23-cv-8292 (class action of trade body with a group of famous writers). Some claims have been already partially dismissed: T Akers, 'DeviantArt and Midjourney deny wrongdoing in copyright infringement lawsuit over in AI image generators' (The Art Newspaper, 10 May 2024) www.theartnewspaper.com/2024/05/10/deviantart-midjourney-stable-diffusion-artificial-intelligence-image-generators; B Brittain, 'OpenAI gets partial win in authors' US copyright lawsuit' (Reuters, 13 February 2024) www.reuters.com/legal/litigation/openai-gets-partial-win-authors-us-copyright-lawsuit-2024-02-13.

[293] Except in Section 4.3.2 on providing access to public domain works.

[294] 'The enjoyment and the exercise of these rights shall not be subject to any formality; such enjoyment and such exercise shall be independent of the existence of protection in the country of origin of the work' (Berne Convention, art 5(2)).

[295] For reasons, see generally: EF Schulze, 'Orphan works and other orphan material under national, regional and international law: analysis, proposals and solutions' (2012) 34(5) *EIPR* 313, 313; DWK Khong, 'The (abandoned) orphan-works provision of the Digital Economy Bill (Legislative Comment)' (2010) 32(11) *EIPR* 560, 560–61; S Van Gompel, 'Unlocking the Potential of Pre-Existing Content: How to Address the Issue of Orphan Works in Europe?' (2007) 38 *IIC* 669, 674.

kind works that are held in archives are more likely to never be published and are subject to different concerns. By their nature, unpublished works were never in commercial distribution, so it is possible to interpret them as a sub-category of out-of-commerce works, which is the current approach in some jurisdictions that are addressed below.

4.4.1. Unpublished Works

If we go back to balancing the author's rights with the public's interests, unpublished works need a more sensitive approach, in the sense that the authors have not made their works accessible and some of them were possibly not intended for publication. The reasons for protecting unpublished works are twofold: (i) the author should be the one to determine when the work is ready for publication; and (ii) if there was no protection for unpublished works, then the author would have to use their resources for self-protection, meaning that they would be kept more hidden.[296]

Even the concept of 'publication' is subject to different meanings in different areas of law (not only copyright, but also confidential information, privacy and defamation), also taking factors into consideration such as the intention of the author, conditions for dissemination and whether it was commercial – these factors are even more blurred in the digital environment.[297] Since there is no requirement to register works, it is hard to determine whether an unpublished work has already entered the public domain.

At the European level, unpublished works are touched on in some Directives: the Orphan Works Directive refers to unpublished works but only those 'which have been made publicly accessible by the organisations referred to in paragraph 1 with the consent of the rightholders, provided that it is reasonable to assume that the rightholders would not oppose the uses referred to in Article 6'.[298] But it is difficult to predict when this would be the case. The Term Directive gives 25 years of protection to persons who lawfully publish or communicate to the public a work that was previously unpublished.[299] Before CDSM, some EU countries specifically mentioned that the preservation exceptions apply only to 'published works'.

[296] WM Landes and RA Posner, *The Economic Structure of Intellectual Property Law* (Cambridge MA, Belknap Press, 2003) 124. For the discussion on justifications for protecting unpublished works: P Masiyakurima, *Copyright Protection of Unpublished Works in the Common Law World* (Oxford, Hart Publishing, 2021) 122–58.

[297] Masiyakurima (n 296) 9–15.

[298] Directive 2012/28/EU of the European Parliament and of the Council of 25 October 2012 on certain permitted uses of orphan works Text with EEA relevance OJ L 299/5 ('Orphan Works Directive'), art 1(4).

[299] Directive 2006/116/EC of the European Parliament and of the Council of 12 December 2006 on the term of protection of copyright and certain related rights (codified version) OJ L 372/12 ('Term Directive'), art 4.

CDSM Directive Recital 37 suggests that the licensing mechanisms and exceptions provided in this Directive can be used for works that 'have never been commercially available', which can include 'posters, leaflets, trench journals or amateur audiovisual works, but also unpublished works or other subject matter, without prejudice to other applicable legal constraints, such as national rules on moral rights'.[300]

In the UK, unpublished works are currently in copyright until 2039. According to section 43 of the CDPA, these works can be copied only in response to a request, thus limiting the possibility for large scale digitisation. Before the CDPA, copyright in unpublished works was perpetual.[301] Afterwards, the copyright term for works whose authors had died after 1969 became life plus 70 years, whereas for unpublished works whose authors had died before 1969 and for works that remained unpublished until August 1989, the term was calculated to be until December 2039.[302] This term has been criticised for being too long.[303]

There was also an IPO Study on these works, where it was recognised that these institutions had to show 'disproportionate effort' in identifying rightholders.[304] Since unpublished works were not dealt with at around the same time as the orphan works, the criticism was also made that some heritage institutions would have to go through the diligent search for orphan works for unpublished works.[305] Furthermore, when December 2039 finally arrives, a great deal of new works will enter into the public domain, where anyone can digitise and then try to claim copyright.[306] and a new wave of 'copyfraud' on digitised unpublished works might also begin.

In the US, changes were made to legislation to end the 'potentially perpetual common law protection' for unpublished works in 1978,[307] thus giving such

[300] CDSM Recital 37.

[301] A O'Connell, 'Copyright in Unpublished Works: 2039 and Orphan Works' (2015) 39(121) *Library and Information Research* 41.

[302] Due to the Duration of Copyright and Rights in Performances Regulations 1995 (SI 1995/3297) extending the term of protection from 50 to 70 years, the 2039 rule applies only where the author died prior to 1969: IPO, 'Consultation on reducing the duration of copyright in unpublished ("2039") works in accordance with section 170(2) of the Copyright, Designs and Patents Act 1988' (2014) 4.

[303] V Stobo, 'Will UK unpublished works finally make their public domain debut?' (CREATe, 2 June 2014) www.create.ac.uk/blog/2014/06/02/will-uk-unpublished-works-finally-make-their-public-domain-debut; Masiyakurima (n 296) 182–89.

[304] IPO, 'Consultation on reducing the duration of copyright in unpublished ("2039") works in accordance with section 170(2) of the Copyright, Designs and Patents Act 1988' (2014) assets.publishing.service.gov.uk/media/5a7ed3ac40f0b62305b836cd/consultation-on-unpublished-works.pdf; IPO, 'Government response to the consultation on reducing the duration of copyright in certain unpublished works' (2015).

[305] LACA, 'Consultation on reducing the duration of copyright in unpublished ("2039") Works – Response from The Libraries and Archives Copyright Alliance (LACA)' (uklaca.org, December 2014) uklaca.org/2019/01/03/reducing-the-duration-of-copyright-in-unpublished-2039-works.

[306] See Section 2.7 for copyfraud.

[307] RA Reese, 'Preserving the Unpublished Public Domain' in RC Dreyfuss, H First and DL Zimmerman (eds), *Working Within the Boundaries of Intellectual Property* (Oxford, OUP, 2010) 55; Hirtle, Hudson and Kenyon (n 243) see Table 3.2.1 and 3.2.2 in this source.

works limited protection. Works that had been created before 1 January 1978 benefited from having a term that was either for the life of the author plus 70 years or until 2003, whichever was longer.[308] Therefore, in 2003, many unpublished works entered the public domain.[309] Section 108(b) of the US Copyright Act allows the reproduction of unpublished works but limits digital copying within the premises of the institution,[310] which means that they cannot be included in mass digitisation projects.

The 2015 US Copyright Office Report on Orphan Works and Mass Digitisation evaluated the idea of including unpublished works under the ECL scheme, but did not recommend including unpublished works for the following reasons: (i) the administrative costs of including such a massive portion of works under licensing would be too great; (ii) it is not possible to determine reasonable licensing fees for works that have never been on the market; and (iii) it would not be compatible with the right of first publication.[311] Unpublished status of works does not prevent claiming fair use for their copying, however it should be noted that Google asserted that the works that it digitised were all published when arguing for fair use.[312] The 2017 Discussion Document on section 108 was also undecided on how remote access to preservation copies of unpublished works should be provided and gave three options in its Model Statutory Language (access on premises, one off loans, or limited time single user digital access).[313]

For unpublished works, it is impossible to determine what their authors intended. But it seems that moral rights should play a bigger role here, especially the divulgation right.[314] Their inclusion under CDSM provisions for out-of-commerce is not very well justified, and there are also questions on whether they should be controlled by CMOs.[315] At the same time, CDSM does recognise moral rights as a limit, therefore leaving the treatment of unpublished works open to different interpretations.

4.4.2. Orphan Works

The definitions of orphan works are similar in the chosen jurisdictions: a work is considered an orphan if its rightholder cannot be identified or located.[316] There

[308] Reese (n 307).
[309] ibid.
[310] US Copyright Act, s 108(b).
[311] US Copyright Office, 'Orphan Works and Mass Digitization' (2015) 84–85.
[312] US Copyright Act, s 107, last para. See also Crews, *Copyright Law* (n 83) 220–22; *Authors Guild, Inc. v Google Inc.*, 954 F. Supp. 2d 282 (SDNY 2013).
[313] 108 Discussion Document 2017, 26.
[314] See Section 2.5.5 on moral rights. See also V Bronder, 'Saving the Right Orphans: The Special Case of Unpublished Orphan Works' (2008) 31(3) *Columbia Journal of Law & the Arts* 409.
[315] 'LIBER Statement Regarding Out-Of-Commerce Works' (LIBER, 18 July 2022) libereurope.eu/article/liber-statement-regarding-out-of-commerce-works/.
[316] 'A work or a phonogram shall be considered an orphan work if none of the rightholders in that work or phonogram is identified or, even if one or more of them is identified, none is located despite a

have been several studies on the percentage and challenges of orphan works in heritage collections for the past two decades: A 2005 study from the United States showed a random sample with 19 per cent unidentifiable works and a specific fine and rare book collection with 13 per cent.[317] Other US studies focusing on specific rights clearance projects provide percentages between 13 per cent and 31 per cent of the entire collection consisting of undetermined copyright status.[318] According to an EC study in 2010, orphan works constitute 13 per cent of the books and 21 per cent of the films in the EU.[319] A British Library study from 2011 show that, of the chosen sample (a book per year from between 1870 and 2010) 57 per cent of books were in copyright. Of those in copyright, 43 per cent were orphans. When permission was sought for the some of the books in copyright, there was no response for 26 per cent and no contact details could be found for 31 per cent.[320] Another UK study from 2009, pointed out that the average portion of orphans in UK public sector ranged between 5–10 per cent, and that the percentage was higher in archives.[321]

Some of these studies also shared how they handled orphan works in their projects: the Covey Case Study, consisting of three different projects, found that requesting authorisation per publisher (instead of per title) reduced transaction costs, however the likelihood of positive response and the future restrictions placed on digitised material depended heavily on the type of institution and materials.[322] The Dickson Study on the digitisation of Thomas F Watson papers at the University of North Carolina at Chapel Hill decided to take risks and make the collection available, relying on fair use.[323] The Akmon Study at the University of Michigan also reached a similar result on being more risk-averse and questioned whether non-response should be taken as denial.[324] The EC Study by Vuopala showed that percentages of orphan works are high in all categories of works, especially photographs and audiovisual material, and recommended there should be a more efficient way to clear rights.[325] The British Library Study by

diligent search for the rightholders having been carried out and recorded in accordance with Article 3: Orphan Works Directive); a term used to describe the situation where the owner of a copyrighted work cannot be identified and located by someone who wishes to make use of the work in a manner that requires permission of the copyright owner': US Copyright Office, 'Report on Orphan Works' (2006).

[317] D Troll Covey, 'Acquiring Copyright Permission to Digitize and Provide Open Access to Books' (2005) Digital Library Federation Council on Library and Information Resources, 11–38.

[318] D Akmon, 'Only with your permission: how rights holders respond (or don't respond) to requests to display archival materials online' (2010) 10 *Archival Science* 45; M Dickson, 'Due Diligence, Futile Effort: Copyright and the Digitization of the Thomas E. Watson Papers' (2010) 73 *The American Archivist* 626.

[319] A Vuopala, 'Assessment of the Orphan works issue and Costs for Rights Clearance – European Commission DG Information Society and Media Unit E4 Access to Information' (May 2010).

[320] B Stratton, 'Seeking New Landscapes' (British Library 2011) 5.

[321] N Korn, 'In from the Cold: An assessment of the scope of "Orphan Works" and its impact on the delivery of services to the public' (JISC, April 2009): naomikorn.com/wp-content/uploads/2020/09/SCA_CollTrust_Orphan_Works_v1-final.pdf.

[322] Covey (n 317).

[323] Dickson (n 318).

[324] Akmon (n 318).

[325] Vuopala (n 319).

Stratton also identified the amount of orphans in British Library Collections and emphasised the need to find more efficient solutions.[326] The Wellcome Collection Study showed the importance of setting up risk criteria and take-down policies for sensitive material and how taking more risks allowed them to make a significant amount of material available online.[327] The Edwin Morgan Study put forth that the lack of clarity around diligent search was problematic and it 'fatally compromises' large-scale digitisation efforts.[328]

In the EU, orphan works first received attention in 2005 in the i2010 Digital Libraries Initiative.[329] This Initiative was a reaction to the rise of digitisation activities in the USs, which prompted the EU to take similar steps and has facilitated existing attempts to digitise European heritage. In 2006, Member States were recommended to 'create mechanisms to facilitate the use of orphan works, following consultation of interested parties'.[330] In June 2008, the 'Final Report on Digital Preservation, Orphan Works, and Out-of-Print Works' was published, and recommended determining criteria for diligent search and having a database of orphan works information.[331]

Prior to the Directive, the Impact Assessment laid out six main options for dealing with the orphan works problem in the EU:[332] (i) Doing nothing: This option was dismissed quickly, since it would prevent the emergence of a European digital library and would create the risk of US and Google becoming a global leader, after which it would be impossible to catch up.[333] This option is included in the Impact Assessment to draw attention to the passive behaviour of Member States, which frustrated the Commission.[334] While the Impact Assessment recognised the risk management approach of 60 per cent of EU libraries, this was not a feasible option for large-scale digitisation.[335] (ii) A statutory exception for libraries providing online access to orphan works: This is for a harmonised exception for non-commercial online access by libraries and other cultural organisations.

[326] Stratton (n 320).

[327] V Stobo, R Deazley and IG Anderson, 'Copyright & Risk: Scoping the Wellcome Digital Library Project' (2013) CREATe Working Paper 2013/10.

[328] R Deazley, K Patterson and V Stobo, *Digitising the Edwin Morgan Scrapbooks* (2017).

[329] MD Papadopoulou, 'The Issue of "Orphan" Works in Digital Libraries' in I Iglezakis, TE Synodinou and S Kapidakis (eds), *E-Publishing and Digital Libraries: Legal and Organizational Issues* (Hershey, Information Science Reference, 2011) 217.

[330] Commission Recommendation of 24 August 2006 on the digitisation and online accessibility of cultural material and digital preservation ((EC) 2006/585) [2006] OJ L236/28, art 6(a).

[331] i2010: Digital Libraries High Level Expert Group – Copyright Subgroup, 'Final Report on Digital Preservation, Orphan Works and Out-of-Print Works' (2008).

[332] European Commission, 'Impact Assessment on the Cross-Border Online Access to Orphan Works' SEC (2011) 615 Final ('Orphan Works Impact Assessment').

[333] 'Statistically, Europe is already lagging behind in the creation of text based digital libraries: whereas Google has already digitised 10 million books … by contrast there are presently approximately 2 million digitised books in EU libraries and cultural institutions' (Orphan Works Impact Assessment, 7).

[334] K De La Durantaye, 'H is for Harmonization: The Google Book Search Settlement and Orphan Works Legislation in the European Union' (2010) 55 *New York Law School Law Review* 157, 164.

[335] Orphan Works Impact Assessment, 22, citing Korn (n 321).

This option was advocated by libraries who were unwilling to go through individual licensing and overlapping searches.[336] (iii) Extended collective online licensing: Once set up, orphans would be included in the agreement.[337] However, the lack of a diligent search element was deemed to make it less suitable as a common European solution to orphan works.[338] (iv) Specific licences for libraries to provide online access to orphan works: This option was deemed as too complex, because an orphan works collection would require licences from each collecting society in the country of first publication; especially when there were works from different jurisdictions in one collection.[339] (v) Centrally granted licences for libraries to provide online access to orphan works: This would mean that, after diligent search and determining the status of an orphan, the public body of the Member State may give a licence that can be for a limited term and only for certain uses. This was criticised for not facilitating an EU-wide solution to the problem and being too complex for libraries that would have to do it separately for each work.[340] (vi) Mutual recognition of the orphan status: This was the option deemed to be one of the most suitable solutions under the Impact Assessment, especially since it removed the pressure to find a common solution, by leaving the decision to the Member States.[341] When these options were ranked based on their benefits for legal certainty, reducing transaction costs, cross-border access, protection against liability, facilitating diligent search, avoid duplication of searches and facilitating the identification of rightholders, options (ii) and (vi) scored the highest.[342]

The Orphan Works Directive (Directive (EU) 2012/28) determines its subject matter as print works, cinematographic or audiovisual works, phonograms and embedded protected works.[343] The Directive makes it clear that it only applies to works that are 'published' or 'made publicly accessible'.[344] Its beneficiaries are 'publicly accessible libraries, educational establishments and museums, as well as … archives, film or audio heritage institutions and public-service broadcasting organisations'.[345] The emphasis on the 'public interest' was also related to the ongoing Google Books case, and the hesitance over leaving access to European heritage in the hands of a commercial entity.[346] The Directive urged Member States to

[336] Orphan Works Impact Assessment, 24.
[337] ibid 27.
[338] ibid 27.
[339] ibid 29.
[340] ibid 31.
[341] R Kerremans, 'A critical view on the European draft directive for orphan works' (2012) 2(1) *QMJIP* 38, 60.
[342] Orphan Works Impact Assessment, 37.
[343] Orphan Works Directive, art 1 and recital (15).
[344] ibid.
[345] ibid.
[346] MC Janssens and R Tryggvadóttir, 'Orphan Works, Out-of-Commerce Works and Making the European Cultural Heritage Available: "Are We Nearly There Yet?"' in IA Stamatoudi (ed), *New Developments in EU and International Copyright Law* (Alphen aan den Rijn, Kluwer International, 2016) 196.

provide a copyright exception for the reproduction and making available of orphan works under Article 5. The Directive determines the scope of diligent search,[347] and advises mutual recognition of the orphan status,[348] meaning that, once a diligent search is made in a Member State and is recorded, the other Member State can consider the work an orphan. The Accessible Registries of Rights Information and Orphan Works (ARROW) was launched in 2008, which now carries a different title (Orphan Works Database).[349]

The Orphan Works Directive was up for review in 2015,[350] but this did not take place. An EUIPO Study from 2017 showed that participants are 'largely satisfied with the overall experience of using the Orphan Works Database', although diligent search requirements were reported as 'too complex', requiring significant time and effort.[351] Following a Study on the Application of the Directive in 2021,[352] a Report was finally released in 2022.[353] The 2021 Study made it clear that the diligent search hindered the usefulness of the Orphan Works Directive, and stakeholders preferred various amendments, differing from each other.[354] The 2022 Report also recognised that the Directive has only partially fulfilled its goal.[355] There are no plans to extend the scope to standalone artistic works, considering the likely resistance from the image sector.[356] The report also mentioned continuing the dialogue and observing the impact of CDSM out-of-commerce and ECL provisions on orphan works,[357] therefore leaving the fate of orphans uncertain again in the hopes that CDSM would improve the situation.

[347] Diligent search must be carried out prior to the use. Sources should be appropriate; Member States determine what the appropriate sources are. If there is evidence, other countries' sources will be consulted. Diligent search should be recorded and Member States should ensure that it is recorded in a publicly accessible database: Orphan Works Directive, art 3. See also U Suthersanen and M Frabboni, 'The Orphan Works Directive' in IA Stamatoudi and P Torremans (eds), *EU Copyright Law – A Commentary* (Cheltenham, Edward Elgar, 2014).

[348] Orphan Works Directive, art 4.

[349] Orphan Works Database: euipo.europa.eu/orphanworks.

[350] Orphan Works Directive, art 10.

[351] EUIPO, 'Orphan Works Survey 2017 – Summary Report' (November 2017). Given the challenges of diligent search, some scholars also assessed the suitability of relying on crowdsourcing to reduce the burden on the institutions: M Borghi, K Erickson and M Favale, 'With Enough Eyeballs All Searches Are Diligent: Mobilizing the Crowd in Copyright Clearance for Mass Digitization' (2016) 16(1) *Chicago-Kent Journal of Intellectual Property* 135.

[352] European Commission, 'Study on the application of the Orphan Works Directive (2012/28/EU) Final Report' (2021) ('2021 OWD Study').

[353] European Commission Staff Working Document, 'Report on the application of the "Orphan Works Directive" 2012/28/EU', SWD(2022) 412 final (Brussels, 6 December 2022), ('2022 OWD Commission Report'). The report explained that the delay was caused due to the late implementation of the Orphan Works Directive by 12 Member States, and the copyright debates shifting to the CDSM Directive also made it difficult to gather evidence on orphans.

[354] 2021 OWD Study.

[355] 2022 OWD Commission Report, 13.

[356] ibid 11.

[357] Review of CDSM is 'due no sooner than 7 June 2026: 2022 OWD Commission Report, 13.

In the UK in 2014 the Orphan Works Directive was implemented, and a parallel UK licensing system was also introduced.[358] Section 77 of the Enterprise and Regulatory Reform Act 2013 inserted a new section into the CDPA: section 116A confers 'Power to provide for licensing of orphan works', in which a licence can be given for a specific action involving an orphan work (but not the exclusive right) after a diligent search.[359] Unlike the Orphan Works Directive, the UK orphan works licences also cover photographs and could be relied on by commercial entities.[360] Licences are valid for a maximum of seven years, but can be renewed.[361] Following Brexit, the EU Orphan Works scheme is no longer applicable.[362] UK institutions were advised to remove orphan works made available under the EU scheme, and instead seek licensing through the UK scheme.[363] The low uptake, and criticisms of the UK system are not painting a very promising picture,[364] however future changes might be possible without the impact of EU laws.

In the US, there were three reports by the US Copyright Office that deal with orphan works. The 2006 Report recognised that the orphan problem is a real one, and that a threshold for diligent search needed to be determined.[365] It also recommended limitation of remedies (once the search is proven, the re-appearing rightholder's remedies will be limited).[366] The 2011 Report urged stakeholders to agree on a mutual licensing system (voluntary collective licensing, mandatory

[358] Copyright and Rights in Performances (Certain Permitted Uses of Orphan Works) Regulations 2014 (SI 2014/978). Interviews conducted for an IPO study between 2012–2013 showed that the introduction of an orphan works system was necessary and beneficial, although there were concerns about the complexity of the system: IPO, 'Orphan Works in the UK and Overseas' (2013/17).

[359] Furthermore, ss 116B and 116C provide for ECL, allowing a licensing body representing a specific percentage of rights holders to grant copyright licences upon payment of fees. Non-members, including re-appearing rights holders, can opt out. It does not exclude orphan works, but it is 'not intended to be the default solution for licensing works': KE Baker, 'It's a Hard Knock Life: A Critique of the Legislative Response to the Orphan Works Problem in the UK' (2016) 5 *UCL Journal of Law and Jurisprudence* 1, 10.

[360] For criticisms of this system's legitimacy under EU laws, see E Rosati, 'The orphan works provisions of the ERR Act: are they compatible with UK and EU laws?' (2013) 35(12) *EIPR* 724.

[361] Having to renew every 7 years is likely to discourage heritage institutions: Deazley, Patterson and Stobo (n 328).

[362] 'As of the withdrawal date, the mechanism of mutual recognition provided for by Directive 2012/28/EU will no longer apply between the United Kingdom and the EU. Consequently, orphan works which have been recognised in the United Kingdom by the withdrawal date will no longer be recognised in the EU under Directive 2012/28/EU and the same will apply for orphan works recognised in the EU …' (European Commission 'Notice to stakeholders: withdrawal of the United Kingdom and EU rules in the field of copyright' (28 March 2018)).

[363] IPO, Guidance: Orphan works and cultural heritage institutions: www.gov.uk/guidance/orphan-works-and-cultural-heritage-institutions.

[364] M Martinez and M Terras, '"Not Adopted": The UK Orphan Works Licensing Scheme and How the Crisis of Copyright in the Cultural Heritage Sector Restricts Access to Digital Content' (2019) 5(1) *Open Library of Humanities* 36; KT O'Sullivan, 'Reforming Irish copyright law: the question of orphan works' (2017) 40(1) *Dublin University Law Journal* 165, 175–84; Baker (n 359). The number of registered works can be seen here: www.orphanworkslicensing.service.gov.uk/view-register.

[365] United States Copyright Office, 'A report on orphan works – A report of the register of copyrights' (January 2006) 92–93.

[366] ibid 115–20.

collective licensing, or statutory licensing) because doing so on an individual basis was deemed impossible.[367] The 2015 Report started a new phase with the suggestion of ECL as a solution, compared with the suggestion of multiple licensing options in the 2011 Report.[368] This was met with mixed reactions, with some parties referring to it as a 'license to steal bill' while others criticised the downplaying of the effectiveness of fair use for orphan works.[369]

The orphans also affected the *Google Books* case: if the proposed 2009 settlement with Google's Book Registry was successful, Google would have had a monopoly over orphans since there would be no one to opt-out on behalf of them. This was one of the main reasons that it was rejected by the court.[370] Currently there is no solution to orphan works in the US, although reliance on fair use is an option.[371]

There are multiple stakeholders in the orphan works problem, but it might be hard to achieve a balance when one stakeholder (the author) is missing from the discussion. These works can be preserved but making them available is trickier. Clearing the rights can be time-consuming, while taking a calculated risk might pay off if no author resurfaces (which seems to be the case based on the reviews of the EU Orphan Works Directive scheme). The legal developments for orphan works seem to be inconsistent and insufficient, but the main problem seems to be the diligent search requirement in the EU and the UK. Even when it is possible to streamline the process by preparing rights clearance lists, the search usually requires significant resources from heritage institutions. This makes the existing schemes more appropriate for digitising a few specific works, that need more legal clarity. However, for large scale digitisation, the fastest solution can be either ECL or introducing 'orphan work notices' promising to take works down, when rightholders appear.

4.4.3. Out of Commerce Works

Out-of-commerce works can be defined as 'when the whole work, in all its versions and manifestations is no longer commercially available in customary channels of commerce, regardless of the existence of tangible copies of the work in libraries and among the public (including through second hand bookshops or antiquarian

[367] US Copyright Office, 'Legal Issues in Mass Digitization: A Preliminary Analysis and Discussion Document' (October 2011).

[368] US Copyright Office, 'Orphan Works and Mass Digitization' (2015).

[369] FX Mattingly, 'If You Don't Use It, You Lose It: What the U.S. Could Learn from France's Law on out-of-Commerce Books of the 20th Century' (2017) 27 *Indiana International & Comparative Law Review* 277, 305.

[370] O Fischman Afori, 'The Battle over Public E-Libraries – Taking Stock and Moving Ahead' (2013) 44 *IIC* 392, 396.

[371] See also Crews, *Copyright Law* (n 83) 257–58.

bookshops)'.[372] The commercial life of a work is usually shorter than its copyright term, which could result in works that are no longer available through sale. According to a study mentioned earlier, only 21 per cent of the selected works from between 1870 and 2010 were still in print (some out-of-print works were in the public domain).[373]

Out-of-commerce works are usually confused with orphan works. They are both results of long copyright terms, and both types are likely not profitable. Most orphan works are likely no longer in commercial circulation (since there is no one to authorize them) and can be treated as out-of-commerce works. But unlike orphan works, whose authors are unknown or unreachable, other out-of-commerce works can belong to known authors, or the work just might be temporarily unavailable.[374] Also, orphan works are meant to qualify as 'orphans' as a result of a diligent search, which is not the case for out-of-commerce. This wide interpretation means that the solutions for out-of-commerce works can complement the solutions for orphan works by providing a (potentially easier) alternative. Similarly, if the scope of 'out-of-commerce' is defined widely enough to include works that have never been in commercial circulation (such as the situation in EU since CDSM), they can include unpublished works. But whether it is fair to place the other two under the same treatment as out-of-commerce works, is not clear.

At the EU level, in 2006 the Commission recommended 'to improve conditions for the digitisation of, and online accessibility to, cultural material by: … (b) establishing or promoting mechanisms, on a voluntary basis, to facilitate the use of works that are out of print or out of distribution, following consultation of interested parties' in 2006.[375] In 2011, a Memorandum of Understanding of Key Principles on the Digitisation and Making Available of Out-of-Commerce Works was signed by European libraries, publishers, authors and collecting societies, which defines its scope as 'books and journals which have been published for the first time in the country where the Agreement is requested, and are to be digitised and made available by publicly accessible cultural institutions as contained within Art 5.2(c)'.[376] It had foreseen voluntary agreements between the parties for the digitisation of out-of-commerce works, that can allow commercial uses and ECL after being widely publicised, allowing rightholders to opt out.[377]

[372] Memorandum of Understanding: Key Principles on the Digitisation and Making Available of Out-of-Commerce Works (2011).

[373] Stratton (n 320) 5. For statistics from EU institutions on works in collections, see also Orphan Works Impact Assessment 116.

[374] For example, the publishers might be selling newer editions, or the work might be temporarily out of print. Borghi and Karapapa, *Copyright and Mass Digitization* (n 200) 89.

[375] Commission Recommendation of 24 August 2006 on the digitisation and online accessibility of cultural material and digital preservation ((EC) 2006/585) para 6(b).

[376] Memorandum of Understanding: Key Principles on the Digitisation and Making Available of Out-of-Commerce Works (2011).

[377] ibid.

The Memorandum had no binding effect, although it has influenced national decisions, such as including ECL in the UK system.[378]

Regarding out-of-commerce works in the EU before CDSM, it might be helpful to remember the 2012 developments in France,[379] and the subsequent case of *Soulier and Doke v Ministre de la Culture*.[380] On 1 March 2012, France adopted a new system for out-of-print books. It involved Bibliothèque nationale de France (BNF) managing a database of out-of-commerce works (works published before 1 January 2001 and no longer commercially distributed). When a book remained on this database for more than six months, a collecting society could give a licence for its digitisation and communication to the public for five years (renewable), in return for a fee.[381] If the author has not opted-out within the six month period, they could still do it afterwards under certain circumstances. The authors could rely on their moral rights, but they would have to show that copying and making their work available might 'affect their honour or reputation'.[382]

This system has been criticised for its scope, as it only covers works before 2001 and those with a publishing contract (thus excluding self-published books).[383] Another issue is the extra opportunity that this system gave to publishers, who can oppose the digitisation of the work even if their original publishing contracts did not extend to digital uses.[384] It was also argued that the French system went beyond the normal ECL regimes by establishing a mandatory system instead of the voluntary one in the 2011 Memorandum of Understanding.[385]

In the *Soulier and Doke* case, the authors lodged a complaint to annul the abovementioned law, claiming it is incompatible with EU copyright law.[386] The Advocate General clarified that the reproduction allowed in French legislation was not covered by the exceptions, and did not satisfy the three-step test.[387] Therefore the author's express and prior consent should be needed, even if remuneration or compensation was provided.[388] The AG also touched upon the

[378] Janssens and Tryggvadottir (n 346) 206.

[379] LOI n° 2012-287 du 1er mars 2012 relative à l'exploitation numérique des livres indisponibles du XXe siècle. (Law No 2012-287 of 1 March 2012 on the digital exploitation of out-of-print 20th century books).

[380] Case C-301/15 *Marc Soulier, Sara Doke v Premier ministre, Ministre de la Culture et de la Communication* ECLI:EU:C:2016:878 [2017] 2 CMLR 9.

[381] ibid para 15.

[382] O Bulayenko, 'Permissibility of Non-Voluntary Collective Management of Copyright under EU Law: The Case of the French Law on Out-of-Commerce Books' (2016) 7 *JIPITEC* 51; A Bensamoun, 'The French Out-of-Commerce Books Law in the Light of European Orphan Works' (2014) 4 *QMJIP* 213, 217–24.

[383] Bensamoun (n 382).

[384] J Ginsburg, 'Fair Use for Free, or Permitted-but-Paid?' (2014) *Columbia Law School Center for Law and Economic Studies, Working Paper* No 481,43.

[385] Tryggvadóttir (n 88) 378–79.

[386] *Soulier* (n 380) para 53.

[387] ibid, Opinion of AG Wathelet, paras 27–31.

[388] ibid 41.

Orphan Works Directive, and argued that it would be 'paradoxical' if more stringent requirements are applied to orphan works when out-of-print works can be exploited based on national legislation.[389] The AG also emphasised that the 2011 Memorandum of Understanding is not legally binding and only supports 'voluntary agreements'.[390] The subsequent judgment stated 'every author must actually be informed of the future use of his work by a third party'.[391] It continued to state that the authors might not even be aware within those six months and their lack of opposition cannot be interpreted as implicit consent.[392] The French system was found to be not in line with Articles 2(a) and 3(1) of the InfoSoc Directive. The judgment not touching on some of the abovementioned points raised by the AG contributed to the uncertainty caused by this case.[393]

Shortly after *Soulier*, the matter was addressed at a wider level: Under CDSM Directive, Articles 8 to 11, Member States shall provide that a collective management organisation (CMO), that is sufficiently representative of the rightholders in the relevant type of works, should conclude non-exclusive licences for non-commercial purposes with cultural heritage institutions for the reproduction, distribution, communication or making available to public of out-of-commerce (Article 8(1)). Where such collective management organisations do not exist, Member States should provide an exception or limitation to the reproduction, adaptation and communication of original databases; the extraction and re-utilisation of sui generis databases; reproduction, adaptation and distribution of computer programs and the reproduction and communication of other works (Article 8(2) and (3)). This was a later addition to CDSM, which originally only focused on the licensing mechanism in Article 8(1).[394] Under Article 8(4), the rightholders can 'at any time, easily and effectively' exclude their works. CDSM Directive Recitals 30–43 provide the rationale and the concerns, mentioning the challenges of cultural heritage institutions digitising such material to be balanced with the protecting the interests of the rightholder who should be able to opt-out, within systems individually set up by the MS depending on their individual national circumstances (types of CMOs, percentage to sufficiently represent, procedure to opt-out).

The system foreseen in Article 8 is further supported by other Articles under CDSM: Article 9 allows the cross-border uses for out-of-commerce works that are authorised under Article 8(1) and (2), Article 10 foresees the information on such works to be added to an online portal for all MS, and Article 11 facilitates stakeholder dialogue between MS, rightholders, CMOs and heritage institutions.

[389] ibid 52.
[390] ibid 64.
[391] *Soulier* (n 380) Judgement, para 38.
[392] ibid 43.
[393] '... CJEU has created further uncertainties, and opened the gate for a potential flow of complaints against national collective management schemes', C Sganga, 'The eloquent silence of Soulier and Doke and its critical implications for EU copyright law' (2017) 12(4) *JIPLP* 321, 330.
[394] Rosati (n 58) 166.

The narrow scope of this system seems to be in line with the three-step test.[395] But it also has shortcomings. Determining if a work is out-of-commerce requires a reasonable effort to assess the availability to the public in the customary channels of commerce, taking into account the characteristics of the particular work, what amounts to 'reasonable effort' is to be determined by MS (Recital 38). Similar to the 'diligent search' required for orphan works, this would still require time and effort. Given the uncertainties around 'reasonable effort' and 'customary channels of commerce',[396] this provision has the potential to be misunderstood or misused.

The determination of 'representativeness' is another big issue, which will vary by sector and country, and cannot be subject to strict numbers/percentages.[397] Furthermore, opting out from ECLs foreseen in Articles 8 and 12 should not be 'complicated and onerous as to discourage authors'.[398] The interpretation and implementation of out-of-commerce provisions are still ongoing,[399] and seeing more examples of current practices of heritage institutions for out-of-commerce would be helpful.[400]

CDSM Article 12, on the other hand, is not limited to out-of-commerce or heritage institutions like Article 8. It gives the MS the option of creating ECL regimes where CMOs with sufficient representation enter into licensing agreements that can extend to outsiders, as long as it is 'only applied within well-defined areas of use, where obtaining authorisations from rightholders on an individual basis is typically onerous and impractical' and rightholders are given the option to easily opt-out at any time.[401]

Recital 44 suggests that ECL is a 'well-established practice in several Member States', and hints at the intention to remedy the impact of the *Soulier and Doke* decision.[402] It is an optional provision, although the level of flexibility that Member States have in their implementation is uncertain (whether it has to follow the exact wording of CDSM, or can be changed based on national differences, as hinted in Recital 46).[403] Such a system could work to supplement the already mandatory

[395] Rosati (n 58) 196.

[396] Rosati (n 58) 172–73.

[397] L Guibault and S Schroff, 'Extended collective licensing for the use of out-of-commerce works in Europe: a matter of legitimacy vis-a-vis rights holders' (2018) 49 *IIC* 916.

[398] European Copyright Society, 'Comment of the European Copyright Society on the Implementation of the Extended Collective Licensing Rules (arts 8 and 12) of the Directive (EU) 2019/790 on Copyright in the Digital Single Market (2020).

[399] For up-to-date resources on these works post-CDSM, see Europeana Out of Commerce works Working Group pro.europeana.eu/project/out-of-commerce-works-working-group. For their ongoing overview of national implementations, see europeana.atlassian.net/wiki/spaces/EF/pages/2406514779/Out+of+commerce+works+National+Implementations+Overview.

[400] For example, M Stockton-Brown, 'Out-of-Commerce: How the Existing Copyright Practices in Film Archives Impact on Widening Public Access to Cultural Heritage' (2022) 13 *JIPITEC* 3.

[401] CDSM, art 12. The ECL system was previously introduced in Section 4.3.3.

[402] Rosati (n 58) 225.

[403] European Copyright Society (n 398).

ECL foreseen for out-of-commerce works in Article 8. Article 12(6) required a report on the use of licensing mechanisms by April 2021, which demonstrated that such systems were used in Member States for varying purposes.[404]

Since Recital 37 foresees this system to also be applicable for different types of works (including photographs – not covered by the Orphan Works Directive) and 'never-in-commerce' works, this provision then applies to other special cases addressed in this chapter. While it would be easier for their digitisation, this could be too broad a brushstroke. It is understandable that most orphan works are out-of-commerce, but the inclusion of unpublished works under ECL might be a step too far.

Turning to the UK out of commerce system, CDSM provisions for out-of-commerce will not be implemented following Brexit. An ECL system was adopted in 2014 in section 116B and 116C of CDPA. The short licence period foreseen in the ECL is seen as an opportunity to get the digitisation projects off the ground and then review the scheme when the renewal time arrives.[405] Only one application for ECL was made by the Copyright Licensing Agency, which was subsequently withdrawn in 2018 citing the 'evolving legal framework that may affect the regulation of national extended collective licensing systems'.[406] The status of UK ECL is also currently uncertain.[407]

In the US, section 108(e) of the Copyright Law states that reproduction and distribution of full works are allowed 'if the library or archives has first determined, on the basis of a reasonable investigation, that a copy or phonorecord of the copyrighted work cannot be obtained at a fair price'.[408] The 2017 Discussion Document on section 108 recommends including more types of work under the preservation clause, so that it is not limited to unpublished works.[409] Their mass digitisation is problematic, as it requires proving that works cannot be obtained through normal commercial channels. If the settlement agreement in *Google* had

[404] Commission report on the use of collective licensing mechanisms with an extended effect under Article 12(6) of Directive 2019/790/EU on copyright and related rights in the Digital Single Market SWD(2021) 337 final (Brussels, 29 November 2021). For responses from Member States (from 2021), see digital-strategy.ec.europa.eu/en/library/reports-collective-management-and-extended-licensing.

[405] Tryggvadóttir (n 88) 255–63.

[406] 'CLA's application for extended collective licensing: update' (ALCS, 30 April 2018) www.alcs.co.uk/news/clas-application-for-extended-collective-licensing-update/.

[407] UK IPO, 'Extended Collective Licensing (ECL): Guidance for relevant licensing bodies applying to run ECL schemes' (2016). But this was withdrawn in 2021 'as a court ruling made the legal status of ECL uncertain': www.gov.uk/government/publications/extended-collective-licensing. Despite the ECL schemes being unworkable since Soulier case (due to supremacy of EU law), the UK can now consider and approve ECL applications: IPO, 'Policy Paper: Collective Rights Management in the UK' (1 January 2024): www.gov.uk/government/publications/ensuring-high-standards-in-collective-rights-management/collective-rights-management-in-the-uk.

[408] US Copyright Act, s 108.

[409] 'there are instances in which a preservation copy of a published work may be necessary, such as when that work is out-of-print or is orphaned. By allowing copies to be made of works disseminated to the public, the Model Statutory Language allows preservation copies to be made of all works that may need to be preserved': 108 Discussion Document 2017.

been successful, and if Google had been allowed to set up a Book Registry to track opt-outs, this would have minimised the out-of-commerce issue.[410]

In the 2015 US Copyright Office Report, the suitability of fair use for the digitisation of out-of-commerce works is questioned and setting up ECL (but with a narrow scope) is suggested as a solution, also giving examples from the European jurisdictions that involved some form of ECL (the UK, France and Germany).[411] The 'pilot programme' for ECL included only literary works, photographs and pictorial or graphic works published as illustrations, diagrams or similar adjuncts to literary works.[412] The recommended beneficiaries of this ECL system were the stakeholders acting on non-commercial research and education purposes,[413] so the report did not directly limit itself to the digitisation acts of libraries and archives. For non-members' works, CMOs would be responsible for conducting the diligent search.[414] But the 2015 US Copyright Office report did not determine who would bear the costs of setting up a CMO infrastructure. Setting up such CMOs and the system for them to negotiate on behalf of all rightholders is particularly risky when this 'pilot programme' was only foreseen as running for five years.[415]

In summary, when dealing with the legal developments for out-of-commerce, two lessons emerge: First, there is an overlap between such works and other special cases handled here. This difference in classification and overlapping solutions already creates some confusion. Second, the brief overview of legal developments shows a lot of incomplete developments in the chosen jurisdictions. In the EU and the UK, the solution of collective management of rights for out-of-commerce is put forward, then quashed with *Soulier and Doke*, then re-ignited with CDSM in the EU and with Brexit in the UK, but more time will be needed to assess the full extent. Furthermore, the ECL system for other works (beyond out of commerce) now exists as an optional provision in Article 12 CDSM – which still leaves some flexibility of interpretation by Member States. Similarly, the US also shows some back and forth, first with the Google Books Proposed Settlement, its refusal, and US Copyright Office recommendations – also not solved. Any such solution that requires an organisation acting on behalf of non-members will need a solid tracking system, and easy opt-out mechanisms. What Google's Book Registry, or the French BnF mechanism were planning to achieve might not be possible in every sector and jurisdiction due to the availability of resources and the willingness of stakeholders.

[410] US Copyright Office, 'Orphan Works and Mass Digitization' (2015) 14.
[411] ibid 83–86.
[412] ibid 7.
[413] ibid 89.
[414] ibid 8.
[415] US Copyright Office, 'Orphan Works and Mass Digitization' (2015) 102; P Samuelson, 'Extended Collective Licensing to Enable Mass Digitisation: A Critique of the US Copyright Office Proposal' (2016) 38(2) *EIPR* 75, 77.

Unfortunately, this seems to be a pattern for all access solutions and special cases; they are subject to different concerns and inconsistent legal solutions (inconsistent over time, and inconsistent between jurisdictions), that are also affected by the practice (stakeholder reactions, projects and cases). This confirms that the existing law clashes with the digitisation of cultural heritage but also leaves us with an incomplete picture of its extent and how it can be improved.

4.5. Role of WIPO

The final question to ask is whether all of the inconsistencies in legal approaches are addressed at the international level. WIPO Standing Committee on Copyright and Related Rights (SCCR) has been focusing on libraries and museums, and has produced valuable resources and contributions from the stakeholders. Although the idea of a wider exception emerged a long time ago, there is also resistance from the rightholders, their representatives, and some governments against the creation of a new exception and a preference for soft law approaches, while others want to continue gathering more evidence.[416] A few of the SCCR outputs should be recognised here.

The first category is the comprehensive comparative studies. One of these is the 'Study on Copyright Limitations and Exceptions for Libraries and Archives' by Kenneth Crews (first in 2008, then in 2014, 2015 and 2017),[417] analysing the 191 WIPO countries and their copyright statutes specifically focusing on general library exceptions, research and study, making available, preservation and anti-circumvention – highlighting the vast range of practices. A similar study was done for museums in 2015, showing that the digitisation activities were falling into the uncertain territory, where museums were rarely permitted (45 out of 188 WIPO members at the time).[418] A revised report focusing on museums included 37 interviews, demonstrating lack of awareness and understanding on copyright impact, and diverse licensing practices in acquiring works.[419]

The second category is textual suggestions, such as the 'Working Document Containing Comments on and Textual Suggestions towards an Appropriate International Legal Instrument (in whatever form) on Exceptions and Limitations for Libraries and Archives', first in 2012, then 2013. The proposed texts from Member States focused on topics of: (i) preservation, (ii) right of reproduction, (iii) legal deposit, (iv) lending, (v) parallel imports, (vi) cross-border uses, (vii) orphan, retracted and withdrawn and out of commerce works, (viii) limitation

[416] S Wyber 'WIPO, Copyright and Libraries' in Coates (n 149) 220–44.

[417] Crews Study (n 44), this report has been used for comparing EU exceptions prior to CDSM changes in Sections 4.2.2.1, 4.3.4.1 and 4.3.4.2.

[418] Canat and Guibault (n 204).

[419] Y Benhamou, 'Revised Report on Copyright Practices and Challenges of Museums' WIPO SCCR/38/5 (2019).

of liability for libraries and archives), (ix) technological measures of protection, (x) contracts, and (xi) right to translate.[420]

Other WIPO resources include the 'Informal Chart on Limitations and Exceptions for Libraries and Archives' that proposed limitations and exceptions to enable digital preservation and digital lending, orphan works provisions that adequately compensated the rightholders, and limited liability for good faith activities of libraries and archives.[421] There was also a round of typology analyses in 2019, separate for libraries, then museums and archives.[422]

As of 2024, WIPO is addressing the matter with toolkits – a preservation toolkit was released in 2023,[423] and a toolkit on access is expected by the end of 2025.[424] The toolkit on Preservation provides a background on preservation activities and considerations, and charts with recommendations and example language that can be utilised by Member States that are planning to create a preservation statute. The categories are:

- Category A: Who may use the exception? (libraries, archives, museums, research and education …)
- Category B: What works may be copied or used? (provisions on works in collection, unpublished, digital works, availability of work on market …)
- Category C: Why may works be copied or used? (provisions on preservation, replacement, copies for other libraries, preserving a work in the collection of another institution, completion …)
- Category D: How may works be copied or used? (provisions on digital uses, copyright notices …)
- Category E: Additional provisions and conditions (three-step test, limitation of liability, circumvention of TPM, defined statutory terms …)[425]

As one of the Toolkit's authors, Kenneth Crews suggested elsewhere that treaties can become 'contentious, time-consuming, and politically charged' and finding any common ground amongst all WIPO members is difficult, so it could make sense to choose to offer guidance instead of a treaty[426] – which currently seems to be the case. While the benefits of such toolkits might be limited for jurisdictions with (partially) functioning systems for preservation and access, including those

[420] 'Working Document Containing Comments on and Textual Suggestions Towards an Appropriate International Legal Instrument (in whatever form) on Exceptions and Limitations for Libraries and Archives' WIPO SCCR/26/3 (2013).
[421] 'Informal Chart on Limitations and Exceptions for Libraries and Archives' WIPO SCCR/34/5 (2017).
[422] KD Crews, 'Copyright Limitations and Exceptions for Libraries: Typology Analysis' WIPO SCCR/38/4 (2019).
[423] Preservation Toolkit (n 5).
[424] 'Draft implementation plan for the work program on limitations and exceptions and preliminary comments received by March 29, 2024' WIPO SCCR/45/6 (2024).
[425] Preservation Toolkit (n 5) Appendix: The Charts of Statutory Elements, pp 26–38.
[426] Crews, *Copyright Law* (n 83).

addressed here, they might be very useful to other jurisdictions who need guidance on these matters.

There has also been some criticism of handling preservation and access as separate issues.[427] However, it is understandable that preservation was picked first, being the less problematic area. So far, WIPO's impact is incomplete, which might change depending on how the Toolkit on Access will address the matters. It will also be challenging to determine to what extent will the Toolkits be used by Member States to improve their laws on digitising heritage, and whether the outcome will prompt another set of studies and discussions – which is likely, given the patterns observed in this book.

4.6. Conclusion

This chapter addressed the impact of the laws in the chosen jurisdictions and demonstrated that all three areas (preservation, access and special cases) are subject to different legal problems. Preservation triggers reproduction and adaptation, and can be achieved with defences specifically for preservation. Providing access is more complicated as these acts can trigger reproduction, communication, distribution, public performance/display and lending rights, and access to in-copyright works require licensing or copyright defences. Special cases are subject to different rules in how they are identified and handled, limiting access to them.

For this clash, specific issues that require further clarification and amendments include:

- classification of the activities of heritage institutions in the light of unclear boundaries of economic rights;
- different approaches to digital exhaustion and lending based on relevant CJEU case law;
- interpretation of CDL following *Hachette*;
- over-reliance on licensing in most activities, giving the power to publishers;
- US section 108 not being amended despite the efforts in the past decades;
- AI/TDM providing a new type of access and causing a new wave of lawsuits;
- Brexit putting the UK in an unfortunate position, which was partly softened by 2014 changes, but the difference will only grow;
- The orphan works system is dysfunctional – but is handled with out-of-commerce provisions in the EU and fair use in the US;
- WIPO being unable to solve the matter due to differences of Member States.

[427] InfoJustice, 'Libraries, archives and museums call on WIPO to finalize the Toolkit on Preservation without further changes' (Infojustice.org, 31 May 2023) infojustice.org/archives/45283. See also Presentations by Sutton, Crews and Pantalony for the SCCR 44th Session: www.wipo.int/meetings/en/details.jsp?meeting_id=78391.

CDSM only partially harmonises the matters. It is also difficult to determine how the case law is going to develop post-CDSM, and to determine the direction the UK will take. In comparison, the US system seems to work better because of the fair use exception but has not been significantly revised in this area lately. WIPO is also not providing a definitive solution, which could lead to different uptakes and interpretations in the future. This leaves us with a piecemeal legal picture. If the goal is to increase digitisation, can this be achieved through smaller changes or new legal instruments? How we answer this will change based on the theory we choose and the stakeholder we prioritise. But there is also a limit to how much law can be changed.

This chapter confirms the outcomes of the previous chapters: that copyright clashes with digitisation – from the perspective of cultural heritage institutions. Despite the many attempts at changing them, the laws in this area are still narrow, unclear and inconsistent as regards their purposes and jurisdictions. The next chapter on practice will also demonstrate how stakeholders embrace different approaches and the uneasy balance this causes.

5

Clash in Practice: Competing Interests, Reactions and Interview Findings

Theory, laws and practice are all connected, so it is time to turn to the final clash. As multiple parties have different priorities for the digitisation of cultural heritage, it makes sense to consider the needs of stakeholders.[1] It is possible to divide them into two main sides for this specific problem of copyright. We can place the public on one side of the debate, wanting heritage to be safe and, more controversially, easily accessible. Cultural heritage institutions could also be placed on the side of 'more access'. Then on the other side we can have the rightsholders, publishers, producers and other representatives, who are more concerned about keeping own works less accessible, so that they can enjoy the benefits of exclusive rights.

But this division is imperfect, as the distinction between what is owned by an individual versus the heritage of all humankind is the passage of time, and even then, heritage belongs to everyone and no one, as suggested in chapters one and three. Furthermore, the changes in copyright law, as illustrated in chapters two and four, also require constantly re-evaluating the position of stakeholders. This chapter will evaluate the relevant stakeholders again, before delving into past reactions to projects and cases. This will be followed with findings from interviews conducted between 2023–2024 for this book.

5.1. (Re)Introducing the Stakeholders: Competing Interests

The first group is the cultural heritage institutions. This group of stakeholders consists of libraries, archives and museums.[2] They are not a homogenous body: they hold different objects (eg, rare/common or 2D/3D), have different attitudes

[1] U Suthersanen, 'Copyright Law: A Stakeholders' Palimpsest' in F Macmillan (ed), *New Directions in Copyright Law: Vol 5* (Cheltenham, Edward Elgar, 2007).

[2] See also Section 2.4.

towards handling of objects (eg, archives are more accustomed than libraries to discarding items) or towards cooperating with private companies (eg, US libraries were more eager than EU ones on participating in Google Books). Some, but not all, receive government funding. As the custodians of cultural heritage, these institutions are responsible to the public for keeping works safe and accessible.[3] In ideal conditions, this group would seek to digitise the maximum amount of works for the minimum amount of money. They would ideally also provide (or be obliged to provide, due to conditional funding) some level of access to their digitised content while also ensuring that certain sensitive works are not released to the public. For this group, arguing for wider copyright exceptions and/or easier and cheaper licensing solutions is likely the most logical path. At the same time, these institutions are responsible for other societal goals, such as supporting artists: therefore they also need to maintain good relationships with the rightsholders and their estates, and embrace different levels of appetite for legal risks.

The second group is the users of heritage, including parties both with commercial and non-commercial motives. While the defences introduced in previous chapter have a clear line between commercial and non-commercial users, it is not as clear in practice, even to the users themselves. Copies that start out as non-commercial could end up being included in commercial projects by some parties. It is also common that public projects rely on commercial partners, supporting otherwise impossible and expensive research needing digital materials. The materials in the public domain might not be sufficient for more complicated and niche research.[4] For the users, copyright is an obstacle to freely using digitised material, especially for access off premises. Commercial users will have the added complexity of not being able to rely on copyright exceptions since most have the 'non-commercial' or 'not-for-profit' condition, in line with the three-step test. A cultural heritage institution can take a risk-based approach in what it shares, and take works down if the rightsholder comes forward, whereas a commercial user cannot take the same risk so easily, necessitating licensing solutions.

Because of their unique nature, this chapter hesitates to identify 'the digitiser' as a separate stakeholder. Digitisers include both parties digitising for own projects (such as Google), and parties digitising for other institutions (such as contractors). While their initiative helps increase the digitisation of heritage, private digitisers are not really a sub-group of either side in the debate. They are very likely to be closer to the 'users' category with their commercial motives. But at the same time, their actions and motives might be shaped by their contracts with heritage institutions and/or publishers.[5]

[3] But it was also argued that public libraries cannot be seen as just one of the stakeholders, because they carry greater importance based on their public role: (O Fischman Afori, 'The Battle over Public E-Libraries – Taking Stock and Moving Ahead' (2013) 44 *IIC* 392, 393). See also J Band and B Butler, 'Why Libraries Need Limitations and Exceptions' in J Coates, V Owen and S Reilly (eds), *Navigating Copyright for Libraries* (Berlin, De Gruyter Saur, 2022).

[4] J Purday, 'Think Culture: Europeana.eu from Concept to Construction' (2009) 1 *DigItalia* 105, 109.

[5] However, this book is focused on the digitisation activities of heritage institutions with mostly non-commercial nature.

The interests of authors, publishers and producers are similar. For authors, it makes sense to rely on copyright protection.[6] Understandably, they are also less likely to argue for the expansion of copyright expansions. At the same time, they are not a homogenous body either, consisting of individuals with different priorities and attitudes towards the circulation of their works, with some authors willingly relying on open access. An additional problem is what happens when the author is missing or dead, and therefore not part of decision making. Even if such works are no longer profitable, it is necessary to remember that any re-emerging author could still be concerned with attribution, integrity, or wanting to keep their works hidden, especially if they are unpublished.[7]

Publishers and producers would also likely argue for stronger copyright protection. These groups also enter into contracts with heritage institutions, that are sometimes more restrictive than what copyright exceptions allow. But if these contracts are the only way of accessing these works (for example, the example of e-lending), or if the institutions are unaware of the exceptions, publishers could be successful in reaching advantageous terms. The latest developments on online libraries during the pandemic, and the reaction to the Internet Archive's controlled digital lending (CDL) practices, hints that this group is consistent in their position favouring stronger copyright protection, even in unusual circumstances.

Parties representing authors, such as the CMOs, can potentially be placed on the same side as authors. But CMOs have to also pay attention to how to set up systems that benefit them and their members.[8] They also represent non-members under circumstances explained in the previous chapter (ECL). This group is also unlikely to lobby for wider copyright exceptions for access to digitised heritage.

Although not really a stakeholder in the same sense, the policymakers are the final category. The main priority for this stakeholder group should be listening to all stakeholders equally and creating a working system that generates enough compliance, whilst not causing too much formality and workload.[9] They need to decide on what is the ideal solution, whether to create or harmonise copyright exceptions, or to solve the issues with licensing. If the solution is to rely on ECL, which seems to be the current direction in the EU, then they need to work together

[6] See generally JC Ginsburg, 'Exceptional Authorship: The Role of Copyright Exceptions in Promoting Creativity' in S Frankel and D Gervais (eds), *The Evolution and Equilibrium of Copyright in the Digital Age* (Cambridge, CUP, 2014).

[7] The justifications for their protection were in ch 3.

[8] Gervais points out the Recital 3 of Directive 2014/26 on CMOs and questions how they can both be on authors side and also fulfil their cultural functions to 'promote the diversity of cultural expression': D Gervais, 'The cultural role(s) of collective management organizations' (2018) 40(6) *EIPR* 349.

[9] For impact of lobbying, see A Vetulani-Cęgiel, 'EU Copyright Law, Lobbying and Transparency of Policy-Making: The cases of sound recordings term extension and orphan works provisions' (2015) 6(2) *JIPITEC* 147; B Farrand, 'Lobbying and Lawmaking in the European Union: The Development of Copyright Law and the Rejection of the Anti-Counterfeiting Trade Agreement' (2015) 35(3) *Oxford Journal of Legal Studies* 487; C Spillane and R Heath, 'Copyright power matrix' (Politico.eu, 16 February 2017) www.politico.eu/interactive/copyright-reform-power-matrix-gunther-oettinger-european-commission-eu-policy.

with the CMOs and carefully decide what should count as adequate representation. If there are additional conditions, such as setting up a register to track certain works, these systems also need to function properly. However, if the other stakeholders are unclear about the scope of defences or not willing to apply for licences, it means that this category of stakeholders is failing their responsibilities.

Therefore, there are multiple stakeholders in this problem with differing attitudes and priorities. This situation amplifies the clashes on legal developments covered so far, which are struggling to reach a balance between the different needs, in line with the theoretical clash. That is why multiple approaches to the same problem emerge, appealing to different stakeholders in varying degrees.

5.2. Overview of Past Developments and Reactions

This section will provide an overview of publicly available reactions to legal developments in the US, EU and UK, through court documents (such as amicus curiae briefs), stakeholder responses to public consultations, and public statements made by the relevant stakeholders. This section will then be followed by interviews with the heritage sector, therefore reaching a balanced overview of the practice.[10]

5.2.1. United States

Reactions to the Google Books Project and the subsequent lawsuit are an excellent example of clashing interests of the parties in practice. We are now familiar with how it ends,[11] but we should also consider how it began. The motives behind the project are largely utilitarian; as identified by its creators, Google's company mission is 'to organize the world's information and make it universally accessible and useful'.[12] The project envisioned by Google was two-fold: for the first part, the Google Partner Programme was based on contracts with publishers, which directed users to purchasing from publishers without interfering too much with the publishers' interests (only three snippets per search term, and excluding certain reference books).[13] However, some of them also still ended up suing Google in the *Association of American Publishers v Google* case, as there were concerns that

[10] The order of jurisdictions is different from the previous chapter since US developments were taking place slightly ahead of EU. See also Section 2.1 for early digitisation developments.

[11] See Section 4.3.4.5 for fair use.

[12] 'About': about.google/.

[13] K Gbegnon, 'Digitized Scholarship and the "Library" Concept: Allowing the History of the Library Exemption to Inform How We View Google's Digitized Library' (2007) 29 *Hastings Communications and Entertainment Law Journal* 75, 77.

Google would become the dominant portal for both current and out-of-commerce books and disrupt traditional publishing models.[14]

The second part was the Google Book Search. Early copyright concerns did not prevent Google from going ahead.[15] Some parties found it worrying that Google could control which items had exposure; there were additional concerns about the 'bucket effect' in which works become less accessible due to the sheer volume.[16] However, it is likely that some participants did not notice at first that the material was for the machines, not regular library users.[17] It is not certain whether Google earned enough from the project to justify its investment through the advertisement revenue,[18] but the project allowed them to improve their search results and to use the data for various non-display purposes. Another problem was Google's secretive approach towards partner libraries. When the contracts were being negotiated for the Google Library project, the libraries had no way of knowing the terms that Google negotiated with other libraries, which was unusual at the time.[19] Due to the risks they perceived, library partners had embraced different approaches to what they provided.[20]

Concerned by Google's scanning without permission, the Authors Guild filed a class-action lawsuit. A month later, five publishers (McGraw Hill, Pearson, Penguin, Simon & Schuster and John Wiley & Sons) also sued Google, followed by a French publishing company suing it separately.[21] It is noteworthy that none of those parties went on to sue the libraries, who made their collections available to Google for scanning. This is interesting because these libraries also received digital copies, which would not have been achieved by §108 of the US Copyright Act.[22]

[14] M Hirschorn, 'The Hapless Seed' *The Atlantic* (June 2007) www.theatlantic.com/magazine/archive/2007/06/the-hapless-seed/305892. Marcum and Schonfeld also suggest: 'publishers were generally supportive when they thought they were Google's only partners': D Marcum and RC Schonfeld, *Along Came Google: A History of Library Digitization* (Princeton, Princeton University Press, 2021) 76.

[15] Wu questions whether Google should have declared the project a non-profit from the start, to alleviate parties' concerns: T Wu, 'What Ever Happened to Google Books' *The New Yorker* (11 September 2015) www.newyorker.com/business/currency/what-ever-happened-to-google-books. Stromberg and Sheth also question whether digitisation should be under the direction of a governmental or intergovernmental organisation, 'akin to NASA for space exploration or, at a global level, the United Nations, instead of a private for-profit corporation': E Stromberg and R Sheth, 'Google Books: Liberating the World's Information, or Appropriating It?' (The Kenan Institute for Ethics, 2018).

[16] R Litwin, 'On Google's Monetization of Libraries' (*Library Juice*, 2004) libr.org/juice/issues/vol7/LJ_7.26.html#3.

[17] M Borghi and S Karapapa, 'Non-Display Uses of Copyright Works' (2011) 1 *QMJIP* 21, 25.

[18] It was calculated in 2007 that the cost of scanning 32 million books would cost 800 million dollars: J Toobin, 'Google's Moon Shot' *The New Yorker* (28 January 2007) www.newyorker.com/magazine/2007/02/05/googles-moon-shot.

[19] Marcum and Schonfeld (n 14) 83–84.

[20] Oxford, Harvard and Stanford only allowed the digitisation of public domain works and Stanford did not allow anything published after 1964: Toobin (n 18). See also Marcum and Schonfeld (n 14) 91–94.

[21] Gbegnon (n 13) 80.

[22] A Alterwain, 'Google Books and Digitisation of Libraries: Fair Use or Extension of Copyright?' (2007) 3 *Convergence* 139.

But it is more beneficial generally to target Google as both the party who digitised and made available, and who is more likely to provide satisfactory compensation, instead of heritage institutions with limited resources.

Initially it was expected that Google would pay the plaintiffs more than the court would order, so as to avoid a lawsuit.[23] Lessig argued that it would be in both Google's and the publisher's interest to settle, because Google did not want to wait and the publishers wanted to set a precedent of being paid in such circumstances.[24] So, it was in the interests of multiple stakeholders not to go to trial. On the other hand, many observers wanted to follow the case, to see how other similar business models could go forward.[25]

The main elements of the proposed settlement agreement were as follows: '(i) Google would pay compensation, (ii) Google would be able to digitise and use books, provided that it shares 63 per cent of the revenue with the copyright owners, (iii) Google would set up a Book Rights Registry at its own expense, in order to distribute compensation payments and revenue share and to locate missing owners, (iv) participating libraries would have access to entire repertoire, (v) Google and Book Rights Registry may decide on new commercial systems to exploit books and (vi) US public would have access to greater portions of texts.'[26]

Nevertheless, more than 400 letters were filed with the court: some were amicus curiae briefs, while others were objections and opt-out requests.[27] Some letters supported the agreement because it fitted their goals, such as helping with distance learning,[28] or increasing the volume of available e-books to enliven the market.[29] The preservation and access benefits of digitisation were also raised by parties as reasons for supporting Google.[30] Some letters were not convinced by their representation as a group.[31] One major aspect that received much criticism

[23] Toobin (n 18).

[24] ibid.

[25] K De La Durantaye, 'Finding a Home for Orphans: Google Book Search and Orphan Works Law in the United States and Europe' (2011) 21 *Fordham Intellectual Property, Media & Entertainment Law Journal* 229, 258.

[26] S McCausland, 'Googling the Archives: Ideas from the Google Books Settlement on Solving Orphan Works Issues in Digital Access Projects' (2009) 6(2) *SCRIPT-ed* 377, 386.

[27] *The Authors Guild et al v Google Inc*, 1:2005cv08136. For court documents, including ones below, see dockets.justia.com/docket/new-york/nysdce/1:2005cv08136/273913.

[28] 'Approval would have a powerful impact on the critical issues of quality standards, research, teacher preparedness and new technologies': Letter addressed to Judge Denny Chin from John G Flores, dated 17 August 2009 re: The United States Distance Learning Association (19 August 2009) Filing 139.

[29] Amicus Curiae Brief of Sony Electronics Inc in Support of Proposed Google Book Search Settlement (8 September 2009) Filing 274.

[30] 'Prior to our partnership with Google, we digitized between 5,000 and 10,000 works each year, a rate that put us ahead of other digitizing libraries and well behind the books, which were already decomposing before we could get to them. At that rate, we estimated that it would take us 900 years … Our partnership with Google, which the settlement will preserve, will enable us to preserve eight million works in a decade': Letter addressed to Judge Denny Chin from Paul N Courant (on behalf of University of Michigan)(10 September 2009) Filing 514.

[31] 'Writers are individuals. We are not a "class" that's somehow reachable with one shout … If someone wants the rights to my books, they can take a few minutes to ask. That's not too much to

was the opt-out mechanism, going against the general rule of seeking permission and giving a default permission to Google. In the 2009 statement of Marybeth Peters, US Register of Copyrights, it was argued that this was not a settlement agreement but an instrument that solves past infringements and gives Google the right to keep scanning without any legal issues.[32] It was also suggested that compulsory licences should only be used when the market fails, but that was not the situation there.[33]

Concerns about competition law were also brought up,[34] especially on how: (i) Google would be the agent in price setting; (ii) the opt-out system would give Google monopoly over orphan works; and (iii) there was a need to mitigate the market power created by the potential approval of the settlement.[35] Another issue that received attention was the cut-off date in the settlement agreement. The definition of 'book' included works written or published in the United States and published before 5 January 2009. This was argued to be too wide because it covered more books than Google had scanned at that point,[36] and was also too narrow because it meant that Google would not actually achieve its goal of scanning every book ever written.

After the court hearing on 7 October 2009, the parties had to go back to negotiations and come up with a narrower settlement agreement (the amended settlement agreement).[37] The amended settlement agreement included: (i) an independent fiduciary for unclaimed works; (ii) a 10–year period for unclaimed works, then the money goes only to charity; (iii) restrictions on the discounts that Google can apply; (iv) well-defined future business models; and (v) more time to decide whether to remove the works from Google. The amended agreement applied only to books published in the United States, Canada, the UK or Australia or registered in the United States. The registry proposed by Google was impressive in terms of shouldering the costs of launching and initial operations of a new registry ($34.5 million).[38] But the amended settlement agreement was met with negative reactions (on adequacy of class notice and representation, scope of relief, competition, privacy and copyright). From a copyright perspective, the problem with the amended settlement agreement was the opt-out model and its

request': Letter addressed to Judge Denny Chin from Scott James (aka Kemble Scott) (13 August 2009) Filing 131.

[32] Statement of Marybeth Peters the Register of Copyrights before the Committee on the Judiciary, 'Hearing on Competition and Commerce in Digital Books: The Proposed Google Book Settlement' (2009).

[33] But there was also a positive attitude towards the aspects of setting up a registry and offering books in formats accessible to the blind and print-disabled: ibid.

[34] Objection of Amazon.com, Inc to Proposed Settlement (2009) Filing 206.

[35] RC Picker, 'The Google Book Search Settlement: A New Orphan-Works Monopoly?' (2009) Working Paper No.462, 3.

[36] Peters (n 32).

[37] Amended Settlement Agreement, Filing 770, also available at authorsguild.org/app/uploads/2012/08/Amended-Settlement-Agreement.pdf.

[38] ibid.

incompatibility with international instruments.[39] Fair use criteria were applied, and Google's use was found to be transformative. The case was rejected by the Supreme Court in 2016, but its influence remains. The same time period also saw the creation of HathiTrust, a large repository including books both scanned by Google and other libraries, who were also sued by the Authors Guild (also found to be fair use).[40] The project still exists, but at a slower pace.[41]

There are lessons to be learned from Google; such as how to plan a project of this size, how to manage the expectations of the parties and when to take legal risks.[42] But this outcome is unique to US copyright law, as the outcome would have been very different without 'fair use'. However, there was also disappointment in how this project did not fulfil its promise, but instead breathed 'commercial air into manner we deal with our cultural legacy'.[43] The availability of digitised materials would be very different if the Google settlement was successful, both positive for greater access but also negative for placing heritage under the control of a private party.

The US Copyright Office Report on Orphan Works and Mass Digitization dated June 2015 also referred to the *Google Books* case and the legal developments in other countries especially around ECL, recommending: (i) a limited liability model for commercial and non-commercial use of orphan works following a diligent search, (ii) an ECL regime as a long-term solution to mass digitisation, starting with a pilot project.[44] This received responses including from libraries wanting to continue with fair use, and authors and publishers organisations supporting ECL, with the parties also noting the size difference between the US and the countries that had ECL systems in place at the time.[45] Whether the embracing of ECL on a wider scale at the EU level will encourage the US to reconsider their approach remains to be seen.

[39] *Authors Guild v Google, Inc* 770 F Supp 2d 666, 679–680 (SDNY 2011).

[40] See Section 4.3.4.5 for fair use criteria and its application to Google Books and HathiTrust. See also Marcum and Schonfeld (n 14) 160–87.

[41] It was mentioned in a 2017 article that there is still a Google team that is responsible for digitising books, but the process is more selective and much slower than it was between 2010 and 2011: S Rosenberg, 'How Google Book Search Got Lost' (*wired.com*, 4 November 2017) www.wired.com/2017/04/how-google-book-search-got-lost; A Marini, 'How the Google Books team moved 90,000 books across a continent' (Google, 27 January 2023): blog.google/products/search/google-books-library-project.

[42] A recent study on the impact of Google Books on the market for physical books suggests that the digitisation has increased the sales of an average book by 5%: A Nagaraj and I Reimer, 'Digitization and the Market for Physical Works: Evidence from the Google Books Project' (2023) 15(4) *American Economic Journal: Economic Policy* 428.

[43] C Castro and R de Queiroz, 'The Song of the Sirens: Google Books Project and copyright in a digital age' (2013) 16(9) *Information, Communication & Society* 1441.

[44] Section US Copyright Office, 'Orphan Works and Mass Digitization' (2015). See Section 4.3.3 for ECL.

[45] 'U.S. has a population of roughly 318 million compared to the combined population of Denmark, Finland, Iceland, Norway and Sweden equally approximately 27 million': American Association of Law Libraries response to 2015 report. For this reply and responses to the 9 June 2015 Notice of Inquiry regarding Mass Digitization, see www.copyright.gov/policy/massdigitization/comments/.

Public reactions to the recent case of *Hachette v Internet Archive* also show the same pattern.[46] Prior to the Appeals decision, amicus curiae briefs in support of the appellant explain how it should be treated as transformative use and therefore fair use, supported with additional arguments such as: (i) how the CDL audience is different from market for licensed e-books,[47] (ii) how CDL does not reduce incentives for authors,[48] (iii) how nonprofit educational activities should not be treated as commercial,[49] (iv) how this decision would endanger the purpose of increasing public access to information,[50] and (v) how libraries can guard reader privacy more than commercial parties when it comes to who borrows what.[51] But there was also some neutrality, due to concerns on whether this case will cause the assumption that all CDL activities are the same.[52] Despite all the positives raised by the parties, the Appeals Court has upheld the decision on it not being fair use.[53] Unless it goes to the Supreme Court and gets overturned, this case will likely continue to be criticised by some stakeholders, while also encouraging caution regarding CDL. It would be interesting to see a narrower CDL application going to court in future in the US on whether fair use would lead to a different outcome.

Although it is outside the scope of this book, recent cases about generative AI have also demonstrated the similar pattern between two sides, authors/publishers versus big companies using their data with the former claiming that they lost the ability to license their works, and that this is already negatively affecting the profession.[54]

[46] See also Sections 4.3.1.4 and 4.3.4.5. For court documents, including ones below, see www.courtlistener.com/docket/67801014/hachette-book-group-inc-v-internet-archive/.

[47] Amicus Brief, on behalf of Jonathan Askin, Patricia Aufderheide, Dr Patrick Goold, Stacey M Lantagne, Sari Mazzurco, Sunoo Park, Aaron Perzanowski, Blake E Reid, Jason Schultz, Pamela Samuelson, and Jessica Silbey (18 December 2023) Filing 92.

[48] Amicus Brief, on behalf of Authors Alliance, Inc (21 December 2023) Filing 102.

[49] Amicus Brief, on behalf of Wikimedia Foundation, Creative Commons, and Project Gutenberg Literary Archive Foundation (22 December 2023) Filing 113.

[50] Amicus Brief, on behalf of Former and Current Law Library Directors, Professors, and Academics (22 December 2023) Filing 106.

[51] Amicus Brief, on behalf of Democracy & Technology, Library Freedom Project, and Public Knowledge (20 December 2023) Filing 100.

[52] Brief of Amicus Curiae Hathitrust in Support of Neither Party (22 December 2023) Filing 109.

[53] *Hachette Book Group Inc v Internet Archive* 115 F.4th 163 (2 Cir 2024).

[54] 'In a survey of authors conducted by The Authors Guild in March 2023 (early in ChatGPT's lifecycle), 69 percent of respondents said they consider generative AI a threat to their profession': Complaint against OpenAI: www.courtlistener.com/docket/67810584/1/authors-guild-v-openai-inc/; 'result in a shrinking of the profession as fewer human authors will be able to sustain a living practicing their craft, and shut out important, diverse voices': Authors Guild statement, authorsguild.org/advocacy/artificial-intelligence; *Complaint in Getty Images v Stability AI*, docs.justia.com/cases/federal/district-courts/delaware/dedce/1:2023cv00135/81407/1; Society of Authors, 'Long-awaited but vague – the SoA view on the government's artificial intelligence white paper' www2.societyofauthors.org/2023/03/31/long-awaited-but-vague-the-soa-view-on-the-governments-artificial-intelligence-white-paper.

5.2.2. European Union

Turning to the digitisation at the EU level, shortly after the announcement of the Google Books project, Jacques Chirac, along with the Premiers of Germany, Spain, Poland, Italy and Hungary, sent a letter to the President of the European Commission asking for the rich heritage of Europe to be digitised and made available,[55] which gave support to the European Digital Library, the European Information Society i2010 Initiative and the creation of Europeana. In terms of similarity to Google Books, the framework foreseen by the Commission also included a book rights registry, having a centralised database and requiring diligent searches. The scope, however, was not limited to books but also included other kinds of works.[56]

The competition with the American digitisation initiatives was emphasised more often in the early stages.[57] Google Books initially had only one European institution among the first five library partners: The Bodleian Library had already started digitising its collections in 2000 and was initially contacted by Google in 2002.[58] In the meantime, the rest of the European heritage sector was becoming aware of Google's digitisation attempts and making its own assumptions about what would happen to European heritage. One of the European parties that reacted to the Google Books Project was *Bibliothèque nationale de France* (BNF), expressing concern on Google dominating the digitisation efforts, and the available digitised heritage being mostly in the English language.[59] It was argued that if the same project were to take place in Europe, Google would be sued much faster because none of the European copyright exceptions covered digitising full works as Google was doing.[60] It was also predicted, before the lawsuit, that the philosophical differences in the European system and the existence of moral rights would prevent Google's actions (even though it was not removing attributions or affecting the works' integrity).[61]

There were also harsher reactions, one of them being from the President of the French Publishers Association (*Syndicat national de l'édition*) describing the

[55] 'Letter of 28 April 2005' available at ec.europa.eu/newsroom/dae/document.cfm?doc_id=5978; Purday (n 4) 105.

[56] De La Durantaye, 'Finding a Home' (n 25) 271.

[57] 'I do understand the fears of many publishers and libraries facing the market power of Google … if we do not reform our European copyright rules on orphan works and libraries swiftly, digitisation and the development of attractive content offers will not take place in Europe, but on the other side of the Atlantic.' (V Reding, 'Digital Europe – Europe's Fast Track to Economic Recovery' europa.eu/rapid/press-release_SPEECH-09-336_en.htm?locale=en.

[58] R Milne, 'The Google Library Project at Oxford' in W Miller and RM Pellen (eds), *Libraries and Google* (New York, Routledge, 2006) 24.

[59] JN Jeanneney and TL Fagan, *Google and the myth of universal knowledge: a view from Europe* (Chicago, University of Chicago Press, 2007).

[60] M Warnecke, 'Google's Legal Stance on U.S.'s Book Search May Have Less Support Under European Law' (2005) 71 *BNA Patent, Trademark & Copyright Journal* 206.

[61] ibid.

Google Books project as 'cultural rape'.[62] European Publishers reacted to Google's proposed settlement agreement in 2009, and expressed their concerns about American libraries digitising European works, especially the lack of representation of non-US rights holders in the plans for a rights registry and the narrow definition of 'commercially available books' in the settlement agreement.[63] There was an objection on behalf of France, claiming that the opt-out regime threatened French authors and cultural diversity and it disadvantaged them in a class action 'where they have no voice or representation'.[64]

Since the adoption of the i2010 Digital Libraries Initiative by the European Commission on 1 June 2005, bringing European heritage into one place emerged as a shared target. The report identified six main goals for European heritage: (i) providing wider access to the digitised public domain and complying with the Directive on the re-use of public sector information; (ii) stimulating digitisation and accessibility of in-copyright material and dealing with orphan works and out-of-distribution works by licensing solutions; (iii) giving Europeana a key role in European digital heritage; (iv) guaranteeing the sustainability of digitised and born-digital content; (v) finding sustainable funding for digitisation; and (vi) using public–private partnerships.[65] While some of these goals were (arguably) accomplished by the MoU on Out-of-Commerce, and the Orphan Works Directive soon after, and by CDSM much later, identifying Europeana's role is tricky.[66]

Europeana itself is not a digitisation project itself; it is a metadata aggregator bringing existing material together. Several challenges were identified in the early stages of Europeana: the funds were limited, at least compared to Google,[67] which contributed to the need to avoid legal risk from the beginning. Comité des Sages suggested the financial situation of the institutions should also be taken into consideration[68] and Member States were encouraged to make sure that

[62] K De La Durantaye, 'H is for Harmonization: The Google Book Search Settlement and Orphan Works Legislation in the European Union' (2010) 55 *New York Law School Law Review* 157, 158.

[63] 'a lot of European books are currently considered as non-commercially available (while they are still commercially available in Europe)' (letter addressed to Office of the Clerk from Ian Muller dated 31 August 2009 re: Koninklijke Van Gorcum BV objections to settlement agreement (31 August 2009) *Authors Guild v Google*, Filing 370. Other Dutch publishers also sent the same letter, which can be found under filings from 1 September 2009 onwards: dockets.justia.com/docket/new-york/nysdce/1:2005cv08136/273913.

[64] Memorandum of Law in Opposition to The Settlement Proposal on Behalf of the French Republic (8 September 2009) *Authors Guild v Google*, Filing 287.

[65] European Commission, M Lévy, E Niggemann, and J De Decker, 'The new renaissance: report of the Comité des Sages on bringing Europe's cultural heritage online' (2011) 4–7.

[66] Directive 2012/28/EU of the European Parliament and of the Council of 25 October 2012 on certain permitted uses of orphan works Text with EEA relevance OJ L 299/5 ('Orphan Works Directive'); Directive (EU) 2019/790 of the European Parliament and of the Council of 17 April 2019 on copyright and related rights in the Digital Single Market and amending Directives 96/9/EC and 2001/29/EC OJ L130/92 ('CDSM').

[67] Europeana's annual budget in 2010 was €2.5 million, while Google's annual revenue was $23.65 billion: De La Durantaye, 'Finding a Home' (n 25) 245.

[68] 'New Renaissance' (n 65) 13.

public funding for digitisation comes with the condition of adding the content to Europeana for free access,[69] especially with the Creative Commons Zero option (no rights reserved). Based on a 2009 report, only 48 per cent of the participating EU institutions had specific budgets for digitisation and only 30 per cent of the budget came from government grants, with the rest coming from internal resources.[70] In addition, participation in Europeana has not been equal among EU Member States.[71]

One of its main achievements has been deemed to create a consensus among European heritage institutions by taking different cataloguing systems from the participating institutions and turning them into a single metadata schema.[72] Europeana Pro also functions as a support network to provide training and guidance.[73] Several other key cultural heritage stakeholders are also identified by the European Commission in heritage developments in addition to Europeana, both at the European and international levels.[74]

Prior to the CDSM Directive, stakeholders opinions were also sought through a consultation on the EU copyright laws between 2013 and 2014.[75] Although some of the outcomes from this were reflected in the changes in CDSM, the consultation responses can provide more insight to positioning of the stakeholders.[76]

Regarding the scope of exclusive rights, specifically issues caused by multiple rights applying to digital transmissions (reproduction and making available) in cross-border scenarios,[77] end users and institutional users wanted more clarity on 'making available' and asked for the country-of-origin principle to be applied. The rights holders' group (authors, publishers and CMOs) refused changes and rejected the 'country of origin' approach to avoid forum shopping. They also saw the application of two rights to one act as a natural result of copyright and argued that introducing a unitary right would damage their interests and impede their chance to license their works.

[69] ibid 25.

[70] 'NUMERIC Study report: Study findings and proposals for sustaining the framework' (2009).

[71] However it is becoming more balanced. For 2009 statistics: De La Durantaye, 'Finding a Home' (n 25) 245 cf. Europeana, 'MS7: Content Report- Mar 2016 (April 2016).

[72] J Purday, 'Intellectual Property Issues and Europeana, Europe's Digital Library, Museum and Archive' (2010) 10(3) *Legal Information Management* 174, 175.

[73] Europeana Pro: pro.europeana.eu/about-us/mission.

[74] Including UNESCO, OECD, Europa Nostra, Network of National Museum Organisations, ICOM, ICOMOS and ICCROM: culture.ec.europa.eu/cultural-heritage/main-actors-on-cultural-heritage/main-actors-on-cultural-heritage-cultural-heritage-stakeholders.

[75] European Commission, 'Public Consultation on the Review of the EU Copyright Rules' (2013) and European Commission, 'Report on the Responses to the Public Consultation on the Review of the EU Copyright Rules' (2014).

[76] The 2013 Consultation offered its participants nine stakeholder groups to choose from (allowing ticking multiple boxes): (i) end-users or consumers; (ii) institutional users (cultural heritage institutions); (iii) authors or performers; (iv) publishers, producers and broadcasters; (v) intermediaries, distributors or service providers; (vi) CMOs; (vii) public authorities; (viii) Member States; and (ix) others. ibid.

[77] Report on the Responses' (n 75) Questions 8–10.

Regarding making some limitations and exceptions mandatory and adding new ones,[78] end-users suggested optional exceptions caused uncertainty, and institutional users recognised that this was needed for individual needs of MS but agreed on further harmonisation helping cross-border projects. Desired changes included exceptions for e-lending, data mining, extending the scope of preservation and allowing heritage institutions to make out-of-commerce works available online (largely addressed by CDSM). Authors, publishers and CMOs debated that there was no need to change the current exceptions, which have already been found to be too broad. They also did not want further harmonisation and did not want the risk of commercial users using works in copyright without any remuneration.

Regarding introducing greater flexibility for limitations and exceptions,[79] end-users and institutional users mentioned the need for a more open-ended system that could also respond to technological changes. Authors, publishers and CMOs stated that having an optional list of exceptions was flexible enough. They did not want the lack of clarity of 'fair use', which would lead to very different results in Member States' courts and create a less harmonised system.

Regarding preservation,[80] institutional users shared that they had problems with the preservation exceptions and claimed that they were sometimes interpreted narrowly and that 'non-commercial requirement' prevented them from cooperating with private parties. On the opposite side, others advised solving the issue with market-based solutions, namely licensing. Authors found the exceptions sufficient and suggested that any act beyond the public interest should be achieved by licensing, but publishers and producers did not report any problems with preservation. CMOs acknowledged that heritage institutions sometimes digitised for more than preservation purposes and that, even though licensing is an option, such institutions prefer not to use this solution.

Regarding providing access to works off premises,[81] end-users and institutional users mentioned problems with limited on-site access and lack of out-of-commerce works in the online environment and suggested that the scope of dedicated terminal exception should be expanded. Such users suggested an exception allowing digitisation and subsequent remote access for non-commercial purposes. Authors argued that remote access should be done via licensing; publishers and CMOs shared that opinion.

Finally, when asked about mass digitisation,[82] institutional users mentioned that the MoU and the Orphan Works Directive (Directive (EU) 2012/28) were inadequate in dealing with the copyright problems in mass digitisation, and they

[78] ibid Questions 21–23.
[79] ibid Questions 24–25.
[80] ibid Questions 28–31.
[81] ibid Questions 32–35.
[82] ibid Questions 40 and 41.

expressed the need for solutions for cross-border access to works and a copyright exception for mass digitisation of out-of-commerce works. Authors claimed that the national structures were sufficient, and that cross-border access would not be needed for works in national languages. But some suggested having a mutual recognition system for cross-border licences or creating legislation to enable mass digitisation. Opt-out licensing systems were not favoured by this group of stakeholders, since they argued that the consent of an author should be obtained. CMOs had different views on legislation for the cross-border availability of out-of-commerce works, and they emphasised the national systems already in place.

Since then, the CDSM Directive has covered some of these issues raised by stakeholders and provided a mainly hybrid solution of an exception (for preservation), licence and a backup exception (for out of commerce, which now include orphans), while also recognising research and heritage beneficiaries for text and data mining. CDSM was also met with more vocal reactions in other issues outside the scope of this research, especially on platform liability and press publishers' rights.[83]

Other developments include setting up a Creative Europe programme that also supports the European Heritage label (separate from UNESCO lists), a Commission Recommendation on digitisation and online accessibility of cultural material and digital preservation, and funding projects on heritage through Horizon 2020.[84] A recent initiative to create the common European Data Space, and the wider efforts towards improving policy and funding for digital heritage, hint that European developments will continue to go in a positive direction.[85]

5.2.3. United Kingdom

Before Brexit, UK stakeholders had been a part of the European initiatives and reacted similarly to the above in EU policy making. 2014 changes to copyright law have also addressed some of the gaps for the heritage sector.[86] But three examples will demonstrate the different needs of the UK stakeholders.

[83] See also CREATe Resource Page on CDSM: www.create.ac.uk/cdsm-implementation-resource-page/.

[84] European Commission, Mapping of Cultural Heritage actions in European Union policies, programmes and activities (2017).

[85] Commission Recommendation (EU) 2021/1970 of 10 November 2021 on a common European data space for cultural heritage [2021] OJ L401/5; European Commission 'EU Policy for cultural heritage': culture.ec.europa.eu/cultural-heritage/eu-policy-for-cultural-heritage.

[86] B White, 'Changes to UK copyright law and how they could affect you' (CILIP, 28 March 2014) www.cilip.org.uk/news/482821/Changes-to-UK-copyright-law-and-how-they-could-affect-you.htm; 'Response to 2014 copyright changes: post-implementation reviews Call for Evidence by the National Museum Directors' Council (NMDC)': www.nationalmuseums.org.uk/media/nmdc_response_to_2014_copyright_changes_post-implementation_review.pdf.

The first example is the preservation exception. The UK public consultation between 2011–2012 showed that heritage institutions considered the rights clearance process onerous and costly and were wary of technological obsolescence.[87] Other rightsholders were generally in favour of preservation but were concerned about the security of preservation copies and the risk of them being used beyond the scope of preservation exception, with other rightsholders hesitant towards preservation exception being used beyond its scope.[88] The review of the 2014 preservation exception shows that it has achieved its policy objectives, and has streamlined the process for preservation, based on input from heritage institutions and licensing bodies.[89]

The second example is the reaction to the consultation on the unpublished works. Many institutions in the UK held unpublished works in their collections, and the rights clearance process for such works was usually unsuccessful.[90] At the same time, rightholders responding to the Consultation were opposed to changing the policy and argued its removal would amount to 'confiscation of property rights'.[91] Therefore, the Government has decided not to go forward with the proposal in the Consultation, citing (then new) solutions provided in the UK Orphan Works Licensing Scheme and the 2014 changes in exceptions for preservation and dedicated terminals.[92]

The final example is the reaction to text and data mining.[93] Since the CDSM changes regarding TDM were not embraced, the creation of a new and wider TDM exception was considered. Following the findings of the IPO Consultation on AI and IP (on copyright and patent implications), the IPO has announced that they will introduce a new copyright and database exception that allows text and data mining for any purpose.[94] It was also foreseen that under this new exception rightsholders would 'not be able to charge for UK licences for TDM and will not be able to contract or opt-out'.[95] Given that these plans were quietly scrapped within a year citing negative response and the need for a deeper conversation with relevant stakeholders,[96] it looks like the UK will take longer to decide on this issue.

[87] HM Government, 'MODERNISING COPYRIGHT: A modern, robust and flexible framework: Government response to consultation on copyright exceptions and clarifying copyright law' (2012) 44. See also HM Government, Consultation on Copyright (2011) 14–39 and 70–73.

[88] ibid 44.

[89] Copyright exception for archiving and preservation, Post Implementation Review (1 June 2019): www.legislation.gov.uk/uksi/2014/1372/pdfs/uksiod_20141372_en_001.pdf.

[90] IPO, 'Government response to the consultation on reducing the duration of copyright in certain unpublished works' (2015).

[91] ibid 4.

[92] ibid 11.

[93] See also Section 4.3.4.4.

[94] IPO, 'Artificial Intelligence and Intellectual Property: copyright and patents: Government response to consultation' (28 June 2022).

[95] ibid.

[96] HC Deb 1 February 2023, vol 727 cols 152WH–168WH.

5.3. Interviews with Experts on Heritage and Digitisation

5.3.1. Methodology

To understand the practical clash better, interviews were conducted between November 2023 and March 2024 with participants working in the heritage sector that have experience in digitisation and/or copyright law.[97] Since the purpose was to explore the concerns of parties with different expertise and responsibilities in heritage institutions, the selected method was semi-structured interviews. Participants were targeted based on their expertise and contacted using the email addresses available on their institutions' websites. However, there were a few recommendations by existing participants, which allowed them to reach more participants. The interviews were all conducted online, and transcriptions were subsequently sent to participants for confirmation.[98]

It was also necessary to consider the potential hesitation of non-lawyers commenting on copyright, and the uncertainty on needing permission from employers. So, the default option for participation on the consent form was anonymous with direct quotes. However, under 'Additional Permissions', there were two more options: (a) their institutions being included (no name, institution only), (b) being quoted in an identifiable manner (name and institution). Overall, 20 participants were interviewed from the UK, US and EU, and nearly half of them have selected one of the additional permissions. Pseudonyms selected for participants indicate their jurisdictions (eg, UK1, US1, EU1), although where relevant the EU Member State is recognised in text. Named participants were also contacted with the quotes selected for this chapter for their final confirmation.

An interview topic guide was provided to the participants which has then shaped the coding of the findings:

- Non-legal challenges (including funding, planning, maintenance and ethical concerns);
- Legal uncertainty and training opportunities in their institution;
- Whether copyright impacts the prioritisation of what will be digitised;
- Whether copyright rules in their jurisdiction are sufficient and clear enough for preservation and access;

[97] This research project has been reviewed and approved by The University of Manchester Proportionate Research Ethics Committee (Ref: 2023-17942-30890). Copies of Participant Information Sheet, Topic Guide and a template of Consent Form can be provided upon request.

[98] Similar interviews were conducted, mostly in-person, between May 2016 and March 2017 for my PhD degree, based on ethical approval from Queen Mary University of London (QMREC1686a). Those 17 interviews are not used here but served to provide a background (not identifiable and no quotations). These interviews had additional questions on the primary purpose of digitisation, how they started digitising, and included participants' pre-CDSM concerns. Any specific references to issues raised in old interviews are marked with the letter 'O' (eg O1).

- Copyright concerns about cooperating with and providing materials to third parties;
- Any specific concerns on the following: preservation, dedicated terminals, orphan, out of commerce, unpublished works, collective licensing, open access, claiming copyright over digitised material;
- Final comments on the way forward.

5.3.2. Non-Legal Concerns

Participants were asked about non-legal concerns they had before and during digitisation projects, such as funding, planning and ethical concerns. In earlier interviews (2016–2017), as part of these non-legal questions, participants were also asked about what they considered to be the primary benefit of digitisation. The participants viewed digitisation more as a method to increase access, combined with the awareness that it was not a stable preservation method, some even said they were sure that the originals would be taken out and digitised again with newer technology.[99] The responses reflected that their priority was not just limited to old objects, but they wanted to facilitate discussion by also including more recent objects in their collections and digitisation.[100]

In the earlier interviews, participants were also asked how they started digitising. Some mentioned starting with a specific project in mind, such as celebrating anniversaries of events/institutions,[101] others mentioned their one-off photography subsequently expanding to more systematic digitisation once they realised they had the right tools and expertise.[102] A participant from a large heritage institution emphasised that their experience with digitisation is definitely not typical, and smaller and independent institutions have a much harder time even generating enough funding for staying open.[103]

Both in old and new interviews, participants explained the impact of unstable funding for digitisation. Some participants shared that they were led by external funding, as they do not have an internal standing budget set for digitisation which causes difficulty in planning: 'we are having to adjust to whatever happens to be funded at any one time. That can make it hard to plan forward a bit if we are not entirely sure, how many staff you can have in place to do something, or exactly when to schedule the work because we have to wait until money comes in'.[104]

[99] O1, O2.
[100] O3, O4.
[101] O4, O5.
[102] O8.
[103] O4.
[104] UK1.

US participants also referred to funding issues: 'cuts to budgets at the university that are trickling down into big cuts in the libraries as well'.[105] Participants reported an extra layer of bureaucracy with federal funding causing delays, such as the procedures for contracting and hiring taking up to a year.[106] Another participant from the US mentioned having both funding for core digitisation budget, and donations where the funding covers both the accessioning and processing of materials, but also their digitisation and metadata creation.[107]

The availability of funding then affects the availability of the staff with relevant experience and knowledge (including copyright knowledge). When explaining the situation in their institution prior to recent changes, a participant shared that it was 'quite hard to have the skills and knowledge infrastructure as a constant … we lose people at the end of the project and then we have to re-recruit'.[108] Another participant also reported that finding temporary staff for the projects takes a while, so the project term does not fit together with how employees will be sourced.[109] It was also necessary for heritage experts to 'future-proof' their digitisation, such as obtaining equipment and building workflows that can be reactivated, so that they can make the best use of any new funding and project staff in the future.[110] Other institutions reported having a core team working on digitisation, so staff turnover (and loss of knowledge and institutional memory) was not a problem they faced.[111]

Since digitisation was not always funded in a stable way, some participants ended up having multiple digitised collections and systems in their institution, creating an additional need to ensure that collections can be brought together: 'a lot of digitisation projects come from specific project ideas or grant funding or little discrete pockets of funding. And so, people end up putting up this little website here with some digitised stuff and a little database here, and, maybe a little microsite here. And that's not sustainable'.[112] It was reported that it was also common to have 'a very mixed legacy of various file formats'.[113] This creates problems with obsoletion and requiring extra work to keep digitised material accessible: 'we've had in the 2000s with blossoming of digital project sites … they're sort of running on software that nobody can maintain and have security holes.'[114]

Other participants also mentioned having different systems in place, to the point that it became a challenge to ensure the interoperability of their

[105] Interview with Mike Furlough, HathiTrust (1 March 2024).
[106] US2.
[107] US3.
[108] Interview with Aruna Bhaugeerutty, Ashmolean Museum (5 March 2024).
[109] EU4.
[110] Interview with Bernard Horrocks, Tate Gallery (23 November 2023).
[111] US3, US4.
[112] Interview with Christine Madsen, Athenaeum21 (5 February 2024).
[113] EU2.
[114] UK1.

systems: 'we've got multiple complex systems and processes in place. And again, this is a big technical challenge for heritage sectors to work with and because a lot of us have got legacy systems, you need to perhaps have clever API and expert colleagues … to pull the data through to make it presentable'.[115]

In terms of planning, participants stressed that bringing together various teams can be challenging, when input from various teams is needed: 'curators and conservators and collective management, and our photographer to look at objects from all these different perspectives. Is it safe to bring the thing in the studio, does it need to be cleaned, or a more significant conservation effort? What are the views that curatorial prefers? … photographers don't directly go into storage to pull out the objects, and are dependent on our collection management staff and their scheduling …'[116] The availability of teams is then reported to slow down digitisation on a mass scale: '… corralling that many people to come in to look at, say, 40 objects is quite a challenge … we could handle all of the camera and software technology issues just fine, it's really just all of that human effort that piles up that really slows us down'.[117] Having too many teams working on digitisation then also causes confusion on priorities: 'we have a lot of different divisions of the library that are part of the digitisation workflow and process, and no one unit or division that kind of owns the whole process … without one centralised leader being able to say "here is the priority, make this happen"'.[118]

The input of the curation team is important for selection, but this input might not always include the necessary legal information about the objects acquired, therefore creating delays.[119] Participants also reported the challenges associated with digitising objects without metadata or descriptions, which demonstrates how experts think differently about what counts as an 'item': 'archivists are used to thinking about things in aggregations, in groupings, a folder worth of things, that file is an object. When we are digitising things from an archival collection, the metadata that we have that we provide is at the file level … when the material gets digitised, someone goes in and adds additional description and writes and other kinds of metadata for each item in that file'.[120] In other circumstances, participants shared that digitisation has to occur before a description can be created, with very fragile[121] and/or audiovisual material that cannot be seen/heard otherwise, for example to assess what is inside a hard drive.[122]

Within all these planning concerns, there also needs to be an ongoing assessment of file formats still being accessible. Especially with some audiovisual formats, participants reported that the digital preservation needs to be done very quickly.

[115] Interview with Bernard Horrocks, Tate Gallery (23 November 2023).
[116] US1, Name withheld, Harvard Art Museums (5 March 2024).
[117] US1, Name withheld, Harvard Art Museums (5 March 2024).
[118] US4.
[119] UK3, EU3, US3.
[120] US4.
[121] UK3.
[122] Interview with Anne Gant, Eye Film Museum (19 March 2024).

Magnetic tapes (LTO) for keeping films were mentioned as an example, they are only reported to have a 5 to 10 year lifespan which then required migrating to a different tape – therefore creating an ongoing responsibility to constantly migrate the data.[123] Another participant also mentioned being more concerned about how audiovisual works are preserved, as their institution has not traditionally focused on this format: 'they will need migration over and over just because of the formats and working that out is going to be pretty difficult because the files are so large …. so there's got to be a constant workflow'.[124]

The accessibility of the material internally then determines if realistic estimates can be given to funders (even without taking copyright into consideration): 'once it looks like it might happen, there will be a process of getting them more specific numbers. That's the very labour-intensive thing to do …. a lot of projects don't come off, I'd say almost the majority of sort of projects that I know about that may or may not happen, don't end up happening in the end'.[125] If the institution does not know how much of the work can be made available due to copyright, then these proposals to funders cannot be realistic. But if the project is not funded, then all the labour-intensive prior legal and non-legal assessments are wasted.[126]

There are also ethical concerns on digitising sensitive material, such as political or religious sensitivities and human remains.[127] Since they serve the entire public, institutions have to respect all needs: 'there are many materials that Indigenous cultures would not want digitised or would want digitised a certain way or would want us to respect access to a digital asset of something of theirs.[128] Same participants suggested that they view digitisation as a way to 'reinstitute traditions and rituals which have not, because of the history of our country, have been annihilated or diminished. And this is a way to bring them back to a community and their younger members'.[129] But they also noted that if something is shared as open access and the community comes forward at a later stage, it can be challenging: 'we don't have control over those assets that have been already used because it was an open access. … we have no idea how far it's spread'.[130]

A participant mentioned being concerned about imposing the Western idea of property on cultures with different understanding.[131] A more recent interview also mentioned a friction between 'radical changes in how we think about intellectual property and going back the idea of having cultural respect' and that it was hard to ensure both.[132] Participants also mentioned concerns about the digital files they

[123] Interview with Anne Gant, Eye Film Museum (19 March 2024).
[124] US2.
[125] UK1.
[126] UK3.
[127] UK2.
[128] US2.
[129] US2.
[130] US2.
[131] O3.
[132] US3.

created when repatriation is in question, suggesting that they are not very sure if the heritage institutions are thinking about those files.[133] There are also further concerns on allowing data mining on Indigenous material, when the AI might interpret these works in an offensive way.[134]

5.3.3. Copyright Uncertainties

When asked about whether copyright determines what is selected for digitisation, there were mixed responses. The first group of participants said no. They mentioned that their selection is determined more by curatorial decisions.[135] Some participants reported that they have seen examples of selection being treated like a research project, determining what sources would be needed to address a certain area, and then ensuring the rights are cleared.[136] In relation to accepting works into their collections, one participant said 'we don't take copyright into account when we're doing preservation work, and we don't take copyright into account when we accept things into the archive. So, we're willing to take it and take care of it long term. But we take copyright into account when we decide to show these films'.[137]

Others in this group said copyright does not determine what is digitised but suggested that copyright status will play a role only at a later stage: 'copyright doesn't hold us back from digitising any of the things in our collections. It does sway how we provide access'.[138] A similar approach was suggested by another participant: 'more likely, if someone has a compelling reason that they're asking for this thing generally, we will digitise it and then the rights review may affect the level of access that we're able to provide', but said that there is still an initial assessment of 'is copyright going to make this so prohibitively difficult that you should abandon ship … if it is not that I can give it a preliminary yes'.[139]

The second group of participants said that copyright definitely affects what will be included in their digitisation: 'most of the stuff that we public and put online is out of copyright or if deemed to be copyright unknown, unlikely to be a high risk'.[140] A similar approach was reported by a US participant regarding how projects are planned: 'part of that proposal involves getting some copyright analysis. And that is very much part of the selection process. If we're not pretty confident that either something is in the public domain, or that we have a strong, fair use kind of

[133] UK2, US2.
[134] US2.
[135] Interview with Bernard Horrocks, Tate Gallery (23 November 2023).
[136] Interview with Christine Madsen, Athenaeum21 (5 February 2024).
[137] Interview with Anne Gant, Eye Film Museum (19 March 2024).
[138] US1, Name withheld, Harvard Art Museums (5 March 2024).
[139] US6.
[140] UK1.

argument that we can make, it is very unlikely that something will be selected for digitisation'.[141]

Finally, some participants reported that it normally should be considered at the beginning, but sometimes copyright is unfortunately considered at the very end by their colleagues, causing problems: 'it almost comes up as a surprise obstacle after a digitisation project has already been signed off and funded'.[142] A participant provided an example: 'in the last few years where we've put a lot of money in very complex digitisation … nobody researched the copyright status before and afterwards, it turned out that it was really complicated and there were rights holders who didn't want to cooperate. So we have a really expensive, very nice digitisation, or restoration as we like to call it, that we can't do anything with'.[143] Another participant reported that it depends on the team: 'it all depends on the staff coming to the right place, sometimes you might have something right at the end of the project and then intellectual property and copyright only been something that's discussed right at the end of the project'.[144]

Some participants acknowledged that digitising public domain works or works where copyright is assigned to the institution can be very desirable: 'you've got trustees and museum directors very commonly saying, "Hey, look, we sweat the assets, we need to generate more income … a content strategy that is affected by digitising things which are apparently more interesting or unique, which is sensible'.[145] Another participant gave the example of photos that have been assigned to the gallery. 'Where we have been assigned the copyright, the assets are going to be attractive, interesting, and potentially quite lucrative for the licensing team. Let's help push those through'.[146] In any case, digitising public domain is easier from a legal perspective: 'the stuff that's already in the public domain is the low hanging fruit, and so that tends to be what gets digitised'.[147]

There have also been changes in the public's expectations for what should be available online. One of the participants felt that the parties arguing for increased access did not recognise the effort and money that goes into digitisation.[148] These expectations also create a pressure: 'really contentious feeling occasionally between users and archives like they feel like the archives are like hoarders or like they're blocking access to materials … don't understand the cost and requirements of care and also the requirements of copyright'.[149] This became more common recently, with the pandemic reinforcing the expectation for works to be online.[150]

[141] US4.
[142] Interview with Daria Wallace, Ashmolean Museum (5 March 2024).
[143] EU3.
[144] UK2.
[145] EU2.
[146] Interview with Bernard Horrocks, Tate Gallery (23 November 2023).
[147] Interview with Christine Madsen, Athenaeum21 (5 February 2024).
[148] O3.
[149] Interview with Anne Gant, Eye Film Museum (19 March 2024).
[150] Interview with Mike Furlough, HathiTrust (1 March 2024).

Another issue that came up in relation to researcher expectations was the quality of digitisation: 'we have made a policy decision to publish both professional and nonprofessional images online because the primary audience is researchers, and the image quality is less important for them, they just want to know what we have'.[151] Whereas objects that are going to be licensed out and bring income usually have a higher quality: 'you can't do very much with a low-resolution image, but you can do so much more with a higher, and also it costs more and it's seen as a much more higher commodity … and it's quite often withheld'.[152]

In some circumstances, especially in research institutions and university libraries, the role played by researchers requesting digital copies was mentioned: 'requests from people who want to do text based analysis on something in our collection that isn't available digitally. So they ask us to digitise it, and then we assess it and figure out if we can do it, and if we can share it with everybody, or just with them'.[153] In other researcher driven projects, a participant said they often ask themselves whether the researcher who handles these objects should be responsible and would they consider the impact of copyright on their projects: 'we've certainly worked with community members who are surprised at the amount of work that has to go into it'.[154]

The level of copyright awareness among the staff is a concern. Participants reported the challenges associated with obtaining legal advice. Very few of these institutions had an in-house legal expert, so some of them relied on online sources and fair use training by other institutions in the US: 'there's a lot of medium to smaller size university libraries that would like to digitise and don't feel like they have the copyright expertise to even start'.[155] Similar thing was reported from a participant with UK/EU background: 'It's very unusual for all but the biggest institutions to have anyone on the ground …. You get people like me kind of sort of muddling through, advising colleagues. And, of course, in the GLAM sector there are people you can talk to. There's training available. There are resources from various archives, museums, etc. bodies that you can take advantage of and train your staff with'.[156] Others reported having to talk with staff members who can determine when legal advice is needed, but are not providing this advice. This then connects to the funding issues again: 'We don't have necessarily the funding to enable legal advice although we're lucky sometimes to be able to ask somebody informally and they can give us a bit of a steer. But not everybody's going to be in that position to be able to do that, and then what do you do?'[157]

Some participants mentioned delivering copyright training to all staff, at least in a way that allows the detection of which cases are complicated enough

[151] Interview with Aruna Bhaugeerutty, Ashmolean Museum (5 March 2024).
[152] UK2.
[153] US2.
[154] US6.
[155] Interview with Christine Madsen, Athenaeum21 (5 February 2024).
[156] EU2.
[157] Interview with Aruna Bhaugeerutty, Ashmolean Museum (5 March 2024).

to get the specialists involved. They mentioned trying to make 'sure that people feel empowered, to not just default kick it over to me to assess a situation'.[158] Another participant said they aim to make their trainings more accessible and digestible: 'You have to really take away the law side of it. You have to take away everything and try and almost marry it with policy … I end up doing some sort of "content training" or "use of images training", rather than copyright training'.[159] Understandably, there has been some hesitance and resistance from staff members on making legal assessments in addition to their main, non-legal responsibilities: 'socialisation of this is one of the most challenging things right, because people hear the word copyright, and they sort of freak out in their heads … asking people who are already overloaded with backlogs of things that need to be processed, decades of backlogs … Asking them to do more work, it's a hard sell'.[160]

One of the participants suggested that people do not tend to ask when they know the answer is going to be negative: 'sometimes it is "better not to ask a lawyer because it's probably gonna be so complicated and they will say no … let's just go ahead and see what happens"'.[161] This then contributes to the abovementioned issue of copyright only being raised at a later stage as an obstacle.

Some participants decide on certain cut-off dates to increase legal certainty: 'certain collections after certain date in certain areas, we just do not touch that until we've got time and resources'.[162] A description of this calculation was provided by a participant: 'when it comes into, let's say to the edge of the time frame, death plus 70 years. So works that are published around 1900–1920, then they have to make the risk assessment, or have to look which authors are now 70 years dead and who are not? And then there's a little bit of blurry cases with digitisation of newspapers and stuff around that time between, let's say, 1900–1940. So, if it's out of copyright or not. There's a little bit of rights clearing. But the works, let's say, before 1900. I think nobody sees any problem.'[163] Although this kind of assessment makes it easier for non-copyright experts to avoid risks, there is also the question of whether this means too much caution, where some works might be unnecessarily excluded.

Participants reported being equally responsible towards users and the rightholders, so this requires having a strict approach to when in-copyright works can be made available.[164] Participants said they want to keep good relations with authors, so that contributed to their approach to copyright: 'often the archives team especially have quite good relationships with people who have put things

[158] US3.
[159] UK2.
[160] US5.
[161] EU3.
[162] UK1.
[163] EU4.
[164] UK3.

on deposit or the descendants of people who did, if they need to ask and get the copyright secured'.[165] In terms of taking risks when copyright holder is missing, the importance of building good relationships with rightholders was emphasised again: 'If a copyright claimant did come forward, it would fill a gap in our research and we'd build a nice relationship …. It doesn't happen very often that somebody comes forward, but if they did, we would hope to foster and nurture the relationship'.[166]

In connection to this caution around copyright, there were also participants saying that they do not want to be at the forefront of legal changes and wanted to observe legal developments before making any big changes: 'once we start hearing about places having friction with rights holders around a certain topic or a certain idea, it's something we have to pay attention to. It doesn't necessarily in mean that it's going to inform a lower risk appetite or tolerance. But it is something that we have to really keep in mind. Because we can't be out ahead of everybody else. And you'll probably hear this from other institutions as well. Nobody wants to be the only one out ahead, it helps to try to pace things along with our peers'.[167] Similar sentiments were reported in relation to carefully observing current developments around CDL and AI.[168]

As part of low-risk appetite, institutions are also then cautious about what they share with others. For example, a US participant mentioned when they send objects on exhibits travelling in their State (such as civic organizations or public schools), where they are asked to make digital copies of highlights from the exhibit for websites. The participant said that although this would be great for getting more people to the exhibits, the copyright implications concerned them and required further discussion.[169] When asked about sharing material with other institutions, a participant mentioned 'I don't think copyright legislation and practitioners totally got their heads around the copyright status of international image interoperability framework …. It's sort of technical API that that makes it easy to pull images that are held in served in one place into another … a lot of different opinions about whether they're reproducing it or not. Because the images are coming from our servers, they're not taking a copy'.[170] Although the participant said they were okay with this, they said it would be a problem if the other institutions then decided to separately copy the images and put them under a different licence.[171]

Another participant said the different attitudes towards copyright can then affect cooperation between institutions 'we loaned them a collection for a

[165] UK1.
[166] Interview with Bernard Horrocks, Tate Gallery (23 November 2023).
[167] US3.
[168] Interview with Mike Furlough, HathiTrust (1 March 2024).
[169] US5.
[170] UK1.
[171] UK1.

particular project, and their archivists reached out and asked if she would be able to do some digitisation from that collection and put it into their online portal … collaboration has been impacted a little bit because of the fact that we are institutionally pretty risk averse'.[172]

While multiple participants accepted that claiming new copyright over digital copies is common in the sector, they were rarely in favour of it. One participant suggested that the attention on compliance with the law was so focused on avoiding infringement, but there was no penalty for copyfraud other than an awkward conversation.[173] The originality argument arose mostly in relation to 3D objects, as their lighting and positioning required a lot of decisions.[174] Some participants explained that copyright would not arise but this was mainly due to their need for accurate representation of heritage – one mentioned researchers needing very high levels of precision for 3D objects for scientific accuracy.[175] They said that if the purpose was something else, such as publishing in a high end magazine, that would be a different discussion, but their purpose was to facilitate research so they would aim for accuracy and therefore not claim copyright.[176]

Another participant suggested that claiming copyright is seen as an easy way of assuring control: 'in terms of simplification for contract law and general discussions, copyright is used in cultural heritage institutions, because there's actually no alternative, to a certain degree'.[177] They also mentioned the impact of the digital systems, such as difficulties with taking the copyright symbol off their websites when only some of the objects have copyright.[178]

In connection to funding issues discussed above, participants acknowledged some had open access requirements. For example, this being a requirement for the National Heritage Lottery Fund in the UK came up: 'because if you want the money, and you're getting what is essentially public money to do all this stuff, then you shouldn't be coming out the other end saying "oh, now I'm going to assert copyright over the public domain stuff"'.[179]

But there is also some hesitance around embracing open access: 'everything needs to be given away Open Access and for free under CC BY licence. Well, that'll stop us from selling it and therefore actually we're going to stop doing it because there's no funding to do it'.[180] This was not always possible when dealing with third party rights 'if you're talking about conserving a Picasso or a Warhol or another in-copyright work, then you know you can't automatically make that content available under an Open Access license because the rights don't belong to you'.[181]

[172] US4.
[173] EU2.
[174] US2, UK2.
[175] US2.
[176] US2.
[177] UK2.
[178] UK2.
[179] EU2.
[180] UK2.
[181] Interview with Bernard Horrocks, Tate Gallery (23 November 2023).

The Creative Commons requirement was mentioned in relation to Europeana also: 'the metadata had to be CC0, because they realized, noting that was very far sighted even then, that you couldn't, for example, serve decent API services without that'.[182] There was also some hesitance in participating in Europeana in general. Earlier interviews (2016–2017) showed some reservation from the UK in particular (some mentioning Brexit), compared with other EU countries.[183] But the mixed responses continued in 2023–2024 interviews: 'they need to look after their own business rather than worry about contributing a million digital objects to a port, or which is visited by, you know, half a million unique visitors every month. A lot of people aren't excited by that offer … So the mixed reception to Europeana is Europe wide, it's not a UK thing, specifically, even with, say, Brexit in mind.[184]

Finally, some participants, in line with their commercial goals, reported that they cannot rely on exceptions, and have to rely on licensing solutions. They mentioned working in imaging departments which are subject to mixed expectations: 'expected to try and make money for the library, rather than be a cost. They can make money for commercial photography commissions or publishing rights … But there is tension between that sort of setup trying to be commercial, but also during this non-commercial activity, which is digitisation'.[185] Likewise, a participant explained having to often remind colleagues that even when their purpose looks educational, they cannot rely on defences in circumstances when their activity is commercial, that it would not fit fair dealing.[186] Others mentioned that they have to rely on licensing because of their responsibility towards the rightsholders and their goals as an institution: 'we feel that aggressive use of the fair dealing defences is not necessarily the best way to promote art and design, for the benefit of art and design'.[187]

5.3.4. Specific Issues

In relation to preservation, participants reported that exceptions work, but this does not extend to giving access to digitised materials. A participant from a jurisdiction that already had a comprehensive preservation exception prior to CDSM reported that not much has changed for them.[188] However another participant suggested that not being able to emulate software with the EU preservation exception is a problem.[189] Similarly in the UK, preservation exception since 2014 has

[182] EU2.
[183] O7, O12, O13.
[184] EU2.
[185] UK1.
[186] UK2.
[187] Interview with Anthony Misquitta, V&A (23 November 2023).
[188] EU3.
[189] EU1, Name withheld, National Library of Netherlands (5 December 2023).

'given museums and galleries that extra confidence that preservation copying is a real tool for colleagues to help preserve and maintain access to their collection' and that the institution was 'very keen for the preservation exception to be used as widely as possible'.[190] US participants mentioned using the US library defence, especially for audiovisual preservation, but clarified that they do not make preservation copies available until a separate full copyright review.[191] Another US participant explained the trouble with preserving new media artworks, where they definitely ask the living artists about preservation up front and met with mixed reactions: 'it varies widely from artist to artist. Some aren't even thinking about that, and some are very aware of it. And they're like "no, this file format and this CD is the artwork. You can't do anything to preserve it other than put it on the cell and hope it's playable the next time you want to use it"'.[192] The same participant also mentioned making Matterport 3D copies of exhibitions, which served to preserve how the object was presented and what it looked like at that point in time, trying to 'expand the perspective of what it an object is by capturing it in installed in an exhibition'.[193]

The dedicated terminals exception, on the other hand, received mixed reactions. It is suggested that it helps when the items are very fragile or permissions cannot be acquired for digital copies to be placed online, as a fallback solution.[194] However this sometimes surprises the visitors: 'researchers going "wait, you have something digital, but you want me to travel somewhere to see it?"'[195] But other participants shared that they do not rely on it much, at least for books: 'Darmstadt case scenario … is not really used very much here. Because, first of all, it costs to digitise books yourself. And then you can only reach your own reading room. So you have to ponder really the cost and the gain of it. And it's not really worth it in many cases. So you just buy another book, or license the book if possible from the publisher. You still have to pay … to the collecting society the same as the cost for another book. So you have to pay for using the copyright exception'.[196] Another EU participant also mentioned it is not very commonly used in their institution: 'an exception like that have to be applied to all campus, and how feasible is that in terms of IP addresses, so that that feels a bit kind of 1990s'.[197]

Another issue that came up was the treatment of unpublished works. In addition to the ethical concerns and not being able to ascertain what the author would have wanted,[198] the '2039 Rule' was also criticised: 'as a sector we've lobbied

[190] Interview with Bernard Horrocks, Tate Gallery (23 November 2023).
[191] US4.
[192] US1, Name withheld, Harvard Art Museums (5 March 2024).
[193] US1, Name withheld, Harvard Art Museums (5 March 2024).
[194] UK1, UK3.
[195] Interview with Christine Madsen, Athenaeum21 (5 February 2024).
[196] EU4.
[197] EU2.
[198] O9, O4.

for that to be abolished in order to increase access to our collections and that hasn't been the case so far'.[199] Another UK participant mentioned this rule surprises researchers doing research on the nineteenth century and having to figure out the copyright status: 'sometimes they have to figure that out themselves, and sometimes they don't have the expertise to do that and are surprised to find this a problem at all',[200] and 'there's always a lot of pushback on that from some people who don't want to acknowledge that older things might still be in copyright'.[201] At the EU level, one of the participants emphasised that the issue of unpublished works is now covered by the out-of-commerce changes as well.[202] In the older interviews, a US participant suggested unpublished works should be digitised freely, but placed in a virtual reading room.[203]

The rules on orphan works, especially the diligent search requirement for the UK Orphan Works Licensing Scheme, were criticised. In the UK, the problem was mostly caused by the diligent search requirement: 'if you've done the diligence anyway, you might then carefully consider taking the risk of going ahead'.[204] Another UK participant also said the due diligence was a big burden especially when digitising on a large scale, and that licence did not cover what they wanted to do with the work, such as placing them online.[205] The previous participants also noted that the participation in UK orphan works licensing scheme was low.[206] UK participants mentioned that although it seems small per item, it adds up in mass digitisation, and then having to renew all this in a few years made this scheme not very desirable.[207] The UK situation was made worse with the loss of the EU scheme post-Brexit. US participants mentioned that they started to provide lower resolutions, and so people are aware of the collections and can see a small portion, and decide later if they want to contact the heritage institution for more.[208] A US participant referred to the hesitation on solving orphan works problem there: 'very reasonable proposals were put forward in the past couple of decades and the major corporate rights holders, content creators fought hard against them, and we couldn't get them established'.[209]

EU participants reported that the orphan works tool is no longer necessary because of out of commerce rules in the CDSM Directive.[210] Another participant mentioned that 'the out of commerce legislation gives us more certainty in the

[199] Interview with Bernard Horrocks, Tate Gallery (23 November 2023).
[200] UK1.
[201] UK2.
[202] EU4.
[203] O10.
[204] Interview with Bernard Horrocks, Tate Gallery (23 November 2023).
[205] Interview with Daria Wallace, Ashmolean Museum (5 March 2024).
[206] O4, O6, O12, O3.
[207] UK3, O4.
[208] US1, Name withheld, Harvard Art Museums (5 March 2024).
[209] US5.
[210] EU4.

sense that it says non-members are legally included in the CMO licence. So, they don't have any grounds for going to court to ask for a higher compensation'.[211]

But participants also recognised that out-of-commerce systems are still being developed, in connection to how the Directive was implemented very slowly, and even now (as of 2024) the implementation is 'still very varied and inconsistent'.[212] One participant suggested that the negotiations were still going on with CMOs and the bulk licensing was not there yet. Another challenge was the length of the licence if the goal was keeping these works online long-term, especially if the project had one-off funding.[213] Another participant suggested that it will take a while before any real impact is seen: 'maybe a little bit sceptical about the pace of change around Europe wide things like this … you don't hear about medium to small institutions. How are they changing policy and practice regarding things like the Copyright Directive implementation? That is a whole other different story. I wouldn't be expecting kind of immediate revolutions'.[214]

For US participants an ongoing concern was the limits of fair use. Even when asked about training their staff, participants said: 'it's always a judgment call, and it's not black and white. There's a spectrum of whether some are more likely to be a fair use, less likely to be a fair use. And that is a very hard concept to get across to people. It's very complex'.[215] Another interviewer called it 'just a cloud of uncertainty hanging over it if we're relying on fair use'.[216] But there was also the suggestion of how the US system 'thrived on ambiguity', which often favoured users.[217]

The question on fair use also brought up Google Books and Internet Archive cases. Past concerns raised around the Google Books project was their motive. One of the previous interviewees suggested that there was hesitation in European institutions on cooperating with Google, since access to heritage is traditionally provided by public institutions in Europe.[218] Another interviewee suggested that allowing an institution like Google to start digitising was an easy way for institutions to receive copies of their collections, 'if anybody was going to get sued, it was Google'.[219] A previous interviewee mentioned being cautious about Google's terms[220] whereas another one called it a 'devil's bargain', in which all the advantage went to Google, but the same participant also recognised that this was still a more preferable option for institutions than having nothing.[221] More recent interviews mentioned participating in Google Arts and Culture, because they saw it as

[211] EU1, Name withheld, National Library of Netherlands (5 December 2023).
[212] EU2.
[213] EU4.
[214] EU2.
[215] US5.
[216] US6.
[217] Interview with Mike Furlough, HathiTrust (1 March 2024).
[218] O12.
[219] Interview with Christine Madsen, Athenaeum21 (5 February 2024).
[220] O5.
[221] O10.

'educational use',[222] but some said they were very careful on which items are placed there to avoid copyright issues.[223]

The impact of *Hachette v Internet Archive* was taken into consideration (interviews were conducted prior to the Appeals decision): One participant mentioned following the case carefully, as it could impact other digital libraries and emergency access.[224] Another US participant also shared their concern: 'even though fair use is something we should be able to rely on and that the exemptions for libraries are things that mostly we can rely on, it definitely feels as though we're working in an environment that is not friendly to those concepts and it feels a little, there's a foreboding feeling around when is the hammer going to come down … I don't like the idea of libraries getting sued. It makes me very uncomfortable, and I think it does have a chilling effect when we're not thinking about our cultural heritage institutions as partners to society and instead as agencies that are detracting from potential market profits. We're here for the public good and that has to that has to be protected, and that goes across cultural heritage institutions. Because otherwise we're just going to end up with more institutions being forced to side on the conservative side of copyright'.[225]

Another common theme that emerged was the concerns about the future of AI, both on the input and output side. Participants mentioned being aware that their collections were being web crawled by commercial users but having nothing in place to prevent it,[226] also touching on the ethical concerns mentioned above. US participants mentioned how it would be considered as transformative use,[227] although there was some concern that the lawsuits could potentially 'claw back a little bit of the fair use victories we had in the last several years'.[228] It was also noted that some companies are entering into contracts with the rightsholders for mining, potentially turning it into a market matter, instead of fair use.[229]

A participant mentioned how the output can be totally unrelated to the training data and suggested: 'cultural heritage institutions shouldn't have a problem … if they're allowing that, if their stuff is being put in so that the machine learns, and then produces something that is completely different, then it shouldn't be an issue'.[230] In the UK, there was also the mention of proposed (and cancelled) changes to the TDM exception in the CDPA, and participants suggested that the commercial and non-commercial uses should not be grouped together, as this could potentially limit non-commercial uses.[231]

[222] US2.
[223] US1 Name withheld, Harvard Art Museums (5 March 2024).
[224] Interview with Mike Furlough, HathiTrust (1 March 2024).
[225] US3.
[226] EU1, US3, US6.
[227] US5.
[228] Interview with Mike Furlough, HathiTrust (1 March 2024).
[229] Interview with Mike Furlough, HathiTrust (1 March 2024).
[230] UK2.
[231] UK3.

Participants also gave the examples of AI generated works entering their collections, such as an AI-generated cover of *The Economist* and wondering about whether getting permission from *The Economist* was sufficient, given the underlying training data.[232] But it is still early days, as another participant mentioned how they have not time to decide on how to treat such works yet: 'we're faced with potentially either being gifted an AI-generated at work or acquiring something that was created with the assistance of AI … we haven't really had any deep conversations internally about what we would do, given the bigger discussions that are happening in the lawsuits around generative AI services being trained on'.[233]

As a concluding question in the interviews, when asked what kind of solution would help with reducing the impact of copyright on digitisation, there were mixed responses on whether law reform was needed (and could be achieved). One participant commented on the length of copyright being too long (although acknowledging it cannot be addressed anytime soon) and also recommended that collective licensing and risk assessment be made easier, and raise more copyright awareness in the heritage sector.[234] Another participant mentioned that in the US ambiguity worked to a certain extent, but the chances of reforming the Copyright Act soon were slim, even though the changes (such as those brought by the pandemic and generative AI) will eventually require it.[235] Another participant expressed scepticism about supranational bodies like UNESCO and WIPO and instead argued that localism is the solution.[236] There were also participants who reported that their digitisation purposes will require licensing solutions,[237] and carefully planned licensing regimes would provide a more flexible solution for all stakeholders.[238]

5.4. Conclusion

After recognising the stakeholders' different interests, the chapter then moved on to the public reactions and repeated concerns about digitisation projects and cases in the US, EU and the UK. In the US, although more than a decade old, Google Books shows how parties react to large-scale digitisation and have various reservations (copyright being only one of them). While it is unlikely that Google will ever reach its aim of digitising every book ever written, new problems emerged in the US in relation to CDL and AI, with the stakeholders sticking with their usual sides. In the EU, attitudes towards copyright are different from the US, in the sense

[232] Interview with Anthony Misquitta, V&A (23 November 2023).
[233] US1, Name withheld, Harvard Art Museums (5 March 2024).
[234] EU4.
[235] Interview with Mike Furlough, HathiTrust (1 March 2024).
[236] EU2.
[237] Interview with Anthony Misquitta, V&A (23 November 2023).
[238] O6.

that most of the change is pushed at the national and regional level, as opposed to a private company determining the pace of developments. Parties' needs were mostly satisfied by the CDSM Directive, however filling the gaps and setting up ECL will likely lead to more issues. In the UK, the reactions so far are focused on special cases (especially unpublished), while TDM reactions also demonstrate parties with different needs.

The interviews have served their exploratory function and have confirmed the concerns raised in earlier chapters, but also showed some issues might have been underestimated or overestimated, which then helped with revising earlier chapters: (i) interviews illustrated that seemingly non-legal challenges reduced the opportunity to digitise and interpret copyright correctly, (ii) copyright did play a role in what is digitised and shared with the public, (iii) the approaches towards licensing solutions changed based on one-off commercial uses versus mass digitisation, (iv) claiming copyright over digitised material was not necessarily due to lack of awareness, but was a strategic re-interpretation of law in the absence of an alternative, (v) there were varying levels of satisfaction with legal developments and less consensus on how law should be improved even within my limited sample of participants, (vi) finally, that AI is on the minds of the heritage sector, although it is too early to see the full extent.

Although it is possible to frame this issue as a two-sided problem between author versus the public, the situation is much more nuanced than that: the heritage sector is not uniform (across jurisdictions and subcategories) and has different levels of resources and familiarity with copyright law. Although most uses by heritage institutions would benefit from wider copyright exceptions, some of them will continue to require licences. On the (relatively) same side we have the users, but grouping commercial users with researchers is a risky approach. While the former might want licensing for certainty, the latter could rely on more copyright exceptions, and grouping them together would disadvantage non-commercial users, such as researchers. On the opposite side, authors, publishers and producers seek more protection, although their willingness to share works freely, their levels of copyright awareness and their negotiating power is varying (and some parties are missing altogether, in the case of orphans). CMOs are also roughly on the same side as authors, while new responsibilities are placed on them with ECL. The relationship between authors, publishers or producers and CMOs is also not smooth and can lead to conflicts.

The concluding chapter will bring all clashes together and introduce potential solutions, framed as: (i) low impact recommendations (minor tweaks in existing law, producing more guidelines and toolkits), and (ii) high impact recommendations (a new instrument).

6

Conclusion and Recommendations

6.1. Emerging Patterns and Directions

Several themes and concerns have emerged in the preceding discussion. Choosing cultural heritage as the starting point meant that the scope of heritage needed to be determined before any copyright conclusions could be drawn. Since there is no single definition of cultural heritage and every instrument defines it differently according to its context and purpose, there was a need to find a more flexible way of approaching the issue (referred to as the cultural property principles), achieved through discussing the scope of heritage (question of what), ownership and responsibility (question of who), and the dangers surrounding it (question of why). In chapter one, through the analysis of the development of cultural property protection, a pattern was identified on how the willingness to spare and preserve heritage was usually met with an obstacle – such as the military necessity and the other priorities of the current inhabitants (in determining and losing world heritage status). So digital technology and, by extension, the impact of copyright are just the latest layer in the inconsistent treatment of cultural heritage.

It was noted early on that this discipline is shaped by authorised heritage discourse (AHD), which also impacted the scope of heritage in the instruments, and certain types of heritage and certain countries were prioritised. Constant effort is necessary to remember and emphasise how cultural heritage is not just limited to tangible, old, aesthetically pleasing heritage belonging in certain countries – to the point that selection of cultural heritage (for protection and digitisation) needs to be done more consciously regarding what will be transmitted to successive generations.

In connection to this, the 'whose heritage' question involves not just the parties holding physical items, but also who takes necessary steps at the right time, who selects them (for inventories, preservation and display) and who accesses them. Similarly, conflating ownership of heritage with the responsibility of heritage creates this dangerous (and all too common) argument of how certain countries and institutions are more capable of preserving, and therefore are deserving of handling cultural heritage. But another concern emerges: while dematerialised heritage means more even representation and fairer distribution of access to heritage, it also creates the risk of new ownership arguments emerging – therefore the law serves to protect the interests of the same parties again. Heritage should be for everyone, while also not neglecting the ethical and physical dangers that come with certain forms.

Digitisation can combat these concerns, while creating its own set of problems, as explored in chapter two. Copyright law plays a role in every aspect of digitisation by limiting what can be digitised, by whom, using which methods and for which purposes. This requires parties to both understand copyright implications and include them in their decision making. There are also further uncertainties caused by new technologies such as artificial intelligence, which provide previously unimaginable ways of interacting with cultural heritage, treating it more as data to be read by machines instead of the (sometimes shared) heritage of humanity. The risk of copyright limiting what can be digitised also means different attitudes emerge: cautious institutions avoid digitising when they can, and other institutions might overreach and use copyright as a convenient way to claim ownership of copies of works that are normally no longer subject to copyright, therefore pulling heritage back into individual ownership. Through the exploration of the digitisation process through the lens of copyright, it emerges that digitising heritage will clash with copyright law, a clash that is divided into three angles: theory, law and practice.

The first clash is in the theory. Chapter three focused on the underlying incompatibility between two areas of law that look at overlapping subject matter: on one side, we have cultural property law and its wide and imprecise approach to its subject matter, which is trying to address the ownership of the tangibles, wanting to protect their physical integrity and supporting more diverse representations and maximising digitisation. On the other side, copyright is more focused on the private interests of the author, in commodifying their own work and benefitting from it, and it has multiple justifications, usually involving the re-interpretation of theories for private property. Therefore, this chapter had to address how the justification theories measure against the principles established in chapter one, in the specific case of digitisation. In other words, could the motivation of cultural property law and the public interests justify a significant calibration in the existing protection for authors? The simple answer is no.

Labour justification for copyright is strong: the discussion focused on what exactly counts as the 'commons' that one can mix their labour with. Questions emerged: first, where cultural property ends and copyright begins, and second, whether an arbitrary and very long copyright term was the right tool for this, even though this is the current tool we are stuck with. It also leads to an uneasy question on external labour and the public domain, specifically if public domain is more valuable (since it is now 'heritage'), or if it is less valuable now that people can share and edit freely. Turning to the personhood justification caused even more hesitation on digitising and placing works online, which can easily clash with attribution and integrity. This is also an issue with works referred to as special cases, especially orphans and unpublished works, making it even more difficult to ascertain what the author would have wanted.

The last two theories however were beneficial in paying more attention to the side of the public, instead of only focusing on the authors' side. But 'public' is different in cultural property law versus copyright law. Leaving this balance to the parties might not be the most conducive method, when the goal is keeping heritage safe and accessible (as a principle that emerged earlier in chapter one). Turning to culture/social planning theory and increasing State interference might be needed for a fair allocation, but this should not amount to overriding the ability of some parties to participate and decide, just for the sake of just and attractive culture defined according to others.

Since the justifications for copyright are solidly in place, there are also safeguards for the author (such as the scope and duration of copyright, prohibition of formalities, limits to exceptions such as the three-step test), that cannot be easily overridden for the sake of heritage. So, two patterns emerge from this first clash, first there are at least two sides to this (author versus public) and second, continuously readjusting the flexibilities for both sides of the debate is more realistic than trying to removing copyright altogether.

The second clash is framed as the 'clash of laws', specifically focusing on the division based on the purpose of digitisation (preservation and access) and the types of works (special cases), while looking at different jurisdictions (namely the EU, UK and US). This involved examining the rights infringed, and the applicable defences, together with the other option of licensing in chapter four. The division between purposes of digitisation demonstrated a pattern in how preservation was easier to achieve than providing access to the digitised work: the copyright laws of the chosen jurisdictions have embraced 'preservation' as a valid goal – the EU and UK have recently improved preservation provisions whereas the US have supported preservation with both sections 107 and 108 of the US Copyright Act. Even WIPO has first worked on the toolkit for preservation as it is less likely to meet with resistance. The impact of copyright was even less if digitisation only focused on digitising the works in the public domain, as low hanging fruit (while recognising the additional impact of PSI and national heritage codes). At the same time, digitising only for preservation without giving access to anyone, or only digitising works in the public domain, is not in line with the principles established in earlier chapters.

For giving access to in-copyright works, and for digitising special cases, the pattern that emerged is that law is inconsistent and narrow. The boundaries of infringed rights were inconsistent both within the EU (considering the combination of the *UsedSoft, Tom Kabinet, VOB*, and *Darmstadt* cases), and between the EU/US (communication versus distribution rights). While it makes sense that in-copyright works cannot be released freely online, activities such as e-lending are left to the mercy of licensing. In terms of defences, a piecemeal approach exists: in the EU/UK the combination of library use, research and data mining defences do allow some activities, while in the US the section 107 fair use provision is used to complement the weaknesses in the section 108 library provision (while also reducing the urgency of fixing section 108).

For special cases, different problems emerged. In the EU, failing diligent search systems for orphan works are replaced with the new out-of-commerce system in the CDSM (combination of licensing with a backup exception), and the unpublished works were hastily included in the same group (unless it interferes with moral rights). For the UK, Brexit meant losing out on the existing EU orphan works regime and the new approach in CDSM. In the US, solving special cases with extended collective licensing (ECL) is rejected by stakeholders, and the boundaries of fair use are being tested in case law. There are also no international solutions coming soon, as WIPO has now turned its focus to providing toolkits and guidance. This all points to a clash in the law, which is fragmented and narrow and is acting as an obstacle especially to digitising for access and digitising special cases.

The third and final clash was one in practice, in connection with the different sides emerging under the first clash, and in connection with different legal approaches emerging under the second clash. In chapter five, revisiting the stakeholders showed that while it is possible to treat this as balancing two interests, there are more sides to this debate. This then unfortunately amplifies the theoretical clash and also leads to multiple voices emerging on the changes in law, some louder than others. The reactions to *Google Books*, *HathiTrust* and the *Hachette* cases demonstrate the different tolerances towards the use of in-copyright works, and the strength of fair use in the US. The EU and the UK reactions also showed evenly divided reactions from the stakeholders, with some parties arguing for licensing and others arguing for amending the relevant defences. Interview findings also helped in confirming the concerns arguments in the earlier chapters, but they also highlighted the impact of non-legal challenges on copyright decisions, and the impact of copyright on digitisation and access.

Based on the clashes and the patterns that emerge, finding a solution that satisfies all parties and solves all issues does not seem realistic. Instead of limiting the recommendations to defences versus licensing, the conclusion chapter will categorise solutions as low impact recommendations and high impact recommendations.

6.2. Low Impact Recommendations

The first option for addressing the copyright clash is to propose changes in the existing laws, and argue that these minor amendments can improve digitisation of cultural heritage. Based on the earlier clashes, making incremental adjustments can be a safer way to find a balance and move forward, without too much resistance from the stakeholders. There are also a set of specific issues highlighted at the end of chapter four which will be helpful.

As a general recommendation to all jurisdictions, adjusting the protected subject matter and the exclusive rights can reduce the risk of copyright infringement. The scope of cultural heritage is already both vague and expanded through multiple instruments, and it would be unproductive to argue that the scope of cultural heritage should be strictly limited to objects outside of copyright protection. If the scope of subject matter cannot be limited then maybe the scope of exclusive rights under copyright can be reconsidered: since the definition of reproduction is technology-neutral, the activity of digitisation is likely to infringe. Similarly, narrowing down the scope of communication, distribution, lending, public performance and display also do not seem likely, however they could benefit from clarifications. In the EU Consultation on Modernisation of the EU Copyright Rules, participants were asked if the application of two rights (reproduction and communication) to a single act (downloading) was a problem, and whether any measures such as joint licences/bundling of rights was needed.[1] In their response, some end users did consider the practice of separately licensing them caused added complexity, but authors did not see any need for a change, and the academics who responded to the Consultation also did not reach an agreement on whether application of two rights to a single act was a problem: some argued that this was a common occasion.[2] While it could make it easier to obtain licences, currently there are no attempts to create such a unitary right. In any case, such a change would go against the international instruments on copyright and would negatively affect the rights holder.[3]

It would also help to make minor changes to existing defences and increase harmonisation to ensure cross-border use of digitised heritage. In the EU, although some exceptions are now mandatory due to the CDSM Directive, the optional nature of the InfoSoc Directive exception was necessary to meet the different needs of the Member States. Preservation is now less of a problem in the chosen jurisdictions, but it is not fully solved in other jurisdictions that are outside the scope of this book, so WIPO's contributions are valuable.[4]

If these changes are not possible, easier steps can be taken to reduce copyright uncertainties, such as setting aside funding for joint copyright trainings for state institutions, and creating shared guidelines, good practice and toolkits.[5] Similarly, heritage institutions should be supported on how to recognise and avoid restrictive contracts with publishers. But the benefit of such solutions depends on the specific circumstances of the institutions (such as their funding, staffing, organisational structure).

[1] European Commission, 'Public Consultation on the Review of the EU Copyright Rules' (2013) Question 10.

[2] European Commission, 'Report on the Responses to the Public Consultation on the Review of the EU Copyright Rules' (2014) Questions 8 to 10.

[3] It is also necessary to keep in mind that the case law since this Consultation has made the scope of making available clearer.

[4] RE Pantalony, KD Crews and D Sutton, 'WIPO Toolkit on Preservation for Cultural Heritage Institutions' WIPO SCCR/43/4 (2024).

[5] See also the recommendations in Y Benhamou and J Ferland, 'Digitization of GLAM Collections and Copyright: Policy Paper' (2022) 71(5) *GRUR International* 403, 414.

6.2.1. Recommendations for the EU

The improvement of preservation and out-of-commerce rules, and the clarification for public domain in the CDSM has been beneficial for the EU. But seeing the full impact of these changes on heritage institutions will take a while. Few other improvements can reduce the impact of copyright and help the EU heritage institutions.

The first issue is the uncertainty regarding the scope of rights, especially adaptation, public performance and display.[6] Since the protection is not harmonised, it can be confusing for institutions to determine if these rights are infringed. For adaptation, relying on reproduction is still an option so it does not change the fact that copyright is still going to limit what can be digitised. Making changes to works, such as restorations, would also concern moral rights, which are also not harmonised. For public display and performance, it depends on what the institutions are doing with the in-copyright works, and in most examples, it would just be covered by communication/distribution. But there are circumstances where more certainty on what counts as 'public' matters: some events are for all visitors, some are ticketed, some are for a very small audience.

The second issue lies in the overlap and clashes between digital distribution, lending and e-lending.[7] The *Darmstadt* case means institutions can digitise their collection and place them on terminals, and this would have been in line with *VOB* (for lending) and *UsedSoft* (for digital exhaustion), but *Tom Kabinet* has complicated the matter of exhaustion for digital copies other than software, and reduced the benefit of the public lending right system. This requires clarifications on what can be lent electronically by the libraries, and what needs to be limited to dedicated terminals. Currently there is the risk of too much reliance on contracts with publishers, and licensing becoming the norm for all e-books.

The third issue is the setting up of a functioning licensing system for special cases. The non-functioning orphan works system is now overlooked and left as it is, due to the recent alternative route for out-of-commerce works. It made sense that CDSM introduced a back-up exception in Article 8(2) and (3) and prevented potential problems for when there is no CMO. However, seeing its full impact will take time. An additional issue causing uncertainties is the text and data mining defences, and how opt-outs will be taken into consideration.

6.2.2. Recommendations for the UK

Although the UK is losing out on CDSM improvements, the changes made in 2014 have been beneficial for preservation and research. The same concerns for

[6] See Sections 4.2.1.2 and 4.3.1.2.
[7] See Sections 4.3.1.3, 4.3.1.4 and 4.3.4.2.

adaptation, public performance/display and e-lending apply (as they did before Brexit), and the UK will now need separate judicial clarifications. The cancelled plans for improving TDM in the UK could have been the first significant change post-CDSM, but the existing TDM provision (CDPA, section 29(A) is still helpful for the heritage sector (non-commercial research), and more progressive changes might still occur in the future, in line with stakeholder feedback.

Improvements are needed for special cases. For unpublished works, the 2039 Rule has not been helpful for the heritage sector. If an amendment cannot be achieved, as the Consultation shows,[8] then more awareness is needed. Heritage institutions are mostly familiar with this problem, but the other stakeholders seeking certain unpublished works might not be aware of the obstacles. Additionally, once these unpublished works enter into the public domain, the influx of copyfraud should be avoided. Inserting a provision similar to Article 14 CDSM might be a way to achieve this, in addition to a clarification in case law.[9]

As for orphan works, the UK orphan works licence has some weaknesses, but especially the diligent search threshold and the length of licences (seven years then renewal) should be changed to encourage the use of the scheme, especially in the light of Brexit. Similarly, an ECL option can help with such works, and the basis is in the CDPA (sections 116B and 116C), however this will require more time.[10]

6.2.3. Recommendations for the US

In the United States, the existence of fair use seems to reduce the urgency of the other problems. However, some issues would still benefit from improvement.

First, section 108 of the US Copyright Act needs to be amended in line with the changes highlighted by the Study Group: specifically including museums, changing number of copies for preservation/replacement, including preservation of born-digital, reducing the impact of published/unpublished distinction, adding exceptions to public display and performance, and making digital circulation possible.[11] Improvements to this provision could potentially reduce the reliance on fair use, which can be unpredictable.

The second improvement would be clarifying the status of CDL following the *Hachette v Internet Archive* decision, and its chilling effect. There is clarification needed on circumstances differing from the specific example of the Internet Archive: for example, what happens if the work is not available to license from a

[8] See Section 5.2.3 for the IPO Consultation on reducing the duration of copyright in certain unpublished works.

[9] *THJ Systems Limited & Anor v Daniel Sheridan & Anor* [2023] EWCA Civ 1354, [2024] ECDR 4, see also Section 2.7.2.

[10] See Section 4.4.2. for orphans, Section 4.4.3 for out-of-commerce.

[11] See Sections 4.2.2.4 and 4.3.4.5.

publisher? Which forms of CDL will be successful for fair use, would it help to emphasise the public interest more in a less controversial version of it? Another issue that was misinterpreted at first, but then corrected at the Appeals Court, was whether the Internet Archive could be treated as a commercial use, so would the outcome be different if there were different approaches towards donations? Would things change if the works were lent in smaller parts or snippets like Google Books, and not in full – although that would defeat the purpose of a library?

Finally, the recommendations on orphan works and mass digitisation by the US Copyright Office should be considered (and attempted) again. If Google invested in creating a Books Registry, this would have simplified the process, but give the control to a private party, whereas US Copyright Office attempts to improve the situation were also met with negative reactions. That does not mean a ECL system is always going to be impossible, this requires listening to the stakeholders and seeing if attitudes change over time. At the same time, the legal developments involving machine learning seem to have diverted attention from ECL.

6.3. High Impact Recommendations

Greater change could be achieved in the form of an international treaty that creates multiple conditions for a defence for digitising and providing access to their digitised collections. Its effectiveness would depend on its national implementation. This could then be strengthened with further attempts to achieve the low impact changes above, shorten the copyright term, and bring limitations on the liability of the heritage institutions. If this instrument were to be implemented within the jurisdictions party to the Berne Convention, it would have to comply with the three step-test:[12]

1. Is this a special case? It needs to limit the activity by the type of beneficiary and for specific purposes.
2. Does it conflict with the normal commercial exploitation of the work? It needs to limit how much of the work can be shown, so it would not replace the work or discourage people from buying works in copyright.
3. Does it unreasonably prejudice the legitimate interests of the author? This is a question of what is reasonable for using digitised materials, and whether an exception created for single uses could have a greater effect when employed by many end-users.

[12] The test was first introduced in Section 4.1.

6.3.1. Components of a New Instrument

If such a new instrument were to be created, its Preamble should first recognise the dangers faced by heritage (including the impact of the pandemic) and emphasise the impact of digital technologies for preservation and access, and mention that the relevant stakeholders' needs should be balanced.[13] Such an instrument needs wide definitions provided up front. One way to define heritage for a copyright treaty would be 'pictures, paintings and drawings; original engravings, prints and lithographs; rare manuscripts and incunabula, old books, documents and publications of special interest (historical, artistic, scientific, literary); postage, revenue and similar stamps; archives, including sound, photographic and cinematographic archives'.[14] But it could also be drafted in a wider way, such as 'all works held in (permanent) collections', to include works that do not fit into traditional categories, especially born-digital materials.

The beneficiaries would also have to be listed carefully and be limited to publicly accessible institutions without commercial motives: libraries, museums, archives (including audiovisual) and galleries. Including institutions that are attached to an educational institution, such as university libraries, would require acknowledging the public interest in education and research.

The instrument should also define digitisation, for example 'reproducing the work by converting from analogue to digital for the purpose of preservation and access'. But it can also be drafted in a way to embrace new technologies and ongoing maintenance, such as 'transferring to new formats in line with the available technology, as many times as needed'. But such an approach could reduce the precision and would support the argument on how this would be outside 'certain special cases'.

The definition of digitisation should be comprehensive, and include both the preparatory uses prior to digitisation, and the types of subsequent uses: preservation and restoration, on-site uses, online uses (which should then be addressed in separate articles). To ensure that the public domain remains accessible, there should be some clarification similar to Article 14 of the CDSM Directive.

The Preservation Article should aim for proactive preservation (digitising without the risk of any loss) and recognise replacement and restoration as a vital part of preservation, thereby reducing the risk of infringement. There should be no limit on the number of copies and no limit on just preserving the permanent

[13] The wording here could mimic UNESCO and EC recommendations on digital heritage, namely Recommendation Concerning the Preservation of, and Access to, Documentary Heritage Including in Digital Form (2015) and Recommendation concerning the protection and promotion of museums and collections, their diversity and their role in society (2015); Commission Recommendation (EU) 2021/1970 of 10 November 2021 on a common European data space for cultural heritage.

[14] Mimicking 1970 Conventions, but only the overlaps with copyright's subject matter.

collection. Objects on loan should also be included under preservation, provided that a copy is shared with the owner or source institution.[15]

There should be separate Articles on what could be placed online and what could be shared on-premises. On-premises access should provide digitised copies of in-copyright, public domain and special cases in full, while also allowing users to view them on own devices without saving or printing a permanent copy.[16] Said in-copyright works should include both works digitised by the institution and the works acquired through licences, as this cannot just be limited to licensing terms. While this goes beyond what is covered under dedicated terminals in some jurisdictions, this can be justified with the public interest motivation of such institutions and by arguing that it does not conflict with normal commercial exploitation.

The works made available online should still include both digitised and licensed material, but there could be limits to this access determined differently for each type of work to ensure that it does not conflict with the commercial exploitation. For example, literary and musical works could be provided only in snippets, and artistic works could only be provided in low-resolution. This way they could still be beneficial for research and enjoyment, but not sufficient for commercial uses. At the same time, lowering of quality, or editing the work into shorter snippets, could potentially infringe the moral right of integrity, which would not fit the jurisdictions with stronger moral rights.

For online access to special cases, both orphan and out-of-commerce works should be shared in full, but with limitation of liability for heritage institutions. To justify this, heritage institutions should also add any information held on these works, such as attribution and any other information they hold on file (not amounting to diligent search). These should also be linked to a central online register on special cases, and regularly updated. On the other hand, digitised unpublished works should only be shared in part, based on harmonised criteria on what kind of heritage can be categorised as too sensitive to share (which should be developed with individuals, groups and communities); although full access can still be provided on the premises. There should also be measures in place for immediate takedown in the case of re-emerging rightholders.

6.3.2. Potential Problems with this Approach

If an instrument including components similar to the ones above were to be created, the first problem would be the three step test. Creating an instrument

[15] Mimicking CDSM Art.6 and the textual suggestions in WIPO Toolkit on Preservation for Cultural Heritage Institutions (2024).

[16] This requirement would have to be developed together with technology experts, depending on the current technology and the resources of institutions, however it would also be open to the risk of misuse.

that is wide enough to cover all digitisation and subsequent forms of access would have difficulty with satisfying 'certain special cases'. Although similar defences exist, the one foreseen above would go beyond the current preservation, library and research exceptions, as it allows both reproducing the work and making it available to users. The second and third steps should also not be an obstacle if the impact of the individual uses can be reduced. Reasonable amounts of all kinds of digitised content can be made available to users. Making extracts available would be similar to how libraries already allow photocopying works, but instead it would encompass all types of works. The logic behind the snippets shown by Google Books is very specific (showing three snippets per search term and excluding certain reference books), but heritage institutions could have difficulties in setting such technical restrictions for the available extracts. Providing snippets or low-resolution versions would mean that the content available to users would not conflict with the second and third steps. But low quality should not be at a level where it distorts the work and affects the moral rights of the author.

A second problem with such an instrument would be reaching international consensus on the ideal boundaries of the rules. Although not very recent, a close example is the discussions at WIPO level for textual suggestions on a new instrument.[17] The different reactions of Member States to these textual suggestions demonstrate how difficult it would be to find common ground: European jurisdictions commented that it should not be for commercial purposes (Austria, Italy, France, Greece, Germany and Spain).[18] The US delegate repeated that preservation discussions should be clear, as they are a 'distinctive function' of such institutions.[19] While discussing the right of reproduction, the EU delegate emphasised the importance of setting the beneficiaries for research and education goals and remaining in line with the three-step test, while the US delegate highlighted the necessity for a copyright notice, a non-commercial purpose and paying attention to how much is copied.[20] On lending, the EU delegate emphasised the CJEU's strict approach against lending without remuneration, and stated that an exception for public lending right would be detrimental.[21] The US delegate focused on the right of distribution and the 'first sale' doctrine and how it relates to library lending.[22] Orphan, retracted and withdrawn, and out-of-commerce works were also discussed. The US delegate stressed that the use of orphan works sometimes expands beyond libraries and archives, and the EU delegate warned against seeing all such works under the same

[17] 'Working Document Containing Comments on and Textual Suggestions Towards an Appropriate International Legal Instrument (in whatever form) on Exceptions and Limitations for Libraries and Archives' WIPO SCCR/26/3 (2013). WIPO's role was covered in Section 4.5.
[18] ibid 4.
[19] ibid 5.
[20] ibid 9–10.
[21] ibid 24 and 28.
[22] ibid 26.

category,[23] as well as mentioning the licensing possibilities for such works. Not much has changed since these discussions at the WIPO, based on the preference of creating separate toolkits on preservation and access.

Even if a solution could be found in the form of a treaty, such an instrument would still have difficulty in bringing the same flexibility that some countries already have. For example, sections 107 and 108 of the US Copyright Act provide enough flexibility, so it does not make sense to suggest that the US system should embrace a less flexible system. The question of whether EU law and UK law can get closer to the American concept of fair use is also common in the academic literature.[24] It is argued that making EU copyright law more flexible would not necessarily 'go against the tide of legal tradition', as the laws themselves only lost their flexibility in the last century.[25]

The final problem is that it would be impossible to avoid the licensing options even if such a defence was created. When discussing the abovementioned textual suggestions at WIPO, EU delegates repeatedly brought up licensing options for different things (right of reproduction, library lending, limitations for orphan, retracted and withdrawn, and out-of-commerce works,[26] which is reflected in the current EU regime 11 years later (at the time of writing). While seeking individual permissions from CMOs would not support mass digitisation, it is a logical solution for small scale digitisation. It also gives greater clarity when the purpose is commercial.

6.4. Concluding Thoughts

Considering the clashing interests of the stakeholders, it becomes a matter of what is possible, and which stakeholder group is more successful in protecting their

[23] 'European Union: … Whenever we start talking about something that seems very reasonable, which is how can we ensure that when there is no rightholder that can be identified or located after a diligent search, the work can be used and very quickly, this type of discussion turns into discussions on mass digitization, use of works out of commerce, use of works that have never been published and where maybe the author of the work never wanted the communication of such works. These are all very different matters and they are extremely delicate.' (ibid 36).

[24] For different positions on the issue, see I Hargreaves, 'Digital Opportunity: A Review of Intellectual Property and Growth' (2011); J Hughes, 'Fair Use and its Politics – At Home and Abroad' and PB Hugenholtz, 'Flexible Copyright: Can the EU Author's Rights Accommodate Fair Use?' in R Okediji (ed), *Copyright Law in an Age of Limitations and Exceptions* (New York, CUP, 2017); D Gervais, *(Re)Structuring Copyright* (Cheltenham, Edward Elgar, 2017); SW Halpern and P Johnson, *Harmonising Copyright Law and Dealing with Dissonance* (Cheltenham, Edward Elgar, 2014) 148; P Torremans, 'The Perspective of the Introduction of a European Fair Use Clause' in TE Synodinou, *Codification of European Copyright Law* (Alphen aan den Rijn, Wolters Kluwer, 2012); M Senftleben, 'The International Three Step-Test: A Model Provision for EC Fair Use Legislation' (2010) 1 *JIPITEC* 67; S Balganesh, N Wee Loon and H Sun (eds), *The Cambridge Handbook of Copyright Limitations and Exceptions*, paperback edn (Cambridge, CUP, 2023).

[25] Hugenholtz (n 24) 290.

[26] 'Working Document' (n 17).

interests. Making minor changes would be preferable for the group of stakeholders comprising of authors, publishers, producers and CMOs, whereas a new instrument would be met with stronger resistance by this group, as it is more likely to conflict with their interests, even when it is drafted and negotiated very carefully and over a long period of time. Although setting up ECL regimes might be concerning for the authors of works covered under special cases, this seems to be the current direction of the EU. The side of the public (commercial and non-commercial users) and the heritage institutions interested in digitising more of their collections would instead have an easier time with a new instrument that supports digitisation. But, as is evident from the title, a high impact change might also be disorienting for some of the stakeholders in this group, especially heritage institutions which are also concerned with the protection of authors.

As recognised at the beginning of this chapter, finding a solution that satisfies all sides and reduces the impact of all three clashes is not likely. The starting point was cultural heritage, and the aim was reducing the negative impact of copyright on the digitisation of heritage. As we can see from the CDSM and WIPO developments addressed here, the preservation side is easier to solve. But the problem is to ensure that digitised cultural heritage gets to be disseminated and accessed by the public. From an idealistic perspective, it is tempting to argue for significantly reducing copyright to the point that digitising heritage will be free from all obstacles, which also includes overriding long-standing copyright safeguards for authors (such as the copyright term, prohibition of formalities, and the three-step test). However, from a realistic standpoint it must be recognised that each of these clashes are real and hard to solve, that cultural heritage matters are rarely solved though swift and drastic measures, that there is no way to satisfy all stakeholders, and a new 'access to heritage' defence or another equally major change is not likely to happen anytime soon. It is therefore my sincere hope that this book also becomes a part of the ongoing incremental improvements of copyright for the digitisation of cultural heritage over an extended period of time, and that we will all continue to develop our understanding of the patterns, reduce copyright uncertainties, and keep an open dialogue between the various stakeholders.

BIBLIOGRAPHY

Books and Book Chapters

Abdel-Latif, A, 'The Emergence of the A2K Movement: Reminiscences and Reflections of a Developing-Country Delegate' in G Krikorian and A Kapczynski (eds), *Access to Knowledge in the Age of Intellectual Property* (New York, Zone Press, 2010) 99–125.

Albert, MT and Ringbeck, B, *40 Years World Heritage Convention: Popularizing the Protection of Cultural and Natural Heritage* (Berlin, De Gruyter, 2015).

Alexandridis, A and Winkler-Horaček, L (eds), *Destroy the Copy – Plaster Cast Collections in the 19th – 20th Centuries: Demolition, Defacement, Disposal in Europe and Beyond* (Berlin, De Gruyter, 2022).

Alivizatou, M, *Intangible Heritage and the Museum: New Perspectives on Cultural Preservation* (New York, Routledge, 2012).

Ang, S, *The Moral Dimensions of Intellectual Property Rights* (Cheltenham, Edward Elgar, 2013).

Antikainen, M and Jongsma, D, 'The Art of CAD: Copyrightability of Digital Design Files' in RM Ballardini, M Norrgård and J Partanen (eds), *3D Printing, Intellectual Property and Innovation: Insights from Law and Technology* (Alphen aan den Rijn, Kluwer, 2017) 257–74.

Antons, C and Logan, W (eds), *Intellectual Property, Cultural Property and Intangible Cultural Heritage* (London, Routledge, 2018).

Aplin, T and Davis, J, *Intellectual Property Law: Text, Cases and Materials*, 4th edn (Oxford, OUP, 2022).

Arizpe, L, 'The Cultural Politics of Intangible Cultural Heritage' in J Blake (ed), *Safeguarding Intangible Cultural Heritage: Challenges and Approaches* (Leicester, Institute of Art and Law, 2007).

Balganesh, S, Wee Loon, N and Sun, H (eds), *The Cambridge Handbook of Copyright Limitations and Exceptions*, paperback edn (Cambridge, CUP, 2023).

Band, J and Butler, B, 'Why Libraries Need Limitations and Exceptions' in J Coates, V Owen and S Reilly (eds), *Navigating Copyright for Libraries* (Berlin, De Gruyter Saur, 2022) 77–104.

Bannerman, S, *International Copyright and Access to Knowledge* (Cambridge, CUP, 2016).

Belder, L and Figaroa, A, 'Living cultural heritage in the Netherlands: the debate on the Dutch tradition of Sinterklaas' in C Waelde, C Cummings, M Pavis and H Enright (eds), *Research Handbook on Contemporary Intangible Cultural Heritage: Law and Heritage* (Cheltenham, Edward Elgar, 2018) 342–62.

Benjamin, W, 'The Work of Art in the Age of Mechanical Reproduction' (1935), trans. H Zohn, ed. H Arendt, *Illuminations* (New York, Schocken Books, 1968).

Bentham, J, *Introduction to the Principles of Morals and Legislation* (1789).

—— *A Manual of Political Economy* (New York, GP Putnam, 1839).

Bently, L, Sherman, B, Gangjee, D and Johnson, P, *Intellectual Property Law*, 6th edn (Oxford, OUP, 2022).

Blake, J, 'UNESCO's 2003 Convention on Intangible Cultural Heritage – the Implications of Community Involvement in Safeguarding' in L Smith and N Akagawa (eds), *Intangible Heritage* (London, Routledge, 2008) 45–73.

—— (ed), *Safeguarding Intangible Cultural Heritage: Challenges and Approaches* (Leicester, Institute of Art and Law, 2007).

——, *Safeguarding Intangible Cultural Heritage: A Practical Interpretation of the 2003 UNESCO Convention* (Cheltenham, Edward Elgar, 2023).

Blomqvist, J, *Primer on International Copyright and Related Rights* (Cheltenham, Edward Elgar, 2014).

Boast, R, and Enote, J, 'Virtual Repatriation: It Is Neither Virtual nor Repatriation' in PF Biehl and C Prescott (eds), *Heritage in the Context of Globalization: Europe and the Americas* (New York, Springer, 2013).

Borghi, M and Karapapa, S, *Copyright and Mass Digitization* (Oxford, OUP, 2013).

Bruncevic, M, *Regulating Transnational Heritage: Memory, Identity and Diversity* (London, Routledge, 2021).

Burrell, R, 'The Changing Judicial Politics of Copyright Exceptions in the UK' in S Balganesh, N Wee Loon and H Sun (eds), *The Cambridge Handbook of Copyright Limitations and Exceptions*, paperback edn (Cambridge, CUP, 2023).

Caddick N, Harbottle G, Suthersanen U (eds), *Copinger & Skone James on Copyright* 18th edn (London, Sweet & Maxwell, 2021).

Cameron, C and Rössler, M, *Many Voices, One Vision: the Early Years of the World Heritage Convention* (London, Routledge, 2013).

Cameron, F and Kenderdine, S, *Theorizing Digital Cultural Heritage: A Critical Discourse* (Cambridge Massachusetts, MIT Press, 2010).

Carrier, MA, 'Limiting copyright through property' in H Howe and J Griffiths (eds), *Concepts of Property in Intellectual Property Law* (Cambridge, CUP, 2013) 185–204.

Christman, J, 'Autonomy, social selves and intellectual property claims' in A Lever (ed), *New Frontiers in the Philosophy of Intellectual Property* (Cambridge, CUP, 2012) 33–57.

Cooper, E, *Art and Modern Copyright: The Contested Image* (Cambridge, CUP, 2018).

Crews, KD, *Copyright Law for Librarians and Educators: Creative Strategies and Practical Solutions*, 4th edn, (Chicago, ALA Editions, 2020).

Cronin, C, 'Intellectual property implications of 3D printing of cultural heritage' in I Stamatoudi (ed), *Research Handbook on Intellectual Property and Cultural Heritage* (Cheltenham, Edward Elgar, 2022) 565–78.

Cuno, J, *Who Owns Antiquity?* (Princeton, Princeton University Press, 2008).

Daly, A, *Socio-Legal Aspects of the 3D Printing Revolution* London, Palgrave Macmillan, 2016).

Darling, K and Perzanowski, A (eds), *Creativity without Law: Challenging the Assumptions of Intellectual Property* (New York, New York University Press, 2017).

Davies, G and Garnett, K, *Moral Rights*, 2nd edn (London, Sweet & Maxwell, 2016).

De Castell, C 'Unintended Consequences of the Digital Shift' in J Coates, V Owen and S Reilly (eds), *Navigating Copyright for Libraries* (Berlin, De Gruyter Saur, 2022) 153–74.

Depreeuw, S, *The Variable Scope of the Exclusive Economic Rights in Copyright* (Alphen aan den Rijn, Wolters Kluwer, 2014).

Drahos, P, *A Philosophy of Intellectual Property* (ANU eText, 2016).

Dusollier, S, 'The commons as a reverse intellectual property – from exclusivity to inclusivity', in H Howe and J Griffiths (eds), *Concepts of Property in Intellectual Property Law* (Cambridge, CUP, 2013) 258–81.

Dutfield, G and Suthersanen U, *Dutfield and Suthersanen on Global Intellectual Property Law*, 2nd edn (Cheltenham, Edward Elgar, 2020).

Elkin-Koren, N, 'Exploring Creative Commons: A Skeptical View of a Worthy Pursuit' in PB Hugenholtz and L Guibault (eds), *The Future of Public Domain* (Alphen aan den Rijn, Kluwer, 2006) 325–44.

Farrand, B, 'Born Digital: Law, policy and the preservation of videogames as digital cultural heritage' in I Stamatoudi (ed), *Research Handbook on Intellectual Property and Cultural Heritage* (Cheltenham, Edward Elgar, 2022) 502–16.

Ficsor, M, 'Collective Rights Management from the Viewpoint of International Treaties, with Special Attention to EU "Acquis"' in D Gervais (ed), *Collective Management of Copyright and Related Rights*, 3rd edn (Alphen aan den Rijn, Wolters Kluwer, 2015).

Fisher, W, 'Theories of Intellectual Property' in Stephen Munzer (ed), *New Essays in the Legal and Political Theory of Property* (Cambridge, CUP, 2001) 168–99.

Forrest, C, *International Law and the Protection of Cultural Heritage* (London, Routledge, 2010).

Francioni, F, and Lenzerini, F, 'The Obligation to Prevent and Avoid Destruction of Cultural Heritage: From Bamiyan to Iraq' in BT Hoffman (ed), *Art and Cultural Heritage: Law, Policy, Practice* (Cambridge, CUP, 2006) 28–41.

Frederiksen, R and Marchand, E (eds), *Plaster Casts: Making, Collecting and Displaying from Classical Antiquity to the Present* (Berlin, De Gruyter, 2010).

Gasaway, L, 'Archiving and preservation in the U.S. copyright law' in E Derclaye (ed), *Copyright and Cultural Heritage: Preservation and Access to the Works in a Digital World* (Cheltenham, Edward Elgar, 2010) 131–55.

Gervais, D (ed), *Collective Management of Copyright and Related Rights*, 3rd edn (Alphen aan den Rijn, Wolters Kluwer, 2015).

Gervais, D, *(Re)Structuring Copyright* (Cheltenham, Edward Elgar, 2017).

Giblin, R and Weatherall, K, 'Taking Control of the Future: Towards Workable Elending' in J Coates, V Owen and S Reilly (eds), *Navigating Copyright for Libraries* (Berlin, De Gruyter Saur, 2022) 351–77.

Ginsburg, JC and Treppoz, E, *International Copyright Law: U.S. and E.U. Perspectives: Text and Cases* (Cheltenham, Edward Elgar, 2015).

—— and Gorman, R, *Copyright Law* (New York, Thomson Reuters, 2012).

——, 'Exceptional Authorship: The Role of Copyright Exceptions in Promoting Creativity' in S Frankel and D Gervais (eds), *The Evolution and Equilibrium of Copyright in the Digital Age* (Cambridge, CUP, 2014) 15–28.

Gillman, D, *The Idea of Cultural Heritage* (Leicester, Institute of Art and Law, 2006).

Goldstein, P and Hugenholtz, PB, *International Copyright: Principles, Law and Practice*, 4th edn (New York, OUP, 2019).

Greenfield, J, *The Return of Cultural Treasures*, 3rd edn (Cambridge, Cambridge University Press, 2013).

Halpern, SW and Johnson, P, *Harmonising Copyright Law and Dealing with Dissonance* (Cheltenham, Edward Elgar, 2014).

Hegel, GWF, *Philosophy of Right* (1820) trans. by TM Knox (Oxford, Clarendon Press, 1952).

Herman, A, *Restitution: The Return of Cultural Artefacts* (London, Lund Humphries, 2021).

——, *The Parthenon Marbles Dispute: Heritage, Law and Politics* (Oxford, Hart Publishing, 2023).

Hilty, RM and Moscon, V, 'An International Instrument on Permitted Uses in Copyright Law' in S Balganesh, N Wee Loon and H Sun (eds), *The Cambridge Handbook of Copyright Limitations and Exceptions*, paperback edn (Cambridge, CUP, 2023) 59–73.

Hintz, C et al, *Finding Balance: Collaborative Workflows for Risk Management in Sharing Cultural Heritage Collections Online* (The University of Kansas Libraries, 2023).

Hirtle, P, Hudson E, and Kenyon, AT, *Copyright & Cultural Institutions: Guidelines for Digitization for U.S. Libraries, Archives & Museums* (New York, Cornell University Library, 2009).

Hudson, E, *Drafting Copyright Exceptions: From the Law in the Books to the Law in Action* (Cambridge, CUP, 2020).

Huefner, K, *What can save UNESCO?* (Berlin, Frank & Timme, 2015).

Hugenholtz, PB, 'Flexible Copyright: Can the EU Author's Rights Accommodate Fair Use?' in R Okediji (ed), *Copyright Law in an Age of Limitations and Exceptions* (New York, CUP, 2017) 275–91.

Hughes, J, 'Fair Use and its Politics – At Home and Abroad' in R Okediji (ed), *Copyright Law in an Age of Limitations and Exceptions* (New York, CUP, 2017) 234–74.

Hyde, L, *Common as Air: Revolution, Art and Ownership* (New York, Farrar, Straus and Giroux, 2010).

Izquierdo, HA, 'Artificial Intelligence and Text and Data Mining: Future Rules for Libraries' in J Coates, V Owen and S Reilly (eds), *Navigating Copyright for Libraries* (Berlin, De Gruyter Saur, 2022) 497–540.

Janssens, MC and Tryggvadóttir R, 'Orphan Works, Out-of-Commerce Works and Making the European Cultural Heritage Available: "Are We Nearly There Yet?"' in IA Stamatoudi (ed), *New Developments in EU and International Copyright Law* (Alphen aan den Rijn, Kluwer International, 2016) 189–209.

Jeanneney, JN and Fagan, TL, *Google and the myth of universal knowledge: a view from Europe* (Chicago, University of Chicago Press, 2007).
Jongsma, D, 'The Nature and Content of the Three-Step Test in EU Copyright Law: A Reappraisal', in E Rosati (ed), *The Routledge Handbook of EU Copyright Law* (London, Routledge, 2021) 338–53.
Kant, I, 'On the wrongfulness of unauthorized publication of books' (1785) trans. and ed. by MJ Gregor in *Practical Philosophy* (Cambridge, CUP, 1996).
Karapapa, S, 'Exhaustion of rights on digital content under EU copyright: positive and normative perspectives' in T Aplin (ed) *Research Handbook on Intellectual Property and Digital Technologies* (Cheltenham, Edward Elgar, 2020) 483–505.
Kila, JD and Balcells, M, *Cultural Property Crime: An Overview and Analysis of Contemporary Perspectives and Trends* (Leiden, Brill, 2014).
Knopf, K, *Decolonizing the Lens of Power: Indigenous Films in North America* (Amsterdam, Editions Rodopi, 2008).
Kohli, VP and Teilmann-Lock, S, 'Copyright and Public Domain Works: Highsmith v Getty' in E Bonadio and A O'Connell (eds), *Intellectual Property Excesses: Exploring the Boundaries of IP Protection* (Oxford, Hart Publishing, 2022) 71–86.
Kono, T, *Intangible Cultural Heritage and Intellectual Property: Communities, Cultural Diversity and Sustainable Development* (Antwerp, Intersentia, 2009).
——, *The Impact of Uniform Laws on the Protection of Cultural Heritage and the Preservation of Cultural Heritage in the 21st Century* (Leiden, Martinus Nijhoff Publishers, 2010).
Koo, J, *The Right to Communication to Public in the EU Copyright Law* (Oxford, Hart Publishing, 2019).
Koskinen-Olsson, T and Sigurdardottir, V, 'Collective Management in the Nordic Countries' in D Gervais (ed), *Collective Management of Copyright and Related Rights*, 3rd edn (Alphen aan den Rijn, Wolters Kluwer, 2015).
Krikorian, G and Kapczynski, A (eds), *Access to Knowledge in the Age of Intellectual Property* (New York, Zone Press, 2010).
Landes, WM and Posner, RA, *The Economic Structure of Intellectual Property Law* (Cambridge MA, Belknap Press, 2003).
Lending, M, *Plaster Monuments: Architecture and the Power of Reproduction* (Princeton, Princeton University Press, 2022).
Lessig, L, *Free Culture* (New York, Penguin Press, 2004).
Lixinski, L, *Intangible Cultural Heritage in International Law* (Oxford, OUP, 2013).
——, *International Heritage Law for Communities: Exclusion and Re-Imagination* (Oxford, OUP, 2019).
—— and Blake, J, *The 2003 Intangible Heritage Convention: A Commentary* (Oxford, OUP, 2020).
Locke, J, *Two Treatises of Government* (1690).
Macmillan, F, *Intellectual and Cultural Property: Between Market and Community* (London, Routledge, 2021).
Marcum, D and Schonfeld, RC, *Along Came Google: A History of Library Digitization* (Princeton, Princeton University Press, 2021).
Masiyakurima, P, *Copyright Protection of Unpublished Works in the Common Law World*, paperback edn (Oxford, Hart Publishing, 2021).
May, C and Sell, SK, *Intellectual Property Rights – A Critical History* (Boulder, Lynne Rienner Publishers, 2006).
Mendis, D, Lemley, M and Rimmer, M (eds), *3D Printing and Beyond: Intellectual Property and Regulation* (Cheltenham, Edward Elgar, 2019).
Mendis, D, 'Back to the Future'? From Engravings to 3D Printing – Implications for UK Copyright Law' in D Mendis, M Lemley and M Rimmer (eds), *3D Printing and Beyond: Intellectual Property and Regulation* (Cheltenham, Edward Elgar, 2019) 56–76.
Mendis, S, *A Copyright Gambit: On the Need for Exclusive Rights in Digitised Versions of Public Domain Textual Materials in Europe* (Berlin, Springer, 2019).
Menell, PS, 'Intellectual Property: General Theories' in B Bouckaert and G de Geest (eds), *Encyclopedia of Law & Economics: Volume II* (Cheltenham, Edward Elgar, 2000) 129–88.

Merges, R, *Justifying Intellectual Property* (Cambridge MA, Harvard University Press, 2011).
Merryman, JH, *Thinking about the Elgin Marbles: Critical Essays on Cultural Property, Art and Law*, 2nd edn (Alphen aan den Rijn, Kluwer Law International, 2009).
Miles, MM, *Art as Plunder: The Ancient Origins of Debate about Cultural Property* (New York, CUP, 2008).
Milne, R, 'The Google Library Project at Oxford' in W Miller and RM Pellen (eds), *Libraries and Google* (New York, Routledge, 2006) 23–28.
Müller, L, *Neutrality in World History* (New York, Routledge, 2018).
Netanel, NW, *Copyright's Paradox* (Oxford, OUP, 2008).
Nozick, R, *Anarchy, State and Utopia* (Oxford, Blackwell, 1974).
O'Donnell, NM, *A Tragic Fate: Law and Ethics in the Battle Over Nazi Looted Art* (Chicago, American Bar Association, 2017).
O'Keefe, R, *The Protection of Cultural Property in Armed Conflict* (Cambridge, CUP, 2006).
O'Keefe, PJ, and Prott, LV (eds), *Cultural Heritage Convention and Other Instruments – A Compendium with Commentaries* (Builth Wells, Institute of Art and Law, 2011).
Oruc, P and Suthersanen, U, 'Intellectual property and cultural heritage issues for museums of archaeological materials' in I Stamatoudi (ed), *Research Handbook on Intellectual Property and Cultural Heritage* (Cheltenham, Edward Elgar, 2022) 392–412.
Osborn, LS, *3D Printing and Intellectual Property* (Cambridge, CUP, 2019).
Padfield, T, 'Preserving and accessing our cultural heritage – issues for cultural sector institutions: archives, libraries, museums and galleries' in E Derclaye (ed), *Copyright and Cultural Heritage: Preservation and Access to the Works in a Digital World* (Cheltenham, Edward Elgar, 2010) 195–212.
Papadopoulou, MD, 'The Issue of "Orphan" Works in Digital Libraries' in I Iglezakis, TE Synodinou and S Kapidakis (eds), *E-Publishing and Digital Libraries: Legal and Organizational Issues* (Hershey, Information Science Reference, 2011) 198–231.
Parzinger, H, 'Cultural Heritage under Attack: Learning from History' in J Cuno and TG Weiss (eds), *Cultural Heritage and Mass Atrocities* (Los Angeles, Getty Publications, 2022) 59–77.
Patry, W, *How to Fix Copyright* (Oxford, OUP, 2011).
Perrin, JM, *Digitizing Flat Media: Principles and Practices* (Lanham, Rowman & Littlefield, 2015).
Pila, J and Torremans, P, *European Intellectual Property Law*, 2nd edn (Oxford, OUP, 2019).
Polybius, *The Histories*, Volume IV: Books 9-15, trans. by W. R. Paton in 1922, revised by FW Walbank and C Habicht, Loeb Classical Library 159 (Cambridge, Harvard University Press, 2011).
Radin, M, *Reinterpreting Property* (Chicago, University of Chicago Press, 1993).
Rahmatian, A, 'Copyright protection for the restoration, reconstruction and digitization of public domain works' in E Derclaye (ed), *Copyright and Cultural Heritage: Preservation and Access to the Works in a Digital World* (Cheltenham, Edward Elgar, 2010) 51–77.
Raustiala, K and Sprigman, CJ, 'When Are IP Rights Necessary? Evidence from Innovation in IP's Negative Space' in B Depoorter and P Menell (eds), *Research Handbook on the Economics of Intellectual Property Rights* Vol.1 (Cheltenham, Edward Elgar, 2019) 309–29.
Rawls, J, *A Theory of Justice* (1971) rev. edn (Cambridge MA, Belknap Press, 1999).
Reese, RA, 'Preserving the Unpublished Public Domain' in RC Dreyfuss, H First and DL Zimmerman (eds), *Working Within the Boundaries of Intellectual Property* (Oxford, OUP, 2010).
Reinbothe, J and von Lewinski S, *The EC Directive on Rental and Lending Rights and on Piracy* (London, Sweet & Maxwell, 1993).
——, *The WIPO Treaties on Copyright*, 2nd edn (Oxford, OUP, 2015).
Ricketson, S and Ginsburg, JC, *International Copyright and Neighbouring Rights: The Berne Convention and Beyond Vol.1*. 3rd edn (Oxford, OUP, 2022).
Rimmer, M, *Digital Copyright and the Consumer Revolution* (Cheltenham, Edward Elgar, 2007).
Robertson, G, *Who Owns History? Elgin's Loot and the Case for Returning Plundered Treasure* (London, Biteback Publishing, 2019).
Rosati, E, *Copyright in Digital Single Market: Article-by-article Commentary to the Provisions of Directive 2019/790* (Oxford, OUP, 2021).

Rousseau, JJ, *The Social Contract* (1772).
Roussos, K and Stamatoudi, I, 'Management issues for cultural heritage institutions' in I Stamatoudi (ed), *Research Handbook on Intellectual Property and Cultural Heritage* (Cheltenham, Edward Elgar, 2022) 413–38.
Samuelson, P, 'Justifications for Copyright Limitations & Exceptions' in R Okediji (ed), *Copyright Law in an Age of Limitations and Exceptions* (New York. CUP, 2017) 12–59.
Senftleben, M, *Copyright, Limitations and the Three-Step Test: An Analysis of the Three-Step Test in International and EC Copyright Law* (The Hague, Kluwer Law International, 2004).
Shiffrin, SV, 'Lockean Arguments for Private Intellectual Property' in S Munzer (ed), *New Essays in the Legal and Political Theory of Property* (Cambridge, CUP, 2001) 138–67.
Slim, H, 'Choosing Between Human life and Cultural Heritage in War' in J Cuno and TG Weiss (eds), *Cultural Heritage and Mass Atrocities* (Los Angeles, Getty Publications, 2022) 299–308.
Smith, L, *Uses of Heritage* (London, Routledge, 2006).
Spedicato, G, 'Digital lending and public access to knowledge' in JC Lai and AM Dominicé (eds), *Intellectual Property and Access to Im/material Goods* (Cheltenham, Edward Elgar, 2016) 149–75.
Sprigman, CJ, 'Copyright and Creative Incentives: What Do(n't) We Know?' in RC Dreyfuss and ESK Ng (eds), *Framing Intellectual Property in the 21st Century: Integrating Incentives, Trade, Development, Culture, and Human Rights* (Cambridge, CUP, 2018) 32–61.
Stamatoudi, IA, *Cultural Property Law and Restitution: A Commentary to International Conventions and European Union Law* (Cheltenham, Edward Elgar, 2011).
Stamatoudi I (ed), *Research Handbook on Intellectual Property and Cultural Heritage* (Cheltenham, Edward Elgar, 2022).
Sterling, JAL, *Sterling on World Copyright Law* 6th edn (London, Sweet & Maxwell, 2022).
Stokes, S, *Art and Copyright*, 3rd edn (Oxford, Hart Publishing, 2021).
Suthersanen, U, 'Copyright Law: A Stakeholders' Palimpsest' in F Macmillan (ed), *New Directions in Copyright Law: Vol 5* (Cheltenham, Edward Elgar, 2007) 119–34.
—— and Frabboni, M, 'The Orphan Works Directive' in IA Stamatoudi and P Torremans (eds), *EU Copyright Law - A Commentary* (Cheltenham, Edward Elgar, 2014) 653–95.
Tan, D, 'Taking the Mickey out of Disney: A Cultural Approach to the Transformative Use Doctrine in Copyright Law' in RC Dreyfuss and ESK Ng (eds), *Framing Intellectual Property in the 21st Century: Integrating Incentives, Trade, Development, Culture, and Human Rights* (Cambridge, CUP, 2018) 171–209.
Toman, J, *The Protection of Cultural Property in the Event of Armed Conflict* (Brookfield, Dartmouth Publishing Company, 1996).
Torremans, P, 'Legal issues pertaining to the restoration and reconstitution of manuscripts, sheet music, paintings and films for marketing purposes' in P Torremans (ed), *Copyright Law: A Handbook of Contemporary Research* (Cheltenham, Edward Elgar, 2007) 28–48.
——, 'Archiving exceptions: where are we and where do we need to go?' in E Derclaye (ed), *Copyright and Cultural Heritage: Preservation and Access to the Works in a Digital World* (Cheltenham, Edward Elgar Publishing Ltd, 2010) 111–30.
——, 'The Perspective of the Introduction of a European Fair Use Clause' in TE Synodinou, *Codification of European Copyright Law* (Alphen aan den Rijn, Wolters Kluwer, 2012) 319–37.
Truyen, F and Waelde, C 'Copyright, Cultural Heritage and Photography: A Gordian Knot?' in KJ Borowiecki, N Forbes and A Fresa (eds), *Cultural Heritage in a Changing World* (Cham, Springer, 2016) 77–96.
Tryggvadóttir, R, *European Libraries and the Internet: Copyright and Extended Collective Licences* (Cambridge, Intersentia, 2018).
Tylor, EB, *Primitive Culture: Researches into the Development of Mythology, Philosophy, Religion, Language, Art, and Custom, Vol 1* (London, John Murray, 1871).
Vattel, ED, *The Law of Nations or the Principles of Natural Law, applied to the Conduct and to the Affairs of Nations and Sovereigns* (1758), anonymous 1797 translation, edited by B Kapossy and R Whatmore (Indianapolis, Liberty Fund, 2008).

Waldron, J, *The Right to Private Property* (Oxford, Clarendon Press, 1988).
Warren, KJ, 'A Philosophical Perspective on the Ethics and Resolution of Cultural Property Issues' in PM Messenger (ed), *The Ethics of Collecting Cultural Property*, 2nd edn (Albuquerque, University of New Mexico Press, 1999) 1–25.
Wendland, WB, 'Managing Intellectual Property Options When Documenting, Recording and Digitizing Intangible Cultural Heritage' in T Kono (ed) *Intangible Cultural Heritage and Intellectual Property: Communities, Cultural Diversity and Sustainable Development* (Antwerp, Intersentia, 2009) 77–99.
Williams, SA, *The International and National Protection of Movable Cultural Property: A Comparative Study* (New York, Oceana Publications Inc, 1978).
Wyber, S, 'WIPO, Copyright and Libraries' in J Coates, V Owen and S Reilly (eds), *Navigating Copyright for Libraries* (Berlin, De Gruyter Saur, 2022) 220–44.
Xanthaki, A, Valkonen, S, Heinämäki, L and Nuorgam, P (eds), *Indigenous Peoples' Cultural Heritage* (Leiden, Brill Nijhoff, 2017).
Young, K, *An Introductory Sociology* (New York, American Book Company, 1934).
Zukin, S, *Landscapes of power: From Detroit to Disney World* (Berkeley, University of California Press, 1991).

Journal Articles and Conference Papers

Akmon, D, 'Only with your permission: how rights holders respond (or don't respond) to requests to display archival materials online' (2010) 10 *Archival Science* 45.
Allan, RJ, 'After Bridgeman: Copyright, Museums, and Public Domain Works of Art' (2007) 155 *University of Pennsylvania Law Review* 961.
Alterwain, A, 'Google Books and Digitisation of Libraries: Fair Use or Extension of Copyright?' (2007) 3 *Convergence* 139.
Anderson, J, 'Access and Control of Indigenous Knowledge in Libraries and Archives: Ownership and Future Use' (2005) American Library Association and The MacArthur Foundation.
Assael, Y et al, 'Restoring and attributing ancient texts using deep neural networks' (2022) 603 *Nature* 280.
Ayris, P, 'The Status of Digitisation in Europe: Extensive Summary of the Second LIBER-EBLIDA Workshop on the Digitisation of Library Materials in Europe' (2010) 19 (3/4) *LIBER Quarterly* 193.
Baker, KE, 'It's a Hard Knock Life: A Critique of the Legislative Response to the Orphan Works Problem in the UK' (2016) 5 *UCL Journal of Law and Jurisprudence* 1.
Barron, A, 'Copyright Law and the Claims of Art' (2002) 4 *IPQ* 368.
Benhamou, Y and Ferland, J, 'Digitization of GLAM Collections and Copyright: Policy Paper' (2022) 71(5) *GRUR International* 403.
Bensamoun, A, 'The French Out-of-Commerce Books Law in the Light of European Orphan Works' (2014) 4 *QMJIP* 213.
Birnhack, MD, 'The Dead Sea Scrolls Case – Who is an Author?' (2001) 23(3) *EIPR* 128.
Blake, J, 'On Defining Cultural Heritage' (2000) 49 *International and Comparative Law Quarterly* 61.
Blumenthal, A, 'A New Definition of Culture' (1940) 42(4) *American Anthropologist* 571.
Bonadio, E and Lucchi, N, 'How far can copyright be stretched? Framing the debate on whether new and different forms of creativity can be protected' (2019) 2 *IPQ* 115.
—— and McDonagh, L, 'Artificial Intelligence as Producer and Consumer of Copyright Works: Evaluating the Consequences of Algorithmic Creativity' (2020) 2 *IPQ* 112.
Borghi, M and Karapapa, S, 'Non-Display Uses of Copyright Works' (2011) 1 *QMJIP* 21.
——, Erickson, K and Favale, M, 'With Enough Eyeballs All Searches Are Diligent: Mobilizing the Crowd in Copyright Clearance for Mass Digitization' (2016) 16(1) *Chicago-Kent Journal of Intellectual Property* 135.

Boyd, WL, 'Museums as Centers of Controversy' (1999) 128(3) *Daedalus* 185.

Bradshaw, S, Bowyer, A and Haufe, P, 'The Intellectual Property Implications of Low-Cost 3D Printing' (2010) 7 *SCRIPTed* 1.

Bronder, V, 'Saving the Right Orphans: The Special Case of Unpublished Orphan Works' (2008) 31(3) *Columbia Journal of Law & the Arts* 409.

Brown, MF, 'Can culture be copyrighted?' (1998) 39(2) *Current Anthropology* 193.

——, 'Heritage Trouble: Recent Work on the Protection of Intangible Cultural Property' (2005) 12(1) *Intl J Cult Prop* 40.

Bulayenko, O, 'Permissibility of Non-Voluntary Collective Management of Copyright under EU Law: The Case of the French Law on Out-of-Commerce Books' (2016) 7 *JIPITEC* 51.

Busse, TJ, 'Crossing the Digital Rubicon: Google Books and the Dawn of an Electronic Literature Revolution' (2018) 18 *Houston Business and Tax Law Journal* 119.

Butler, KC, 'Keeping the World Safe from Naked-Chicks-in-Art Refrigerator Magnets: The Plot to Control Art Images in the Public Domain through Copyrights in Photographic and Digital Reproductions' (1998) 21 *Hastings Communications and Entertainment Law Journal* 55.

Capell, L, 'Digitization as a Preservation Method for Damaged Acetate Negatives: A Case Study' (2010) 73 *American Archivist* 235.

Carpenter, MM, 'Intellectual Property Law and Indigenous Peoples: Adapting Copyright Law to the Needs of a Global Community' (2004) 7 *Yale Human Rights and Development Law Journal* 51.

Castro, C and de Queiroz, R, 'The Song of the Sirens: Google Books Project and copyright in a digital age' (2013) 16(9) *Information, Communication & Society* 1441.

Chambers, S and Schallier, W, 'Bringing Research Libraries into Europeana: Establishing a Library-Domain Aggregator' (2010) 20 *LIBER Quarterly* 105.

Chon, M, 'Intellectual Property "from Below": Copyright and Capability for Education' (2007) 40 *UC Davis Law Review* 803.

Christen, K, 'Gone Digital: Aboriginal Remix and the Cultural Commons' (2005) 12(3) *Intl J Cult Prop* 315.

Clark, B and Tozzi, S, '"Communication to the Public" under EU Copyright Law: An Increasingly Delphic Concept or Intentional Fragmentation?' (2016) 38 *EIPR* 715.

Clark, D, 'Skill and labour not enough for copyright – but software-generated art still original' (2024) 35(3) *Entertainment Law Review* 128.

Colangelo, G and Lincesso I, 'Law versus technology: looking for a solution to the orphan works' problem' (2012) 20(3) *International Journal of Law and Information Technology* 178.

Combe, P, 'Copyright Protection of Works Displayed in Public Places: Challenges over the Freedom of Panorama Exception' (2018) 23 *Art Antiquity & Law* 313.

Conway, P, 'Preservation in the Age of Google: Digitization, Digital Preservation, and Dilemmas' (2010) 80 *The Library Quarterly* 61.

Corbett, S, 'Immaterial Cultural Property and the Private Owner: How Copyright and Trade Law Might Address Access and Preservation' (2019) 9 *QMJIP* 262.

Craig, CJ, 'Locke, Labour, and Limiting the Author's Right: A Warning Against a Lockean Approach to Copyright Law' (2002) 28 *Queen's Law Journal* 1.

Crews, KD, 'Legal Deposit in Four Countries: Laws and Library Services' (1998) 80(4) *Law Library Journal* 551.

——, 'Museum Policies and Art Images: Conflicting Objectives and Copyright Overreaching' (2012) 22 *Fordham Intellectual Property, Media & Entertainment Law Journal* 796.

Cronin, C, '3D Printing: Cultural Property as Intellectual Property' (2015) 39 *The Columbia Journal of Law & the Arts* 1.

Cruikshank, J, 'Oral Tradition and Material Culture: Multiplying meanings of 'words' and 'things'' (1992) 8(3) *Anthropology Today* 5.

Dahlström, M, Hansson, J and Kjellman, U, '"As We May Digitize"– Institutions and Documents Reconfigured' (2012) 21 *LIBER Quarterly* 455.

Dalbello, M, 'Cultural Dimensions of Digital Library Development, Part I: Theory and Methodological Framework for a Comparative Study of the Cultures of Innovation in Five European National Libraries' (2008) 78 *The Library Quarterly: Information, Community, Policy* 355.
Dasari, H, 'Assessing Copyright Protection and Infringement Issues Involved with 3D Printing and Scanning' (2013) 41 *AIPLA Quarterly Journal* 279.
Davies, P, 'Access v Contract: Competing Freedoms in the Context of Copyright Limitations and Exceptions for Libraries' (2013) 35 *EIPR* 402.
Davis, A et al 'Pilbara Rock Art: Laser Scanning, Photogrammetry and 3D Photographic Reconstruction as Heritage Management Tools' (2017) 5 *Heritage Science* 25.
Dawson, P, Levy R and Lyons, N, '"Breaking the Fourth Wall": 3D Virtual Worlds as Tools for Knowledge Repatriation in Archaeology' (2011) 11 *Journal of Social Archaeology* 387.
Day, M et al, 'The preservation of disk-based content at the British Library: Lessons from the Flashback Project' (2016) 26(3) *Alexandria: The Journal of National and International Library and Information Issues* 216.
Deazley, R, 'Photographing Paintings in the Public Domain: A Response to Garnett' (2001) *EIPR* 179.
——, 'Photography, copyright, and the South Kensington experiment' (2010) 3 *IPQ* 29.
—— and Stobo, V, 'Archives and Copyright: Risk and Reform' (2013) CREATe Working Paper No. 3.
De La Durantaye, K, 'H is for Harmonization: The Google Book Search Settlement and Orphan Works Legislation in the European Union' (2010) 55 *New York Law School Law Review* 157.
——, 'Finding a Home for Orphans: Google Book Search and Orphan Works Law in the United States and Europe' (2011) 21 *Fordham Intellectual Property, Media & Entertainment Law Journal* 229.
Derclaye, E, 'An Economic Analysis of the Contractual Protection of Databases' (2005) 1(2) *University of Illinois Journal of Law, Technology and Policy* 247.
Determann, L, 'Digital Exhaustion: New Law from the Old World' (2018) 33(1) *Berkeley Technology Law Journal* 185.
Dickson, M, 'Due Diligence, Futile Effort: Copyright and the Digitization of the Thomas E. Watson Papers' (2010) 73 *The American Archivist* 626.
Dietz, A, 'The Moral Right of the Author: Moral Rights and the Civil Law Countries' (1994) 19 *Columbia VLA Journal of Law & the Arts* 199.
Dolinsky, K, 'CAD's Cradle: Untangling Copyrightability, Derivative Works, and Fair Use in 3D Printing' (2014) 71 *Washington and Lee Law Review* 591.
Dore, G and Turan, P, 'When Copyright Meets Digital Cultural Heritage: Picturing an EU Right to Culture in Freedom of Panorama and Reproduction of Public Domain Art' (2024) 55 *IIC* 37.
Dryden, J, 'Copyfraud or Legitimate Concerns? Controlling Further Uses of Online Archival Holdings' (2011) 74(2) The *American Archivist* 522.
Dulong de Rosnay, M and Langlais, PC, 'Public artworks and the freedom of panorama controversy: a case of Wikimedia influence' (2017) 6(1) *Internet Policy Review*.
Dunne, A, 'Copyrighting Experiences: How Copyright Law Applies to Virtual Reality Programs' (2019)12 *The Journal of Business, Entrepreneurship & the Law* 329.
Dusollier, S, 'A Manifesto for an E-Lending Limitation in Copyright' (2014) 5 *JIPITEC* 213.
Dworkin, G, 'Moral Rights and the common law countries' (1994) *Australian Intellectual Property Journal* 5.
European Copyright Society, 'Comment of the European Copyright Society on the Implementation of Art. 14 of the DSM Directive 2019/790' (2020) 11 *JIPITEC* 22.
Fabian, C and Schreiber, C, 'Piloting a National Programme for the Digitization of Medieval Manuscripts in Germany' (2014) 24(1) *LIBER Quarterly* 2.
Farrand, B, 'Lobbying and Lawmaking in the European Union: The Development of Copyright Law and the Rejection of the Anti-Counterfeiting Trade Agreement' (2015) 35(3) *Oxford Journal of Legal Studies* 487.
Fischman Afori, O, 'The Battle over Public E-Libraries – Taking Stock and Moving Ahead' (2013) 44 *IIC* 392.
Fisher, K, 'Copyright and Preservation of Born-digital Materials: Persistent Challenges and Selected Strategies' (2020) 83(2) *The American Archivist* 238.

Flynn, J, Giblin, R and Petitjean F, 'What Happens When Books Enter the Public Domain? Testing Copyright's Underuse Hypothesis Across Australia, New Zealand, the United States and Canada' (2019) 42(4) *University of New South Wales Law Journal* 1215.

Foley, JH, 'Enter the Library: Creating a Digital Lending Right' (2001) 16 *Connecticut Journal of International Law* 369.

Foote, KE, 'To Remember and Forget: Archives, Memory and Culture' (1990) 53(3) *The American Archivist* 378.

Fourmile, H, 'Who Owns the Past? Aborigines as Captives of the Archives' (1989) 13 *Aboriginal History* 1.

Frigeri, M, Kretschmer, M and Mezei, P, 'Copyright and eLending in public libraries: an incomplete revolution?' (2024) 15 *JIPITEC* 156.

Frigo, M, 'Cultural Property v. Cultural Heritage: A "Battle of Concepts" in International Law?' (2004) 86 *International Review of the Red Cross* 367.

Galilee, K, 'To what extent should uses of public architectural works be permitted under European copyright law ?' (2018) 1(2) *Stockholm Intellectual Property Law Review* 18.

Garnett, K, 'Copyright in Photographs' (2000) 22(5) *EIPR* 229.

Gbegnon, K, 'Digitized Scholarship and the "Library" Concept: Allowing the History of the Library Exemption to Inform How We View Google's Digitized Library' (2007) 29 *Hastings Communications and Entertainment Law Journal* 75.

Geiger, C, Frosio, G and Bulayenko, O, 'Text and Data Mining in the Proposed Copyright Reform: Making the EU Ready for an Age of Big Data?' (2018) 49 *IIC* 814.

Gerstenblith, P, 'From Bamiyan to Baghdad: Warfare and the Preservation of Cultural Heritage at the Beginning of 21st Century' (2006) 37 *Georgetown Journal of International Law* 245.

Gervais, D, 'The cultural role(s) of collective management organizations' (2018) 40(6) *EIPR* 349.

Gervais, DJ, 'The Machine as Author' (2019) 105 *Iowa Law Review* 2053.

Ghosh, S and Mezei, P, 'The Elusive Quest for Digital Exhaustion in the US and the EU: The CJEU's Tom Kabinet Ruling a Milestone or Millstone for Legal Evolution?' (2020) *Hungarian Yearbook of International Law and European Law* 249.

Giblin, J, Ramos, I and Grout, N, 'Dismantling the Master's House: Thoughts on Representing Empire and Decolonising Museums and Public Spaces in Practice An Introduction' (2019) 33(4–5) *Third Text* 471.

Gilchrist, J, 'Copyright Deposit, Legal Deposit or Library Deposit: The Government's Role as Preserver of Copyright Material' (2005) 5(2) *Queensland University Technical Law & Justice Journal* 177.

Ginsburg, J, 'Fair Use for Free, or Permitted-but-Paid?' (2014) *Columbia Law School Center for Law and Economic Studies*, Working Paper No 481.

Goold, PR, 'Why the U.K. Adaptation Right Is Superior to the U.S. Derivative Work Right' (2014) 92 *Nebraska Law Review* 843.

Green, A, 'Big digitisation: where next?' (Digital Resources for the Humanities and Arts Conference, Belfast, 8 September 2009).

Griffiths, J, 'The "Three-Step Test" in European Copyright Law: Problems and Solutions' (2009) 4 *IPQ* 428.

Griffiths, J, Synodinou, T and Xalabarder, R, 'Comment of the European Copyright Society Addressing Selected Aspects of the Implementation of Articles 3 to 7 of Directive (EU) 2019/790 on Copyright in the Digital Single Market' 72(1) *GRUR International* 22.

Grün, A, Remondino F and Zhang, L, 'Photogrammetric Reconstruction of the Great Buddha Of Bamiyan, Afghanistan' (2004) 19(107) *The Photogrammetric Record* 177.

Guadamuz, A, 'A Scanner Darkly: Copyright Liability and Exceptions in Artificial Intelligence Inputs and Outputs' (2024) 73(2) *GRUR International* 111.

Guibault, L and Schroff, S, 'Extended collective licensing for the use of out-of-commerce works in Europe: a matter of legitimacy vis-a-vis rights holders' (2018) 49 *IIC* 916.

Hansen, DR, 'Copyright Reform Principles for Libraries, Archives, and Other Memory Institutions' (2014) 29 *Berkeley Technology Law Journal* 1559.

Heald, PJ, 'How Copyright Keeps Works Disappeared' (2014) 11(4) *Journal of Empirical Legal Studies* 829.

Hennessy, K, 'Virtual Repatriation and Digital Cultural Heritage: The Ethics of Managing Online Collections' (2009) 50 *Anthropology News* 5.

Hettinger, EC, 'Justifying Intellectual Property' (1989) 18 *Philosophy & Public Affairs* 31.

Hornick, J, '3D Printing and IP Rights: The Elephant in the Room' (2015) 55 *Santa Clara Law Review* 801.

Hudson, E and Kenyon, AT, 'Digital Access: The Impact of Copyright on Digitisation Practices in Australian Museums, Galleries, Libraries and Archives' (2007) 30 *University of New South Wales Law Journal* 12.

Hugenholtz, PB and Van Velze, SC, 'Communication to a new public? Three reasons why EU copyright law can do without "a new public"' (2016) 47 *IIC* 797–816.

Hughes, J, 'Philosophy of Intellectual Property' (1988) 77 *Georgetown Law Journal* 287.

Iljadica, M, 'Copyright and the Right to the City' (2017) 68(1) *Northern Ireland Legal Quarterly* 59.

Jean-Baptiste, O, 'Augmented and virtual reality art: a new frontier of legal protection' (2021) 4(2) *Interactive Entertainment Law Review* 102.

Johnson, EE, 'Intellectual Property and the Incentive Fallacy' (2012) 39 *Florida State University Law Review* 623.

Kaiser, A, 'Exhaustion, Distribution and Communication to the Public – The CJEU's Decision C-263/18 – Tom Kabinet on E-Books and Beyond' (2020) 69(5) *GRUR International* 489.

Kapczynski, A, 'The Access to Knowledge Mobilization and the New Politics of Intellectual Property' (2008) 117 *Yale Law Journal* 804.

Karapapa, S, 'Reconstructing copyright exhaustion in the online world' (2014) 4 *IPQ* 304.

Katyal, SK, 'Technoheritage' (2017) 105 *California Law Review* 1111.

Keller, P et al, 'Re-Use of Public Sector Information in Cultural Heritage Institutions' (2014) 6 *International Free and Open Source Software Law Review* 1.

Kelley, KL, 'The Complications of "Bridgeman" and Copyright (Mis)use' (2011) 30(2) *Art Documentation: Journal of the Art Libraries Society of North America* 38.

Kerremans, R, 'A critical view on the European draft directive for orphan works' (2012) 2(1) *QMJIP* 38.

Khong, DWK, 'The (abandoned) orphan-works provision of the Digital Economy Bill (Legislative Comment)' (2010) 32(11) *EIPR* 560.

Kogan, TS, 'Photographic Reproductions, Copyright and the Slavish Copy' (2012) 35 *The Columbia Journal of Law & the Arts* 445.

Kongolo, T, 'The extent of the public domain in the age of new technologies including artificial intelligence (AI)' (2023) 45(1) *EIPR* 589.

Kretschmer, M, Margoni, T and Oruç, P, 'Copyright Law and the Lifecycle of Machine Learning Models' (2024) 55 *IIC* 110.

Kwall, RR, 'Library Reproduction Rights for Preservation and Replacement in the Digital Era: An Author's Perspective on §108' (2005) 29 *The Columbia Journal of Law & the Arts* 343.

Landes, WM and Posner, RA, 'An Economic Analysis of Copyright Law' (1989) 18 *The Journal of Legal Studies* 325.

Langdalen, J, 'Editing Historical Music in the Age of Digitization' in L Duranti and E Shaffer (eds), *UNESCO The Memory of the World in the Digital Age: Digitization and Preservation Conference Proceedings* (Vancouver, 26–28 September 2012).

LeComte, R, 'Writers Blocked: The Debate over Public Lending Right in the United States during the 1980s' (2009) 44(4) *Libraries & the Cultural Record* 395.

Lemley, MA, 'IP in a World Without Scarcity' (2015) 90 *New York University Law Review* 460.

Lessig, L, 'The Creative Commons' (2004) 65 *Montana Law Review.*

Leval, P, 'Toward a Fair Use Standard' (1989) 103 *Harvard Law Review* 1105.

Lixinski, L, 'A Third Way of Thinking about Cultural Property' (2019) 44(2) *Brooklyn Journal of International Law* 563.

——, 'Digital Heritage Surrogates, Decolonization, and International Law: Restitution, Control, and the Creation of Value as Reparations and Emancipation' (2020) *Santander Art & Culture Law Review* 65.

Loulanski, T, 'Revising the Concept for Cultural Heritage: The Argument for a Functional Approach' (2006) 13(2) *Intl J Cult Prop* 207.
Löbling, L et al, 'Navigating the Legal Landscape: Technical Implementation of Copyright Reservations for Text and Data Mining in the Era of AI Language Models' (2023) 14 *JIPITEC* 499.
Lunney, GS, 'Reexamining Copyright's Incentives – Access Paradigm' (1996) 49 *Vanderbilt Law Review* 485.
Lyons, CL, 'Thinking about Antiquities: Museums and Internationalism' (2014) 21(3) *Intl J Cult Prop* 251.
Macmillan, F, 'The Protection of Cultural Heritage: Common Heritage of Humankind, National Cultural "Patrimony" or Private Property ?' (2013) 64 *Northern Ireland Legal Quarterly* 351.
Magán, JA et al, 'Mass Digitization at the Complutense University Library: Access to and Preservation of Its Cultural Heritage' (2011) 21 *LIBER Quarterly* 48.
Marciszewski, M, 'What Do Andy Warhol and Google Have in Common? Transformative Uses and the Effect upon the Potential Market: The next Question for Fair Use and the Right to Prepare Derivative Works' (2023) 92 UMKC Law Review 291.
Margoni, T, 'The Digitisation of Cultural Heritage: Originality, Derivative Works and (Non) Original Photographs' (2014) Institute for Information Law 54.
—— and Kretschmer, M, 'A Deeper Look into the EU Text and Data Mining Exceptions: Harmonisation, Data Ownership, and the Future of Technology' (2022) 71(8) *GRUR International* 685.
Martinez, M and Terras, M, '"Not Adopted": The UK Orphan Works Licensing Scheme and How the Crisis of Copyright in the Cultural Heritage Sector Restricts Access to Digital Content' (2019) 5(1) *Open Library of Humanities* 36.
Matthes, EH, '"Saving Lives or Saving Stones?" The Ethics of Cultural Heritage Protection in War' (2018) 32(1) *Public Affairs Quarterly* 67.
Mattingly, FX, 'If You Don't Use It, You Lose It: What the U.S. Could Learn from France's Law on out-of-Commerce Books of the 20th Century' (2017) 27 *Indiana International & Comparative Law Review* 277.
Matulionyte, R, 'E-Lending and a Public Lending Right: Is It Really a Time for an Update?' (2016) 38 *EIPR* 132.
Matz, RC, 'Bridgeman Art Library, Ltd. v. Corel Corp.' (2000) 15 *Berkeley Technology Law Journal* 3.
Mazzone, J, 'Copyfraud' (2006) 81(3) *New York University Law Review* 1026.
McCausland, S, 'Googling the Archives: Ideas from the Google Books Settlement on Solving Orphan Works Issues in Digital Access Projects' (2009) 6(2) *SCRIPT-ed* 377.
McCrary, Q, 'The Political Nature of Digital Cultural Heritage' (2011) 20 *LIBER Quarterly* 357.
McCutcheon, J, 'Death rights: legal personal representatives of deceased authors and the posthumous exercise of moral rights' (2015) 3 *IPQ* 242.
——, 'Levola Hengelo BV v. Smilde Foods BV: The Hard Work of Defining a Copyright Work' (2019) 82 *MLR* 936.
Mendis, D,'Clone Wars Episode II – The Next Generation: The Copyright Implications Related to 3D Printing and Computer-Aided Design (CAD) Files' (2014) 6 *Law, Innovation and Technology* 265.
——, 'In Pursuit of Clarity: The Conundrum of CAD Software and Copyright – Seeking Direction Through Case Law' (2018) 40(11) *EIPR* 694.
Merryman, JH, 'Thinking about the Elgin Marbles' (1985) 83(8) *Michigan Law Review* 1880.
——, 'Two Ways of Thinking About Cultural Property' (1986) 80 *The American Journal of International Law* 831.
——, 'The Nation and the Object' (1994) 3(1) *Intl J Cult Prop* 61.
——, 'A Licit International Trade in Cultural Objects' (1995) 4(1) *Intl J Cult Prop* 13.
Michel, JB et al, 'Quantitative Analysis of Culture Using Millions of Digitized Books' (2011) 331 *Science* 176.
Michel, S, 'Digitisation of art in the public domain–museum urges Wikimedia to take down reproductions of out-of-protection artworks' (2019) 14(6) *JIPLP* 427.
Mishra, M and Lourenço, PB, 'Artificial intelligence-assisted visual inspection for cultural heritage: State-of-the-art review' (2024) 66 *Journal of Cultural Heritage* 536.

Moffett, L, 'A Bridge Too Far? Attacks against Cultural Property used as Military Objectives as War Crimes: The *Prlić et al.* Case and the Mostar Bridge' (2020) 20 *International Criminal Law Review* 214.

Morrison, C and Secker, J, 'Copyright Literacy in the UK: a survey of librarians and other cultural heritage sector professionals' (2015) 39(121) *Library and Information Research* 74.

Münster, S et al, 'Artificial Intelligence for Digital Heritage Innovation: Setting up a R&D Agenda for Europe' (2024) 7 *Heritage* 794.

Mwangi, FG, 'The Road to Providing Access to Kenya's Information Heritage' in L Duranti and E Shaffer (eds) *UNESCO The Memory of the World in the Digital Age: Digitization and Preservation Conference Proceedings* (Vancouver, 26–28 September 2012).

Nagaraj, A and Reimer, I, 'Digitization and the Market for Physical Works: Evidence from the Google Books Project' (2023) 15(4) *American Economic Journal: Economic Policy* 428.

Netanel, N, 'Copyright Alienability Restrictions and the Enhancement of Author Autonomy: A Normative Evaluation' (1993) *Rutgers Law Review* 24.

——, 'Copyright and a Democratic Civil Society' (1996) 106 *Yale Law Journal* 283.

O'Connell, A, 'Copyright in Unpublished Works: 2039 and Orphan Works' (2015) 39(121) *Library and Information Research* 41.

O'Sullivan, KT, 'Reforming Irish copyright law: the question of orphan works' (2017) 40(1), *Dublin University Law Journal* 165.

Okediji, R, 'Towards an International Fair Use Doctrine' (2000) 39 *Columbia Journal of Transnational Law* 75.

Oriakhogba, DO, 'Repatriation of ancient Benin bronzes to Nigeria: reflection on copyright and related issues' (2022) 17 (10) *JIPLP* 823.

Oruç, P, '3D Digitisation of Cultural Heritage: Copyright Implications of the Methods, Purposes and Collaboration' (2020) 11(2) *JIPITEC* 149.

——, 'Rethinking who "keeps" heritage: 3D Technology, Repatriation and Copyright' (2022) 71(12) *GRUR International* 1138.

——, 'Documenting Indigenous Oral Traditions: Copyright for Control?' (2022) *International Journal of Cultural Property* 29(3) 243.

Osborn, LS, 'Of PhDs, Pirates,and the Public: Three-Dimensional Printing Technology and the Arts' (2014) *Texas A&M Law Review* 811.

Panezi, A, 'A Public Service Role for Digital Libraries: A Case of Emergency Electronic Access to Library Material and the Unequal Battle against Misinformation through Copyright Law Reform' (2021) 31 *Cornell Journal of Law and Public Policy* 65.

Patry, W, 'Andy Warhol Foundation for the Visual Arts, Inc.v Goldsmith: did the U.S. Supreme Court tighten up fair use?' (2023) 18(9) *JIPLP* 628.

Pavis, P, and Wallace, A, 'Response to the 2018 Sarr-Savoy Report: Statement on Intellectual Property Rights and Open Access relevant to the digitization and restitution of African Cultural Heritage and associated materials' (2019) 10 *JIPITEC* 115.

Picker, RC, 'The Google Book Search Settlement: A New Orphan-Works Monopoly?' (2009) Working Paper No.462.

Pieraccini, M, Guidi, G and Atzeni, C, '3D Digitizing of Cultural Heritage' (2001) 2 *Journal of Cultural Heritage* 63.

Polcak, R, 'Digitisation, Cultural Institutions and Intellectual Property' (2015) 9(2) *Masaryk University Journal of Law and Technology* 121.

Pollock, R, 'Forever Minus a Day? Calculating Optimal Copyright Term' (2009) 6(1) *Review of Economic Research on Copyright Issues* 35.

Porter, G, 'Gender Bias: Representations of Work in History Museums' (1990) 3 *Continuum: The Australian Journal of Media & Culture*.

Prott, LV and O'Keefe, PJ, '"Cultural Heritage" or "Cultural Property"?' (1992) 1(2) *Intl J Cult Prop* 307.

Purday, J, 'Think Culture: Europeana.eu from Concept to Construction' (2009) 1 *DigItalia* 105.

——, 'Intellectual Property Issues and Europeana, Europe's Digital Library, Museum and Archive' (2010) 10(3) *Legal Information Management* 174.

Rasenberger, M, 'Copyright Issues and Section 108 Reform' (2010) 34 *The Columbia Journal of Law & the Arts* 15.

Rasmussen, CH and Hjørland, B, 'Libraries, archives and museums (LAM) Conceptual issues with focus on their convergence' in B Hjørland and C Gnoli (eds), *ISKO Encyclopedia of Knowledge Organization*.

Raustiala, K and Sprigman, CJ, 'The Piracy Paradox: Innovation and Intellectual Property in Fashion Design' (2006) 92(8) *Virginia Law Review* 1687.

Remondino, F, 'Heritage Recording and 3D Modeling with Photogrammetry and 3D Scanning' (2011) 3 *Remote Sensing* 1104.

Romano, R, 'Copyright law and cultural heritage in Italy: work in progress' (2018) 13(9) *JIPLP* 694.

Rosati, E, 'The orphan works provisions of the ERR Act: are they compatible with UK and EU laws?' (2013) 35(12) *EIPR* 724.

Rub, GA, 'Reimagining Digital Libraries' (forthcoming, 2024) 113 *Georgetown Law Journal*, Ohio State Legal Studies Research Paper No. 848.

Samuelson, P, 'Unbundling Fair Uses' (2009) 77 *Fordham Law Review* 2537.

——, 'Extended Collective Licensing to Enable Mass Digitisation: A Critique of the US Copyright Office Proposal' (2016) 38(2) *EIPR* 75.

——, 'Regulating technology through copyright law: a comparative perspective' (2020) 42(4) *EIPR* 214.

Sandalow, C, 'I Did You a Favor by Taking Your Work: Reconsidering the Harm-Based Approach to the Fourth Fair Use Factor' (2022) 46 *The Columbia Journal of Law & the Arts* 457.

Sapir, E, 'Cultural Anthropology and Psychiatry' (1932) 27(3) *Journal of Abnormal and Social Psychology* 229.

Sappa, C, 'Hosting the public domain into a minefield: the resistance to art.14 of the DSM Directive and to the related rules that transpose it into national law' (2022) 17(11) *JIPLP* 924.

——, 'Participating in Cultural Life via Augmented Reality on Cultural Goods: What Role for Copyright?' (2022) 71(7) *GRUR International* 618.

—— and Widla, B, 'Framing texts and images: critical and posthumous editions in the digital Single Market' (2023) 54(9) *IIC* 1359.

Savenije, B and Beunen, A, 'Cultural Heritage and the Public Domain' (2012) 22 *LIBER Quarterly* 84.

Schulze, EF, 'Orphan works and other orphan material under national, regional and international law: analysis, proposals and solutions' (2012) 34(5) *EIPR* 313.

Senftleben, M, 'The International Three-Step Test: A Model Provision for EC Fair Use Legislation' (2010) 1 *JIPITEC* 67.

Sganga, C, 'The eloquent silence of Soulier and Doke and its critical implications for EU copyright law' (2017) 12(4) *JIPLP* 321.

——, 'From Soulier to the EU Copyright Law Reform: What Future for Non-Voluntary Collective Management Schemes?' (2018) 19 *ERA Forum* 137.

——, 'A Plea for Digital Exhaustion in EU Copyright Law' (2019) 9 *JIPITEC* 211.

Shapiro, D, 'A Universalist: Fathering Fields' (2014) 21(3) *Intl J Cult Prop* 237.

Shevlin, C, 'The Difficulties in Finding a Single Theory to Justify Copyright' (2015) 3 *North East Law Review* 49.

Silberman, NA, 'From cultural property to cultural data: the multiple dimensions of "ownership" in a global digital age' (2014) 21(3) *Intl J Cult Prop* 36.

Silverman, I, 'Optimising Protection: IP Rights in 3D Printing' (2016) 38(1) *EIPR* 5.

Solanki, MR and Dongaonkar, A 'A Journey of Human Comfort: Web 1.0 to Web 4.0' (2016) 3(9) *International Journal of Research and Scientific Innovation* 75.

Stein, AM, 'The Italian Code of Cultural Heritage and the "Vitruvian Man" Case Comment' (2023) 45(8) *EIPR* 497.

Stockton-Brown, M, 'Out-of-Commerce: How the Existing Copyright Practices in Film Archives Impact on Widening Public Access to Cultural Heritage' (2022) 13 *JIPITEC* 3.

Sullivan, AM, 'Cultural Heritage & New Media: A Future for the Past' (2016) 15 *John Marshall Review of Intellectual Property Law* 604.

Suthersanen, U, 'Creative Commons – the Other Way?' (2007) 20 *Learned Publishing* 59.

Theodoropoulos, A and Antoniou, A, 'VR Games in Cultural Heritage: A Systematic Review of the Emerging Fields of Virtual Reality and Culture Games' (2022) 12(17) *Applied Sciences* 8476.

Townsend Gard, E, 'Last Twenty (L20) Collections: Applying Copyright's Section 108(h) in Libraries, Archives and Museums including the New Music Modernization Act for Pre-1972 Sound Recordings' (2018) 22(3) *UCLA Journal of Law and Technology i.*

——, 'Nine Copyright Things Every Library and Archive Should Know in 2023' (2023) 41 *Cardozo Arts & Entertainment Law Journal* 485

Tucci, G, Cini, D and Nobile, A 'Effective 3D Digitization of Archaeological Artifacts for Interactive Virtual Museum' (2011) *International Archives of the Photogrammetry, Remote Sensing and Spatial Information Sciences* 414.

Van Buren, ED, 'Museums and Raree Shows in Antiquity' (1922) 33(4) *Folklore* 337.

Van Gompel, S, 'Unlocking the Potential of Pre-Existing Content: How to Address the Issue of Orphan Works in Europe?' (2007) 38 *IIC* 669.

Vathitphund, T, 'Access to knowledge difficulties in developing countries: A balanced access to copyrighted works in the digital environment' (2010) 24(1) *International Review of Law, Computers & Technology* 7.

Vawda, S, 'Museums and the Epistemology of Injustice: From Colonialism to Decoloniality' (2019) 71(1–2) *Museum International* 72.

Vetulani-Cęgiel, A, 'EU Copyright Law, Lobbying and Transparency of Policy-Making: The cases of sound recordings term extension and orphan works provisions' (2015) 6(2) *JIPITEC* 147.

Vizvary P et al, 'Copyright Literacy of Cultural Heritage Workers in the Czech Republic with a Focus on Librarians' (7th European Conference on Information Literacy, 20–23 September 2021).

Wachowiak, MJ and Karas, BV, '3D Scanning and Replication for Museum and Cultural Heritage Applications' (2009) 48 *Journal of the American Institute for Conservation* 141.

Wallace, A and Euler, E, 'Revisiting Access to Cultural Heritage in the Public Domain: EU and International Developments' (2020) 51 *IIIC* 823.

Warnecke, M, 'Google's Legal Stance on U.S.'s Book Search May Have Less Support Under European Law' (2005) 71 *BNA Patent, Trademark & Copyright Journal* 206.

Wojcik, MC, 'The Antithesis of Originality: Bridgeman, Image Licensors, and the Public Domain' (2008) *Hastings Communications and Entertainment Law Journal* 257.

Wu, MM, 'Hachette, Controlled Digital Lending, and the Consequences of Divorcing Law from Context' (2023) 42(2) *Legal Reference Services Quarterly* 129.

Yamada, S, 'Who Moved My Masterpiece? Digital Reproduction, Replacement, and the Vanishing Cultural Heritage of Kyoto' (2017) 24(3) *Intl J Cult Prop* 295.

Yanisky-Ravid, S, 'The Hidden Though Flourishing Justification of Intellectual Property Laws: Distributive Justice, National Versus International Approaches' (2017) 21 *Lewis & Clark Law Review* 1.

Zemer, L, 'The Making of a New Copyright Lockean' (2006) 29(3) *The Harvard Journal of Law & Public Policy* 891.

Zimmerman, DL, 'Copyrights as Incentives: Did We Just Imagine That?' (2011) 12 *Theoretical Inquiries in Law* 30.

Reports and Studies

ALAI, 'Opinion on the criterion "New Public", developed by the Court of Justice of the European Union (CJEU), put in the context of making available and communication to the public' (2014).

Bailey, L et al. 'Position Statement on Controlled Digital Lending by Libraries'.

Benhamou, Y, 'Revised Report on Copyright Practices and Challenges of Museums' WIPO SCCR/38/5 (2019).
Brown H et al, 'The role of microfilm in digital preservation' in J Davidson, S Ross and M Day (eds), *DCC Digital Curation Manual* (2011).
Cambridge Consultants, 'Use of AI in Online Content Moderation' (Ofcom, 2019).
Canat, JF and Guibault, L, 'Study on copyright limitations and exceptions for museums' WIPO SCCR/30/2 (2015).
Crews, KD, 'Archives Copyright Exceptions: Typology Analysis' WIPO SCCR/39/5 (2019).
——, 'Copyright Limitations and Exceptions for Libraries: Typology Analysis' WIPO SCCR/38/4 (2019).
DCMS, 'Government Response to the Independent Review of E-Lending in Public Libraries in England' (2013).
——, Independent Library Report for England (2014).
DC Research and Wavehill, 'Research to understand the levels of public investment in museums' (Arts Council England, January 2024).
Deazley, R, Patterson, K and Stobo, V, Digitising the Edwin Morgan Scrapbooks (2017).
Dore, G and Priora, G, 'The EU imperative to a free public domain: The case of Italian cultural heritage' (2024) Communia Independent Expert Opinion.
'Draft implementation plan for the work program on limitations and exceptions and preliminary comments received by March 29, 2024' WIPO SCCR/45/6 (2024).
European Commission, Lévy, M, Niggemann, E and De Decker, J, 'The new renaissance: report of the Comité des Sages on bringing Europe's cultural heritage online' (2011).
European Commission, 'Public Consultation on the Review of the EU Copyright Rules' (2013).
——, 'Report on the Responses to the Public Consultation on the Review of the EU Copyright Rules' (2014).
——, 'Mapping of Cultural Heritage actions in European Union policies, programmes and activities' (2017).
——, 'Study on emerging issues on collective licensing practices in the digital environment' (2021).
——, 'Report on the use of collective licensing mechanisms with an extended effect under Article 12(6) of Directive 2019/790/EU on copyright and related rights in the Digital Single Market' SWD(2021) 337 final (Brussels, 29 November 2021).
——, 'Study on the application of the Orphan Works Directive (2012/28/EU) Final Report' (2021).
European Commission Staff Working Document, 'Report on the application of the "Orphan Works Directive" 2012/28/EU', SWD(2022) 412 final (Brussels, 6 December 2022).
EC Green Paper, Copyright in the Knowledge Economy, COM(2008) 466 Final.
EUIPO, 'Orphan Works Survey 2017 – Summary Report' (November 2017).
Europeana, 'Recommendations on Copyright and its role in the Digital Transformation of the Cultural Heritage Sector' (March 2021).
——, 'DSI 2-Access to Digital Resources of European Heritage D4.4 Report on ENUMERATE Core Survey' (2017).
——, 'MS7: Content Report- Mar 2016 (April 2016).
European Copyright Society 'General Opinion on the EU Copyright Reform Package' (24 January 2017).
——, 'Comment of the European Copyright Society on the Implementation of the Extended Collective Licensing Rules (Arts. 8 and 12) of the Directive (EU) 2019/790 on Copyright in the Digital Single Market (2020).
Gilbert S, 'Crypto, web3, and the Metaverse' Policy Brief (Bennett Institute for Public Policy, March 2022).
Gowers, A, *Gowers Review of Intellectual Property* (London, HM Treasury, 2006).
Hansen, DR and Courtney, KK, 'A White Paper on Controlled Digital Lending of Library Books' (2018).
Hargreaves, I, *Digital Opportunity: A Review of Intellectual Property and Growth* (2011).
Hatch, P, Morrison C and Secker, J, 'A study of copyright specialists in UK educational and cultural institutions: Who are they and what do they do?' (Copyright Literacy, 2017).

Hilty, R and Richter, H, 'Position Statement of the Max Planck Institute for Innovation and Competition on the Proposed Modernisation of European Copyright Rules Part B Exceptions and Limitations (Art. 3 – Text and Data Mining)' (2017) Max Planck Institute for Innovation & Competition Research Paper No. 17-02.

Historic England, '3D Laser Scanning for Heritage: Advice and Guidance on the Use of Laser Scanning in Archaeology and Architecture' (2018).

Historic England, 'Photogrammetric Applications for Cultural Heritage: Guidance for Good Practice' (2017).

HM Government, 'MODERNISING COPYRIGHT: A modern, robust and flexible framework: Government response to consultation on copyright exceptions and clarifying copyright law' (2012).

House of Commons Library Briefing on Local Museums (March 2018).

i2010: Digital Libraries High Level Expert Group – Copyright Subgroup, 'Final Report on Digital Preservation, Orphan Works and Out-of-Print Works' (2008).

ICOM, 'Museums, museum professionals and Covid-19: third survey' (2021).

IFLA Position on Controlled Digital Lending (2021).

Impact Assessment on the modernisation of EU copyright rules accompanying the document Proposal for a Directive of the European Parliament and of the Council on copyright in the Digital Single Market SWD (2016) 301 final.

'Informal Chart on Limitations and Exceptions for Libraries and Archives' WIPO SCCR/34/5 (2017).

International Centre for the Study of Preservation and Restoration of Cultural Property (ICCROM) 'A Guide to Risk Management of Cultural Heritage (2016).

IPO, 'Orphan Works in the UK and Overseas' (2013/17).

——, 'Consultation on reducing the duration of copyright in unpublished ("2039") works in accordance with section 170(2) of the Copyright, Designs and Patents Act 1988' (2014).

——, 'Exceptions to Copyright: Libraries, Archives and Museums' (2014).

——, 'Government response to the consultation on reducing the duration of copyright in certain unpublished works' (2015).

——, 'Extended Collective Licensing (ECL): Guidance for relevant licensing bodies applying to run ECL schemes' (2016) (Withdrawn).

——, 'Artificial Intelligence and Intellectual Property: copyright and patents: Government response to consultation' (28 June 2022).

——, 'Policy Paper: Collective Rights Management in the UK' (1 January 2024).

Janke, T, 'Minding Culture: Case Studies on Intellectual Property and Traditional Cultural Expressions' (2003) WIPO Publication No. 781.

Korn, N, 'In from the Cold: An assessment of the scope of "Orphan Works" and its impact on the delivery of services to the public' (JISC, April 2009).

Keller, P and Warso, Z, 'Defining best practices for opting out of ML Training' (2023) Open Future Policy Brief #5.

Kretschmer, M, Kretschmer, T, Peukert, A and Peukert, C, 'The risks of risk-based AI regulation: taking liability seriously' (2023) CEPR Discussion Paper No. 18517.

LACA, 'Consultation on reducing the duration of copyright in unpublished ("2039") Works – Response from The Libraries and Archives Copyright Alliance (LACA).

Mendoza, N, 'The Mendoza Review: an independent review of museums in England' (November 2017) DCMS.

Network of European Museum Organisations, 'Final report: Digitisation and IPR in European Museums' (March 2020).

NUMERIC Study report: Study findings and proposals for sustaining the framework' (2009).

Pantalony, RE, Crews, KD and Sutton, D, 'WIPO Toolkit on Preservation for Cultural Heritage Institutions' WIPO SCCR/43/4 (2024).

Peters, M, 'Hearing on Competition and Commerce in Digital Books: The Proposed Google Book Settlement' (2009).
Poole, N, 'The Cost of Digitising Europe's Cultural Heritage' (2010) Report for Comité des Sages of European Commission 30.
Proudman, V et al, 'Transposing the Directive on Copyright in the Digital Single Market: A Guide for Libraries and Library Associations' (2019).
Richly, S, 'Scoping Study on Public Lending Right' WIPO SCCR/45/7 (2024).
Sarr, F and Savoy, B, 'The Restitution of African Cultural Heritage. Toward a New Relational Ethics' (November 2018).
Sganga, C et al, 'D2.3 Copyright flexibilities: mapping and comparative assessment of EU and national sources' (2023) reCreating Europe.
Sieghart, W, 'An Independent Review of E-Lending in Public Libraries in England' (2013).
SPARC Europe, 'The Directive on Open Data and the Re-Use of Public Sector: Information Briefing for national legislative implementation in the interest of supporting Open Access to research data and its re-use' (2019).
Stenou, K, 'Universal Declaration on Cultural Diversity: a vision, a conceptual platform, a pool of ideas for implementation, a new paradigm' (2002) UNESCO.
Stobo, V, Deazley, R and Anderson, IG, 'Copyright & Risk: Scoping the Wellcome Digital Library Project' (2013) CREATe Working Paper 2013/10.
Stratton, B, 'Seeking New Landscapes' (2011) British Library.
Stromberg, E and Sheth, R, 'Google Books: Liberating the World's Information, or Appropriating It?' (The Kenan Institute for Ethics, 2018).
The Conference on Fair Use, Final Report to the Commissioner on the Conclusion of the Conference on Fair Use (November 1998).
The National Archives, 'Guidance on the implementation of the Re-use of Public Sector Information Regulations 2015 for the cultural sector' (January 2019).
'The Section 108 Study Group Report' (2008).
Torsen, M and Anderson, J, 'Intellectual Property and the Safeguarding of Traditional Cultures: Legal Issues and Practical Options for Museums, Libraries and Archives' (2010) WIPO.
Troll Covey, D, 'Acquiring Copyright Permission to Digitize and Provide Open Access to Books' (2005) Digital Library Federation Council on Library and Information Resources.
UNESCO, 'Report of the Expert Meeting on the "Global Strategy" and thematic studies for a representative World Heritage List' (Paris, 20–22 June 1994).
——, 'Museums around the world in the face of COVID-19' (Paris, May 2020).
US Copyright Office, DMCA Section 104 Report' (2001).
——, 'A report on orphan works – A report of the register of copyrights' (January 2006).
——, 'Legal Issues in Mass Digitization: A Preliminary Analysis and Discussion Document' (October 2011).
——, 'Orphan Works and Mass Digitization' (June, 2015).
——, 'Section 108 of Title 17 – Discussion Document' (2017).
——, 'Authors, Attribution, and Integrity: Examining Moral Rights in the United States' (April 2019).
——, 'State Sovereign Immunity Study' (2021).
Vuopala, A, 'Assessment of the Orphan works issue and Costs for Rights Clearance – European Commission DG Information Society and Media Unit E4 Access to Information' (May 2010).
Weinberg, M, '3D Scanning: A World without Copyright' (2016) Shapeways.
WIPO, 'Collective Management of Copyright and Related Rights, Third Edition' (2022).
WIPO Technology Trends 2019: Artificial Intelligence (2019).
'Working Document Containing Comments on and Textual Suggestions Towards an Appropriate International Legal Instrument (in whatever form) on Exceptions and Limitations for Libraries and Archives' WIPO SCCR/26/3 (2013).

INDEX

www.ingramcontent.com/pod-product-compliance
Ingram Content Group UK Ltd.
Pitfield, Milton Keynes, MK11 3LW, UK
UKHW020802290926
15470UKWH00003B/909